WITHDRAWAL FROM EMPIRE
A Military View

WITHDRAWAL FROM EMPIRE

A Military View

WILLIAM JACKSON

St. Martin's Press
New York

Dedication

To my dear wife, Joan, in our
Ruby Wedding year, and in
gratitude for all her help and
support over those forty years

© William Jackson, 1986

All rights reserved. For information, write:
Scholarly & Reference Division,
St. Martin's Press, Inc., 175 Fifth Avenue, New York, NY 10010

First published in the United States of America in 1987

Printed in Great Britain

ISBN 0–312–00552–0

Library of Congress Cataloging-in-Publication Data

Jackson, W.G.F. (William Godfrey Fothergill),
    Sir, 1917–
    Withdrawal from empire.

    Bibliography: p.
    Includes index
     1.   Great Britain––Colonies––History.
2.   Great Britain––History, Military––20th century.
3.   Great Britain––Colonies––Defenses.   4.   Great
Britain––Colonies––Administration.   5.   Great
Britain––Military policy. I. Title.
DA18.J33   1987   941.082   86–29855
ISBN 0–312–00552–0

Photographs by courtesy of the
Imperial War Museum, London

Maps drawn by Patrick Leeson

CONTENTS

LIST OF MAPS

LIST OF ILLUSTRATIONS

CHRONOLOGY

Part I: The attempt to stay: 1945 to 1956

Year	Western Hemisphere and Europe	Mediterranean, Middle East and Africa	India, Far East and Pacific
1945	5. End of the war in Europe.		
	7. Labour Party wins UK general election		
			8. Atomic bombs on Japan.
		10. Jewish revolt begins in Palestine.	9 British troops re-occupy former British, Dutch and French Colonies.
		12. Revision of Anglo-Egyptian Treaty demanded by Egypt.	
1946			2. Indian naval and airforce mutinies.
		6. Arrest of Jewish leaders in Palestine.	
		7. Bombing of the King David Hotel, Jerusalem.	8. The Calcutta killings.
			9. Communist rebellion begins in French Indo-China.

1947

6 Marshall Plan for Europe.

3. Withdrawal of British troops from Egypt to the Canal Zone completed.

4. Palestine referred to the UN.

11. UN vote for the partition of Palestine.

3. Mountbatten Viceroy of India.

8. Indian independence and the Punjab massacres.

1948

1. to 6. Berlin Blockade.

3. Brussels Treaty signed.

2. Accra riots.

5. Last British troops leave Palestine.

6. State of emergency declared in Malaya.

1949

8. First Soviet A-bomb detonated.

Arab League fails to stop formation of Israel.

10. Chinese People's Republic proclaimed.

1950

7. British National Service extended to two years.

6. Makarios elected Ethnarch of Cyprus.

1. Dutch leave Indonesia.

4. Briggs arrives in Malaya.

6. Korean War starts.

1951

10. Churchill wins UK general election.

2. Nkrumah wins first Gold Coast general election.

8. Nationalisation of Anglo-Persian Oil Company and abrogation of Anglo-Egyptian Treaty of 1936.

4. MacArthur dismissed.

10. Murder of Sir Henry Gurney in Malaya.

1952			
	4. NATO formed.		2. Templer takes over in Malaya.
		7. King Farouk overthrown.	
		10. State of emergency declared in Kenya.	

1953	3. Stalin dies.	3. Lari Massacre in Kenya.	
			7. Korean armistice signed.
			9. First area declared 'white' in Malaya.
		10. Anglo-Egyptian talks fail.	

1954		4. Nasser seizes power in Egypt.	
			5. Fall of Dien Bien Phu in Indo-China.
		10. New Anglo-Egyptian Treaty signed.	
			11. Templer leaves Malaya.

1955	4. Eden succeeds Churchill.	4. Grivas opens *EOKA* Campaign in Cyprus.	
		5. USSR offers arms to Egypt.	
			7. Alliance Party wins first Malayan general election.
		10. Harding takes over in Cyprus.	
			12. Abortive meeting with Chin Peng at Baling.

1956		3. Last British troops leave Canal Zone; and Makarios deported to the Seychelles.
		7. Nationalization of the Suez Canal.
		8. British troops start withdrawing from Kenya.
	10. Russian intervention in Hungary.	
		11. Anglo-French landings at Port Said.

Part II: The decision to go: 1957 to 1972

Year	Western Hemisphere and Europe	Mediterranean, Middle East and Africa	India, Far East and Pacific
1957	1. Macmillan succeeds Eden.		
	3. Treaty of Rome signed by original Six.	3. *EOKA* ceasefire and release of Makarios.	
	4. Sandys' 1957 Defence Review published.		8. Malaya independent within the Commonwealth.
		11. Foot succeeds Harding in Cyprus.	

1958		
	4. Grivas re-opens *EOKA* campaign in Cyprus.	
6. De Gaulle returns to power in France.		
7. McMahon Act amended by US Congress.	7. Hashemite dynasty overthrown in Iraq; and US and British military intervention in Lebanon and Jordan.	

1959		
	1. Djebel Akhdar taken by SAS.	1. Armed struggle reopens in Vietnam.
	2. Zurich Agreement on Cyprus.	
10. Macleod appointed Colonial Secretary, and Watkinson Defence Secretary.		

1960		
	2. Macmillan's *Wind of Change* speeches.	
	3. Sharpville massacre.	
	7. Civil war starts in the Congo.	
11. UN decolonisation resolution 1514(XV).		
12. Last British National Service call-up.	12. Central African Federation breaks up.	

| 1961 | | 5. South Africa becomes a republic. | 5. Proposal to form Federation of Malaysia announced. |
| | 8. First British application to join the EEC. | 6. British military intervention to Kuwait. | 11. US MAAG established in Saigon. |

1962	1. De Gaulle vetoes British entry into EEC.	2. Announcement of creation of Aden military base.	
	10. Cuban missile crisis.	9. Pro-Nasser revolution in the Yemen.	9. Azahari wins first Brunei elections.
	12. Polaris agreement with US.		10. Chinese invasion of India.
			12. Brunei rebellion.

1963	1. Last National Serviceman leaves the British Army.	Aden joins the Federation of South Arabia.	
			4. Indonesian 'Confrontation' with Malaysia starts.
			9. Federation of Malaysia formed.
	10. Lord Home replaces Macmillan.		
	11. President Kennedy assassinated.		
		12. State of emergency declared in Aden; and Makarios calls for British help in Cyprus.	

1964			
		1. East-African mutinies.	
		1–6. Radfan campaign.	
		3. UN takes over in Cyprus.	3. Indonesia deploys regular troops against Malaysia.
		7. Announcement of independence for South Arabia by 1968.	
			8. Indonesian landings in Malaya fail; and direct US military involvement in Vietnam starts.
	10. Wilson wins UK general election.		
		11. NFL launch terrorist campaign in Aden.	

1965			
			6. Viet Cong invade South Vietnam.
			8. Singapore leaves Malaysia.
		9. Direct rule imposed in Aden.	
			10. Communist coup in Indonesia crushed.
		11. UDI by Southern Rhodesian Government.	

1966			
	2. Publication of Healey Defence Review.	2. Withdrawal of Aden military base announced.	
			8. 'Confrontation' with Indonesia ends.
		12. *Tiger* talks on Rhodesia.	

1967	5. Second British application to join the EEC.		
		6. Arab-Israeli Six Day War; and police mutinies in Aden.	
			7. British military withdrawal from Southeast Asia by mid-1970s announced.
	11. Devaluation of sterling.	11. Aden evacuated.	
	12. De Gaulle vetoes second British EEC application.		
1968			1. Withdrawal from Southeast Asia advanced to 1971.
		10. *Fearless* talks on Rhodesia.	
1969		6. Franco closes Gibraltar frontier.	
	8. British troops intervene in Ulster.		8. US troop withdrawals from Vietnam start.
		9. Libyan military coup ends Anglo-Libyan Treaty.	
1970			5. US bombing of North Vietnam resumed.
	6. Heath wins UK general election.		
		7. Dhofar campaign begins.	
		9. Nasser dies.	

| 1971 | 6. British EEC entry terms agreed. | 1 to 12. Final phase of military withdrawal from Southeast Asia. |

| 1972 | The British military withdrawal from Empire is complete; and Britain enters the European Community. | |

PROLOGUE
Seventeenth, eighteenth and nineteenth centuries

God of our fathers, known of old,
  Lord of our far-flung battle-line,
Beneath whose awful hand we hold
  Dominion over palm and pine—
Lord God of Hosts, be with us yet,
  Lest we forget—lest we forget!

Rudyard Kipling's *Recessional*, 1897, Verse 1

1 RAGS TO RICHES . . .
1588 to 1920

It is the love of the people: it is their attachment to their government, from the sense of the deep stake they have in such a glorious institution, which gives you your army and your navy, and infuses into both that liberal obedience without which your army would be a base rabble, and your navy nothing but rotten timber.

Edmund Burke 1729–1797

This book is about the military campaigns waged to ensure Britain's orderly withdrawal from Empire after the Second World War. But military stories should not be told in isolation from political, economic and other relevant influences. War, in the second half of the twentieth century, is as much a continuation of politics by other means as it ever was in von Clausewitz's day. British military actions between 1945 and 1972 can only be seen in proper perspective against the background of the three centuries of the creation of the British Empire that held within them seeds of the eventual collapse of British power and the remarkable transformation from the imperial splendour of 1921 to the loosely knit British Commonwealth of nations in the last quarter of this century.

Much has been written about the political and economic aspects of Britain's rise and fall. It is the old story of rags to riches and back to rags. One or two generations make a family's fortune; the next few expand and enjoy it; and then come those who spend it, not necessarily on riotous living: sometimes on altruistic endeavours. In Britain's case it was centuries rather than generations that marked her progress through the cycle. It took the seventeenth and eighteenth centuries to lay the foundations of her Empire; the nineteenth to build upon them; and only half the twentieth to withdraw from her imperial role.

The driving force in the creative period was the quest for wealth to which were added the twin spurs of rivalry with the Spaniards, Portuguese, French and Dutch, and of religious and political escapism that provided the flow of colonists, seeking a new life free from the intolerances of English and European society. But success would not have been possible had it not been for the fighting spirit and skill of the British sailors and soldiers and in recent years airmen, which has stayed constant for three and a half centuries and was so recently demonstrated in the Falklands Campaign.

Imperial success was far less consistent. The First British Empire was acquired largely in opposition to Spain and Portugal, and brought about primarily by settling sparsely populated lands in North America and by sugar farming on islands in the Caribbean. It was lost in the 1770s through failure to apply to the North American colonies the principles of representative government that had been fought for and won by Parliament in the English Civil Wars of the 1640s. American influence was to help to create and destroy the Second British Empire. Blocked to the west, the British drive for colonial wealth turned eastwards where commercial rivalry with the French and the Dutch led to the conquests in the older civilizations of Asia and thus to the creation of her new empire.

American influence in the destruction of the Second Empire was less obvious and more long term. Britain learnt the lesson of failure to apply her own constitutional advances to her settler colonies and gave them the self-government of dominion status when they pressed for it. It took much longer for the same lesson to be applied to territories acquired by conquest rather than settlement, in which the indigenous people remained numerically predominant. Nevertheless, it was the experience of the Great American Rebellion that made transition from Empire to Commonwealth inevitable in the longer term. In North America Britain learnt to seek political rather than military solutions to imperial problems. Unlike other empires, consent with minimal coercion became the bonding material of the second British Empire. That bonding could not have been effective without the stable environment provided by British military prowess, in which good government could generate economic prosperity both for the subject people and for Britain. Being associated with the Union Jack became attractive to 'the lesser breeds without the law' as Kipling expressed it over 100 years later.

The reverse side of the coin of American influence was less constructive and equally long term. As the Second British Empire grew and the United States expanded towards the Pacific coast of North America during the nineteenth century, a love-hate relationship developed between the two. Inbred loyalty to the Anglo-Saxon tradition and way of life held them together: American pride in winning independence from Britain kept them at arms length. American admiration of British imperial success, coupled with the memories of their own rebellion, created the paradox of American anti-colonial imperialism, which was so often displayed when the United States emerged as a world power at the beginning of the twentieth century. Emotional American support of Britain, the mother country, masked an insidious dislike of her Empire. American influence was to play a decisive role in accelerating Britain's eventual withdrawal from Empire.

In the early eighteenth-century struggle with France, two opposing schools of British strategic thought developed, which are still relevant today. The 'Continental' school led by Godolphin and Marlborough, argued that Britain's interests were best served by maintaining, by force if need be, a favourable balance of power in Europe. Success on the

Continent would free Britain to pursue her political and economic interests overseas, knowing that her island base was secure. The 'Maritime' school, on the other hand, led in those days by the land-owning Tory Party, disliked the high taxation that was bound to flow from military involvement in European politics. Not only had a large standing army to be paid for—anathema to most Britons since the Civil War—but financial subsidies were needed to keep the armies of fickle European allies in the field. In the Maritime school's view, the security of the British Isles could be ensured more cheaply by maintaining a strong Royal Navy to control the English Channel; and war with European rivals overseas could be made to pay for itself by capturing their colonies, trading posts and commerce.

The conflict between these two schools has never been resolved. Most British wars since Queen Anne's day have been fought pragmatically, using a compound of the two strategies. In the War of the Spanish Succession (1701–1713) British fleets snapped up French and Spanish overseas possessions, while Marlborough's armies fought his great land battles. The Tories' point was made by the alarming escalation in the slaughter on the European battlefields and outflow of cash in subsidies.

Marlborough's costly victories did not bring peace and stability to Europe, but the Treaty of Utrecht gave Britain most of Canada at the expense of the French, who retained only their Quebec settlements. Spain ceded Gibraltar and Minorca, giving Britain naval control of the western Mediterranean, the start of the shortest route to India.

In the Seven Years War (1754–1761) Pitt used both strategies, but placed the greater emphasis on Britain's Maritime effort. On the Continent, British financial subsidies, and the Army's victory over the French at Minden (1759), helped to keep Frederick the Great's Prussian army in the field against France. Overseas, Clive's victory at Plassey (1757) gave Bengal to the East India Company and set the foundations for British rule in India; and Wolfe's victory on the Heights of Abraham (1758) brought all known Canada under British sovereignty. Under the Treaty of Paris, signed at the end of the war, Britain acquired more islands in the Caribbean, Florida and the right to navigate the Mississippi, so all in all Pitt could claim that the war had paid for itself by the increase in British assets.

The Napoleonic Wars provided a classic example of the most advantageous mix of Britain's Maritime and Continental strategies. In the first phase her effort was principally at sea with minimal Continental commitment, and it ended with Nelson's victory at Trafalgar in 1805. Command of the sea then enabled Britain to attack Napoleon's flank in Portugal and Spain and to blockade Napoleonic Europe, making the second phase from 1807 to 1813 a Maritime/Continental effort. Only in the short third phase did Britain fight Continentally to bring about Napoleon's final defeat at Waterloo in 1815. Britain's losses had been small compared to those of Marlborough's campaigns and her gains were much greater.

Trafalgar and Waterloo, coupled with the Industrial Revolution, which had started in England in the 1760s, made Britain the superpower of the nineteenth century. Her ambition to rise from rags to riches had been fulfilled. As the Georgian period ended and the Victorian age began, she acquired a sense of imperial mission based on liberal morality and religious evangelism. The Victorians and Edwardians developed their imperial heritage through the acquisitiveness of their colonial proconsuls, their naval and military commanders, and their own new-found enthusiasm for exporting British enlightenment. Little thought was given to economic and military consequence of over-expansion. Britain had the wealth and could enjoy shouldering her self-imposed 'white man's burden', taking as much pride in her occasional defeats as in her continuing military successes.

Over-expansion has always been a potent cause for the collapse of families, businesses and empires. It played a major part in Britain's eventual return to rags. Most of the older world empires had been geographically homogenous: the British Empire was divided by the world's oceans and could only be linked by sea power and political consent, both of which were ephemeral. Return to the rags of middle power status was made all the more certain by Britain's own political development and sense of individual and corporate liberty, reaching back through the Civil War to the Magna Carta (1215). After the American rebellion, it took only two minor revolts in Canada in 1837 to set in train the process that was to lead relatively quickly to the imperial formula, which had eluded George III and his ministers when dealing with the American colonists in the 1770s: dominion status for the settler colonies which had remained loyal.

It was no accident that the passage through Parliament of Lord Gray's First Reform Bill (1832), modestly widening the electoral franchise in Britain, and of his Bill for the Abolition of Slavery (1833), occurred in the same decade as the birth of the Chartist movement, the forerunner of the Labour Party. The three events reflected the liberal spirit of the age, though the two bills had to be fought through against determined opposition and the Chartists were far from welcome in British society at the time. On the Christian principle of doing unto others as you would they should do unto you, the concept of granting the settler colonies responsible internal self-government in the Westminster style was set forth in Lord Durham's Report of 1839 on the causes of Canadian political unrest. Canada became the first self-governing dependency under the Canada Act of 1840. Almost simultaneously with Disraeli's Second Reform Bill, which advanced democracy in Britain with a further extension of the franchise, Canada was granted full independence as a dominion under the Crown in the British North America Act of 1867. The precedent was thus set for the other settler colonies. Australia gained dominion status in 1901, New Zealand in 1907 and South Africa in 1910.

In theory the same principles of constitutional development should have applied to all colonies whether settled, conquered or annexed: in practice it seemed unlikely to the Victorians and Edwardians that any of the non-white colonies would be able to stand on their own feet without loss of stability or annexation by some other European power. It was Britain's mission to give them good government, so that they could prosper and develop their own political institutions, preferably, but not necessarily, on British parliamentary lines.

There were obvious differences in the British mind between the white settler colonies and the non-white dependent territories. In the former, Britons and other European migrants came to stay, building new lives for themselves and establishing family roots. In the latter, administrators, soldiers, merchants and missionaries came and went with no intention of settling: inter-marriage with the indigenous people was frowned upon and eventual retirement to Britain, hopefully richer, was their intention. In between the two came hybrids like South Africa, Rhodesia and Kenya where settlers established themselves, providing the government and employing the local people as labourers on their farms, in the mines and in other enterprises. The problems they were to present in due course were only slightly less intractable than Britain's oldest colonial problem of Northern Ireland.

There was another categorization of Britain's colonies, which was to become increasingly important as the Empire waxed and finally waned. Some colonies were strategically significant; indeed, places like Gibraltar, Malta, Cyprus and Aden, were acquired for specific military purposes. Others were of little concern to the Admiralty, the War Office and, latterly, the Air Ministry in Whitehall. The defence of the Empire was based upon maritime power which, in turn, depended upon naval bases and coaling stations in the nineteenth century and air bases as well in the twentieth. The concentration of these bases lay on the imperial line of communication through the Mediterranean, Red Sea and Indian Ocean. When Britain's withdrawal from Empire started most of the military rearguard actions took place along this line of communication: transition elsewhere was relatively peaceful.

The latter half of Victoria's reign was a period of exaggerated confidence in Britain's imperial mission and of inordinate pride in enlightened liberal principles. The two together created a sense of Anglo-Saxon racial superiority. The former was articulated by Disraeli and Kipling, and the latter by Gladstone. Despite the defeat of Napolean at Waterloo, France remained Britain's principal colonial rival, though the two countries were united in repelling the real, and sometimes imaginary, threats to their interests posed by Tsarist Russia.

Anglo-French partnership in the Crimean War (1854–6) did not check colonial competition between Britain and France in the Mediterranean, Middle East and Africa. Only in India were French interests virtually extinguished. The Indian Mutiny (1857–8) led to the demise of the East India Company, its replacement by the British Government of India, and eventually to Disraeli's proclamation of Queen Victoria as Empress of India (1876). The construction of the Suez Canal by de Lesseps and Disraeli's purchase of the Khedive's shares in the Suez Canal Company helped to secure Britain's communications with India, but embroiled her in Egyptian politics with Victorian epics like the Battle of Tel-el-Keber (1882), Gordon's assassination at Khartoum (1885) and the Battle of Omdurman (1898).

In Africa, Cape Colony, which had been taken from the Dutch during the Napoleonic Wars, lost some of its strategic importance with the opening of the Suez Canal, but became Britain's base for expansion northwards into Central Africa. Cecil Rhodes' dream of an all Red route from the Cape to Cairo entangled Britain in the Zulu and Boer Wars. There was less competition in the rest of Africa, the French dominating the Muslim territories of the north-west, the Sahara and parts of the west coast, while Britain confined herself to developing her footholds in West Africa—the Gambia (first annexed in 1686), Sierra Leone (1807), the Gold Coast (1870) and the Niger basin (1870). A *modus vivendi* with the Dutch led to the peaceful development of the Straits Settlement of Penang (1786), Singapore (1819) and Malacca (1824). Penetration south-eastwards into the Pacific was equally peaceful, but efforts to open up trade with China, though successful, proved militarily expensive.

Gladstone disliked overseas commitments. His triumph in driving through the Third Reform Bill, which further extended adult male suffrage, was not to be repeated in his two attempts to introduce Home Rule for Ireland in 1886 and 1894. In the heady days of Victorian enjoyment of empire, bowing to nationalism of any kind, let alone within the British Isles, was politically unacceptable. What chances there might have been for Ireland to follow the Canadian precedent in a peaceful way were lost. Ironically efforts were being made in India at much the same time by British officials to create a national consciousness where none had existed before the establishment of the British Raj. The Indian National Congress met for the first time in 1885, the year of the Third Reform Bill, and demanded the extension of British parliamentary institutions to India. Sinn Fein in Ireland and the Indian National Congress were to become the trend-setters in Britain's withdrawal from Empire.

Despite all the jingoism of the latter half of Victoria's reign, there was serious public debate about whether the Empire, particularly India, actually strengthened or weakened Britain. Disraeli's Conservative and Unionist Party, appealing to considerations of power, prestige and national pride espoused the former view; Gladstone thundered the latter. There was, however, no gainsaying the fact that Britain alone was shouldering the whole burden of imperial defence and was paying for the Royal Navy upon which the security of the Empire depended. Although the grant of dominion status tended to weaken the imperial connection, it was welcome because, as Gladstone put it, 'self-government begets self-defence'. Conversely, it gave the dominions the right to decide when and where their military resources, such as they were at that time, should be used. While Australia and New Zealand with their very recent and almost entirely British immigrant populations could be relied on to spring to Britain's aid in times of military emergency, there was much less certainty about the older Anglo-French and Anglo-Dutch electorates in Canada and South Africa. After all, why should, say, Canada or South Africa help to pick Britain's strategic chestnuts out of some European fire that was not endangering North America or southern Africa?

Doubts as to whether Britain could and should remain a paramount imperial power were fanned by the surprising difficulty she experienced in crushing the Boer rebellion at the turn of the century. Australia, New Zealand and even Canada sent contingents on a voluntary basis, but there was unease, especially in Canada. It was encouraging to Britain that such help should be forthcoming, but worrying that it should have been needed at all. Some means had to be found of harnessing the latent military resources of the Empire without infringing the various degrees of independence reached by dominion governments.

The rise of a unified Germany in the heart of Europe after the Franco-Prussian War of 1870, and of Japan in the Far East after the Russo-Japanese War of 1904–5, both with imperial ambitions, gave urgency to the quest for a sensible burden-sharing formula for British imperial defence. The Anglo-Japanese Alliance of 1902, and Britain's tacit support of Japan in her war with Russia, reduced the threat to British interests in the Far East. The blatantness of the German Kaiser's aggressive imperial policies overcame dominion reluctance to accept Whitehall's co-ordination of defence policies in the run-up to the First World War.

The German challenge at sea, in Europe, and in the world at large, generated unusually rapid action. In 1902 the Committee of Imperial Defence was established in London and was formally recognized by the dominions in 1904. In the following year the Colonial Conferences which had begun in 1887, were renamed the Imperial Conferences. In 1907 the Imperial General Staff was set up with an exchange of staff officers between Britain and the dominions. It concentrated upon standardizing organization, equipment, tactics and training throughout the Empire. Definitive war plans could not be made because it was realized that dominion governments could not commit their electorates to hypothetical situations. It was also accepted that dominion contributions would be in the form of contingents rather than cash contributions to an imperial defence budget. Dominion self-interest—in other words nationalism—tended to outweigh imperial loyalty despite the German threat.

The First World War, when it came, strengthened both the unity of the Empire and dominion nationalism. The British government declared war on behalf of 'all His Britannic Majesty's realms beyond the seas'. The only objections came from the Afrikaners, who were themselves deeply divided over the issue. All Britain's dependencies played their part in the imperial war effort: the Canadians and Indians on the Western Front; the Australians and New Zealanders at Gallipoli and, later, with the Indians in

Palestine and Mesopotamia as well as on the Western Front; the Canadian, Australian and New Zealand navies at sea; and South African contingents in the seizure of Germany's African colonies.

The war was fought perforce with a combination of Maritime and Continental strategies. The existence of the German High Seas Fleet and U-boat flotillas, and the fact that Britain could no longer feed her own population without imports from abroad, made the former inevitable: Germany's central geographical position in Europe, and the need to prevent the establishment of German long-range weapons on the Channel coast and U-boats in the Channel ports, forced Britain into a major Continental effort in support of France and Belgium. Unlike the Napoleonic Wars the emphasis in British strategy became over-Continental: like Marlborough's wars the losses progressively mounted in the cauldron of the Western Front.

Seven million men left the British Isles, 700,000 never to return. The annual British loss during the Napoleonic wars had been about 5,000; in the First World War, it was 170,000. The Empire sent a million and a half men overseas of whom 200,000 were killed: no mean effort, which not only helped in the common war effort, but also brought national pride to the individual dominions and colonies, and to India. In contrast, the United States' emergence from its self-imposed isolationism in 1917 was belated and proved to be fleeting with the American electorate's rejection of President Woodrow Wilson's policies after the war.

The wartime strengthening of the bonds of Empire was furthered in 1918 by the creation of the Imperial War Cabinet and by the acceptance of dominion representatives in the British delegation to the Peace Conference in 1919. The only sour note had been the Easter Rising in Dublin in 1916 when Sinn Fein tried to win by force the national independence that the dominions already enjoyed and which was recognized internationally by their separate signatures on the Treaty of Versailles. Their coming of age was also marked by their individual memberships of the League of Nations.

After the Napoleonic Wars Britain had eschewed territorial aggrandisement at the Congress of Vienna: at Versailles she received, as League of Nations' mandates, the German African colonies of Tanganika, the Cameroons and Togoland, and the Ottoman provinces of Palestine, Jordan and Iraq. The British Empire had reached its zenith in territory, population and power. In Field Marshal Smuts' view the British Empire 'emerged from the war quite the greatest power in the World, and it is only unwisdom or unsound policy that could rob her of that great position'.[1] In the euphoric atmosphere of victory the dominion representatives gloried as much in imperial success as in their own nationhood. Smuts articulated the common feeling:

We are the only group of nations that has ever successfully existed. People talk about a league of nations and international government, but the only successful experiment in international government that has ever been made is the British Empire founded on the principles which appeal to the highest political ideals of mankind.[2]

But, while success may breed success, it also attracts predators. Furthermore, Britain's success had been bought at too great a material and psychological price. The zenith of her imperial power was soon passed and her decline began as totalitarian rivals gathered and as she grappled with the problems of Ireland and India.

2 NEW RIVALS GATHER
1920 to 1945

The British Empire ... is based not on force but on goodwill and a common understanding. Liberty is its binding principle.

David Lloyd-George at the Imperial Conference of 1922

The British Empire in the 1920s was like a newly completed Arc de Triomphe. Britain was the ground on which it stood; the dominions were the solid buttresses either side; and the dependent territories formed the arch ring with the Indian empire as its keystone. Such monuments cannot survive the ravages of time unless the foundations are firm, the material is sound and the arch has symmetrical strength. In the eyes of British and dominion statesmen, common ideals provided the symmetry; to Britain's subject people, confidence held the ring together—confidence in the soundness of British administration, in Britain's will to govern and in her power to defend them against internal subversion and external aggression.

British imperial confidence depended more upon people's general assessment of British power than upon the reality of that power. In 1921 the two coincided: there was no need to fudge the reality. Britain's military forces were victorious; her rivals defeated; and her imperial institutions were developing in a way that suggested still greater achievements. There was confidence also in Britain's ability to lead the newly established League of Nations, which it was hoped would lessen the chances of another world war and would create a more peaceful and prosperous world.

Paradoxically, it was Britain's own desire to build that better world that started her decline. The beginning of her return from riches to rags was typical of any powerful family in which the younger generations become disillusioned with its way of life, conscious of both its wealth and the poverty around it. Trying to put things right has greater attractions for them than accumulating further wealth. The heavy losses suffered by Britain during the First World War increased her idealism, but it also gave her a severe bout of imperial anaemia. British public opinion in the inter-war years indulged itself in peacekeeping fantasies: Britain, as the paramount world power, had only to set an example and the rest of the world would follow; collective security through the League of Nations, led by Britain, was the surest way forward; and disarmament with Britain to the fore was the panacea to the world's ills. The value of the Empire to Britain and the morality of colonialism were questioned as they had been in the days of Disraeli and Gladstone. This time the bitter memories of the Boer War and the scale of national bereavement in the First World War gave birth to many more latter-day Gladstones than Disraelis. The change in national attitudes was soon reflected in the affairs of Ireland, India and the dominions.

In Irish affairs Gladstone's attempts to introduce Home Rule in 1886 and 1894 had been defeated by an unholy alliance between Tory landed interests, Ulster Protestants and middle and working-class jingoism. How could Britain rule an empire, 'on which the sun never sets', if she could not govern her own islands? Few of Gladstone's opponents had doubted that the causes of Irish poverty must be eliminated, but they believed this should be done by sensible administrative action rather than by decentralizing more power from London to Dublin. Home Rule should be killed by the kindness of legislative reform and a greater sensitivity to Irish grievances. The error in this train of thought lay in treating Irish nationalism as a product of economic distress. The Easter Rising in Dublin in 1916 had shown how wrong this was. Nationalism—the feeling of racial difference—was at the root of Irish separatism, as it was also becoming in India as British power declined.

Much has been written and re-written about Lloyd George's sudden volte-face in 1921 when he offered dominion status to de Valera as a way out of full-scale civil war in Ireland. It was a logical step to take. There were the precedents of failure with the American colonies and subsequent success with the Canadians, and of the very recent grant of dominion status to South Africa that seemed to have healed the Anglo-Boer rift. Dominion status gave far more power to Dublin than Gladstone's concept of Home Rule would ever have done, but it involved the partition of Ireland.

The Irish settlement established a number of new precedents. It widened the potential usefulness of dominion status as a constitutional device for harnessing nationalism within the unity of the Empire. But it also established partition, the antithesis of unity, as an undesirable but nevertheless practicable solution to inter-racial antagonism. It had not been used in Anglo-French Canada or Anglo-Dutch South Africa, but it was to become increasingly important as Britain withdrew from Empire. Many colonial boundaries had been drawn with little regard to ethnic origins. Independence for majorities could often spell new bondage for minorities. Where inter-communal distrust was too deep to be bridged by constitutional safeguards partition became the oft-used solution.

From the British point of view the manner of the Anglo-Irish parting had several undesirable by-products. It demonstrated the power of nationalism to move mountains and the vulnerability of British power to popularly-backed terrorism. The days when rebellions like the Indian Mutiny could be crushed by savage reprisal were over. British public opinion and the development of the international press, using the speed of twentieth century communications, lent increasing emphasis to the principle of using minimum force within the law when dealing with all forms of internal unrest.

The most unfortunate by-product was the legacy of Irish racial bitterness that is still so pronounced amongst Irish communities in the United States and the older dominions. Many of their forebears had emigrated from Ireland in the worst periods of economic distress and political frustration. Memories turned into myths and have fuelled anti-British sentiments ever since.

The lessons of the Irish rebellion were not lost on political activists in India. In no other part of the Empire did Britain feel the sanctity of her imperial mission more deeply: and in no other dependency was confidence more crucial to British rule. The British military presence amongst the teeming millions of the Subcontinent was tiny: 45,000 British troops garrisoning the whole of India and Burma. Although India had been conquered by the sword, the stability of the Indian Empire depended more upon mutual benefit and the consequential level of Indian consent rather than continued use of that sword. There was a close partnership between the administrators in the Indian Civil Service—both British and latterly Indian—and the Indian people in the development of better government. The relative incorruptibility and impartiality of the British Raj brought a degree of unity to the Subcontinent that had never existed before. But the voluntary partnership could only last for as long as Britain had something to give through example and education. The latter held the key to India's future. To the British, education was part of their mission: to the Indians, it was a stepping-stone to independence. Growing numbers of Indians wanted to apply the theory they had learnt in British public schools and universities to the practice of their lives in India. Britain did not resist: by 1917 internal self-government had become the common aim on both sides. Differences developed between the educated Indians and their imperial mentors on two scores: the speed at which transfer of power could be accomplished, and the type of constitution needed to maintain the unity of the Subcontinent without the catalyst of a British presence. Arguments about pace were immediate and pressing: constitutional dilemmas came later.

The Indian equivalent of the Irish Easter Rising as a milestone on the road to independence was the massacre at Amritsar in 1919 when British-commanded Gurkha troops opened fire on a supposedly peaceful demonstration in the confined area of the Jallianwala Bagh from which there were too few exits for the crowd to escape. Almost 400 people were killed. The British government, the government of India and the majority of the British people condemned the action of General Dyer, who ordered the troops to fire, but there was a significant minority amongst the British establishment in India and in Britain who applauded him. Victorian folklore about Indian atrocities and British heroism during the Indian Mutiny only 60 years earlier had not yet been crowded out of British minds by twentieth century events. Fear of a recurrence of the Mutiny generated immediate and uncritical support for rapid and decisive military action at the least sign of a repetition. Doubts about the efficacy and moral acceptability of military reprisal were only just beginning to take root in British public opinion, used as it was to the success of Victorian gun boat diplomacy.

As in Ireland there were two ways in which the Indians could bring effective pressure to bear on Britain to speed up constitutional reform: peaceful political pressure or violence. The former was more in keeping with Indian philosophy, but the threat and practice of urban unrest, be it riot or terrorism, was never far below the surface and burst out sporadically when emotions flared, as it had always done throughout India's history. Gandhi's rise to prominence in the leadership of Congress increased the emphasis on peaceful persuasion. He exploited the strengths of Indian religious pacifism and the weaknesses of British liberal morality, but his followers often lapsed into almost medieval beastiality against their fellow men, though rarely against the British.

In the inter-war years there was no lack of effort on both sides to move forward towards an acceptable constitutional solution which would give Indians progressively more say in their own government despite prejudices on both sides. It is fair to say that the impetus for reform on the British side came more from the Westminster Parliament, reflecting British public opinion, than from the British administrators in India, who were faced with day to day problems rooted in the backwardness of the great majority of the many different peoples that inhabit the Subcontinent. Progress would certainly have been much slower had it not been for the unrelenting political pressure applied by Congress, which in the inter-war years was an all-India party representing Hindus, Muslims and Sikhs, and was only at odds with the Indian princes. The Montague-Chelmsford reforms in the latter half of the First World War had set in train the development of self-governing institutions with, in the words of the declaration, 'a view to the progressive realization of responsible government in India as an integral part of the British Empire'.[1] Dominion status was not mentioned, but the precedents were obvious and were confirmed in 1929 by the Viceroy, Lord Irwin, who was authorized by the British government to say that 'the natural outcome of India's constitutional progress . . . is the attainment of Dominion Status'.[2]

The pace of reform was still too slow for India's intellectual leaders and too fast for Britain's proconsuls. The Congress Civil Disobedience Campaigns maintained the pressure on the government of India and on British public opinion. In the early 1930s there was a flurry of constitutional activity with the First and Second Indian Round Table Conferences in London, and the passage of the Government of India Act of 1935, which gave India fully responsible internal self-government on federal lines. The constitution, though brilliantly drafted, was fatally flawed. It had been devised by British politicians and officials, principally in Whitehall, and not by Indians in Delhi. It proved unacceptable to both the nationalists of the Congress Party and to the princes. The former were none the less prepared to accept office in the provincial assemblies as stepping stones to greater power, but the latter blocked the institution of responsible self-government at federal level, leaving the Viceroy to govern with a nominated rather than elected executive council.

The Irish and the Indians were not the only inhabitants of the British Empire dissatisfied with their constitutional status during the inter-war years. Whilst Australia and New Zealand were happy to accept the precedents of membership of the Imperial War Cabinet and of the League of Nations as evidence of their independence, Canada and South Africa were not, and they were joined in their disquiet by the Irish Free State. Each had different reasons for wanting a legal instrument that defined their status in a way which foreign countries and their own people could understand: Canada, because she wished to develop direct relations with United States; South Africa, to satisfy the Boers that they did not need to strive for a republic; and the Free State, to prove its right to secede from the Commonwealth. Australia and New Zealand preferred to follow the British practice of avoiding the inflexibility of written constitutions. They sided with Britain in her reluctance to define in theory how free the dominions really were: practice was sufficient for them.

But it was practice that reinforced the calls for clearer definition. A series of incidents occurred in the early 1920s, starting with the Chanak affair of 1922, in which Britain acted in an apparently high-minded way without adequate consultation with dominion governments. Exhaustive debates at the Imperial Conferences of 1923 and 1926 led to the Balfour Declaration, which described Britain and her dominions as:

... autonomous Communities within the British Empire, equal in status, in no way subordinate one to another in any aspect of their domestic or external affairs, though united by a common allegiance to the Crown, and freely associated as members of the British Commonwealth of Nations.[3]

There was something in this declaration for everyone: all could applaud the concept of equality of status. Australia and New Zealand could delight in the continuing existence of the British Empire; Canada, in freedom in foreign as well as domestic affairs; and South Africa and Ireland, in acceptance of their autonomy.

The Balfour Declaration formed the basis of the Statue of Westminster which was enacted in the Westminster Parliament in 1931, and was confirmed, with some reservations, in the Canadian, South African and Irish legislatures. Australia and New Zealand did not bother to do so until much later, feeling that the whole exercise was an unnecessary piece of pedantry. The Statute was silent on the right of secession, but the separatists in South Africa and the Irish Free State took this to be the import of the words 'freely associated'. The Irish put the matter to the test after the abdication of Edward VII in 1937 by introducing a new constitution that was republican in all but name. With the tacit agreement of the other dominions, the new Eire remained associated with the Commonwealth, setting a precedent for republics as well as monarchies within its membership. Eire finally seceded in 1947, the same year that the Republics of India and Pakistan joined the Commonwealth. The device of accepting the British monarch as Head of the Commonwealth preserved the Crown's essential symbolism, which was reinforced by mutual self-interest and the affinity of a common recent history and political tradition.

In the non-self-governing dependencies of the British Empire controversy in the inter-war years was economic rather than political. The idea of trusteeship had taken root in the British mind, but colonial coming of age seemed a long way off. Each colony was expected to be financially self-sufficient, paying for its Governor and his government and finding its own development capital. With Britain wedded to free trade since the mid-nineteenth century, there had been no call for an imperial economic policy, other than *laissez-faire*. Shortages of food and raw materials during the German U-boat campaign of the First World War did encourage some economic co-ordination but it did not last for long after the war.

In the 1920s British colonial development policy was selfishly negative. Instead of viewing the Empire as a great family estate which required methodical development, the British Treasury sought to ensure that no part of it became a drain on the British taxpayer. Such colonial development projects that were put forward, and there were not many, were judged by the impact they would make on the high levels of unemployment in the United Kingdom. By 1929, however, Britain's colonial conscience was beginning to stir. The Colonial Development Act of that year provided a modest cache of funds, but it was ringed around by so many restricting criteria that the available money was consistently underspent.

During the world Depression of the early 1930s, the prices of colonial products slumped, bringing poverty to many British colonies which highlighted their economic difficulties and social distress. The protectionist lobbies gradually won the upper hand and ushered in the era of imperial preferences, which, together with the upturn in the world's economy when it came, did much to help the colonial producers of primary products back onto their feet. Paradoxically there had been little internal unrest during the black days of the Depression, but as soon as the tide turned widespread disturbances occurred in the Caribbean, in the Rhodesian Copper Belt and in West Africa. The causes were primarily economic though with some racial undertones. Wages had not kept pace with inflation and the indigenous people felt they were not receiving their share of the economic revival.

The public display of colonial dissatisfaction between 1935 and 1938 had an impact in Whitehall where those who believed in the theory of trusteeship received a better hearing. They were helped by Italy and Germany claiming their places in the colonial sun, and by American criticism of Britain's performance as the leading colonial power. Treasury objections to use of imperial funds to help colonial governments to improve social conditions were overcome, and projects to build new housing, schools and hospitals were accepted. Much larger sums were allocated henceforth under the Colonial Development and Welfare Acts than hitherto. The stark fact began to emerge that the Empire was no longer self-financing and renewed doubts were expressed about the value to Britain of many of her overseas possessions. Her ability to find the resources needed to meet her commitments as a responsible colonial power was also called into question. The outbreak of the Second World War stilled these doubts but only for its duration.

The gentlemanliness of the internal debates about constitutional reform for the dominions and about economic ways and means in the colonies was not matched in international relations in the 1920s and 1930s. The high hopes, which Britain had placed in the League of Nations in the 1920s, were shattered in the 1930s. The flimsiness of collective security was demonstrated first by Fascist Italy's invasion of Abyssinia (1935); then by Nazi Germany's march into the Rhineland (1936); and finally by Imperial Japan's invasion of China (1937). Despite Britain's efforts at appeasement, the three totalitarian powers became Britain's new and overtly hostile imperial rivals, all three harping on the 'colonial question' as one of the justifications for their aggressions.

The Second World War, when it broke out in 1939, strengthened the bonds of Empire as its predecessor had done. This time each dominion entered the war of its own volition and in its own time. The Australian and New Zealand governments declared war before consulting their parliaments, the New Zealand Prime Minister saying 'Where Britain goes, we go; where she stands, we stand.' Mackenzie King made his point by consulting the Canadian Parliament first, so Canada's declaration was delayed four days. In South Africa, General Hertzog's cabinet was divided. He and five ministers favoured neutrality; General Smuts, his deputy, and seven colleagues wanted to follow Britain's lead. Smuts triumphed in the subsequent debate in the South African House of Assembly. Hertzog asked for a dissolution of Parliament. The Governor-General refused as Smuts was able to form an alternative government and did so, holding power until 1948. Unhappily Hertzog's eclipse enabled militant Afrikaner nationalists, led by Doctor Malan, to emerge as the main opposition party, undermining the attempted fusion of the English and Boer political traditions.

Britain declared war for all her other dependent territories. The Viceroy of India declared war on behalf of India without consulting the Indian political leaders: a grave lapse of political judgement, although constitutionally correct. His action enabled Congress to adopt the attitude of 'how could an unfree India support Britain in her fight for freedom?' The Congress governments in the provinces, which had been established under the 1935 Government of India Act, resigned and there was a wartime reversion to direct British rule. Nevertheless, Indian sentiment was pro-British in the struggle with Germany and Italy, though ambivalent in the case of Japan. The Indian Army provided no less than two and a half million men to fight with great distinction in almost all the great battles of the Middle East and Mediterranean campaigns: Keren, Tobruk, El Alamein, Cassino, Rome, the Gothic Line and the Po to mention but a few of the battle honours of its regiments. It provided the bulk of the armies which stopped the Japanese on India's eastern frontier, drove them back and out of Burma, re-occupied Malaya and Singapore, and took the Japanese surrender in the French and Dutch Far-Eastern empires.

In the desperate days of 1940 and 1941, when Britain stood alone, the Empire responded with an unprecedented surge of military effort. The First World War's figure of one and a half million men sent abroad by the dominions and colonies was more than trebled to five million. The large dominion contingents fought under British, and later American, higher commanders with a degree of co-operation that belied the increase in dominion independence and nationalism since 1918. Most of the British and dominion generals had won their spurs in the unimaginative attritional fighting on the First World War's Continental battlefields. Their success in the Second World War which the British Empire fought largely with a marine and air bombardment strategy, was shown in the steep decline in the casualty figures (900,000 killed out of eight million in the First World War and 370,000 out of 11 million in the Second, which lasted a year longer).

While the fighting against Italy and Germany increased the cohesion of the British Empire, the same cannot be said of the war against Japan. The destruction of the American fleet at Pearl Harbor, the capture of Singapore, and the occupation of all British, French and Dutch colonial territories up to the India-Burma border, shattered the myth of European racial supremacy in Asian minds. Japan's much vaunted Asian Co-prosperity Sphere became a reality. The fact that Britain's defeat in the Far East had been primarily due to her extraordinary single-handed military effort west of Suez against the Germans and Italians, went unnoticed in the bazaars of India and Southeast Asia. Although Japan was beaten in the end, and British forces re-occupied most of the territories lost by the French and Dutch as well as her own, previously unthinkable challenges to European rule had become thinkable and remained so in Asia and Africa.

The damage done to British imperial pretensions by the Axis might have been repaired had it not been for the hostile post-war policies of the two emergent superpowers, who had been Britain's wartime allies. The roots of Russia's idealogical hostility needs no cataloguing. Her defeat of the German invasion of Russia and her occupation of the whole of Eastern and much of Central Europe gave her the base from which the Communist Party could pursue its policies of world revolution with greater imperial ambition than any of the Tsars. There were also many areas in the British Colonial Empire where conditions were ripe for the successful mating of nationalism with communism to produce an attractive alternative to

British paternalism. The danger was so obvious that it gave a spur to British post-war colonial development. The Colonial Development and Welfare Act of 1945 placed much more cash with fewer strings at the disposal of the Colonial Office than it had ever been given in pre-war days.

The effects of American policies were more subtle and potentially more damaging, and so need to be charted briefly. The United States emerged as a world power at the turn of the century. The principle of barring European interference in the American hemisphere, annunciated by President Monroe in 1823, had not stopped American governments meddling in other people's affairs as soon as they had the power to do so. American involvement in the Cuban revolt against Spain led to the Spanish-American War of 1898 and to the US becoming a colonial power with the acquisition of Puerto Rico, Guam and the Philippines, followed by the occupation of Hawaii, part of Samoa and Wake Island. The thrust of American colonialism was westwards across the Pacific, avoiding entanglement with the European powers and building upon the American penetration of Japan, which had begun during the Japanese revolution of 1868.

American ambitions began to influence European affairs and British imperial interests immediately after the First World War. Despite America's belated entry into the war, the US delegation dominated the Peace Conference in 1919 and Washington hosted the World Disarmament Conferences of 1921 and 1922. The latter were to have a decisive impact upon the British Empire. For the first time since Trafalgar, Britain was faced with the loss of naval supremacy upon which her imperial power had rested for so long.

During the nineteenth century the Royal Navy's strength was geared to the Two Power Standard, i.e. numerical superiority over any other pair of naval powers. This was a practicable policy as long as Britain's rivals had metropolitan populations of no more than about 50 millions. The emergence of the United States, and later the USSR, able to govern populations numbered in hundreds of millions, progressively changed the scale of world power to Britain's disadvantage. The Washington Disarmament Conference brought the first British acknowledgement that maintaining the Two Power Standard in the twentieth century was beyond her means.

It was not only the change in scale that led to Britain abandoning naval supremacy. The twin factors of post-war financial stringency and determination to prevent another world war through moral leadership were combined to lead Lloyd George's government in 1919 into formulating the 'Ten Year Rule' as the basis for British defence planning in the post-war era. Churchill, who was a member of the Cabinet at the time, supported the policy, that assumed:

that the British Empire will not be engaged in any great war during the next ten years and that no Expeditionary Force is required for this purpose.[4]

Britain had ended the war with her customary naval supremacy, but her ships were ageing. America and Japan, who had replaced France and Russia as the yardsticks against which British naval strength should have been measured under the old criteria, had in hand large naval building programmes of post-Jutland ships. A British replacement programme on the scale needed to compete with the new US and Japanese fleets was politically out of the question in war-weary and idealistic Britain. The unavoidable corollary was the decline to a One Power Standard. Superiority, or at least equality, would be maintained with the US fleet but not with the Japanese as well. The risks were to be reduced by renewing the Anglo-Japanese Treaty of 1902, in spite of American objections, in order to safeguard British interests in the Far East.

The British negotiators at the Washington Conferences seemed successful at the time. Naval strengths were pinned to a ratio of 5:5:3, with the British and US fleets co-equal at five and the Japanese at three. The Anglo-Japanese Treaty was not renewed but was replaced by a Four Power Pact by which the US, Britain, France and Japan would settle any differences in the Pacific on an amicable basis. Neither measure worked: German naval rearmament upset the 5:5:3 ratio, and the intensity of American and Japanese rivalry destroyed the Four Power Pact. The British government had to choose between the Pacific rivals and chose to support the United States despite misgivings about American hostility to British colonial policy.

The United States went from the international rags of self-imposed isolationism to the riches of superpower status in as short a time as Britain was to return to the rags of a middle power. US self-interest was joined by an American sense of mission far more quickly than had been the case in Britain. Though isolationism remained a political force to be reckoned with, the Americans took a justifiable pride in exporting the three major elements of their success: the American democratic way of life, which had created political stability without monarchy; the ingenuity of their mass-production of food and manufactured goods, which out-stripped the innovations of the British Industrial Revolutions; and the American brand of Anglo-Saxon liberal morality, which placed colonialism high on their list of anathamae despite their own colonial possessions. Missionary zeal in evangelizing the American way of life was later joined by an anti-Communist fervour that distorted the American message and brought the US some strangely reactionary, monarchical protegés.

A decisive struggle between American isolationism, self-interest and sense of mission took place during the first two years of the Second World War. At first isolationism and self-interest went hand in hand to keep the US determinedly neutral, most Americans thinking in terms of a localized conflict in Europe from which it was the duty of the US government to stand well clear. Hitler's early triumphs brought about a change of mood. Self-interest joined sense of mission in opposition to isolationism as Americans realized that they might not be able to avoid embroilment in Britain's struggle with the dictators. After Roosevelt's re-election in

November 1940 'Save America by helping Britain' became a credible slogan, which was given substance in the lend-lease legislation of February 1941. It was a generous gesture which kept Britain fighting while America armed. Nevertheless, opinion polls at the time showed that isolationism was far from dead. The majority of Americans still wished to avoid the conflict, though they felt their entry sooner or later was inevitable. Their sense of mission was enhanced by the high moral tone of the Atlantic Charter, which was the product of Roosevelt's first meetings with Churchill off the coast of Newfoundland in August 1941, where they met on board the battleships *Augusta* and *Prince of Wales* anchored in Placentia Bay.

It is tempting to read into their statement of Anglo-American war aims an overt declaration of support for Britain, as the mother country, coupled with covert American hostility to the British Empire from which they were proud to have freed themselves and wished to free others. The third clause read:

Third, they [Britain and the USA] respect the rights of all peoples to choose the form of government under which they will live; and they wish to see sovereign rights and self-government restored to those who have been forcibly deprived of them.[5]

But this was not American drafting. Churchill himself presented the first draft after the President had suggested that the centre-piece of the meeting should be a joint declaration of political principles. In discussions of Churchill's draft two extra clauses were added and one was substantially amended. The third clause remained much as Churchill had written it.

The Atlantic Charter, in fact, expressed the common theme of Anglo-American political tradition. Breach of that tradition had led to the original loss of the North American colonies; adherence to it had created the dominions; and its elaboration under post-Second World War American pressure was to turn Empire into Commonwealth far quicker than the two great leaders could ever have anticipated.

The third clause, indeed the whole Charter, had been drafted with the countries of Europe in mind. Cables were soon arriving in Whitehall from British colonial governors questioning its relevance to the peoples of their territories. They were reassured by Churchill, who stated in the House of Commons in September 1941 that the Charter did, indeed, refer to the 'Nations of Europe now under the Nazi yoke.' As far as Britain's dependent peoples were concerned Britain had made:

declarations on these matters which are complete in themselves, free from ambiguity and related to the conditions and circumstances of the territories and peoples affected. They will be found to be entirely in harmony with the high conception of freedom and justice which inspired the Joint Declaration.[6]

Churchill had either relied too much on his memory or overstated his case. Harold Macmillan, then Parliamentary Under-Secretary in the Colonial Office, minuted that he did not think:

that the Prime Minister can have realised the true nakedness of the land when he made his statement ... The declarations are not complete in themselves, nor are they free from ambiguity. They are scrappy, obscure and jejune.[7]

However, a Statement of Policy on Colonial Development and Welfare, issued at the time of the 1940 Act had said:

H.M.G. are the trustees for the well-being of the peoples of the Colonial Empire. The primary aim of colonial policy is to protect and advance the interests of the inhabitants.[8]

Trusteeship rather than guidance towards self-government was still the British concept of the colonial way ahead at the time of the Atlantic Charter. Despite Churchill's disclaimer, the significance of its third clause was not lost on indigenous political leaders in India, Burma, Ceylon and others of the more advanced British dependencies.

Before the Japanese attacked Pearl Harbor in December 1941, the United States was well on the way to becoming what Roosevelt called 'the Arsenal of Democracy'. Isolationism was finally subdued with that attack, and sense of mission took over with self-interest trailing in second place. Once in the war the massive scale of the American mobilization of manpower and resources gave the United States the political and military leadership of the Allied counter-offensives in Europe and the Pacific. US land, sea and air forces first overtook and then dwarfed those of the British Empire, large though they were. The close friendship and co-operation that developed between Churchill and Roosevelt and in the Combined Anglo-American Chiefs of Staff Committee, was reflected downwards, creating one of the most successful wartime international partnerships ever achieved and on the vastest scale. The Allied victory cloaked, for a time, the relative decline of British power.

The Second World War ended with the United States standing where Britain had stood after Waterloo: the paramount power, able to influence decisively the shape of the post-war world and determined to impose a new political order free from old fashioned spheres of influence, imperial pretensions and, as soon as the closeness of their relations with Britain would allow, free from colonialism, including her own.

The Second World War had wrought profound changes amongst the British dominions as well. The theories propounded in the Balfour Declaration had been tested in practice and had proved workable. The dominions were indeed independent, and yet were able to work successfully together in a common cause when under an external threat. All the potential dangers of the Ten Year Rule, the 5:5:3 naval disarmament ratio, and the failure to renew the Anglo-Japanese Treaty were realized too. Britain could no longer defend the dominions. Canada drew closer to the United States in the defence of North America, and Australia and New Zealand had to look to Washington rather than London for a return of stability to the Pacific. Washington had replaced London as the capital of the Western world.

The affairs of the Colonial Empire had not stood still either. The emphasis upon social as well as economic development, which had been triggered by Hitler harping on the 'Colonial Question' before the war, was further encouraged by forthright American criticism of the backwardness of many British territories to which American servicemen had been sent during the war, and by Anglo-American strategic considerations. There was particular American pressure in the Caribbean where stability was especially important to the United States. Not only did the arc of British West Indian islands lie like a protective screen of unsinkable aircraft carriers defending the Panama Canal, but it was also feared that unrest amongst their African and mixed-race populations could spill over onto the American mainland. The Anglo-American Caribbean Commission had been established in 1942 under President Roosevelt's prompting to secure the approaches to the Panama Canal and to help the US with its own colonial problems in Puerto Rico and the American Virgin Islands. By the end of the war far more ambitious colonial development plans had been authorized under the Colonial Development and Welfare Act of 1945.

In preparing the British position for the Dumbarton Oaks Conference in the autumn of 1944, the United States and United Kingdom delegations exchanged memoranda. The British paper stated that the objective of good colonial administration was to promote to the utmost the well-being of colonial peoples within the world community. So far as the United Kingdom was concerned, this objective implied:

(i) the development of self-government within the British Commonwealth in forms appropriate to the varying circumstances of colonial peoples;
(ii) their economic and social advancement; and
(iii) recognition of the responsibilities due from members of the world community one to another.[9]

The general concept of trusteeship with good government as its immediate aim was being replaced by a more specific commitment to work towards self-government at a speed appropriate to each colony.

Britain herself emerged from the Second World War exhausted but less so than in 1918. Her financial state was precarious but her casualties had been fewer, and her sense of achievement was all the greater because she had stood alone and had successfully resisted the totalitarian challenge. The arch of imperial confidence had just withstood the shock of the early German and Japanese victories. Dominion collaboration was closer than ever, and her special relationship with the United States had been strongly reinforced. Furthermore, there was a much greater sense of realism in the country. Enthusiasm for the myths of collective security had waned: in its place had come guarded support for the United Nations and a determination to build a better world based upon strength rather than appeasement. Soviet ambitions were recognized by the British sooner than the Americans as a potential cause of a third world war.

The victory parades following VE Day and VJ Day in London and the dominion capitals proclaimed the British Empire's recovery from the malaise of the interwar years. But, in truth, they celebrated *pyrrhic* victories. Though Britain occupied a seat at the top table it was more in recognition of her great war effort than a reflection of actual power. The arch of imperial confidence still stood, but it had been fatally weakened by the sentiments expressed in the Atlantic Charter and by the Japanese demonstration of the fallibility of Europeans.

PART 1

THE ATTEMPT TO STAY
1945 to 1956

If drunk with sight of power, we loose
  Wild tongues that have not thee in awe,
Such boastings as the Gentiles use,
  Or lesser breeds without the Law—
Lord God of Hosts, be with us yet,
  Lest we forget—lest we forget!

Rudyard Kipling's *Recessional* 1847, Verse 4

3 The Trend Setters
India and Palestine: 1945 to 1947

His Majesty's Government wish to make it clear that it is their definite intention to take the necessary steps to effect the transference of power into responsible Indian hands by a date not later than June 1948.

Mr Attlee's statement to Parliament, 20 February 1946

Victorious once more in 1945, Britain had no intention of abandoning her imperial role. Churchill had set the tone in the dark days of 1942 when he growled at a Mansion House dinner:

I have not become the King's First Minister to preside over the liquidisation of the British Empire.[1]

Gradual transition from Empire to Commonwealth, yes: abandonment of so many different peoples around the world whose future Britain held in sacred trust, no. The British way of life had survived the challenge of the totalitarian powers: there was no reason to bow to the idealist anti-colonial pressures of the United States nor to the blatantly subversive policies of the Soviet Union.

Neither of the major British political parties had serious doubts about the aim of transforming the Empire into the Commonwealth. Any gap there may have been before the war had been narrowed through Conservative and Labour leaders working together in Churchill's wartime coalition. There was less agreement on the speed at which the metamorphosis could and should take place. The pace of constitutional development would depend, as it had done in the eighteenth and nineteenth centuries, more upon the outcome of British internal politics than upon any deeply considered imperial design. The British electorate in 1945 sought radical change but with more money spent upon creating a better Britain than on building a more powerful Commonwealth. And so it was Gladstone's rather than Disraeli's heirs, who dictated immediate post-war imperial development.

Mr Attlee's Labour government inherited a British Commonwealth and Empire undiminished in territory and population since it had reached its zenith under Lloyd George's Liberal government in 1921: indeed, it was temporarily and embarrassingly enlarged during the aftermath of the war. British troops remained in occupation of all the Italian colonies, which they had conquered in Africa, and in most countries of the Middle East including Iran. The Mediterranean Sea, Red Sea, Persian Gulf and Indian Ocean were virtually British lakes. In the Far East British troops, principally Indian Army divisions, were occupying not only the British territories of Malaya, Singapore, North Borneo and Hong Kong, but also the Dutch East Indies and French Indo-China. And nearer home the British Army of the Rhine had been formed to garrison the British Occupation Zone of Germany and other troops were likewise stationed in Austria, in the divided city of Trieste, and in strife-torn Greece. All this amounted to a costly military burden which could not be carried for long if the Labour government was to honour its election pledges to introduce the welfare state and to carry through its programme of nationalisation. Nevertheless, the electorate had swung away from the idealism of the 1930s and was able to stifle hopes of rapid and total demobilization such as occurred after the First World War. National Service was to remain part of the British way of life until the early 1960s, and there was no reneging on Britain's self-imposed commitment to lead each of her colonies and protectorates to a secure independence, free from fear of external or internal predators.

A chronology of the period 1945 to 1956 during which Britain attempted to convert her Empire into a Commonwealth without loss of influence in world affairs is in the front papers of this book. Military thinking was not yet dominated by the philosophies of nuclear deterrence. Only the United States owned the hardware of atomic bombs, although Britain had the know-how to build them. Britain's military strategy was based on three pillars: the defence of the United Kingdom, of her sea lanes, and of her line of communication through the Middle East to India and Australasia. Before the Second World War the first had depended upon insuring a favourable balance of power in Europe; with the wartime devastation of Germany it had come to mean the Anglo-American defence of their occupation zones from the Baltic to the Adriatic. The sea lanes were not under threat because the Soviet navy was insignificant at that time. Most thought had to be given to the Middle East where local nationalist ambitions and Soviet subversion could combine to threaten the sea and air routes through Suez and Western oil supplies in the Persian Gulf. The Chiefs of Staff judged that the stability of the whole area between the Caspian and Red Seas was vital to the Empire and to the West as a whole.

As the Attlee government surveyed its inheritance in 1945, four areas of strategic concern were evident: in Europe there was the power vacuum left by the annihilation of Nazi Germany; the Middle East was a cauldron of conflicting interests; India was in constitutional and inter-communal turmoil; and in the Far East a struggle for succession had begun between the former colonial powers and the indigenous liberation armies. The European situation was well seized by the Americans who were moving towards the generous Marshall Aid Plan. How Britain dealt with the threats to her interests in the Middle East, India and the Far East would set the trends in the post-war development of her power and influence. Of the four, the quest for an acceptable solution to the Indian problem was deemed by the Attlee government to be by far the most urgent.

There were few doubts amongst the political parties in Britain that India should be granted some form of independence now that the war was over. The only questions were how soon and in what way this could be achieved without partitioning the Subcontinent between the Hindus and the Muslims. Paradoxically, while the Indian political parties had not been able to rid themselves of the suspicion that Britain had no real intention of leaving and had, therefore, tried to exploit all her wartime difficulties to bring pressure to bear on her to do so, the Indian Army had continued to serve Britain and India with outstanding courage. In India itself the teeming millions, who make up the many different races of the Sub-continent, retained an almost child-like faith in the British Raj, despite the intense political agitation to replace it with a home-spun alternative.

The Indian struggle for independence had been a triangular contest ever since the All India Congress had been formed in 1885. Up to the Government of India Act of 1935 the contestants had been the British government holding paramount power, the Congress representing all shades of opinion in British India, and the princes of the Indian states whose autocratic rights were enshrined in each state's treaty with the British Raj.[2]

The 1935 Act led to a radical change in the triangle of forces. All the Indian political parties sensed, as they were intended to do, that the British government was intent upon following the Canadian, Australian, New Zealand and South African precedents by granting India independence in stages: responsible internal self-government would lead to dominion status and then possibly to total independence after the Irish precedent. Congress saw itself as the heir-apparent to the British Raj: the Muslim League, a relatively minor party in the 1930s, had other ideas. A Congress Raj would be dominated by the Hindu majority and would not necessarily be preferable in Muslim eyes to the British Raj. As so often happens when a community's interests are endangered it finds an outstanding leader. The Indian Muslims found Mohammed Ali Jinnah. By 1940 the three sides of the triangle had become Britain, Congress and the Muslim League. Congress still claimed itself to be *the* non-communal body representing Indians of all classes and creeds. That claim was progressively challenged by the League as far as the Muslims were concerned.

Jinnah, a brilliant lawyer, had been a prominent exponent of Hindu/Muslim unity in the Congress Party in the 1920s. He became disillusioned with Indian politics in the early 1930s. After the Second Round Table Conference he resigned and settled in England, despairing of Indian unity because he could see no way of changing the Hindu majority's determination to ignore the rights of large minority communities like the Muslims. In 1935 he was persuaded by Liaquat Ali Khan, not without difficulty, to return to India to lead the Muslims in their struggle for recognition. His

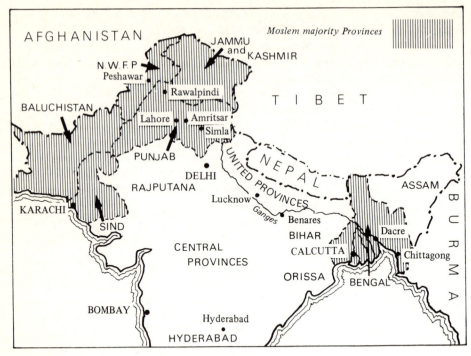

1. Muslim majority provinces of India in 1945.

Muslim nationalism drowned his earlier enthusiasm for Indian unity. With single-mindedness of purpose and great tactical skill, he propagated the concept of the Muslim nation. In Lahore in March 1940 the League, under Jinnah's leadership, passed a resolution proclaiming that India was not one but two nations: Hindu and Muslim. The three north-western provinces of British India (North West Frontier Province, Sind and the Punjab) together with the states of Baluchistan and Kashmir and two north-easterly provinces (Bengal and Assam) were predominantly Muslim and should form independent Mohammedan states within whatever Indian federation replaced the British Raj.

Hindu/Muslim antagonism was not new to India. The Muslims had been the rulers of India since 1018 and had lorded it over the Hindus. Much of the inter-communal strife had been damped out during the British Raj's communally impartial administration, backed by effective provincial police forces and the highly efficient Indian Army, both of which were mixed-manned, containing Hindus, Sikhs and Muslims, all of whom worked loyally together under British officers. Beneath the British imposed unity there could not have been a deeper divide between the philosophies and practices of the Hindu and Muslim creeds. It was far deeper than the chasm separating Catholics and Protestants during the bitterest period of the Wars of Religion in Europe. The Hindu and Muslim faiths demanded fundamentally opposite ways of life, the practices of one being anathema to the other in everyday routine. The divide was further magnified by the Hindu caste system which lowers a series of iron curtains between classes of its own people and a doubly thick one between them and every other religion and political system. It lauds division rather than unity, treating its own labouring classes as 'untouchables' with the Muslims still lower in their scale of values. It is hardly surprising that the Muslims with their conquering, proselytizing faith and with their memories of Mogul power in pre-British India should distrust the Hindu, who, in his turn, saw the opportunity to reverse not only the two centuries of British hegemony but the seven of Muslim rule as well. Ironically it was the Hindu who was demanding unity despite his religious practices: the Muslim naturally sought separation, having lost the power, though not the will, to rule.

At the time of Dunkirk and the Battle of Britain, the position of the three protagonists in India clarified. Congress demanded immediate independence so Indians could devise their own constitution in their own way: the League wanted a constitution first with cast-iron safeguards for minority communities; and the British government was determined that any concession they might choose to offer to win Indian support for the war effort should only become effective after the war was won. There was clearly a great deal to be said for the Muslim arguments about two nations. Why then did the British government initially side with Congress in trying to preserve the unity of India?

There were three principal reasons: political, economic and geographic. The British were proud of their unique achievement of unifying the Sub-continent. They did not want to see their creation destroyed. All the different communities were living together relatively peacefully, often intermingled in the villages and not entirely segregated in the towns. Ethnically, the difference between the twelfth and thirteenth century Muslim invaders and the indigenous Hindus had faded over the years as the latter absorbed the former in all but religion. The Indian Army was an outstanding example of what could be done in bridging the communal divide.

From the economic point of view, partition would be extraordinarily difficult. The early years of British administration in India had coincided with the Industrial Revolution in Britain. Its fruits had been applied to India as a whole and not provincially. Trunk roads, railways and telegraphic and radio communications were on an all India basis, as were the patterns of trade, the legal system and the administrative machine. At a time when enlargement of trading communities was in vogue around the world to take advantage of scale, partition seemed economic nonsense.

Geographically, separation of the Muslim majority provinces was even more difficult. The Pakistan Jinnah envisaged would be in two blocks: five provinces in the north-west with two in the north-east. There could be no physical communication between them. The two provinces bordering

Hindustan, the Punjab and Bengal, though containing overall Muslim majorities, had large Hindu populations in their eastern and western districts respectively. All Muslim arguments in favour of partitioning India could be applied with equal force to the need to divide the Punjab and Bengal, and Congress was not slow to use them. A Muslim state, however, without the eastern Punjab and western Bengal, which included the great port of Calcutta, would in Jinnah's words be a 'moth-eaten' Pakistan. Without Calcutta, which was unmistakably Hindu, the eastern provinces of Pakistan would hardly be economically viable.

To complicate matters further the lands of the warlike Sikhs straddled the divide between the Muslim west and Hindu east of the Punjab. Arguments for Pakistan could equally well apply to a Sikhistan and to the claims of other distinctive warlike peoples such as the Jats. Acceptance of Pakistan, motheaten or not, could be the start of a slippery slide into the Balkanization of India.

In attempting to preserve the unity of India despite its religious divisions, the British were ignoring their recent experiences in Ireland and were pinning their faith upon their success in Canada and South Africa. They misjudged the depth of the Indian divide, the singleness of purpose of the Muslim leaders and the inflexible arrogance of the Hindus. They underestimated the catalytic effect of their presence, which had enabled the two communites to live together for so long under their neutral administration. For India to remain united the Muslims had to feel secure: the British Raj provided that security. The search for a constitutionally acceptable alternative to British rule was doomed to failure. Nevertheless, three British negotiators came close to success: Sir Stafford Cripps, Lord Pethick-Lawrence and Earl Mountbatten.

Sir Stafford Cripps' attempt was made in March 1942, when British fortunes were at their lowest ebb. The Japanese armies were almost up to India's eastern frontier with Burma. Japanese radio stations were blaring out invitations to Indians to revolt against the British: how could they claim to be India's defenders when they could only hold Malaya, Singapore and Burma for a few weeks? Attractive though this propaganda may have seemed to the Japanese, it had surprisingly little effect on Britain's overall military effort. It says much for the strength of the British Raj that India never ceased to play her full part in providing logistic support for the Allied forces operating in the Mediterranean, Indian Ocean and Far East. Britain would, of course, have liked whole-hearted Indian political support, especially in opposing the Japanese on the Burma frontier, but it was not this desire which triggered the Cripps mission. The pressure came from President Roosevelt and from China's Generalissimo Chiang Kai Shek, both of whom wished to widen the political as well as the military front against the Japanese. The Labour members of Churchill's War Cabinet supported their plea that Britain should make one more attempt to find a solution to the Indian constitutional problem. Sir Stafford had just returned from Moscow where he had been British

Ambassador during the most critical days of the German invasion of Russia. He had a keen interest in Indian affairs and had many influential Indian friends. Churchill, with some reluctance, agreed that Cripps should offer a three-point plan: when the war was over new elections would be held and a constituent assembly established; the resulting constitution would be accepted by Britain provided any province or state, which rejected it, was entitled to retain its existing relationship with Britain; and meanwhile an interim government would be established in which Indian political leaders would hold all portfolios except Foreign Affairs and Defence. A treaty would be negotiated for the transfer of power in which the Indian Union would be free to decide its future relationship with the Commonwealth.

The League welcomed the proposals because provinces were given the right to secede from an Indian union. Congress would not accept the separatist clause. All Cripps' genuineness of purpose and negotiating skill failed. Gandhi dubbed his proposals as 'a post-dated cheque on a bankrupt empire'. Cripps packed his bags and went home, and Congress initiated its vicious 'Quit India' campaign, which had all the hallmarks of open rebellion. The Muslim League took no part in what was essentially a Hindu revolt.

Fully forewarned of the Congress intentions the Viceroy and his Executive Council acted promptly and effectively. Gandhi and all the important Congress leaders of the campaign were arrested and imprisoned. For a time the British writ did not run in Bihar and parts of the United Provinces. Communications were cut and for about three weeks supply of the Burma front was in jeopardy. Leaderless, the revolt died away. The British Raj was still too strong: Indian administrators and police officers had not yet begun to re-insure their futures with Congress or its rival, the Muslim League. The Raj was never again challenged on such a scale, but the Cripps mission negotiations formed a watershed: there could be no going back on the British government's offer of independence when the war ended. The British will to govern started to seep away; instability gathered momentum; and at every level, from senior officials down to lowly villagers, the future began to look dangerously uncertain.

As soon as the war with Germany ended, Lord Wavell, who had succeeded Lord Linlithgow as Viceroy in October 1943, attempted to implement the first two steps of the Cripps plan: the establishment of a constituent assembly and the formation of an interim government with Indian leaders holding the principal portfolios, which did not exclude, as the Cripps plan had done, Foreign Affairs and Defence, although the Commander-in-Chief would remain British with a seat in the government. The Simla Conference, which he called in June 1945, resulted in neither a constituent assembly nor a representative interim government. Superficially the arguments revolved around the allocation of seats between the communities: in fact, Congress and the League were manoeuvring to influence a decision as to whether there should be one or two constituent assemblies. The Congress cry remained 'quit first and Indians will decide the future': the League responded with the demand 'divide, then quit'. Wavell closed the conference when it became clear that he could not reach agreement on the allocation of seats, let alone portfolios, in the interim government which he wished to form.

The only positive result of the Simla Conference was agreement to call elections for the central and provincial assemblies early in 1946 (the last elections to these assemblies had been in 1937 and 1939). Two events outside India reset the political stage and left the actors disorientated for about six months. At the end of July, Mr Attlee's Labour government, with early independence for India enshrined in its election manifesto, won its landslide victory in the 1945 general election in Britain. A month later came the Japanese surrender after the destruction of Hiroshima and Nagasaki with atomic bombs. The greater certainty that Britain was going to quit India, coupled with the inherent uncertainties associated with the aftermath of any war, gave fresh impetus to the slide towards political instability and internal disorder.

In the autumn of 1945 sporadic rioting broke out in many Indian cities and was primarily anti-British in character. The embers of the 'Quit India' campaign still smouldered and were easily fanned into flame by irresponsible and often malicious local press reports. Much more serious rioting broke out in Calcutta in February. They were still anti-British in tone but with undercurrents of Hindu-Muslim bitterness. They were made worse by the criminal element of Calcutta, the Goondas, trying to profit by the disorders. After two days of rioting the police acknowledged that they had lost control and the Army was called in. It took the 2nd Green Howards, 2nd York and Lancasters, 1st North Staffords and 4th/3rd Gurkhas four days to bring the disturbances to an end. This was the first serious warning of deterioration in the police's capacity to control the Calcutta mobs.

This poor showing by the once highly efficient Calcutta police was symptomatic of the crisis of confidence that was beginning to grip most of India. Indianization of the officer cadre of the police forces had begun in the 1930s and had been accelerated during the war years. Standards of administration had slackened and operational efficiency had been reduced. Moreover, Indian officers, with the best will in the world, were bound to come under increasing political and communal pressure to be less than communally impartial. They could resist these pressures as long as there was confidence that the British Raj would last until they retired; a possibility that was becoming less and less likely for all but the older age groups. Loss of impartiality was serious enough: more serious was the disintegration of the police Intelligence system. Sources just dried up as confidence waned. A vicious circle set in. Lack of timely information meant less effective pre-emptive action, which, in its turn, led to more frequent failure, further loss of confidence and an increasing dependence upon the Indian Army to help keep the peace.

But the Indian Army had its own troubles, stemming from very different causes. In British eyes, its continuing loyalty and discipline were essential to the orderly transfer of power. It was the guarantor, and indeed exemplar, of a united India which they still hoped would emerge in the end. In Indian eyes, the Army was the British buttress for further prevarication over the grant of independence and as such was a target for denigration and disruption by the extreme nationalists and their press. A weapon lay close at hand, which the Congress and League leaders were not slow to grasp. After the fall of Malaya, Singapore and Burma, the Japanese had some 60,000 Indian troops as prisoners of war. A former militant left-wing leader of Congress, Subbas Chandra Bose, who had quarrelled with Gandhi over his policy of non-violence, first sought Hitler's help, then joined the Japanese and helped them to recruit 20,000 of these prisoners into a force called 'The Indian National Army' which was to help in the 'liberation' of India. It put up a remarkably poor performance against the regular Indian divisions in Burma, but its repatriation to India after the Japanese surrender presented the Commander-in-Chief, Field Marshal Auchinleck, and indirectly the Viceroy, with a hideous politico-military dilemma. In British eyes the members of the INA were traitors; in Indian eyes they were heroes. To apply the full rigour of military law to them could fire the tinder dry political bonfire: to show leniency would strike at the roots of the Indian Army's discipline. A sensible compromise was reached whereby only the leaders and those charged with atrocities were to be tried. Unfortunately the trials were badly handled, giving those who wished to weaken the morale of the Army every opportunity to do so. The sentences were severe but commuted by the Commander-in-Chief, who was sensitive to the political environment. Most of India heaved a sigh of relief; the British officers of the Indian Army and the British civilian community were horrified; and the British will to rule was seen by everyone inside and outside India to be weakening.

Concurrently with the INA trials, a 'strike' by RAF National Service-men at Dum Dum and other airfields was dealt with just as leniently. The infection spread to the RIAF and then to the Royal Indian Navy. Mutinies broke out, first, in warships at Bombay and then at Karachi. There were accompanying disturbancs in both cities in support of the sailors. The Indian Army put down both mutinies, suffering only minor unrest itself, mainly caused by administrative lapses in the handling of troops returning from abroad.

There was an important difference between the Indian Army and its sister services, which perhaps holds the secret of British success with indigenous forces in India and the American failure later in Vietnam. British officers were commissioned into Indian regiments and were part of the regimental family: they were not advisers. Between the British officers and the sepoys there was the unique rank of Viceroy's Commissioned Officer (VCO) filled by the best and most experienced men drawn from the ranks of the regiment. The newer Royal Indian Navy and Royal Indian Air Force did not have this rank as they were organized on RN and

RAF lines. The VCO's were far more than the warrant officers of the British services. They were the father figures to the sepoys and interpreters of their feelings to the British officers. At the same time they were the counsellors to the British officers, relaying British orders to the sepoys in a language they understood and representing the sepoys' domestic problems, religious customs and simple fears in a way that enabled the British officers to appreciate the sepoys' point of view. In the VCO the wide gap between the British and Indian mentalities and ways of life was bridged to the benefit of the regimental family, and the strengths and weaknesses of the two races were dovetailed: British forward planning and insistence on the highest professional standards was complemented by Indian concentration on the present and enjoyment on the sense of achievement in reaching the standards required. The Indian Army's regimental families withstood, with few exceptions, the grim tests with which they were confronted during the transfer of power and its bitter aftermath.

The Indian elections, which took place in the early months of 1946, polarized the political situation by eliminating most of the minor parties and leaving the field clear for a joust to the death between Congress wearing the colours of Indian unity and the League waving the green flag of Pakistan. Surprisingly at provincial level the results belied the League's claim to speak for 90 per cent of the Muslim community. In two Muslim majority provinces, the North West Frontier and Assam, Congress won enough Muslim seats to form the government. In Sind and Bengal the League was forced into a coalition with such minority parties as had survived to do so. And in the key province of the Punjab Sikhs tipped the scales against the League in favour of a non-Muslim government. However, in the central assembly elections, the League took all the Muslim seats: non-League Muslim politicians at both central and provincial level decided the time had come to jump on the Pakistan bandwagon before it was too late. The League's claim to speak for all Muslims became more credible.

The completion of the elections served as an appropriate moment for a major initiative by Mr Attlee's government in fulfilment of their election promises. They decided to send out a Cabinet Mission composed of three senior ministers of Cabinet rank: Lord Pethick-Lawrence (Secretary of State for India), Sir Stafford Cripps (President of the Board of Trade) and Mr A. V. Alexander (First Lord of the Admiralty). Its task was to seek the agreement of the Indian leaders to the 'principles and procedures' whereby the Indians could frame their own constitution. They arrived on 24 March 1946 and, after seven weeks' hard negotiations in the growing heat of the Indian spring, concluded that no agreement was possible. Rather than return empty handed they set out their views on the way ahead, in what came to be known as the Cabinet Mission plan.

In putting forward its plan the Mission first gave its reasons why it believed partition was neither desirable nor practicable. Instead it proposed a three tier system of government for a united India. At the top the central government and legislature would be responsible for foreign affairs, defence and fundamental rights with corresponding financial powers: everything else would be vested in the provincial governments. In between the central and provincial governments, the provinces could be grouped on a communal and geographic basis. Three groups were suggested:

Group A (predominantly non-Muslim)
> Madras, Bombay, United Provinces, Bihar, Central Provinces, Orissa.

Group B (West Muslim provinces)
> Punjab, North West Frontier Province, Sind.

Group C (East Muslim provinces)
> Bengal and Assam.

The Indian states would join the groups of their choice, and communal and minority interests would be protected at central level by a special voting system.

The League accepted the plan because it came near to recognizing Pakistan without partition: Congress also went along with it conditionally because it preserved the Union. The Sikhs objected that they would be left in the Muslim Group B if the Punjab was not partitioned. To have won both League and Congress agreement, albeit conditionally, was certainly a triumph for Lord Pethick-Lawrence, but it did not last. Within a month the whole delicately balanced edifice collapsed over the allocation of seats in the interim government and a politically explosive speech by Pandit Nehru, who in effect said that Congress had only accepted proposals for a constituent assembly. This would be a sovereign body which need not necessarily follow the Cabinet Mission plan. In his view the grouping system would probably never work. The Mission's provisos about proper arrangements for minorities was a domestic Indian matter: 'we accept no outsiders' interference with it,' he said, 'certainly not the British government's'.[3]

The League's reaction was immediate, understandable and disastrous to the Mission's plan and to India. On 27 July it revoked its acceptance and authorized its working committee to draw up a plan for 'direct action' to achieve Pakistan. Events moved fast. On 6 August, Wavell, with much misgiving, asked Pandit Nehru to form an interim Indian government without the League. On 8 August Congress authorized Nehru to accept the invitation. The League declared 16 August to be 'Direct Action Day', Jinnah proclaiming: 'This day we bid farewell to constitutional methods.'[4] The measures to be taken were not spelt out but violence was clearly intended. It came with ghastly consequences in Calcutta on that day.

The police and military intelligence systems had been expecting further trouble in Calcutta for some weeks. General Sir Francis Tuker, the commander of Eastern Command, which was responsible for the north-eastern third of India from Delhi to the Burma border, had ordered three extra battalions to reinforce the garrison. Only the 7th Worcesters had actually arrived on 16 August to join the 2nd Green Howards and the 2nd York and Lancasters. The 1st/3rd and 3rd/8th Gurkha Rifles had still some distance to travel. Tuker expected a repetition of what had become normal anti-government rioting with targets relatively clearly defined and easily defended. No one expected the horrors of the 'Calcutta killings'.

During the first fortnight of August the local Congress and League politicians, together with the Calcutta press, had been reflecting events in Delhi with inflammatory speeches and articles all directed at the opposite community. The Muslim Chief Minister of Bengal, Mr Suhrawardy, opened Pandora's box by declaring 16 August a public holiday to mark 'Direct Action Day'. He proposed to address a mass rally of Muslims in Calcutta as part of the 'celebrations'. Satan finds work for idle hands at the best of times: with communal passions already inflamed his opportunities were all the greater!

The day started ominously as Muslim crowds tried to stop Hindu shops opening, and in their excitement set fire to some of them. The Hindus retaliated by blocking the routes of Muslim processions heading for Suhrawardy's mass meeting. A number of these processions had been deliberately routed through predominantly Hindu areas. As early as 3 p.m., the time Suhrawardy was due to speak, the Commissioner of Police reported the situation was out of hand. No sooner had his men dispersed the crowds than they reformed with unusual speed and persistence. The acting Area Commander, Brigadier Sixsmith, toured the city with the Commissioner. They saw hooliganism and some arson but nothing to warrant intervention by the Army. Nevertheless, it was agreed that if things got worse the Army would clear and hold the main roads, leaving the police to deal with the labyrinth of alleys between them. Due to lack of Intelligence they did not know that mass killings had started in the back streets, isolated Muslim groups in Hindu areas being slaughtered and vice versa. They did, however, notice both Hindu and Muslim Goondas gathering ready to exploit whatever opportunities the growing turmoil might present for blood and loot.

An immense crowd thronged Suhrawardy's meeting at which he declared that Direct Action Day was the first step in the struggle for Muslim emancipation from Hindu domination. As the Muslim crowds started to make their way back through the Hindu areas the general human conflagration started. At 6 p.m. a curfew was clamped on the worst affected areas and at 8 p.m. the Army started to move in to the support of the police. The first impression of one of the battle experienced company commanders as he led his troops down one of the main roads was that 'an armoured division had swept through on the tail of a heavy bombardment'. Shops and houses were burning, their contents littered the roads and the air was dank with the fumes of police tear gas shells. Surprisingly there was no evidence of the killings which were taking place: there were no bodies in the streets. It was not until daylight that they began to appear, dumped in the roads or heaped on coolie handcarts.[5]

For the next two days, 17 and 18 August, the three British battalions and 1st/3rd Gurkhas struggled to gain control of the centre of Calcutta and the main roads while the inter-communal killing went on unabated. The poor who could not defend themselves suffered most. The Goondas and the Sikhs did much of the killing. The latter were the mechanics and taxi drivers of Calcutta and thus had the mobility to move from place to place, avenging the killing of Hindus as well as their own people. Inter-communal hatred, unbridled fear and a disdain for the sanctity of human life, turned Calcutta into a carnal house in which only the strong and those who could seek safety within the mass of their co-religionists survived.

The British and Gurkha troops made a supreme effort on 19 August and succeeded in regaining control of the worst affected northern half of the city. Next day the combined effects of the arrival of more troops (3rd/8th Gurkhas and 4th/7th Rajputs, followed later by 2nd Royal Norfolks, and 2nd East Lancashires) and the sating of the Hindu/Muslim blood lust dampened down the fury. The hideous debris had to be cleared up. The municipal services, like the police, had collapsed. Normality was gradually established by the action and example of the Army. British officers and soldier volunteers from the battalions cleared the putrifying corpses from the streets and alleys with the help of the few Doms (the only Hindus allowed to handle dead bodies) who could be found and pressed into service. Many of the bodies had been horribly mutilated: old men, women and children had not been spared in the savagery. The Army's administrative services set up refugee camps and helped to feed the city while Army doctors strove to prevent epidemics with innoculations and supervision of rudimentary hygiene. The death toll will never be known. The official estimate was 4,000 dead and 10,000 seriously injured, but most accounts suggest that this was a gross under-estimate.

The Muslims had provoked the Calcutta killings, but, being the minority in the city and no match for the Sikhs, they had been worsted. Rumours spread to other Indian cities with large Muslim or Hindu minorities and the vernacular press inflamed inter-communal tension. Reprisal and counter-reprisal spread outwards as the sparks of Calcutta lit other inflammable areas. In September Bombay suffered. Then Muslim vengeance in east Bengal led to a mass flight of Hindus to Calcutta and western Bengal. This in turn triggered even more savage Hindu assaults on the Muslim minorities in Bihar and the Central Provinces. The madness was viciously contagious and showed no sign of burning itself out. In January it spread to the Punjab where Sikh and Muslim bands waged bitter war against each other at the expense of the villagers. In the twin cities of Lahore and Amritsar, the former with a Muslim majority and the latter Hindu and Sikh, mobs murdered, pillaged and burnt the homes and people of rival communities. In March the Muslims in the rural area of

Rawalpindi massacred the Hindu and Sikh minorities. 'Remember Rawal-pindi' was to become a Sikh battle cry later that summer.

Two things stood out during the period from August 1946 to March 1947. First, the rioting had ceased to be anti-government and was now inter-communal. The British were no longer the enemy, only the scape-goats. The Muslim policy of direct action might have led then and there to full scale civil war had it not been for the second factor. The discipline and loyalty of the Army did not crack despite the communal stresses within it and brought to bear upon it. A large proportion of the Army was recruited in the Punjab. The men were naturally worried about their families and they were free to read the ragings of the communal press; yet it was the Army that contained and gradually quietened each area when the police lost control. In Bihar a police mutiny had to be suppressed by the Army. Most of the regiments concerned were made up of Hindu, Punjabi Muselman and Sikh companies: loyalty to the regimental family—for the time being at least—transcended communal bitterness.

Credit for helping to stop all out civil war must also be given to Mahatma Gandhi, who, in his seventy-seventh year, journeyed on foot from village to village in areas where tension was high, preaching Hindu-Muslim brotherhood. His prayer meetings, which were fully reported in the press, did have a calming effect worth many battalions.

The series of atrocities which followed the 'Calcutta killings' made their impact in Delhi and London. Wavell, who visited Calcutta and many of the other disaster areas, returned to Delhi determined to persuade the League to join the interim government to reduce communal tension and to enable him to call the proposed constituent assembly in December to demonstrate Britain's good faith in pressing on with arrangements for the transfer of power. He succeeded in the former, but not in the latter. The League took up its five seats in Nehru's government. Jinnah did not join, preferring to be represented by Liaquat Ali Khan. Despite the flames of civil war licking around the edges of India's body politic, high-level bargaining went on. In desperation Wavell called the constituent assembly which the League refused to attend. At its first session in December Congress enforced the passage of a resolution proclaiming that India should become an independent sovereign republic. This was hardly the conciliatory approach that would soften the rift between Hindu and Muslim or endear it to the British who hoped India would become the keystone of the new British Commonwealth.

In London the Attlee government was fast losing patience. It seemed to British ministers that a way would have to be found to compel a consensus amongst the Indian leaders, otherwise a solution would be imposed by civil war. Wavell was clearly at the end of his political resources. The only solution he could propose was the announcement of a finite programme for withdrawal, which would be carried out in military style, province by province, starting with the less politically fraught areas of southern India. The whole operation, he suggested, could be completed by March 1948.

Mr Attlee could not agree. He wrote later that such a policy amounted to 'an ignoble and sordid scuttle, and I wouldn't look at it'.[6] A new man with new policies was needed.

Mr Attlee's choice was Admiral Viscount Mountbatten of Burma. A number of points commended him as Wavell's successor. He was an acknowledged leader with a great flair for making people of diverse races and creeds work together, as his successful period as Supreme Allied Commander Southeast Asia had demonstrated. He had shown great originality earlier as Churchill's Director of Combined Operations in laying the foundations for the invasions of North Africa, Sicily and finally Normandy. He was also known to hold liberal views, and as a member of the Royal Family he was extraordinarily well cast to be the last Viceroy of India at a time when prestige could be vital to a successful and friendly transfer of power.

Before accepting the appointment Mountbatten pressed for the government's agreement to two things: first, there should be a specific date for the ending of the British Raj, which was to be announced with his appointment; and second, that he be given full plenipotentiary powers to negotiate and carry through the transfer of power by that date. There was no argument about the necessity for a date: it was generally agreed to be one of the few ways left of compelling an Indian political consensus. The actual date took more resolution. A balance had to be struck between flexibility to meet the unforeseen and rigidity to impose a decision making discipline. The formula 'not later than July 1948' was adopted. Plenipotentiary powers were even less easy to grant, but in the end Mountbatten won his point in practical terms though not in constitutional theory. His membership of the Royal Family helped to sway the arguments in his favour.

The Mountbattens (the plural is appropriate because Countess Mountbatten was to play a major role in the creation of a favourable atmosphere for the transfer of power) arrived in Delhi at the end of March 1947 as the Punjab was reacting to the Rawalpindi killings; the Calcutta Gurkha police and the Bihar police were in mutiny; and curfews were being imposed in cities as widely separated as Bombay, Benares and Calcutta. The hot wind of communal hatred was still blowing. Worst of all the British senior officers of the Indian Army were beginning to fear that the contagion would spread to their mixed regiments if a decision about India's future was much further delayed by political prevarication. The slide towards ungovernability was accelerating.

Mountbatten spent April and May treading the paths of Sir Stafford Cripps and Lord Pethick-Lawrence before him, seeking a solution to the insoluble: how to maintain the unity of India in a way which satisfied both Hindu and Muslim. At times he came near to success with various versions of the three-tier Cabinet Mission plan. In a nutshell both sides accepted the provincial tier; Congress wanted a strong upper tier at central government level and disliked but would tolerate the intermediate group tier; and the

League would not have the upper tier at any price and would only accept Pakistan, the combination of groups B and C under a Muslim government. In the end, confronted by Jinnah with the threat of the bitterest civil war in Asia's long and bloody history, if he persisted in trying to impose unity, Mountbatten gave way and began to discuss the problems of partition with both sides, always hoping that, when faced with the actual difficulties of dividing India, the Muslims would pull back and the Hindus would seek reconciliation: neither happened. The League pushed all the harder for Pakistan; Mountbatten had to find a way of making it acceptable to Congress.

Mr. V. P. Menon, one of the Viceroy's senior Indian officials of the Indian Civil Service (ICS) is credited with suggesting the successful way forward: the transfer of power to two new dominions. If there could not be unity in India, there could be amity within the overall embrace of the Commonwealth. It would be possible for British officers in the ICS, Army and police to go on serving the two dominions in the difficult early stages of their existence without any change in their loyalty to the Crown. Indeed, the two new dominions could have a common Governor General to help ease the problems of transition. The suggestion did not fundamentally change the harsh realities of partition, but acted as the solvent which brought the three sides of the triangle—the British government, the Congress and the Muslim League—together in relatively friendly agreement at the highest level.

On 3 June Mountbatten announced the British government's agreement to partition as the only practical solution, and the acceptance by the other dominion governments of the two new dominions to which the power and responsibilities of the British Raj would be transferred 'immediately' (no date was given in the announcement because it had yet to be decided). The people of each province would decide through their provincial assemblies to which dominion they wished to belong. In the case of the Punjab and Bengal special voting systems were to be arranged so that districts in the new frontier areas could decide on which side of the line they wished to live. A boundary commission of eminent judges under Sir Cyril Radcliffe's chairmanship would be set up to delineate the final line of the frontiers. A partition council would be established to reach agreement on the division of assets, including the armed services, which would be split between the two dominions.

It was some days before Mountbatten announced what he meant by 'immediate' transfer of power. Fearing that his interim government would collapse if there was any delay, he chose the earliest administratively practical day: 15 August 1947, only ten weeks ahead. In this time the necessary legislation had to be drafted and passed through all its parliamentary stages before the Westminster summer recess; the provinces had to opt; the Boundary Commission had to settle at least the provincial frontiers; and plans had to be made for the division of the army. The last would be the responsibility of the Army Reconstitution Committee, working under the Partition Council. There seems to have been a general belief that, with the decision to 'divide and quit' by 15 August, the inter-communal violence would die away as both sides settled down to make the new dominions work. The problems of maintaining the peace while partition went ahead were subsumed in the general principle of 'the quicker the better' and by the fact that any delay could lead to uncontrollable anarchy and the bitterest civil war.

In retrospect, the reasoning behind the 15 August decision put the cart before the horse. The most difficult part of the transfer of power was not parliamentary drafting or administrative action; it was the actual division of India at bazaar and village level. Much more thought should have been given to how the division was to be made without minorities on either side of the new borders fearing for their lives. The brutal fact is that none of the political leaders at national level or the senior officials, including the Viceroy and the Commander-in-Chief, saw this as the limiting and most dangerous factor in the transfer of power. Mountbatten confessed later:

But I freely confess that I did not anticipate the scale and extent of what was going to happen, nor, so far as I am aware, did anyone in authority in India, Pakistan and the United Kingdom anticipate this.[7]

It was hardly a wise decision to begin the division of the Army, the only force left in India with the impartiality to stamp out inter-communal violence, before the peaceful partition of the Subcontinent had been achieved. At the time there seemed to be compelling political reasons for doing so: the military dangers were gravely misjudged.

The Indian Army was not just a symbol of the British Raj: it was the power that had created the political unity of the Subcontinent and, in the last resort, maintained it. As long as British viceroys were responsible for the good government of India and still hoped to hand over to one successor government they were reluctant to do anything which might jeopardise the unity of the ultimate instrument of their power. When in the early 1940s it was becoming clear that a Hindu/Muslim partition of India might become a reality, a number of senior British officers suggested that it would be wise to start reorganizing the Army on communal lines so that partition, if it came, would be easier. This could have been done for valid administrative reasons, because the differences of religious custom in mixed regiments complicated discipline and supply. Wartime expansion or post-war de-mobilization could have provided the pretext for making the change. It was never seriously contemplated: to have done so would have been an admission of failure at a time when the policy of maintaining the unity of the Subcontinent was being determinedly pursued.

There were deep-seated emotional prejudices on both sides about the Indian Army. One of the earliest demands made by Nehru, when he became Wavell's Chief Minister in August 1946, was the 'nationalisation' of the Army. By this he meant Indianization of the officer corps and a drawing nearer of the Army to the people of India so that it could become 'their army'. Indianization had been in train since the 1930s, but it was being accelerated in the approach to independence. All the British commanders accepted Indianization: they were much less certain about the possibility of dividing the Army if partition was decided upon. Wavell, Auchinleck and General Lord Ismay, who had been Churchill's wartime Military Secretary and accompanied Mountbatten, had spent most of their working lives in the Indian Army and were convinced that it could only be split with the greatest difficulty. Field Marshal Auchinleck, C.-in-C., wrote in April 1947 just before the partition decision was taken:

The Armed Forces of India, as they now stand, cannot be split up into two parts each of which will form a self-contained Armed Force . . .

   The formation of two separate Armed Forces is not just a matter of redistributing certain classes of men. It is a matter of great complexity and difficulty. . . . Any such drastic reorganisation would have to be carried out in stages over a period of several years, and during this period there would be no cohesive Armed Force capable of dealing with any serious defensive operations on the North West Frontier.[8]

He might have added 'or with internal security operations', but he presumably took that as read. Mountbatten expressed his views at about the same time when reporting a conversation which he had had with Mr Jinnah, to London:

I told him that while I remained statutorily responsible . . . for the preservation of law and order in India, I would not agree to the partition of the Armed Forces, which have already been so weakened by nationalisation that they could not stand partition as well . . .[9]

It is a pity that both men did not stick to their sensible military views. When the partition decision was taken they bowed to the political inevitability of dividing the Army and set about making the best of a difficult job, hoping to mitigate the adverse effects on the Army and the Subcontinent.

   Auchinleck headed the Armed Forces Reconstitution Committee. He insisted on the title 'Reconstitution' as less psychologically damaging than 'Division' or 'Partition'. He was helped in his task by the creation of the two successor dominions rather than foreign states. British officers, essential to the reconstitution, could stay on without becoming mercenaries in the service of alien powers. It was also possible to win acceptance of the need for the temporary establishment of a Supreme Headquarters under Auchinleck, as Supreme Commander, to handle the reconstitution. It would have no operational functions and would be dissolved as soon as its administrative tasks were over. It would be answerable to a Joint Defence Council chaired by Mountbatten with the Defence Ministers of the two dominions and Auchinleck as its principal members. The appointment of senior British officers to be the Chiefs of Staff of the two dominions, also helped.

   The Reconstitution Plan for the Army, when it emerged, envisaged a

1. Field Marshal Lord Wavell, Viceroy, 1943–7

2. Field Marshal Sir Claude Auchinleck, C-in-C India, 1941 and 1943–7, talking to India's youngest VC, Sepoy Kamal Ram

3. Admiral Lord Louis Mountbatten,
   Viceroy, 1947, with Major General
   Reese, Commander of the Punjab
   Boundary Force

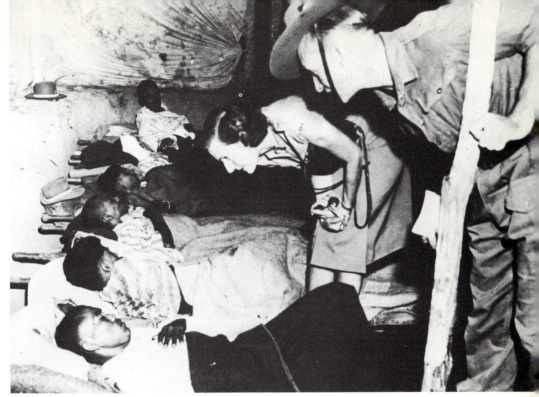

4. Lady Mountbatten, talking to wounded Gurkha soldiers

5. An illegal Jewish immigrant ship, the *Langev*, after being boarded by the Royal Navy (white helmets): 650 people were packed into this 600 ton wooden hulled vessel

6. An arms cache unearthed in a Jewish settlement by 6th Airborne Division

7. The bomb explosion at the King David Hotel, Jerusalem

8. The damaged wing

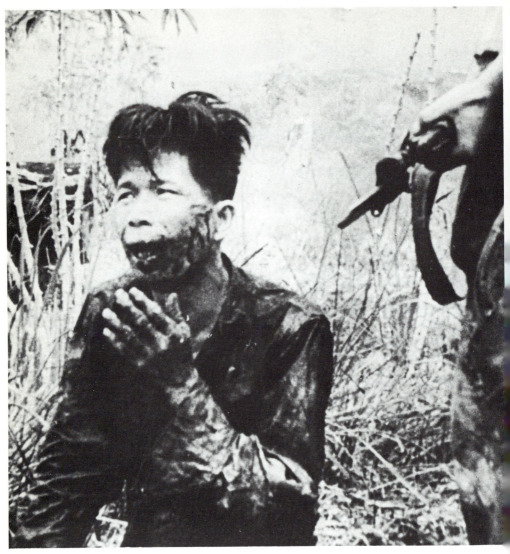

9. A wounded Communist terrorist

10. An SAS patrol in eastern Malaysia
11. A resettlement 'new village' under
    construction in Malaya

12. General Sir George Erskin (*centre*), Director of Operations, Kenya, 1953–5

13. Clearing the tracks into the Aberdare forests

two phase operation. In the first, which was to be completed by 15 August, there was to be a rough and ready division of the Army's major fighting units. The predominantly Muslim units in India would move to Pakistan and vice versa, leaving behind their Hindu or Muslim sub-units, as the case might be, for reallocation to other units in each dominion. In the second phase there would be a detailed comb out of individuals from staffs and the mixed units of the administrative services who would be permitted to opt for either dominion. The Brigade of Gurkhas was to be divided between the British and the new Indian armies, the former taking four regiments (2nd, 6th, 7th and 10th, each of two battalions) off to Malaya for the defence of Southeast Asia. The longest task would be the division of training and logistic establishments, the latter involving the cross movement of large tonnages of equipment, spares, ammunition and supplies of all types. It was hoped that enough of these transfers would be completed satisfactorily for the supreme headquarters to be disbanded by April 1948. The broad division of troops was 260,000 to India and 140,000 to Pakistan.

While Auchinleck went along loyally with his task of planning the division of the Army which he loved, he did not remain silent about the operational risks that were being taken in the wake of the partition decision. He recommended to the Viceroy that the British troops should remain on active service ready to protect British lives and property and to help maintain law and order. Mountbatten could not agree for a number of political reasons. Once power had been transferred it would be the responsibility of the two dominion governments to discharge both tasks. If British troops became involved it would be very difficult to extricate them. Moreover, holding British troops in reserve would show total lack of confidence in the successor governments. Nevertheless, with the British government's approval, Mountbatten did ask both governments if they wanted British troops to stay after 15 August or leave as soon as the necessary administrative arrangements could be made. Jinnah was not averse to the temporary retention of British troops: Nehru was quite emphatic saying 'I would sooner have every village in India put to the flames than keep the British Army here after August 15'.[10] And so the invaluable reserve of the *Gora Paltan*, as the British regiments were known to the villagers, was steadily withdrawn. There had been 30 major British fighting units left in India at the turn of the year: by 15 August these had been reduced to 14.[11]

Auchinleck had reason to be worried. Long before 15 August the security situation in the disputed future frontier areas of the Punjab, particularly around the Sikh homelands, showed signs of further deterioration. The very experienced Governor of the Punjab, Sir Evan Jenkins, described the situation as a 'communal war of succession'. The rival communities had settled down since the announcement of partition to do maximum damage to each other in a wave of mass terrorism and village burnings. In and around Amritsar organized Sikh bands destroyed isolated Muslim villages at the rate of three or four a night. Muslim bands based in

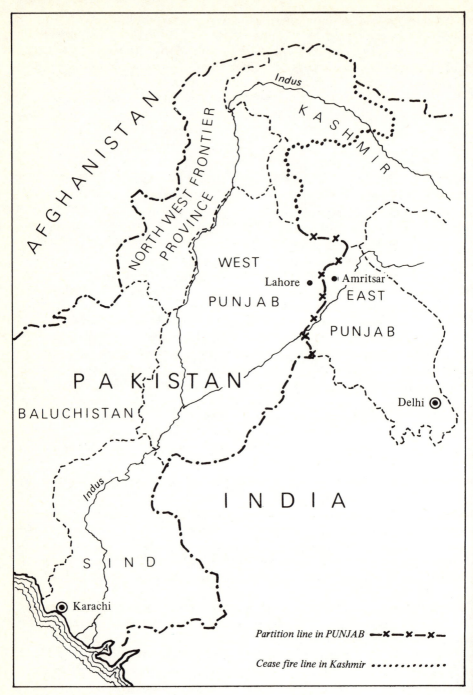

2. The Partition of the Punjab in 1947.

Lahore took revenge, but were less well organized. Delhi itself was not immune from the savagery. In the countryside just to the west of the capital the Hindus tried to exterminate the primitive Meo people, who were Muslims, but the Meos fought back. Villages over a 50-mile front were burnt out before the Army brought the human conflagration under control.

On 22 July, only three weeks before Independence Day, the Partition Council heeded Auchinleck's warning and decided to establish a special military force to support the civil authorities in the disputed areas of the Punjab. Major General T. W. Rees' 4th Indian Division of Middle East fame was given the task of forming the Punjab Boundary Force (PBF) and was reinforced up to 55,000 men, all its units being reliable mixed regiments. Rees was a highly experienced commander, who had led his division with great success throughout the war. He was to be responsible directly to Auchinleck as the Supreme Commander, but he was given an Indian and a Pakistani brigadier as advisors and liaison officers linking the PBF with the governments of the two dominions. The PBF became operational on 1 August. It was considered fully adequate for its task and so it might have been if the goodwill engendered at the highest level by the dominion solution had been reflected downwards. That it was not was no fault of the national leaders like Nehru and Liaquat Ali Khan, who worked hard and persistently to reassure the people by touring the most troubled areas. Habits of a lifetime die hard: local politicians and the provincial press could not change their communal and anti-British spots overnight. They continued to inflame the respective community passions and to blame the British for the results. On 5 August hard evidence emerged of the implication of the Sikh national leadership in planning the extermination of Muslim minorities in their areas and of attempting Jinnah's assassination. Mountbatten considered their arrest but was advised by the Governor of the Punjab and the Governors-designate of the two new provinces of East and West Punjab that the Sikhs were so tightly knit as a community that this could only make matters worse. He has been blamed ever since for not doing so.

By 15 August the PBF was no longer a military reserve in aid of the civil power; it had become the only security force left in the border areas. Seventy per cent of the old Punjab police had been Muslim: those in East Punjab were disarmed and were waiting to be sent back to Pakistan, while the Hindu policemen in the West Punjab refused to serve on. Such police as remained on duty sided with their own co-religionists in the communal struggle. Fifty-five thousand troops may have seemed a large force on 1 August: by 15 August it was trying to quieten an area of 37,500 square miles populated by over 14 million people, living in 1,800 towns and villages; and Rees was being blamed by ministers of both dominions for partiality.

While Delhi celebrated Independence Day on 15 August, the Punjab blew up in violence and terror. Almost simultanously minorities on either side of the border decided to leave homes that their families had lived in for generations and to make for the supposed safety of Pakistan or India. The two minority populations uprooted themselves and fled despite the dangers of doing so, which they judged, in their terror-stricken state, to be less than staying in their old towns and villages. Attacks on minority villages turned into much more devastating attacks upon straggling columns of defenceless refugees and massacres on refugee trains. By October the savagery of August and September had exhausted itself. The problem became one of resettling the destitute and improving the conditions in the quickly improvised and primitive refugee camps. In all it is estimated that four to five million people moved in each direction. How many died will never be known. Conservative estimates put the figure at 200,000; propagandists talk of a 'million dead'.

The PBF did not survive the holocaust. Political attacks on it for not being able to achieve the impossible led Auchinleck to recommend its disbandment as a joint force. At the end of August it was split up and its units joined the side to which each was allotted under the Army Reconstruction Plan. The two halves went on striving under the direction of its own dominion to quench the embers of the tragedy.

The atmosphere in Bengal was no less tense, but recent memories of the 'Calcutta Killings' had their effect. Tuker's troops were ready and the people had less inclination to repeat their earlier savagery. When trouble did start, Gandhi, who had taken up residence in one of the poorer districts of Calcutta, declared 'a fast unto death' until the violence stopped. It did: one man achieved more in Bengal than 55,000 troops could do in the Punjab.

At the height of the crisis in the Punjab, the Indian leaders were big enough men to accept that the situation was beyond their inexperienced capabilities. They asked Mountbatten, in effect, to cease to be a constitutional head of state and to grip the situation by executive action. He set up an emergency committee and war room, which he headed himself, and brought rapid military decision making back into play. He has been described by Lord Ismay as working in his old capacities of 'Captain of a Destroyer Flotilla, Chief of Combined Operations, Supreme Commander, and Governor-General, all rolled into one'.[12] Lady Mountbatten played her part too in galvanizing the organizations working on the relief of the refugees. Many of the decisions Mountbatten took in the run up to the transfer of power can be and are still criticized. No one can deny the service he and his wife rendered to India in the grim summer and autumn of 1947.

Many attempts have been made to play down the horrors of the Punjab massacres and the lesser disorders elsewhere which marred the transfer of power. For instance, it has been pointed out that the 1943 famine in Bengal, caused by the loss of Burmese rice during the Japanese occupation, killed one and a half million people. Bad though things were in the Punjab they could have been very much worse had partition not been accepted nor carried through so quickly: civil war would have cost many more lives. Gandhi and other Hindu and Muslim leaders felt the actual losses were a small price to pay for freedom. Perhaps they were, but they were also a warning to be heeded as other British dependencies advanced from Empire to Commonwealth. Inter-communal hatred was not unique to India, nor were the politico-military problems of transition.

As any established power weakens, a struggle for succession inevitably occurs. How violent it becomes depends on the peoples' confidence in the security forces—the police and the army. Many an Indian and Pakistani minister had reason to rue the day when he attempted to undermine them in India. The causes of India's violence can be blamed upon irresponsible agitation, on the excitable temperament of the people, on their lack of respect for human life in spite of their beliefs in non-violence, on administrative weakness caused by Indianization, on communal bias in the police and other services, and on political misjudgement. But two fundamental military mistakes were made, the one consequent upon the other. The age-old military principle of always having one foot on the ground was broken. At the time of greatest potential danger reconstitution of the armed forces was allowed to go ahead with only one toe on the ground, the luckless Punjab Boundary Force. Not only was the Army in the process of breaking up and moving; the government and police were too. There was no stability at any level when it was most needed. The cause of this breach of principle was more fundamental. The military commanders paid too much attention to the political factors and failed to impress the military realities of the situation upon their political masters. This was unusually difficult for the subordinate military commanders to do in India in 1946 and '47 because the leading political figures—Viceroys Wavell and Mountbatten—were themselves outstanding military men grappling with supreme political problems. The usual checks and balances of separate political and military responsibilities were missing. And India's own political leaders were only interested in achieving independence and partition: the cost to them was immaterial.

The British left India with great sadness, feeling that their mission to the Subcontinent's people was incomplete. The people at the grass roots felt so too, but there could be no turning back the pages of history. A very different story was unfolding in Palestine where there were no such nostalgic feelings.

Britain is often said to have built her Empire in a fit of absent-mindedness: her acceptance of the League of Nations' Mandate to establish a Jewish home in Palestine turned out to be a high-minded error of judgement. The anti-semitic pogroms in Russia and Central Europe in the nineteenth century had led to three to four million Jews seeking refuge elsewhere. Some did go to Palestine, but the majority found sanctuary in the United States, especially in New York. By the end of the First World War there were only 66,000 Jews living in Palestine amongst almost 600,000 Arabs, while in the United Kingdom the Jewish population was small and well integrated into British society; and yet it was Britain who saddled herself with what was to be the thankless and impractical task of creating a new Israel without dispossessing the Arabs who had tilled the Holy Land since Roman times.

In the early 1920s it seemed appropriate that the British, as latter-day crusaders, who had successfully driven the infidel out of Jerusalem, should help to return the Israelites to their Promised Land. It was appreciated that there was conflict between Britain's wartime pledges to the Arabs and the concept of a Jewish national home in Palestine enshrined in the Balfour Declaration. Allenby's victories had, however, freed such vast areas of the Arab lands from Turkish rule that it was felt the Arabs would not 'grudge that small niche . . . being given to the people who, for all these hundreds of years, have been separated from it',[13] as Balfour put it.

The Mandatory responsibilities that Britain accepted from the League of Nations in 1920 indeed spoke of a *national home* for the Jews, which was to be established in Palestine without prejudice to the civil and religious rights of the existing inhabitants, the Palestinian Arabs. There was no direction to establish a Jewish state. It was hoped that Jewish immigration would help to develop the backward Arab economy of Palestine. The fear was that too few Jews would be prepared to stay once they found that the land did not 'flow with milk and honey': the life was harsh, the soil poor, water scarce and the Arabs hostile.

In the initial burst of Jewish enthusiasm in the 1920s young men and women flocked from Europe and the United States to make the dry soil of Palestine bloom. By the end of the decade, the Jewish population had doubled but the physical difficulties and Arab hostility, highlighted by the brutal massacre of Jews in Hebron in 1929, had become so discouraging that there was a small net outflow of Jews looking for a better life elsewhere.

Hitler's rise to power in Germany rekindled Jewish enthusiasm for the Promised Land. By 1935, Jews were arriving in Palestine at a rate of 60,000 per year. This was too much for the Arabs. The Arab Revolt began in 1936 and drew into Palestine the equivalent of two British divisions before it was mastered. Most of the Arab leaders were deported to the Seychelles and the death penalty was ruthlessly imposed for the carriage of arms. Although the revolt was successfully crushed, the Jews came to believe that the Arab use of force had reversed British policy from being pro-Zionist with sympathy for the Arabs to pro-Arab with sympathy for the Jews. The 1939 White Paper on Palestine did nothing to disabuse them of this idea. In it, the British government restricted Jewish immigration to a final quota of 75,000 spanning a five-year period. Thereafter no Jews would be allowed to enter Palestine without Arab consent. It also set up self-governing institutions with the aim of leading a Palestinian state to independence in ten years, subject to Jewish consent. It was hoped that Arab control of immigration and Jewish control of the speed of advance to independence would induce the two communities to co-operate. Neither side accepted this judgement of Solomon; nor did political opinion in Britain and the United States. In the House of Commons the Conservative majority of 248 dropped to 89 when the White Paper was debated. In Washington President Roosevelt questioned Britain's right to restrict Jewish immigration. He did not support the British view that it would be illegal to establish a Jewish state (rather than a Jewish home) in Palestine against the wishes of the Arabs; indeed, he had always assumed this was the purpose of the Mandate. The Second World War broke out before the League of Nations could pronounce on the White Paper's legality, but the dragon's teeth of Anglo-American discord over Palestine had been sown.

It was the Jews rather than the Arabs who made the best use of the war years. The Arabs' Grand Mufti of Jerusalem, who had escaped deportation to the Seychelles, alienated British sympathy by seeking Hitler's support. The Jews naturally supported Britain in her struggle with their mortal enemy, Nazi Germany. Nevertheless, they sought every means of undermining the provisions of the 1939 White Paper and of preparing themselves for the armed struggle, which they knew must come with the Arabs before the state of Israel could be born. Planning was carried out by the Jewish Agency, which had been established under the Mandate to advise the British administration in Palestine on Jewish affairs. Three lines of policy were pursued: defeat of the immigration quotas by illegal entry; obtaining military training and equipment by offering to serve in the British forces defending the Middle East against German invasion; and organizing support in the United States. The last was by far the easiest to carry out. Not only did American Jewry have the financial resources but it had political clout as well. No presidential candidate, other than Woodrow Wilson in 1916, had ever reached the White House without winning New York where the Jews held the political balance of power.

Playing the illegal immigration card had two advantages: it increased the Jewish population and it embarrassed the British government by giving the impression that its White Paper restrictions were inhuman. Those refugees from Nazi-occupied Europe, who often reached the coast of Palestine in over-crowded and unseaworthy steamers, were interned until the official immigration quota allowed their release into the Jewish community or they were reshipped to Mauritius for the duration of the war. The internment of each batch of new illegal arrivals caused a storm of protest amongst the Jewish communities in Palestine and the United States. Britain, despite her single-handed struggle with Nazi Germany, was branded as barbaric.

Churchill saw obvious advantages in arming the Jews to help fight the Germans. He would have liked to have raised a Jewish division, but the Chiefs of Staff considered the risk of alienating Arab opinion was too great. Only one brigade was raised, which fought in Italy during the latter stages of the war. Jews were also recruited into British Special Service units operating in the Eastern Mediterranean and Middle East and into local defence units in Palestine. The build up of trained Jewish military manpower was helped too by the arrival of Jews in General Anders' Polish forces and of ex-soldiers amongst the illegal immigrants.

The main Jewish military force, the Hagana, had its origins in the days of the Ottoman Empire when the Jewish settlements were allowed local home guards to protect them against Arab attack. The Hagana was reborn in the 1920s as a part-time settlement protection force and was connived at by the British authorities as long as it confined its activities to local defence. It became perforce the foundation of the future Jewish national army, clandestinely built up for more than local defence of settlements. Within the Hagana there was an elite group, the Palmach, whose members had seen service in the British and other European armies. They were full-time underground soldiers, accepting Jewish military discipline, and were organized and trained for offensive operations.

In 1937 a breakaway group was formed by extreme Zionists called the Irgun Zvai Leumi, dedicated to establishing a Jewish state. Whereas the Jewish Agency, which controlled the Hagana believed in political methods, Irgun espoused the use of force. When the Second World War broke out Irgun decided to co-operate with the British. A small group of its followers, led by Abraham Stern, disagreed and formed the *Lechamey Heruth Israel* (Hebrew Freedom Fighters), to continue violent opposition to the British administration. The LHI became known as the 'Stern Gang'. Its *modus operandi* was assassination. Stern himself was killed in a gun battle with the Palestine police in 1942.

Neither of the extremist groups had much support until 1943 when news began to seep out of occupied Europe of the horrors of Hitler's 'final solution' to the Jewish problem. Moderate leaders of the Jewish Agency realized that the Allies could do little at that time to help the Jews in Occupied Europe other than pressing on with their preparations for the invasion of Normandy. The extremists thought differently: in their view, only force would shift Britain from her apparently pro-Arab policies. In February 1944 Irgun, now under Menachim Begin, a Polish refugee, who had arrived in Palestine with Anders' army and who was to become Israel's Prime Minister in the 1980s, declared war on the British Mandatory Government of Palestine. His hostility was directed against the Palestine police and other organs of government. Irgun had no quarrel with the British Army's operational divisions, which rested and retrained in Palestine before returning to the Italian front.

The Irgun campaign began on 12 February 1944 with the blowing up of the immigration offices in Jerusalem, Haifa and Tel Aviv. A fortnight later the tax offices in the same towns were destroyed, and on 23 March the CID offices were dynamited too. Both British and Jewish public opinion was shocked by these outrages. It seemed that the Zionist cause was being prejudiced just as it was being strengthened by the news of the Nazi holocaust. The Jewish Agency publicly condemned Irgun, and the Hagana took steps to hunt down its terrorists. The Jewish moderates had good

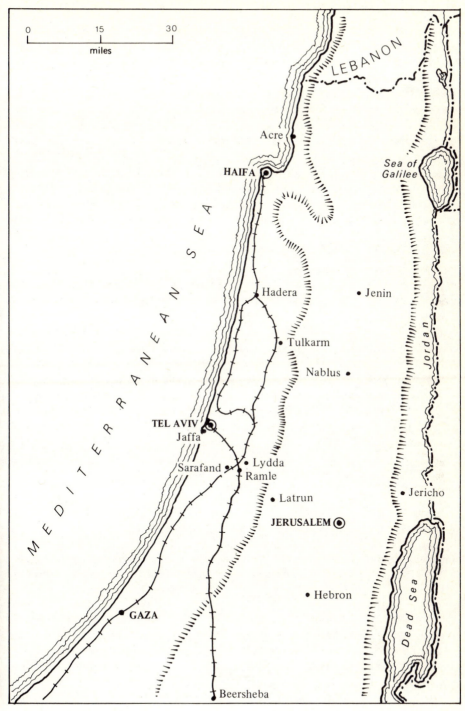

3. Palestine in 1945–7.

reason for opposing Irgun. In London and Washington Churchill and Roosevelt were moving ahead of and in opposition to their foreign policy advisers in their support of the Zionist cause. Churchill had always been pro-Zionist, but the Foreign Office and the Chiefs of Staff believed that British interests would be better served by maintaining Arab rather than Jewish friendship. The former could be jeopardized if Britain helped to set up a Jewish state, however small, in Palestine. In Arab eyes, such a state would become a Jewish bridgehead in the Arab world that would be progressively expanded to Arab detriment. The most that the Arabs were likely to accept was some form of cantonization of Palestine, in which the Arab majority would be maintained. Roosevelt had also been consistently pro-Zionist and could not ignore the Jewish vote in the 1944 presidential elections. On the other hand, the State Department, the American Chiefs of Staff and the oil lobby in Congress, saw the dangers to their interests in loss of Muslim confidence in US policy. The delicate balance in both capitals could be swung by some rash Irgun operation.

It was not, however Irgun but the Stern Gang that upset the apple cart in November 1944. Roosevelt was returned to the White House, having sided with the Zionists during the election. A British Cabinet committee, set up to advise on post-war policy in Palestine, had recommended a partition plan favourable to the Jews. The Stern Gang, with the obtusest of timing, murdered Lord Moyne, British Minister Resident in Cairo and a close personal friend of Churchill just after the US Presidential elections. The Prime Minister lost his Zionist inclinations and allowed the pendulum of British offical opinion to swing back into a neutral position, in which Arab interests were given full weight despite increasing American political criticisms of British policy. Just before he left office in 1945 Churchill minuted the Colonial Secretary and Chiefs of Staff:

I do not think that we should take the responsibility upon ourselves of managing this very difficult place while the Americans sit back and criticize. Have you ever addressed yourselves to the idea that we should ask them to take it over? I believe we should be the stronger the more they are drawn into the Mediterranean. At any rate, the fact that we show no desire to keep the mandate will be a great help. I am not aware of the slightest advantage which has ever accrued to Great Britain from this painful and thankless task. Somebody else should have their turn now. However, the Chiefs of Staff should examine the matter from the strategic point of view.[14]

The Chiefs of Staff rejected Churchill's ideas. They feared that handing over to the United States would adversely affect Britain's position in the Muslim world and would place British vital interests in the Middle East in the hands of another country. They expected that the renegotiation of the Anglo-Egyptian Treaty, which Egypt was demanding, would lead to the British evacuation of the Nile Delta and possibly the Canal Zone. Palestine was the next most suitable location for Britain's Strategic Reserve for the Mediterranean and Middle East.

The end of the war in Europe added a further dimension to the Palestine problem: how to resettle the Jewish survivors of the Holocaust. It was clear to the new Attlee government that Palestine could not take all the displaced European Jews, even if the Arab States were willing to accept them, which they certainly were not. The war had been fought and won to make Europe safe for everyone, including the Jews, who should therefore return to their own home towns and help in the reconstruction of a new and more civilized Europe. The Zionists took a different view: how could the Jews be expected to return to the scenes of their agony? Other anti-semitic regimes could arise in the future. The Jews needed their own state that could look after their interests world wide. Hitler's 'final solution' had, in fact, created a nation of European Jews without a home: Palestine was the right place and they were prepared to fight for a Jewish state there.

Matters came to a head in the autumn of 1945. There were enough pro-Zionists in both the British and American governments for policy decisions to be leaked from time to time to the Jewish Agency. Two important leaks about British policy occurred in September. In London, the Agency became aware that the Attlee government had decided to maintain the 1939 White Paper policy until a new United Nations' trusteeship agreement had been negotiated. In the meantime, subject to Arab agreement, 1,500 immigration permits would be issued per month as Palestine's contribution to the European refugee problem. In Washington, correspondence between Attlee and Truman was leaked, which showed that the Prime Minister had turned down a request from the President for the immediate issue of 100,000 permits. A wave of fury swept through the Jewish communities, bringing the moderates and extremists together in a determination to change British policy by both military as well as political means.

The Jewish leaders decided to adopt a two-handed strategy. Doctor Chaim Weizemann, the ageing Zionist who had negotiated the Balfour Declaration in 1917, was to lead the political offensive to bring the pressure of American and world opinion to bear on Britain and the Arab States. Ben Gurion, Chairman of the Jewish Agency Executive and later Israeli's first Prime Minister, would mount the military operations to unnerve the Palestine Government. The actions of the Hagan, Palmach, Irgun and Stern Gang were to be co-ordinated by a special committee called 'X Command' on which Irgun and Stern representatives sat. Financial and logistic support was to come from American Zionist organizations like the 'Sonnenborn Institute', which ostensibly supplied agricultural machinery and medical supplies to the Jewish settlements, but in reality helped the Hagana by buying ships, aircraft, trucks, surplus weapons and ammunition from wherever they could be acquired. There was no shortage of cash.

The Zionist military plan was to concentrate on headline catching acts of sabotage in anticipation of or in reaction to specific political events. Loss of life was to be avoided to reduce adverse political reaction in Britain and America. Particular attention was to be paid to targets associated with immigration control, and a further attempt was to be made to flood the system with illegal immigrants. Hagana agents worked hard in the European refugee camps, persuading Jews to opt for settlement in Palestine; and the Jewish underground smuggled tens of thousands of East-European Jews westwards to swell the queues for Palestine. In July 1945 there had been only 50,000 Jewish refugees in the British and American refugee camps: by the end of 1946 there were 250,000. Immigrant ships were purchased and manned by armed Hagana crews. Refugees were then sent clandestinely to them in Mediterranean ports for passage to Palestine.

The British security forces in Palestine in October 1945 consisted of the Palestine police (5,000 British, Arab and Jewish constables under British officers), the Arab-manned Transjordan Frontier Force and the Bedouin Arab Legion under Glubb Pasha. The 1st Division was resting and retraining in Palestine after the Italian campaign, and the 6th Airborne Division was on its way to Palestine to form the Middle East Strategic Reserve. Both these field force divisions were to be available to support the police, but their primary task was training for general war. The 1st Division occupied camps in the northern half of the country and 6th Airborne Division was concentrated around Gaza in the south. The independent 7th Infantry Brigade was stationed near Jerusalem under GHQ control and Naval and RAF forces in the eastern Mediterranean were also available.

The Jewish revolt opened on 31 October 1945 with a demonstration of the strength and co-ordination of their resistance organization. The Palestine railway network was cut in 154 places, a train and three locomotives were destroyed, three police patrol craft, used for intercepting illegal immigrant ships, were sunk, and slight damage was done to the Haifa oil refinery. The Jewish Agency blandly disclaimed responsibility, saying that it repudiated violence. It blamed British policies for the 'spontaneous upsurge amongst the Jewish people, who feared for their future'. Such protestations rang hollow in Whitehall. British Intelligence had broken the Agency telegraphic code and were well aware of the depth of its involvement.

Throughout the painful birth of the state of Israel, which lasted for almost two years, Britain sought to reconcile the irreconcilable without going to war with the Jewish people or alienating the Arab States. The birth contractions came in five spasms, each in response to a specific political initiative associated with an international committee of inquiry or a major conference which the Jews wished to impress with their total dedication to the rebirth of Israel.

The target during the first spasm was the Anglo-American Palestine Committee, which was set up to examine how many Jewish refugees wanted to settle in Palestine and how many Palestine could actually absorb. Ernest Bevin, Britain's Foreign Secretary in the Attlee government, had become personally convinced during the Potsdam Conference of the malign hostility of the Soviet Union and the need for continuing close

Anglo-American co-operation in the post-war world. On the Palestine issue he was at one with Churchill in objecting to American criticism without responsibility. As soon as the dust of the New York elections had settled, President Truman agreed to Bevin's proposals for a joint committee of enquiry. Unfortunately, in announcing its formation in the House of Commons on 13 November, Bevin was over-forthright. He stressed that Britain had never promised to bring about a Jewish state, only a Jewish home in Palestine. That might still be achieved, if it was recognized that Palestine alone could not solve Europe's Jewish refugee problem, and if the Jewish people would stop trying to jump the post-war resettlement queues. They were not the only people without a home. Next day the Jewish population of Jerusalem and Tel Aviv blew up in a genuinely spontaneous wave of anger, not orchestrated by the Agency. Anti-British rioting gripped both cities.

The Jerusalem riots of 14 November were quickly contained by the police. In Tel Aviv, 3rd Parachute Brigade was called in to assist the police. On the first night 8th Parachute Battalion, which had been training for internal security duties since its arrival in early October, was deployed and it used the regulation drills for dealing with riots. The troops showed the usual restraint under barrages of stones thrown at them, but when injuries began to mount fire was opened after repeated warnings. A small number of rounds aimed and fired by marksmen under direct supervision of an officer at prominent ring-leaders dispersed the crowds and a curfew was imposed. Next day the rest of the Brigade was deployed to enforce the curfew that was being broken by large crowds. After due warning fire had again to be opened before the curfew could be re-imposed. It lasted until 20 November. By the time it was lifted six Jews had been killed and 60 wounded: 12 British soldiers had been taken to hospital and another 30 treated for less serious injuries. Damage to property was extensive: the post office, income tax office and other government buildings suffering most. The firmness and discipline of the 3rd Parachute Brigade left its mark. The Jewish community, well-versed in evading the Gestapo, never again resorted to rioting to express their anger as long as Britain held the Mandate.

During the Anglo-American Committee's deliberations the combined Jewish resistance movement mounted three offensives with a large number of minor incidents interspersed between them. On Boxing Day police stations and armouries were the main targets. Between 20 and 26 February 1946 it was the turn of the Royal Air Force. Dispersed aircraft were attacked on three airfields. Seven were destroyed and eight damaged, most being transport aircraft for the Airborne Division's training. An attack on the 3rd Hussars' camp at Sarafand failed with two of the raiders being captured. The third offensive came on 2 April and was directed once more at the railway system, but with diminishing returns: a third of the saboteurs were killed or captured.

In the follow up operations mounted after each of these attacks the police and Army met with a wall of silence and obstruction when they searched the nearby Jewish settlements. The biblical curse on all informers ensured silence was kept; and random burial of scrap iron neutralized the effectiveness of mine detectors in uncovering arms caches. Young British National Servicemen were no match for the cunning of the East-European Jews.

General Sir Alan Cunningham had succeeded Lord Gort in November as High Commissioner. He had conquered Italian Somaliland and Abyssinia in 1941, but had been less successful commanding 8th Army in the Western Desert. He believed that it was the role of the police and Army to hold the ring with peace-keeping operations while a political solution was sought. Every effort was to be made to win the support of the moderate majority of the Jewish community, thereby isolating the extremists. When the Chiefs of Staff suggested disarming the Jews, Cunningham objected: politically it would alienate the moderates, and militarily it would be extraordinarily difficult as recent experience in follow-up searches had shown. The Chiefs of Staff did consider an alternative suggested by Cunningham: the occupation of the Jewish Agency offices and the arrest and deportation of Jewish leaders as had happened to the Arab leaders during the pre-war Arab revolt. Cunningham was authorized to plan the operation (codenamed 'Agatha'), but it was to be held in abeyance until after the Anglo-American Committee had reported. The security forces were also strengthened by the arrival of 3rd Division from Germany, which initially relieved 1st Division. The 1st Division was temporarily withdrawn to Egypt to reorganize after losing large numbers of its older men in the post-war demobilization.

Just as the Anglo-American Committee was about to report events took an ugly turn. So far there had been no deliberate attacks on British servicemen. The Hagana and Irgun had confined themselves to sabotage. Officers and men were only armed when on duty. The atmosphere was one of strained normality with the police rather than the Army in control. On 25 April 1946 the Stern Gang murdered in cold blood seven unarmed soldiers of the 2nd Parachute Brigade, who were guarding a recreational transport park in Tel Aviv against vandalism and petty theft. The revulsion felt by the whole Army was deep and lasting. Most soldiers had come to Palestine in a pro-Zionist frame of mind, having either seen or read about Hitler's extermination camps. The transport park outrage, added to a growing dislike of Jewish methods, changed their attitudes: 'We beat the Nazis for them didn't we; why pick on us?' With a few minor exceptions, however, discipline was always maintained.

The same could not be said of the Jewish side. 'X Command' first lost control of the Stern Gang and then of Irgun. The GOC Palestine, General John D'Arcy, and the Chiefs of Staff pressed the British government to allow the introduction of the standard pre-war imperial policing penalties: dynamiting houses known to have harboured dissidents; imposing collective fines on towns and villages; and using curfews to make life uncomfortable in hostile areas. Much as he appreciated the trials faced by the troops, the Prime Minister decided that political considerations must be given precedence. He was still not prepared to put plan 'Agatha' into operation either. In his view:

To put into operation the full plans against the Jewish Agency and *Hagana* on account of outrage for which they cannot be proved responsible would have widespread repercussions at a time when it is hoped to deal with Palestine through Anglo-American co-operation.[15]

The Anglo-American Committee reported on 1 May 1946. It accepted the Jewish demand for 100,000 immigration permits, but not the establishment of a Jewish state. Truman gave immediate public support for the former, but avoided mentioning the latter. Bevin stated two pre-conditions for their implementation: both Jews and Arabs should be disarmed and agreement must be reached on the future constitutional structure of the Palestine government. In putting these conditions to James Byrnes, US Secretary of State, Bevin warned that Britain was contemplating giving up the Mandate. The only thing that made the Attlee government hesitate was the danger of Russian penetration into the Middle East in the wake of British withdrawal. The aggressive attitude of the Jews was poisoning Anglo-American relations and would continue to do so unless the United States was prepared to share the responsibilities and difficulties of imposing a solution. Both men agreed that a group of American and British officials should examine the practical problems of implementing the Anglo-American Committee's recommendations.

The group of experts was led by Henry Grady of the State Department and Sir Norman Brook, Secretary to the British Cabinet. Its deliberations spanned the summer months of 1946 and marked the second spasm of contractions in the re-birth of Israel. In response to British refusal to grant the 100,000 permits immediately, the Hagana launched a major attack on road and rail bridges linking Palestine with its Arab neighbours on 16 June; and next day Irgun kidnapped five British officers from the Tel Aviv Officers' Club and held them hostage against the lives of the two of their own men captured in the raid on the 3rd Hussars' camp. The kidnapping was not difficult because British servicemen off-duty still went about unarmed. Ben Gurion disingenuously assured the Colonial Secretary that there were no links between the Agency and the extremist groups. On Cunningham's recommendation Operation 'Agatha' was authorized by the British government.

The operation took place on 28 June. It had been well planned and came as a complete surprise to the Jewish community in spite of the fact that some 17,000 troops took part. The Jewish Agency offices were occupied and Jewish leaders were arrested all over Palestine. Two important men escaped: Ben Gurion, who was abroad, and Doctor Moshe Sneh, the holder of the Security portfolio in the Agency executive, who eluded capture. Those arrested were not sent to the Seychelles as the Arab leaders had been. They were held in Palestine at Latrun and Rafiah. The operation proved to be a military but not a political success. The Hagana ceased operations, but hopes of the emergence of a new and more moderate Jewish leadership were not fulfilled. Instead, the extremists' grip on the Jewish community tightened. There had been too little Intelligence about their organizations for many of Irgun's or the Stern Gang's members to be picked up.

In response to 'Agatha' the surviving Jewish leadership planned a series of attacks including blowing up the King David Hotel which housed the government secretariat and the GHQ. Though it was heavily guarded, it was still in use as a hotel, which made it possible to introduce the explosives through the catering department. Irgun took charge of the operation and managed to place seven milk churns of explosive in the cafe on the ground floor. A warning was to have been given so as to gain maximum political effect without risk of adverse reaction to large numbers of casualties. The warning was mismanaged and came too late. Ninety-one people died (41 Arabs, 28 Britons, 17 Jews and five others) when the whole of one wing collapsed into a pile of rubble on 22 July.

International and local reaction was one of horror, but the British political and military response was muted because there were high hopes that Anglo-American agreement on the way ahead was near. The British government confined itself to issuing a White Paper setting out the evidence connecting the Jewish Agency with the sabotage and terrorist attacks of the previous nine months. The Army mounted a massive search operation in Tel Aviv into which the King David Hotel bombers were thought to have escaped. It was code-named Operation 'Shark'.

'Shark' started on 30 July and lasted four days. It was carried out by 6th Airborne Division's 1st, 2nd and 3rd Parachute Brigades and 2nd Infantry Brigade from 1st Division plus three independent infantry battalions and three armoured car regiments. The operation was again well planned and methodical, but searching a hostile city with 170,000 inhabitants was far from easy. A cordon was first established round the city, which was then divided by inner cordons into manageable brigade search areas. A strict curfew was imposed and the inhabitants were allowed only two hours per day for shopping within their brigade cordons. One hundred thousand people were screened and almost 800 were detained. Arms and ammunition were unearthed on a modest scale. While the population generally co-operated in this massive show of force, the troops were made well aware that Jewish sympathies lay with the extremists and not with the moderates. Begin escaped detection cooped up in a secret compartment in his house without food or water while troops camped in the garden.

Meanwhile, British hopes of an agreed Anglo-American plan began to fade. There was little difficulty in agreeing the constitutional proposals for Jewish and Arab provinces with a neutral province for the Jerusalem area governed until independence by the Mandatory power. No agreement could be reached on the immigration issue. The American Chiefs of Staff advised against the use of American troops to help impose a settlement but pointed out to the President that US military forces and the American standard of living depended upon oil, and hence on Arab co-operation. Truman was faced with the more immediate problem of the New York elections in October. He demanded the immediate issue of the 100,000 permits but without offering military support to deal with the consequences. Attlee, for his part, insisted that the constitutional proposals should be put to a conference of Arab and Jewish leaders, which Bevin was convening in London, before any decisions were taken on the immigration quotas.

The London Conference and negotiations between its sessions lasted through the autumn and winter of 1946–47 and constituted the third re-birth spasm. The Conference opened on 9 September with only the Arab delegations present. The Jews refused to attend unless their leaders were released from Latrun and Rafiah. However, they continued to negotiate outside the Conference, at which the Arabs rejected the Anglo-American partition proposals and demanded a unitary state based upon majority rule. The Arabs were implacably opposed to partition in any shape or form because they could see it could lead to the re-birth of Israel and that they were determined to abort.

Outside the Conference the Jews seemed to be in a more conciliatory mood. Bevin decided to make one last effort to reach a compromise with them. As a goodwill gesture the Jewish leaders were released, and he delayed the reconvening of the London Conference until after the World Zionist Conference in Basle in December.

None of this diplomatic activity was to the liking of Field Marshal Montgomery, who had become CIGS in June. In his characteristically abrasive way he declared that the policy of appeasing the Jews had failed; Cunningham was a ditherer; and there was no discernible political or military plan. He asked that Cunningham should be directed to use all the large military forces at his disposal to enforce strict law and order. In his view the only way to stamp out terrorism was to take the offensive and hold the initiative. If 'Agatha' had been pursued ruthlessly, he believed that the illegal organizations would have been destroyed; instead they had been allowed time to reorganize and recruit. Cunningham, to his credit, was not prepared to be overawed by the Field Marshal. He resisted Montgomery's intervention on the grounds that such action would only increase Jewish hostility without necessarily defeating the extremists. It was better to let the Jewish Agency and Hagana impose restraint upon them as they appeared to have been doing since the King David Hotel outrage.

Montgomery's points were made for him by events in November and December. Irgun attacks on the rail and road networks were stepped up and, on 29 November, they succeeded once more in blowing up the income tax office in Jerusalem. A week later there were violent scenes in Haifa, orchestrated by the Hagana, when some 3,900 illegal immigrants were transferred to British ships and sent off to Cyprus. Then, in December, two

Irgun youths were given jail sentences and 18 lashes. Irgun kidnapped the brigade major of 2nd Parachute Brigade and three sergeants and lashed them in retaliation. It was some satisfaction to the victims that the perpetrators were later caught with whips still in the back of their car. Then, in January, further kidnappings occurred to enforce the reprieve of Irgun prisoners under death sentence. Faced with continuing violence despite every effort to reach a political solution, the British government authorized the clearing of decks for decisive military action. All British families were sent home; administrative staffs were withdrawn into specially protected areas; and three divisional sectors were established with 3rd Division in the south, 1st Division in the centre and 6th Airborne Division in the north. The Army was well balanced to act decisively if the second session of the London Conference were to fail.

The winter of 1946–47 was particularly depressing for the British people. The weather was severe; food rationing was still in force; there were shortages of everything; and clearing up the aftermath of the war seemed to be never-ending at home and abroad. Trying to reconcile Arab and Jew in Palestine was generally felt to be a quite unnecessary additional burden. No vital British interests were at stake. Why not let the Jews and Arabs fight it out without the British Army acting as referee? Churchill as leader of the Opposition, articulated this feeling on a number of occasions in the House, demanding the return of the thankless task to the United Nations.

The World Zionist Conference in Basle ended in defeat for moderate Jewish opinion and this did not bode well for the London Conference when it reopened on 27 January. The Jews again refused to attend, but carried on negotiations outside the Conference, which did serve to crystallize the views of the two sides. The Jews would accept partition: the Arabs would not. Bevin saw that he had three options: sacrifice Britain's wider interests in the Middle East by imposing partition on the Arabs; go to war with the Jews to impose majority rule, thereby risking the loss of American financial support to Britain; or to hand the Mandate back to the United Nations with the consequent loss of British prestige and the opportunity to station the British Strategic Reserve in Palestine. British public opinion was running strongly in favour of the third option, and the Chiefs of Staff saw withdrawal from Palestine as the lesser of two evils: friendship of the Arab States was strategically more important than military camps and training areas in Palestine.

On 18 February 1947, after the London Conference had failed, the British government referred the problem to the United Nations, but did not, at that stage, surrender the Mandate. If the United Nations could produce an agreed solution that Britain felt she could impose, she might be willing to stay on. Bevin felt that Soviet antipathy to Zionism would ensure that a solution based upon partition, which the Jews favoured, would not win the necessary numbers of the UN votes. Before the matter could be fully debated the standard diplomatic minuet was danced, setting up a United Nations Special Committee to establish the facts about Palestine.

The appointment of the Special Committee ushered in the fourth and decisive spasm of action and reaction to the re-birth of Israel. Irgun decided to impress the United Nations with Jewish resolve to win the whole of Palestine and the British Army struck back. On 1 March Irgun blew up the Jerusalem Officers' Club killing 13 people and injuring 16. They also perpetrated another 16 acts of terrorism and sabotage. In retaliation, martial law was imposed on the Jewish quarter of Jerusalem and on the whole of Tel Aviv on 2 March. Trade came to a standstill and economic ruin stared the Jewish community in the face. Had the commanders on the spot appreciated that the damage done to trade had come closer than anything else in breaking Jewish resolve it might not have been lifted on 17 March. Their intention, however, was to teach the Jewish community a lesson, and this had been achieved. At the end of the fortnight the commanders on the spot saw that unemployment created was helping Irgun to gather recruits and support.

The decision to lift martial law was not taken without considerable debate in Whitehall. The Cabinet sought its extension to the rest of Palestine and its indefinite prolongation, but the Chiefs of Staff advised against its retention. The Army was not organized for, nor did it have the resources to administer the country single-handed for a prolonged period. In their view, close co-operation between the civil government, the police and the Army in administration of tightly drawn emergency regulations was a better method. The Cabinet concurred. A fortnight later Irgun demonstrated its resilience by blowing up a section of the Haifa oil refinery, which blazed for three weeks. On 4 May they breached the walls of Acre prison with explosive charges and released 41 Jews and, incidentally 214 Arab prisoners. Their escape was intercepted: eight Jews were killed and 13 captured, including three Irgun men whose trial and death sentence were to contribute to the final re-birth of Israel.

The United Nations Special Committee arrived in Palestine in the middle of June and took evidence for six weeks. Two major incidents proved decisive so far as the British were concerned. The first was the failure to win international support in stopping the Hagana's chain of illegal immigrant ships sailing from European ports. The crisis came over the *President Warfield*, a specially converted Great Lakes ferry, renamed the *Exodus*, which the Hagana brought into Séte in Southern France and embarked 4,500 refugees. She had been specially fitted to accommodate these people in grossly overcrowded conditions, and she had also been given anti-boarding devices, including a heavily-protected bridge, an alternative wheel house below decks, and a sharp-edged boom around her hull to prevent British destroyers coming alongside. The French authorities let her sail in spite of the strongest British diplomatic protests. She reached Palestinian waters on 18 July and, after a prolonged struggle, was boarded by the Royal Navy and taken into Haifa where the refugees were trans-shipped to British ships and sent back to France. There the French authorities refused to make them land, and so they had to be sailed round to the British zone of Germany and disembarked there. All the while anti-British propaganda was swirling round the world, particularly in America, where public opinion became increasingly pro-Zionist.

The second incident had a greater effect on British public opinion. The Stern Gang, not to be outdone by Irgun, kidnapped two British NCOs, Sergeants Martin and Pain, and held them hostage for the lives of the three Jews sentenced to death after the Acre prison raid. There was no reprieve. The day after the three were hanged in Acre prison, Martin and Pain were hanged by the Stern gang. Their bodies were strung up in an olive grove and booby trapped. The British officer, who cut them down, was injured in the explosion and one corpse was blown to pieces. A wave of revulsion swept Britain at what the *Daily Express* called 'medieval barbarism'. Anti-semitic demonstrations occurred in London, Manchester, Liverpool, Newcastle, Gateshead and Holyhead, all areas hit by the post-war economic depression. In Tel Aviv some troops and police took the law into their own hands. Their rampage was short-lived: otherwise discipline was maintained throughout the Army in Palestine. If there had ever been a chance of Britain carrying on in Palestine under a new trustee agreement with the United Nations, it died with the murder of the two sergeants. Terrorism had triumphed because no British vital interests were at stake.

The Special Committee's report, which was debated at the General Assembly in September, recommended the ending of the British Mandate, the partition of Palestine, the continuation of British administration for two years after which the Arab and Jewish states would be given their independence, and the immediate admission of 150,000 Jewish immigrants. The British government was not prepared to implement such proposals and made it clear at the beginning of the debate that it would withdraw British troops and administration if a solution acceptable to both sides was not found and a sensible plan was made to carry it through. Few diplomats present believed that Britain would do such a thing and took it as a tactical ploy to engineer a request by the UN for a continuation of the Mandate. They were all proved wrong. Lobbying became intense. Russia surprised everyone by supporting the Zionists and voting for partition. Even so the vote would have gone the other way if it had not been for the American use of unscrupulous economic blackmail to make up the minds of the smaller states in favour of partition. Britain abstained and, after partition was agreed, refused to play any part in its implementation. She insisted only upon enough time to wind up her administration, to evacuate the vast tonnages of military stores and equipment accumulated in Palestine, and to withdraw her troops. The date 15 May 1948 was set for ending the Mandate and 1 August for the completion of the evacuation.

The final United Nations vote had been taken on 29 November. Next day the first Arab-Israeli war broke out. Until the end of March the Arabs held the initiative, but, through their lack of preparation, disunity and military incompetence, failed to abort the re-birth of Israel. From April onwards the Jews fought back and exposed the Arab feet of clay. The

British Army held the two sides in check only to the extent necessary to complete an orderly withdrawal southwards into the Canal Zone in Egypt and by sea from Haifa to Cyprus and the United Kingdom. As with most withdrawals, the time-table was accelerated as the weeks went by. The last troops and stores left Haifa on 30 June.

There was no disguising the defeat. The British government had given way to terrorism and this lesson was not lost in anti-British circles around the world.

The saddest outcome of the struggle was the damage done to Anglo-American relations, certainly in the Middle East, at a time when close co-operation was needed to check Soviet ambitions. The power of ethnic and other congressional lobbies to hold the United States government to ransom in international affairs had also been demonstrated. The anti-Communist syndrome had not, as yet, taken a firm enough grip on the collective mind of the American electorate to dowse Anglo-American post-war rivalry and to demonstrate the need for Anglo-American interdependence in the Cold War.

4 Riding the Communist and Nationalist Tides

The beginning of the Cold War in Europe and the Hot War in the Far East: 1948 to 1951

The British, though willing ... to concede independence to Asian dependencies, wanted to do so in conditions of their own choosing, having first re-established their authority. The French, though willing to concede a degree of autonomy within the French Union, were not psychologically prepared to give full independence. The Dutch, broadly speaking, had learnt nothing and forgotten nothing.

Brian Crozier on the Cold War in Southeast Asia[1]

While post-war military trends were being set in India and Palestine, the first shots were being fired in the twentieth century's wars of religion between Communism and Western-style democracy. Ernest Bevin's worst fears of the malignancy of Soviet hostility were borne out as Communist regimes were installed in all the countries of Central and Eastern Europe occupied by the Red Army; but so, too, were his hopes of a renewal of the Anglo-American special relationship, which began to bloom again as the Americans subordinated their anti-colonial instincts to their greater dislike of Communism.

In Europe, thanks to American political efforts and financial generosity, the Cold War was kept cool. The Truman Doctrine saved Greece and Turkey. The Marshall Plan helped restore Western Europe's shattered economies and general political confidence. The Soviet blockade of Berlin was defeated; NATO came into being; and the Western Occupation Zones of Germany were welcomed into the community of Western nations as the Federal Republic of Germany. By the middle of 1949 a precarious stability had been achieved and a clearly defined frontier established between the two ideologies along the Iron Curtain.

Neither stability nor a recognized frontier was created in the Far East; nor was the post-war struggle for power a cold war. It turned warm, then hot almost as soon as the Japanese surrendered in August 1945. In its early stages it was a quest for freedom from colonial rule. In each of the four colonial empires (the British in Malaya and North Borneo, the Dutch in their East Indies, the French in Indo-China and the Americans in the Philippines) the mix of Communist and Nationalist influences was difference; so was the approach of the superpowers. Russia provided the inspiration and support for the indigenous Communist parties until the end of 1949 when the People's Republic of China was proclaimed; thereafter Mao Tse Tung's philosophy of revolutionary war and Chinese material aid became the more important. The opposite was initially true of the exemplar of liberty, the United States. After their unfortunate wartime experiences in China, where everything they touched seemed to turn sour, the Americans had no wish to be drawn southwards into Southeast Asia. In the American view, Britain had come to terms with the nationalist spirit of Asia in her withdrawal from India and was well placed to provide post-war leadership in the area. There was general agreement that American political and economic philosophy had little appeal in Asia where almost all progressive thought was socialist. Asian nationalists tended to see the choice for the future lying between Democratic Socialism and Communism: in effect between the British and Russian or Chinese ways of life. Britain was willing to provide the political leadership in Southeast Asia, but hoped for American economic support.

The suddenness of the Japanese collapse caught all sides unprepared. The Japanese had recognized that their co-prosperity sphere with its cry of 'Asia for the Asians' could only succeed if their conquered territories were given a measure of independence. They took the deliberate decision to install indigenous governments favourable to themselves. The process had barely begun when the Americans landed in the Philippines in the autumn of 1944. Moreover, signs of Japanese defeat had not gone unnoticed by the peoples of Southeast Asia and their experience of three years under Japanese rule had not endeared the majority to Japan. Anti-Japanese resistance groups grew in size and confidence. They were just as determined to resist the return of colonial rule as to unseat the Japanese, but their preparations to seize power were far from complete when the atomic bombs were dropped. Amongst the colonial powers, only Britain and America were ready to reassume their colonial administrations. The British were just about to invade Malaya from India and Burma with Operation 'Zipper'. They had a full panoply of military government ready to take over in the wake of the landing forces. The Americans were already in full administrative control of the Philippines. The French and Dutch, however, were just recovering from German occupation and had hardly begun to assemble colonial expeditionary forces to resume sovereignty over their empires.

The wartime allies—Britain, America, Russia and Nationalist China— were not taken entirely by surprise. They had agreed at Potsdam how the Japanese surrender should be handled. Mountbatten's Southeast Asia Command was to be responsible for accepting the Japanese surrender and the repatriation of Allied prisoners of war from Malaya and the British North Borneo territories, from the Dutch East Indies, and from French Indo-China as far north as the 16th Parallel. The Chinese Nationalists would occupy northern Indo-China. And in Northeast Asia the Russians would occupy Manchuria and Korea down to the 38th Parallel, while the Americans took over the Japanese Islands and South Korea.

The British reoccupation of their own territories went remarkably smoothly. There was some delay while the 'Zipper' forces were reorganized

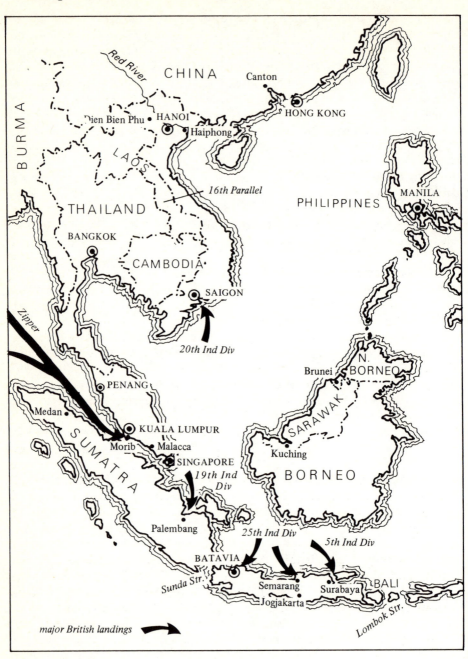

4. The Allied re-occupation of Southeast Asia in 1945.

for unopposed landings and quick establishment of temporary British military governments. The Japanese surrendered on 14 August: the first British troops landed in Malaya and Singapore at the beginning of September; in Indo-China in the middle of the month; and in the Dutch East Indies at the end of it. Most of the troops employed were Indian divisions.

In the aftermath of the war British and Americans rode with the tide of nationalist aspirations in their territories. The French and Dutch did not. The United States acted first, giving the Philippines their independence in return for the retention of American military bases. Britain did not go as far in Malaya because she did not need to do so. Her pre-war rule had not been oppressive. It had been indirect through treaties with the rulers of the nine Malay states by which she provided external protection and internal advice; and, in return, she had created the wealth and prosperity of Malaya as a whole. Only the early trading ports of Malacca, Penang and Singapore were colonies under direct British administration. The British were generally welcomed back. The Japanese had not endeared themselves to the Malayan and Singaporean populations. They had treated the Chinese inhabitants particularly brutally. Many Chinese had decamped from the towns and had set themselves up as squatters in remote areas, eking out a meagre living by subsistence farming on small plots cleared along the jungle fringe. Others had taken to the jungle itself as anti-Japanese guerrillas, joining the Communist-led Malayan People's Anti-Japanese Army (MPAJA). They collaborated with the British officers, who had stayed behind in the jungle after the fall of Singapore, and were later loosely controlled and directed by British Force 136 officers, who returned secretly to Malaya to organize anti-Japanese action before the 'Zipper' forces landed. They had armed themselves initially with weapons either stolen from the Japanese or found abandoned after the British surrender. Later more arms and supplies were dropped to them through the agency of Force 136.

The Japanese had not set up a puppet government in Malaya and so they handed over direct to their British counterparts as they arrived. The Malayan Communist Party overtly co-operated with the returning British administration as wartime allies and was recognized by the British as a legitimate political party. Covertly the Party aimed to take over the government by political infiltration. They assumed that this would not be difficult in view of the British government's proclaimed objective of leading its dependent people to independence. Mountbatten, who established his Southeast Asia Command Headquarters in Singapore, had relatively little difficulty in persuading the guerrillas to leave the jungle, hand in their arms and return to normal life in the community. Each guerrilla was given a lump sum for his services. More arms than had been dropped into the jungle by Force 136 were handed in; many more weapons were buried in secret jungle caches. The guerrillas' principal wartime liaison officer with the British, Chin Peng, received an OBE and marched in the London victory parade!

In Indo-China things were very different. The Japanese had allowed Vichy France to continue governing Indo-China under their supervision until March 1945. Suspicion that the French might collaborate with the Americans in landings on the Asian mainland led to their disarming the French garrison and imposing a puppet regime under the Vietnamese Emperor, Bao Dai, in Saigon. The 20th Indian Division under Major General Douglas Gracey took the Japanese surrender in Indo-China south of the 16th Parallel and the Chinese Nationalists did the same north of the Parallel. In the south a disunited group of mainly non-Communist factions came to power, whereas in the north Ho Chi Minh's Communist Viet Minh were predominant. Both the British and Chinese withdrew as agreed when their task of disarming the Japanese were over, leaving the French, as the recognized sovereign power, to determine the future constitutional arrangements for Indo-China. The French Expeditionary Force, under General Leclerc of North African fame, arrived in time to take over internal security responsibilities before the British and Chinese left.

While protracted negotiations were carried on with all the rival factions, General Leclerc tried to re-establish a French military and police presence throughout the country, but the French writ never ran beyond those cities and towns that his troops managed to reoccupy. In the negotiations, the French offer of autonomy within the French Union did not go far enough to satisfy the local demand for total independence in association with France; and conversely mere association would give Indo-China more independence than the succession of shaky French governments could grant in the charged political atmosphere of post-war France.

Negotiations broke down finally in September 1946. Ho Chi Minh withdrew his Viet Minh forces from Hanoi into the remote mountain area north of the city, close to the Chinese border, where his military commander, General Giap, had prepared a base area from which an armed insurrection against the returning French could be sustained. He proposed to follow Mao Tse Tung's formula based upon rural rather than Russian-style urban revolution. Communised villages were to surround the towns rather than the towns exporting Communism to the villages.

The first two phases of the revolutionary struggle—the guerrilla and protracted warfare phases—lasted for almost four years. The strength of the French Expeditionary Corps rose to 152,000 and was supported by another 120,000 non-Communist local troops, but it was never strong enough to impose a military solution. In trying to do so the French lost 2,500 men, including 800 officers, the equivalent of the total output from St Cyr for the period.

The military situation changed dramatically at the end of 1949 with the arrival of the Chinese Communist armies on the northern frontier of Indo-China. Ho Chi Minh was recognized by both Russia and the People's Republic of China as the sole representative of the people of Indo-China.

General Giap was able to expand and re-equip his Viet Minh forces for the final phase of his campaign—the war of movement. There was an equal and opposite reaction in Western capitals. The Americans dropped their reluctance to become involved in Southeast Asia and rallied to the side of the French to forestall the domino effect of a Communist victory in Indo-China. Despite American repugnance to colonialism, a US military aid programme was begun. It was designed to modernize the equipment of the French army and air force, and to raise enough Indo-Chinese divisions to relieve the French of static defensive tasks so that they could concentrate on offensive operations.

It took Giap, with full Chinese support, five more campaigning seasons to defeat the French.[2] In 1950–1 the French lost all their garrisons on the Chinese frontier and were forced to withdraw to a large defensive perimeter around the Red River Delta, protecting Hanoi and the port of Haiphong. In 1951–2 Giap attempted to destroy key posts in the French perimeter. He used orthodox Chinese tactics of massed infantry attacks with disastrous results. For instance, in one attack he launched 22,000 Viet Minh against a French garrison of 6,000 and suffered 6,000 fatalities, 8,000 wounded and 600 men were taken prisoner without managing to overrun the position. Such losses forced a change of tactics in the 1952–3 campaign. Instead of hammering at the Red River defences he attempted to draw the French into the open by advancing into Laos. The French, now equipped with American transport aircraft, countered with an increasing use of mobile forces, moved and supplied by air. A series of successful operations suggested to the French High Command that they had found the way of neutralising Giap's mobility that was based upon 'coolie power'. In the 1953–4 campaign they threw down the gauntlet by occupying the remote but strategically important area of Dien Bien Phu on the Laotian border, intending to supply the garrison of 12 battalions by air. The challenge failed: coolie power won. By prodigous efforts the ant-like columns of North Vietnamese manhandled anti-aircraft guns and ammunition through the mountains and jungles, and reduced the French air supply to a trickle. The crisis came on 22 April 1954 when the weather broke, stopping air supply and offensive air support altogether. Dien Bien Phu fell on 1 May, bringing French rule in Indo-China to an end. Independence came to Vietnam but not peace or unity. The Communists had won the first round: the Americans replaced the French for the second and were to be just as unsuccessful.

In the Dutch East Indies it was the Nationalists who triumphed and in a much shorter time. The Communist Party of Indonesia had been crushed by the Japanese, whereas the Indonesian Nationalist Party of Doctor Sukarno had managed to win overt Japanese support while clandestinely organizing an extensive underground movement dedicated to winning independence from the Japanese or from anyone else who might replace them. Such was the popular disillusion with the Japanese policies that Sukarno was able to command widespread support, particularly amongst the Indonesian officials serving the Japanese administration. It was to Sukarno that the Japanese turned when they decided in the autumn of 1944 to prepare Indonesia for independence within the Japanese co-prosperity sphere; but, due to the delaying tactics of the local Japanese military commanders, it was not until 17 August, three days after their surrender, that Sukarno was allowed to proclaim the Republic of Indonesia under his leadership.

It was six weeks before the first British troops landed at Batavia, the capital of Java, which is now Djakarta. Sukarno had ample time to take over from the Japanese and to establish his government. Mountbatten announced that the 25th Indian Division under Major General Philip Christison was 'to accept the surrender of the Japanese, on behalf of the United Nations, and to protect the people and maintain law and order until such time as the lawful government of the Netherlands East Indies is once again functioning'.[3] This was a clear indication to the Indonesians that the British were intent on restoring Dutch rule. British troops became *persona non grata* and vicious rioting broke out in Batavia and at Semarang. To add insult to injury Mountbatten called upon the Japanese instead of Sukarno's Republican government to restore law and order. When the 5th Indian Division tried to land at the former Dutch naval base of Surabaya, it was opposed by the local Indonesians. The Royal Navy had to open fire, doing considerable damage to the city, before a truce could be arranged by Sukarno, who realized that it would be foolish to alienate the British. The atmosphere was not improved by the murder of Brigadier Mallaby by Indonesian extremists while he was touring Surabaya two days after the cease-fire.

Mountbatten was in a difficult position. Britain had to be loyal to her Dutch ally and yet had no wish to re-impose Dutch colonial rule against the genuine wishes of the Indonesians. But what were their wishes and who should speak for them? The Dutch quite naturally disparaged Sukarno's government as Japanese puppets, who did not reflect the deep attachment of the ordinary Indonesians to the Dutch Crown. The Indonesian political factions were sufficiently divided to make it difficult to discover the depth of political support enjoyed by Sukarno, and in Holland opinion was equally divided on whether to negotiate with Sukarno or not. The main British contribution was to act as honest-broker in trying to settle matters by negotiation, while Dutch troops gradually took over from British units in the few coastal towns which they had occupied. The last British troops did not leave until November 1946. The Dutch attitude to their East Indies was much the same as the French in Indo-China. They were prepared to grant a measure of autonomy to a 'United States of Indonesia' within the Dutch empire, but never enough to satisfy Indonesian nationalist demands which were, by British and American standards, quite modest. When they thought they were strong enough, the Dutch tried to settle matters by military means. They made two major attempts to crush the Republican government. In the 'First Military Action', which started on 20 July 1947,

Dutch mechanized army units supported by the Dutch air force, made deep penetrations into Republican-held territory. Towns fell, but nothing decisive was achieved because the Republican troops melted into the countryside that remained hostile to the Dutch. The subsequent guerrilla war negated such successes as the Dutch troops did achieve. For a brief moment the Indonesian Communists started a rebellion of their own, claiming that Sukarno was collaborating with the Dutch as he had done with the Japanese. Republican troops put down the rebellion without Dutch help, disproving Dutch claims that the Republican government was Communist rather than Nationalist at heart.

The 'Second Military Action' began just before Christmas 1948. It was an all out effort to re-establish Dutch sovereignty once and for all. Jogjakarta, the Republican capital in central Java, was bombed and captured. Sukarno and most of his ministers were arrested. The Dutch had little difficulty in taking all the strategically important towns, but they did not have the resources to pacify the vast, heavily populated rural areas. The guerrilla war intensified with the united support of the great majority of the Indonesian people.

It was not the military failure of the 'Second Military Action' that was most damaging to the Dutch cause: its adverse effect on world opinion proved to be decisive. The newly found voice of Afro-Asia could be clearly heard in two fora: at the United Nations where a Special Commission on Indonesia was set up; and in the first Afro-Asian Conference convened by Pandit Nehru at Delhi in January 1949 in direct response to events in Indonesia. Britain and the United States had been ambivalent up to this point, trying to support their Dutch ally in Europe, and yet, hoping that the Hague would follow their example in India and the Philippines. After Mao's victory in China, an independent nationalist Indonesia would be infinitely preferable to a Communist state that might emerge if the Dutch persisted in trying to put the colonial clock back. The Americans held the trump card. Holland could not continue her costly colonial war without the Marshall Aid funds, which were regenerating her economy. American economic persuasion worked. New negotiations under United Nations auspices brought independence to the United States of Indonesia on 27 December 1949. Indonesian nationalism had triumphed, on this occasion, without much international Communist support.

In Malaya the opposite happened. The Communist Party, which was predominantly Chinese, tried to oust the British administration by military means. The Malayans, to whom independence was just as dear, accepted the validity of British colonial policy and co-operated in the struggle with the Chinese Communist insurgents, whose challenge started almost as soon as the victory parades were over.

The Malayan Communist Party had been led since 1939 by Loi Tak, a Vietnamese with professional Marxist training who has always been suspected of being a triple agent. The evidence is only circumstantial: the British, then the Japanese and finally the returning British found it relatively easy to penetrate the Party during his leadership. In February 1947 he disappeared mysteriously and so did the Party funds. He was succeeded by Chin Peng, OBE, as Secretary of the Central Committee. The Party policy up to that time had been to develop an urban revolution on orthodox Soviet lines. The numerous local grievances, thrown up in the aftermath of the Japanese occupation, were exploited and trades union activity was developed in ways which would discredit the British administration. The year 1947 was one of Communist sponsored strikes throughout Malaya and Singapore; 1948 brought an upsurge in intimidation, extortion and violence up and down the Malay Peninsula and on Singapore Island. The government reacted with corresponding firmness by introducing new trades union legislation, which made it much more difficult for hardcore Communist agitators to use the unions for political purposes and by re-introducing the pre-war power to deport non-Malayan citizens. As most of the Chinese still held Chinese passports, this proved an effective weapon. From the Communist point of view the most depressing thing was the absence of any sign of a popular rising against the British. The Party also ran out of money.

Failure brought with it a change in Party policy. Chin Peng's experience as the Guerrilla liaison officer with the British during the war had given him a leaning towards clandestine warfare rather than political revolution. He and his Central Committee found further encouragement from the international Communist conferences held in Calcutta early in 1948 at which Southeast Asian Communist Parties were encouraged to seize power by any available means and to drive out the Europeans. As in Indo-China the successes of the Communist armies in China inspired the adoption of Mao's policy of rural rather than urban revolution. In March 1948 the Malayan Communist Party's Central Committee decided upon armed insurrection, incorporating features of both the Maoist and Russian revolutionary philosophies. They planned to remobilize the MPAJA in the jungle, this time under the title the Malayan Peoples Anti-British Army. Following the teachings of Mao they aimed to 'liberate' remote rubber estates where they would establish small people's republics, which they could expand by gradually absorbing nearby villages and then towns until they were strong enough to challenge the government's security forces in mobile operations. They hoped to speed up the process by continuing the Soviet philosophy of triggering popular risings in the towns through the creation of chaos by sabotage and urban violence, thereby discrediting the British administration.

The topography of Malaya was extraordinarily favourable for the type of campaign Chin Peng had in mind. The mountain spine of the Malaya Peninsula is nearer to the west coast than the east. Between the mountains and the western sea board lies the developed fifth of Malaya, which is well-roaded and contains the main towns, rubber estates and tin mines. The remaining four-fifths of Malaya is dense tropical rain forest. It was easy enough to establish terrorist bases in the jungle fringe from which to attack

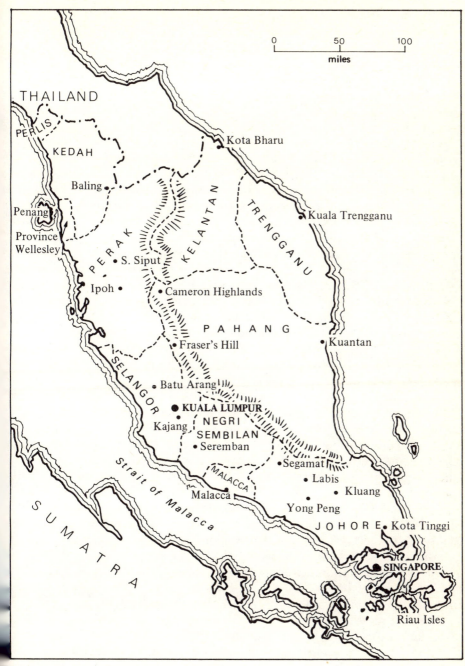

5. Malaya and Singapore in 1945–1960.

or intimidate the estate and mine workers, and these could be supported from more secure camps established deep in the jungle. Food and other essential supplies could be obtained from the 400,000 Chinese squatters working their small plots of land close to the jungle edge.

The make-up of the population of Malaya was less favourable to Chin Peng's mode of warfare: the sea of the people was not as warm and hospitable to the terrorist fish as he hoped. Out of a population of five million (excluding Singapore) 49 per cent were Malays, 38 per cent Chinese, 12 per cent Indians and only one per cent Europeans. There was no love lost between the indigenous Malays and the imported Chinese and Indian communities. The Chinese had been brought in by commercial firms to work the rubber estates and the tin mines; and the Indians by the British administration to operate the railways and to maintain the roads. The Chinese were still loyal to China and, as Mao's success grew, so did their support for the Malayan Communist Party. The Indians were also influenced by events in their home lands, but they did not have the political leadership or numerical strength to be more than awkwardly anti-British. The Muslim Malay majority on the other hand, was determinedly anti-Communist and tended to side with the British, though far from critically, in order to bring back their pre-war economic prosperity and to maintain their political dominance over the Chinese.

In March 1948 the hardcore Communists from both the overt and covert Party organizations went underground. Out of 10,000 ex MPAJA guerrillas, some 3,000 returned to the jungle and reactivated the eight regiments of the anti-Japanese days with approximately one regiment per Malay state, though regimental and state boundaries did not always coincide nor were regimental strengths uniform: they depended upon the level and enthusiasm of support in each area. Another 8,000 part time guerrillas, including a high proportion of new recruits, remained living in villages and squatter areas where they could be called upon by the regiments for specific tasks from time to time. The wartime supply organization was also reactivated amongst the rural Chinese under the title Min Yuen, or the Masses Organisation. Of the two million Chinese in Malaya, some 60,000 were probably active supporters and another half million could be depended upon to help the Communist cause.

The Communist mobilization was inevitably patchy as it depended upon the action of faceless men isolated from each other by the cell system. Internal communication was by the usual chain of dead-letter boxes, used by most clandestine organizations, with couriers never being allowed to meet each other to reduce the chances of betrayal. Initially, the more experienced and hardened guerrillas were formed into a Special Service Corps of mobile killer squads of four to five men each, whose role was to impose a reign of terror by murdering managers, government officials and policemen. While they were carrying out the earlier atrocities, the eight regiments (later raised to ten) were being trained in jungle camps set up to accommodate up to 300 men each. The standard size of camp varied, but they generally consisted of living huts, classrooms and a parade ground, all hidden from air reconnaissance by the high leaf canopy of the primary jungle. Each was protected from ground attack by sentries hidden on the few jungle tracks leading to it. If the alarm was given all the guerrillas in the particular camp would disperse and make their way to an agreed rendezvous when the danger was passed. Most terrorist operations were carried out by platoons of about 50 men though companies of 200 to 300 were sometimes used.

In the early days of the insurrection the Communists had separate political and military chains of command. Chin Peng and the Central Committee left Singapore and established themselves in a secret jungle hide-out in South Johore. Within the central organization there was the Politburo and the military high command. At state level, there was a state committee linked to the local regimental headquarters, and a similar linkage worked lower down with District and Branch Committees working to companies and platoons. At the grass roots level the Min Yuen worked in the villages and squatter areas to support the local regiment with intelligence, supplies and recruits.

The first Communist plan was militarily over-ambitious and politically misconceived. They hoped to discredit the government by ruining the economy and terrorizing the people. Three targets were specified: murder of European and Asian estate and mine managers; slashing of rubber trees, burning estate smoke houses, in which the rubber was cured, and the destruction of mine machinery; and attacks on police and government officials. Attacks on management, police and officials was logical: destruction of economic assets was counter-productive as it threw the very people, whose support they sought, out of work. Some committee members appear to have believed that a people's republic could be declared by August 1948, the British having cut their losses and left as they appeared to have done in India and Palestine.

April and May saw a general upsurge in lawlessness throughout Malaya. Labour disputes became more violent, Communist propaganda more strident, and sporadic murders of managers and overseers pointed to increased Communist intimidation and enforced fund raising. There was division in government circles about the causes of the unrest. Some officials argued that it was due to low wages and the general post-war malaise, which was affecting most countries; others saw the directing hand of international Communism. The Cominform (Communist Information Bureau) had been established in September 1947 and was generally seen as the fount of all evil in the Western world. Events in Indonesia and in Indo-China corroborated the view that there was a Soviet master plan to uproot Western influence in Asia. The balance struck between these two views undoubtedly erred on the side of complacency. Nevertheless, the High Commissioner to the Malayan Federation, Sir Edward Gent, was not taken by surprise. While pressing on with measures to improve standards of living, his staff were drafting emergency regulations. Much of the government complacency was due to lack of specific intelligence of the Communist plan and a belief in the adequacy of the security forces—police and army.

In June the situation deteriorated alarmingly. On 16 June brutal murders were perpetrated by the killer squad of the 5th Regiment in Perak. Three of the victims were British planters, who were executed in cold blood. That evening a state of emergency was declared in Perak and Johore, and two days later it was extended to the whole of Malaya. Large scale arrests of known Communist activists were made and, on 23 July, the Malayan Communist Party and its front organizations were declared illegal.

At the beginning of the emergency the Malayan police force was 9,000 strong. It was only just recovering from the psychological effects of the British defeat in 1942 and of the very different policing methods used by the Japanese. The force was almost entirely Malay with a poor knowledge of the Chinese language and customs because in pre-war days Chinese affairs had been looked after by the Chinese Protectorate under the Secretary for Chinese Affairs, based in Singapore. There was a Chinese Protector and staff in each state. Unfortunatey, this paternal anachronism of earlier colonial days was not reinstituted at the end of the war, leaving a wide gap in the government's knowledge and advice about the Chinese.

The Army's order of battle looked impressive. There were four sub-districts: North, Central, Johore and Singapore, controlling a total 11 battalions[4] and one artillery regiment. The GOC Malaya was Major-General A. Galloway, whose headquarters was in Kuala Lumpur alongside the federal government. But there were weaknesses. Apart from the two Malay Regiment battalions, the Army was looked upon as an imperial force with immediate responsibility for the external defence of Malaya and the wider task of assisting in the general defence of Southeast Asia. The Gurkha battalions, though ideal for jungle operations, had only recently arrived from India and Burma; and some were seriously under strength, having left behind those who had chosen to stay with the Indian Army. They were all in the process of retraining and absorbing large numbers of recruits. The formation of the new 17th Gurkha Division of all arms and services had only just started. The artillery regiment, 26th Field Regiment RA was training the 7th Gurkhas as gunners. The conversion was stopped and 7th Gurkhas took the field as infantry as did 26th Field Regiment with some success. The British battalions had their problems too. They had lost most of their experienced wartime soldiers who had been replaced with young National Servicemen with scant knowledge of the jungle, but with no lack of enthusiasm for the excitements of active operations: they had much to learn.

The learning curve on both sides was long and erratic: neither Chin Peng's Communists nor the government's security forces had much practical experience of guerrilla and counter-guerrilla operations. Both made glaring mistakes. Initially the Communists recognized their errors quicker than the government, which started with two grave disadvantages: it was still in its formative stages and it lost its three top men responsible for security at the very beginning of the emergency. The British government had orginally proposed to replace their old treaties with the Malay sultans by a new comprehensive treaty, establishing a Malayan Union to which the temporary British military government would hand over. The Malay rulers objected and the British government wisely accepted their alternative proposal for a federation, which excluded Singapore with its predominantly Chinese population. The negotiations took time; and it was not until January 1948, only six months before the emergency was declared, that the new agreement was signed, establishing the Federation of Malaya. The federal and state governments had no time to find their feet before the pressures and problems of the emergency were thrust upon them. Sir Edward Gent, the Federation's first High Commissioner, was killed in an air crash on his way back to London on 4 July and was not replaced by Sir Henry Gurney, who had been Chief Secretary in Palestine, until 6 October.[5] The Commissioner of Police, Mr Langworthy, retired on grounds of ill-health and was replaced in August by another 'Palestinian', Colonel W. N. Gray, a former Royal Marine officer, who had been Inspector General of the Palestine Police. There was plenty of room for cynical comments about Malaya becoming a second Palestine. The third change had come slightly earlier when General C. H. Boucher, an experienced Gurkha commander, had relieved Galloway in a routine chain of military postings.

In the first year of the emergency the government's worst error was not so much its complacency as its gross underestimate of the time it would take to master the Communist insurrection. Policy was devised and directed in terms of months rather than years. Nevertheless, it must be given credit for two fundamentally correct decisions. Countering the Communist threat was seen to be primarily political and economic rather than military. The civil administration and police were kept in the driving seats with the Army in support. The second decision was to recognize from the start that the security forces must always act within the law. This was to become a cardinal principle in all the military campaigns fought by the British Army to ensure an orderly withdrawal from Empire. It was no use claiming to uphold the law if the law had to be broken to do so. Such action would alienate the very people the law was designed to protect. Law-abiding citizens are usually prepared to accept the toughest emergency regulations, even those temporarily reducing personal liberty, provided they are duly passed through the legislative process and, thereafter, are seen to be applied impartially. The four most crucial provisions of the first set of Malayan emergency regulations were: arrest and detention without trial to counter the intimidation of witnesses; the right of search without warrant to speed up operations; the registration of all the population and the issue of identity cards to help in the identification of suspects; and the strict control of fire-arms, including the mandatory death sentence for their illegal possession. A fifth came later in January 1949. It was the notorious Regulation 17D, which empowered the High Commissioner to order collective detention and the banishment of non-Malayan citizens whom he was satisfied had been collaborating with the Communist guerrillas.

There was an early clash between the civil and military over operational policy. The planters and tin miners needed immediate protection to maintain their morale and to prevent economic collapse. The police did not have enough men to protect some 3,000 rubber estates let alone the tin mines and other commercial enterprises as well. Raising enough police would take longer than anyone envisaged the emergency would last. The Army was called on to fill the gap. General Boucher objected strenuously to the dispersal of his troops on static guard duties: he believed in the orthodox military view that seizure of the initiative by offensive military action with forces concentrated and mobile would produce decisive results much quicker. A compromise was reached. The Army agreed to help train 15,000 armed special constables (a figure later raised to 24,000) to undertake the estate guard duties, and so free itself to mount major offensive sweeps through the worst affected areas. Meanwhile, the police force was to be doubled by accelerating the peace-time training pro-gramme with the help of 500 men from the Palestine police; all police stations were to be strengthened, given radio communications and their numbers increased; and mobile police jungle squads of 20 to 40 men were to be set up in vulnerable districts to carry out quick follow-up operations to reduce the calls on the Army. The jungle squads became para-military forces and later formed part of the 3,000 strong Police Field Force.

Three additional forces were raised as quickly as recruiting, training and equipment would allow. Former Force 136 officers, who knew the old MPAJA operational areas and camps, formed Ferret Force to operate within the jungle to help locate and destroy the guerrillas either by themselves or in conjunction with the Army and RAF. Ferret Force consisted of some 20 patrols each of about 15 men. The Gurkha and Malay battalions provided specially picked soldiers to form the majority of each patrol to which were added civilian volunteers with specialized knowledge of the jungle and Dyak trackers from North Borneo. The Police Frontier Force was the second addition. It was composed of 6000 men locally recruited on the Thai border to patrol and watch the jungle tracks across it. And the third was the Auxiliary Police Force of 15,000 part-time volunteers (eventually raised to 100,000) to help the regular police locally. Raising, training and equipping the Frontier Force and the Auxiliary Force placed a great load on the shoulders of Colonel Gray and the police headquarters' staff, who were also responsible for the overall direction of security operations. The strain, in the end, grew too great.

The Army, though at first reluctant to call on Whitehall for reinforce-ments, received a battalion from Hong Kong in early August and the 4th Hussars from the United Kingdom later that month. The Hussars came without their armoured cars because it was thought that the Malayan road bridges would not carry their weight. This was soon found to be a mistake and the cars were shipped out to them, proving invaluable for escort duties. By the autumn the security situation had deteriorated so much that the 2nd Guards Brigade was sent out in October: the first time the Guards had operated east of Suez since the Shanghai crisis between the world wars.

In the early months of the emergency the Army was largely on call to help the police to deal with terrorist incidents as they occurred. There was, as yet, too little information on which to mount a major military sweep. It had few successes because the CTs (Communist Terrorists), as the Army called the guerrillas, had usually made good their escape before the troops arrived. The Communists, for their part, made three unsuccessful attempts to establish 'liberated areas'. The occupation of the Batu Arang coal-mining area, just north of Kuala Lumpur, was defeated by 2nd/6th and 2nd/7th Gurkha Rifles and 26th Field Regiment, who killed 26 CTs. The second attempt, which was made in a remote area in Kelantan, was frustrated by the Malay Regiment. And the third attempt at Kajang, just south of Kuala Lumpur, resulted in the death of Lau Yew, the highest ranking military member of Central Committee, who was surprised and shot down by a police patrol.

It was not until September 1948 that the pattern of CT operations became clear enough to warrant major military operations. General Boucher had stated in the Legislative Council that his object was:

To break up the insurgent concentrations, to bring them to battle before they were ready, and to drive them underground or into the jungle, and then to follow them there . . . I intend to keep them constantly moving, and deprive them of food and of recruits . . .[6]

He decided to start his operations in Johore where the CTs were operating in gangs up to 300 strong. Ferret Force and three British and two Gurkha battalions were concentrated, and began a series of offensive sweeps through the most likely areas of jungle. Two particularly inaccessible areas were dealt with by amphibious landings, and full use was made of strikes by RAF Spitfires and of air supply. The results, at the time, seemed meagre for the effort expended. Twelve CT camps were found and burnt; and some ammunition and food dumps were uncovered; but main CT units slipped away. Similar operations in Selangor and Perak over the next six months brought just as few rewards.

Boucher's sweeps were largely counter-productive. Major operations denuded other areas of troops deployed to support the police and this led to local criticism of lack of soldiers for follow-up operations after serious incidents. It was also becoming clear that the conventional military sweep against a line of stops was not the answer, but old habits and trains of thought die hard. New brigade and battalion commanders arriving in Malaya fresh from large scale manoeuvres in the Rhine army and with memories of Second World War operations etched on their minds, clung to a belief in their effectiveness far longer than they should have done. The first two years of the emergency can be called the period of the 'big battalions' on *both* sides.

Boucher's big battalions had made a much greater impact on Chin Peng than was realized at the time. In the first four months of the emergency 206 Chinese civilians and 17 Europeans had been killed in terrorist attacks, but 343 CTs had also been killed by the security forces. While the Communists clearly had the tacit support of most of the rural Chinese and of the Chinese town dwellers in such intensely Communist areas as Kluang in Johore, Kajang in Selangor and Sungi Siput in Perak, they saw no signs of any spontaneous uprisings for which they had hoped. The Central Committee recognized that the British had not been taken by surprise and a quick collapse of their administration was most unlikely. The British reaction, though considered complacent and indecisive by the European community, had been much quicker and tougher than the Communists had expected. Popular support for the Communist cause, though worrying to the government, had been disappointing. Chin Peng and his colleagues took a decision to face up to a long war in December 1948, a year earlier than the British authorities.

The December debate in the Central Committee led to the issue of the Second Communist Operational Directive (the First ordered mobilization). All regiments were to withdraw into safer camps deep in the jungle, many sited east of the mountain watershed in Pahang and Kelantan, where they were to improve their organization, training and equipment. They were to depend on the aboriginal tribes for food supplies. About one third of each regiment was to stay in smaller camps on the jungle fringe west of the range with two tasks: to maintain the level of terrorist incidents and to build up the Min Yuen organization ready to supply the regiments when they returned to resume the offensive. The Second Directive started on its way down the tortuous CT chain of command early in 1949 but did not become effective until April. The title Malayan Races Liberation Army was introduced at the same time to broaden the guerrilla forces' appeal.

The government's Intelligence services had been improving all the time. Moves of the gangs over into Pahang and Kelantan and towards the Thai frontier were detected in part, but their purpose was misconstrued as a withdrawal due to defeat rather than a recoil for riposte. Corroboration was to be found for this optimistic view in the halving of terrorist incidents from 200 to 100 per month in the spring of 1949. Sir Henry Gurney concluded that the campaign could be won as far as the imperial military forces were concerned by the end of the year. All that would remain to be accomplished would be the pursuit and final destruction of the gangs which would probably wither in the discomforts of the jungle and the disappointment of defeat. Thereafter, it would be the task of the police and the Malay Regiment to do the tidying up and to make sure that Mac

Tse Tung's continuing successes in China did not trigger another Chinese revolt in the Federation.

The Communist-inspired pause in the campaign was not wasted by the government, although it had been misinterpreted. The crash programme of police expansion went ahead and new equipment was bought to improve operational efficiency. The Army, however, believed it had enough troops for the final mopping up phase and did not call for reinforcements. Indeed, Ferret Force was disbanded to let experienced regulars return to their battalions and the specialist volunteers go back to their civilian jobs. The Dyaks were re-allocated to battalions to increase tracking efficiency. With success apparently achieved by the policy of keeping the enemy on the move, there was no pressure for a change of tactics. Many thousands of man-hours were wasted methodically combing hundreds of square miles of jungle to the discomfort and exhaustion of the troops who had to plough their way through it in the hot, humid climate. Intelligence was still too poor for precisely directed operations: conventional sweeps had to go on. Such contacts that did occur were more often than not due to random chance. CT camps were rarely surprised because there was ample warning of the troops' approach and more than enough cover into which to disappear until the troops had left. The strategic and tactical keys to success were recognized early in the emergency: winning the loyalty of the majority of the Chinese community, and improving Intelligence to give specific rather than general information so that operations could be targetted accurately. Winning Chinese loyalty faced the government with a dilemma: the rigorous measures needed to stop them supplying the CTs would alienate them still further, and yet lack of such measures would leave the Min Yuen unchallenged. Moreover, measures taken to favour the Chinese would inevitably upset the Malays, who had always objected to the Chinese being treated as adopted Malayan citizens.

At the highest political level, Gurney encouraged the formation of the Malayan Chinese Association to give the Chinese a political voice. Until the military tide turned, however, the MCA remained a group of loyalist leaders with no party followers. At the lowest levels, the government, police and Army were faced with the Chinese squatter problem. There were two broad categories of people living illegally on land to which they had no title: the small farmer working his plot of land to feed his family and to market his produce; and the commuter, who lived in a shack because there was nowhere to live in the nearby town or village where he worked. Many squatter areas were beyond the reach of the government's existing administrative and police services. It was hoped that squatter loyalty might be won by resettling them in new areas where they could be properly administered and protected, provided they were given legal title to the land on which they were resettled.

Finding the land and meeting the physical and financial burden of resettling some 400,000 squatters was more than the federal or state governments were prepared to face in 1949. Instead it was decided to use the newly enacted Regulation 17D to uproot known collaborators and their families and to send them back to China. Seven operations to clear squatters from areas where the level of collaboration with the CTs was considered intolerable, were carried out in the first half of 1949. The experience of doing so led to a revolt within the government itself because of the obvious inhumanity of the process, the adverse reaction of world opinion and the propaganda advantages presented to the Communists. These objections were not, however, entirely responsible for a halt being called to 17D operations. Mao's Communist armies had captured most of the Chinese coastal ports and had closed up the Hong Kong Frontier, making deportation to China impractical. The government's 'Squatter Committee', originally set up in January 1949, was given the task of finding new ways of carrying out resettlement within Malaya without deportation. Conventional methods had failed; fresh ideas were needed.

The same was largely true in the Intelligence field. There was a tendency to assume that the expansion of the police CID and the confidence given to the Chinese community by the more obvious presence of the security forces and their growing operational success would result in a greater flow of useful information, as, indeed, they did. It was noted, however, that the best Intelligence had come from the hundred or so terrorists who had surrendered. After much debate it was decided to offer an amnesty to CTs who gave up voluntarily, provided they were not implicated in murder. The timing was difficult to decide: if announced too early it might be construed as a sign of government weakness; if too late the effect would be lost and the emergency prolonged. By the autumn of 1949 the tide seemed to be running strongly enough in the government's favour for the risk to be taken. On 6 September the amnesty was announced together with the suspension of the mandatory death sentence for the illegal carriage of arms. One hundred and sixteen CTs took advantage of the surrender terms but were mainly waverers of little Intelligence value. The rate of surrender soon fell away. Chin Peng re-opened his offensive within days of the amnesty announcement.

The resumption of the Communist offensive was not recognized by the security forces as such until the cold statistics of the number, size and types of incident revealed the marked increase in CT activity. The incident graph rose steeply from 100 to 400 per month with road and a few rail ambushes predominant. The morale of the population dipped as the attacks multiplied in frequency and audacity. Matters were made worse by news of Mao's final victories in China and the proclamation of the People's Republic of China in October 1949. Britain's over-hasty *de facto* recognition of Mao's regime may have helped to ward off the Communist threat to Hong Kong, but it made winning Chinese confidence in Malaya all the more difficult. The last straw could have been the admission of Communist Chinese consuls into Malaya, which was proposed by the Foreign Office as part of the price to be paid by Britain to protect Hong Kong.

Fortunately, Gurney won his battle to stop their appointment, though it was a close run thing.

The general feeling in the Chinese community in the small towns in Malaya is well illustrated by a contemporary police report from a village in Perak:

The local village and *kampong* talk, more or less openly, goes like this: 'The Government is getting weaker and weaker—Communism, which is to liberate us all, is triumphant in China and will shortly be the same in Siam and then here. Russia has the biggest and best bomb. This Government is terrified and has recognised Communism in China and will shortly hand over to Communism here or will have power wrested from it by the liberating armies. . . . Do you want to be a man marked as a running dog, a helper of Imperialism, and so if you do not want to be tortured and have your throat cut, you had better help the liberating army and the peoples' government now..'[7]

By the end of 1949 British complacency and faith in conventional methods was fading fast. The government began to accept what Chin Peng had acknowledged a year earlier that the emergency was going to be a prolonged struggle which had to be fought as a war and not just as an annoying abberation in peacetime administration. General Boucher, who was about to leave Malaya at the end of his tenure in command, reversed his previously held view by stating behind closed doors that the Army had temporarily shot its bolt. It needed to introduce a rolling programme of rest and retraining for its battalions if they were to fight a long campaign. For this he needed more units to provide reliefs and to strengthen his striking force. The only source of immediate reinforcements was Hong Kong. Despite the presence of the Communist armies on the colony's border with China, the pressure to restore morale in Malaya was so great that General Sir John Harding, GOC-in-C Far East Land Forces, was authorized by London to move, first, 26th Gurkha Brigade with one British and two Gurkha battalions to Malaya in February 1950, followed by 3rd Commando Brigade in May. The formation of a fourth battalion for the Malay Regiment was accelerated and the 13th/18th Hussars were sent from the Middle East to help 4th Hussars with armoured-car escort duties. The RAF was also reinforced with bomber, fighter and transport aircraft. The Royal Australian Air Force sent a squadron of Lincoln bombers to help make life more uncomfortable for the CTs in the jungle.

General Sir John Harding had been Field Marshal Alexander's Chief of Staff in Italy and was the architect of the great battles which destroyed Hitler's Gustav and Gothic Lines. He had one of those minds which distils the most complex problems into their essential components and shapes them into a comprehensible pattern from which operational policy can be evolved. In his view the battle in Malaya could never be won by providing extra troops alone: the road to success lay in the development of effective government administration throughout the Peninsula, which could win the confidence and support of all races. The purpose of the extra troops was two-fold: to boost civilian morale and to provide a breathing space for the civil administration and police to gain the upper hand.

Harding was supported in his analysis by Field Marshal Sir William Slim, who had taken over from Field Marshal Montgomery as CIGS, and who was no stranger to the problems of the Far East. He felt that not only was effective civilian administration a vital military requirement, but its attainment should be achieved with all the vigour of a military operation. What was needed was a man who could help the High Commissioner weld the civilian and military authorities together as a team. So far the burden of co-ordination had fallen upon Colonel Gray, the Commissioner of Police, who had all the problems of the rapid expansion of the police forces on his hands as well. What was needed, Slim concluded, was a director of operations, responsible only to the High Commissioner, who could devise and direct a long term plan for the restoration of government authority and the defeat of the Communist insurgency. Sir Henry Gurney did not demur. The choice of Lieutenant-General Sir Harold Briggs for the post was Slim's inspiration. Briggs had served under him with distinction in the Burma campaigns and had retired to Cyprus. He agreed to Slim's request that he should accept the post for a minimum of a year, and, for personal reasons, not more than 18 months. It was a happy choice. He was an imaginative and incisive man, but was also modest and tactful. He needed all these qualities to master the anomalies of his position: a retired lieutenant-general acting in a civilian capacity, directing security force operations in support of the civil power. He ranked co-equal with the High Commissioner's Chief Secretary and was given full powers to initiate police and military action, subject only to the right of the Commissioner of Police to appeal to the High Commissioner and the Army, Naval and Air Commanders to their respective Cs-in-C in Singapore.

Briggs arrived in Kuala Lumpur in April 1950. The toll of casualties since the emergency had risen to 863 civilians, 323 policemen and 154 soldiers killed, totalling 1,340. The CT casualties were assessed at 1,138 killed, 645 captured and 359 surrendered, a loss of 2,142. Although CT recruiting kept pace with losses, Chin Peng and the Communist Central Committee were becoming as worried about lack of success in bringing about a governmental collapse as the general public were in the government's failure to reduce the level of terrorist attacks. In their Third Operational Directive, disseminated early in 1950, the Central Committee announced two policy decisions which were a few months ahead of similar changes on the government side. First, they abandoned the Maoist philosophy of establishing liberated areas because the government forces could reach them too easily anywhere in Malaya. Instead they decided to develop temporary bases in places where the government administration was weak enough for the Min Yuen to prosper. Their main effort was to be concentrated upon extending their Min Yuen infra-structure, the very target which Harding and Slim had singled out for attack. Secondly, they abandoned 'big battalions' in favour of much smaller gangs, operating from the jungle fringes wherever Min Yuen support was adequate. They had found that the larger the gang the more difficult it was to withdraw after a successful ambush. Large gangs also presented the security forces with easier targets for their more heavily equipped units and their supporting air forces.

Briggs' great contribution to the defeat of the Communists in Malaya was the development of his long term master plan—the Briggs Plan—and the successful execution of its earlier phases. Paradoxically, he, a soldier, made a much greater impact on the emergency with his civil administrative measures than through his direction of military operations. This was exactly what Harding and Slim intended. There were enough able soldiers available to develop new military techniques; the more difficult task was to bring the federal and state governments onto a war footing in the enervating climate of Malaya. If Briggs had arrived a year earlier, his policies might not have been accepted: the Communist onslaught during the winter of 1949–1950 created the necessary consensus which enabled him to act. It was clear to everyone in government that short term measures had had their day: his long term plan was generally welcomed, certainly at first, in spite of its probable cost in money, manpower and time.

While developing his plan Briggs took a number of preliminary steps to create a more responsive civil/military infra-structure. The first step was to improve the speed of decision making by establishing a combined civil/military command structure. At the top a federal war council of senior officials was set up, comprising himself (Chairman and Director of Operations), the Chief Secretary, the Commissioner of Police, the Commanders of the Armed Services and later the Director of Intelligence when one was appointed. Its task was the formulation of federal war policy, planning and allocation of resources. Execution of policy and planning within each state or settlement was the responsibility of the State War Executive Committee (SWEC) with similar but fewer members: the *Mentri Besar* (The Sultan's Chief Executive), the British Adviser, the Chief of Police and the Senior Army Commander (usually a brigadier). As each Mentri Besar was burdened with the day to day running of the state the British adviser usually took the Chair. At the lowest level the District War Executive Committee (DWEC) carried on the day to day prosecution of the war under the chairmanship of the District Officer with the senior police commander and the local battalion commander as the principal members. At all levels, experts such as information officers, heads of specialized police, military and Intelligence branches were co-opted as required. While the SWECs and DWECs drove the execution of operational policy, they were still politically subordinate to the federal and state governments.

Briggs' second step was to strengthen the Intelligence system. In this he was helped by Sir William Jenkin, formerly of the Indian police. The principal change was the formation of a police Special Branch to gather tactical Intelligence within the Chinese and Indian communities. At first, most of its superintendents were British working with Chinese and Indian inspectors. They wore plain clothes in the villages and used the local police post as a base. They became just as well-known for what they were as their Communist opposite numbers, but their presence gave the villagers some confidence, which enabled them to gather the village gossip and to piece together the pattern of local Communist activity. Special Branch operations were helped by a system of rewards introduced at the same time. Information leading to the capture of CTs ranged from Malay $40,000 for Chin Peng down to $2,000 for an ordinary CT ($100 represented about one month's wages). At a later stage in the emergency these rewards were greatly increased and led to some decisive defections of gang leaders.

Briggs' third step was to insist that all governmental departments were combed for suitable officers, particularly Chinese speakers, who could reinforce the administration at district level to bring the government to the villages and the squatter communities. The most important posts created were Chinese Affairs officers at every level from village up to the Federal Secretary for Chinese Affairs in Kuala Lumpur.

Briggs' fourth preliminary step was to strengthen the Information service. He was helped in this by Hugh Carlton Green, who later became Director General of the BBC. Information and Psychological Warfare Services were concentrated under him as Head of Emergency Information Services. His task was to see that the government's case and its operational successes and failures were seen in a favourable light by the general public and in a correspondingly gloomy light by the Min Yuen and CTs.

The Briggs' plan, which started to evolve within a month of his arrival, had two distinct components: civil and military. The former was based upon a crash programme of squatter resettlement, the object of which was to bring all rural Chinese under government administration, and to protect and cut them off from the CT gangs. Existing villages and estate labour lines were to be given defensive perimeter wire and outlying families were to be moved inside it; and some 400 new villages were to be constructed to house the illegal squatters where there were no existing villages into which they could be moved. Resettlement was not to consist merely of herding people inside compounds like concentration camps: the new villages were to be provided with the full range of social services—schools, medical facilities, community centres, shops and so forth—and a major effort was to be made to create a community spirit within each village through elected village councils and general encouragement in self-help from the resettlement officer appointed to run the village. Each family was to be given its plot of land to which it would receive legal title. Protection was the responsibility of the police, who were to establish a post in each village and recruit local home guards to help them patrol and watch the perimeter wire. At first the home guards would be unarmed watchers, but, as confidence grew in a village's loyalty, they were to be armed with shotguns.

The re-settlement plan was dauntingly costly in terms of administrative effort, finance, manpower and material resources. Much of the basic planning had been done by the 'Squatters Committee', but the scheme would never have got off the ground had it not been for Briggs, who cut through administrative difficulties in response to a desperate security situation. By the end of the programme in the mid-1950s, 740,000 Chinese had been moved either into the new villages or protected labour lines and existing villages.

The military component of the Briggs Plan had two elements: the creation of a security 'framework' throughout Malaya, superimposed on which were the main striking forces whose role was to destroy the CT gangs district by district with a progression of systematic military clearance operations, starting in Johore and moving northwards until the remnants of the Malayan Races Liberation Army were driven over the Thai border. The framework was based upon the grid of static police stations and posts, which were increased in numbers and given better communications. In the worst areas the Army reinforced the police cover with infantry company bases located near the jungle fringe, where the troops lived, patrolled and watched for long periods, thus getting to know not only the terrain but the local people and their habits. Police and Army framework operations were designed to build up a detailed tactical Intelligence picture of each district upon which the major clearance operations could be planned when the striking force reached the particular district. They were also used to help sever the links between the CTs and their Min Yuen supporters, and for immediate follow-up operations after incidents.

Framework operations were slow, tedious and unexciting, but in the end proved to be the true military complement to the civilian resettlement programme as battle winners. Briggs' first clearance operations, which started in June 1950, were not a success. For them, two thirds of the Army was deployed in Johore, Negri Sembilan and South Pahang. Terrorist incidents declined, and arms hauls and surrenders increased, but no lasting improvement was achieved. The CT gangs continued to evade the nets drawn round them and returned to their old haunts as soon as the troops were withdrawn to start another operation. The incident rate also climbed back to its original level. Briggs recognized that his major operations had been mounted too soon, but argued that they were essential to civilian morale and for buying time for the longer-term measures of bringing effective government to the people to take effect. While he did not stop the major operations, he directed greater emphasis and more of the Army's resources should be given to the framework so that clearance operations could be mounted with better Intelligence and more specific and accurately defined targets.

In implementing the civil component of his Plan, Briggs ran into considerable difficulties. There were many sceptics amongst the older Malayan hands in the government services and the police, who saw no reason to believe that Briggs had hit on the right longer-term formula: on the contrary, they considered his plans over-ambitious and beyond the capability of the government agencies to fulfil. The most critical shortage was in suitable officers for the rapidly expanding administrative service and the police. Recruiting and training the right sort of men took time. Moreover, the SWEC and DWEC system only thinned the jungle of government bureaucracy and did not clear it, particularly in the financial departments. Briggs managed to goad the federal and state governments into a trot: it was to take a more dynamic personality than Briggs to spur them into a war-winning gallop.

The most worrying feature of the latter half of 1950 was a drop in police morale. In Colonel Gray's view this was due to the forces' over-rapid expansion from 10,000 to 62,000 in two years. In his own words it was 'bottom heavy', lacking adequate leadership. Whereas the Army could relieve its units in rotation, the police had no such opportunities for rest and retraining. The cadre of experienced police officers was over-stretched, over-diluted, and over-tired. The addition of Briggs' requirements for his resettlement programme led to a number of unfortunate clashes between Gray and himself. Gray believed that resettlement should be delayed until the police morale had improved, whereas Briggs, with Gurney's support, insisted that resettlement should take priority over routine police work. Briggs' policy went forward despite police objections. It was only partially successful in that the new villages were not well enough protected and their links with the CTs were not completely cut.

International events also conspired against Briggs. The continuation of the Cold War in Europe and the outbreak of the Korean War in June 1950 made the despatch of more troops to Malaya most unlikely; indeed, some reductions were expected as Britain rallied to the American call to build up the United Nations' force defending what little was left of South Korea. Britain's military manpower books could only be balanced by extending National Service to two years in August 1950. It was not, however, the expected loss of troops that worried Gurney and Briggs. Communist successes, first in China, and then in Korea, reconfirmed in many Chinese and Malay minds that European days in the Far East were numbered. While the majority of the Malayan Chinese did not join the Communists neither did they increase their support for the British or for the Malayan Chinese Association, in spite of great efforts made to encourage them to do so. CT losses rose steeply due to Briggs' major operations in southern Malaya and the framework operations throughout the Peninsula, but the flow of recruits into the jungle did not dry up. The strength of the Malayan Races Liberation Army had risen from the original 3,000 to some 7,000 to 8,000 men in the active gangs.

The years 1950 and 1951 were black for both sides. The figures speak for themselves:

	1948	1949	1950	1951
Civilians killed and missing	401	494	752	668
Police and soldiers killed	149(60)	229(65)	393(70)	504(124)
	550	723	1,145	1,172

(Military killed shown in brackets)

	1948	1949	1950	1951
CTs eliminated (killed, captured or surrendered)	693	1,207	942	1,401

By the summer of 1951 receding public confidence in the government's ability to end the emergency was being reflected in the Press and the Legislative Council debates. In the latter, speakers pointed to the continual changes in military policy. One respected Malay member said:

We have under Major General Boucher driven the bandits deep into the jungle, and under Lieutenant-General Sir Harold Briggs we have tried with all our might to drive them out again ... looking at the matter as a layman, I am inclined to believe all this chopping and changing of policy is as confusing to the public as it is to the bandits![8]

A critical notion that day was defeated by 61 votes to four; nevertheless, it was an indication of restlessness with the slow returns for the governments' very considerable effort and financial outlay. The latter might have caused more difficulty had it not been for the boom in rubber and tin prices caused by the Korean War and the British and American rearmament programmes which flowed from it. The buoyancy of Malaya's revenue came at just the right time when maximum expenditure was needed for the resettlement programme.

On the Communist side the situation seemed no better. Dearly held dogmas were being proved fallible by events. Lack of spectacular success and rising losses caused rifts over policy at Central Committee level and disillusion amongst the lower ranks, who were losing faith in the faceless men of the Party leadership. In October 1951 the Fourth Operational Directive was issued by the Central Committee. It admitted to two errors of judgement: the party had placed too much emphasis on the needs of the revolution and too little on the interests of the masses; and the party had failed to distinguish between the 'incorrigible big bourgeois' and 'the exploitable medium bourgeois'. In future as much emphasis was to be given to the political struggle to win wider support as to military operations. Special efforts were to be made to penetrate the new villages and to establish the Min Yuen within them. Destruction of economic assets, upon which the people were dependent for their livelihood, was to stop. And terrorist murder was to be confined to government officials, police, Army and informers. Care was to be taken to avoid killing government health officers and engineers, who were helping to improve the lot of the people and who had their confidence. Military attacks were to be confined to platoon level with an emphasis on ambush.

The October 1951 directive was not just a change of gear for an even longer pull: it was a tacit acceptance that the armed struggle had failed and there was to be a gradual rekindling of the political struggle while the Malayan Races Liberation Army concentrated on survival to fight another day when conditions were more propitious. The directive took even longer than the previous ones to reach the lowest levels of the Party because many of the links in the Communist communication system had been parted.

Before the Communist acceptance of military defeat became known to the Intelligence services, four of the government's principal officers had left the scene: Gurney had been murdered in a chance ambush on his way up to Fraser's Hill for a weekend rest; Briggs had given up his appointment and died soon afterwards; Gray had been dismissed by the new Colonial Secretary, Oliver Lyttelton, in response to pressure from commercial interests in Kuala Lumpur; and Jenkin had been retired with an incipient nervous breakdown. Churchill had won the October 1951 election. The new teams which took over in London and Malaya were to find 1952 an even grimmer year than 1951. The watershed of the emergency had, however, been reached, though this was not realized at the time. It was sad that Gurney and Briggs did not live to see their policies vindicated, but they were both tired and might not have been able to carry the government over the broad and difficult summit.

While the British were resisting the Communist insurgency in Malaya and the French were being submerged by it in Indo-China, the United States was embroiled in the Korean War. The Russians had allowed the North Korean forces, which they had trained and equipped with modern tanks, guns and aircraft, to invade the south on 25 June 1950. At that time, the Soviet delegation to the United Nations was boycotting the Security Council because the Communist Chinese had not been allowed to take the Nationalists' seats. In consequence, Russia was unable to veto the Security Council resolution, branding North Korea as the aggressor and calling for a United Nations force to intervene and demonstrate that aggression was not to be allowed to pay in the post-war world. The United States was the only power with forces near enough to intervene, and so was able to don the United Nations' mantle unopposed. Even so the intervention nearly failed. The US occupation forces in Japan were far from ready for the war that was thrust upon them. Had it not been for General Douglas MacArthur's leadership the small South Korean Army, which the Americans had equipped only with light weapons suitable for a gendarmarie, would have been swept into the sea. As it was the American troops rushed from Japan barely managed to retain a precarious toe-hold on the southeastern tip of Korea around the small port of Pusan.

Ernest Bevin, though a very sick man, was still British Foreign Secretary.

Under his leadership Britain rallied to support her Atlantic partner, though not without misgivings. Americans had lurched from their immediate post-war reluctance to risk burning their fingers again in Chinese politics to the anti-Communist extremism of the McCarthy era. Many in Britain feared that American military involvement on the mainland of Asia could lead to the Third World War in which atomic weapons would be used. British support to the United States in Korea was not extended to the American refusal to recognize the Communist regime in China, nor to their determination to help Chiang Kai Shek defend Formosa.

The British Commonwealth contributed the only significant non-American land, sea and air contingents to the United Nations force in Korea. The 27th Brigade was rushed north from Hong Kong to Pusan in British warships in mid-August 1950 and arrived just in time to help fend off the last North Korean attacks on the Pusan bridgehead. The 41st Royal Marine Commando joined the American amphibious forces and the Royal Navy and Royal Air Force contributed ships and aircraft. Australia sent ships, aircraft and two infantry battalions, and New Zealand provided an artillery regiment. With the arrival of the 29th Brigade from the United Kingdom and the 25th Brigade from Canada, the 28th Commonwealth Division was formed and played its full part in the advances and withdrawals to and fro across the 38th Parallel. Britain's worst fears were realized when MacArthur's cavalier actions led to Chinese intervention and the possibility of extending the war to the Chinese homelands. The American 'hawks' were prepared to risk a major war in an area of no vital strategic importance to the Atlantic Alliance. General Omar Bradley, Chairman of the American Chiefs of Staff, dubbed it a wrong war, in the wrong place, at the wrong time, and against the wrong enemy. A crisis of Anglo-American confidence arose when President Truman did not rule out publicly the use of atomic weapons. Attlee flew to Washington in December 1951 to advise caution. He was successful in softening Truman's approach, but he failed with his further suggestion that peace negotiations might be possible if America would recognize the Chinese People's Republic. MacArthur finally over-stepped the mark in April 1952 and was sacked by Truman. MacArthur's views were encapsulated in the open letter he wrote to a US Congressman, which led to his sacking:

If we lose the War to Communism in Asia, the fall of Europe is inevitable: win it, and Europe most probably would avoid war and yet preserve freedom. . . . There is no substitute for victory.[9]

MacArthur was to be proved wrong. Although the hot war continued in Korea for another two years, stalemate rather than victory occurred without the war's extension to the Chinese mainland or to the world. The armistice negotiations eventually established a recognized frontier between Communist and Western democracy in Northeast Asia: it was to take many more years to do the same thing in Southeast Asia.

5 The Struggle for Hearts and Minds
The defeat of the Mau Mau in Kenya and victory in Malaysia: 1952 to 1956

The answer lies not in pouring more soldiers into the jungle but rests in the hearts and minds of the Malayan people.

General Sir Gerald Templer, 1952[1]

The return of Churchill to power in October 1951 did not lead to any major changes in British colonial policy, which had remained in the main, bi-partisan during Attlee's post-war Labour government. Oliver Lyttelton, the new Conservative Colonial Secretary, accepted his predecessor's definition of Britain's Colonial purpose:

to guide the Colonial territories to responsible Government within the Commonwealth in conditions that ensure to the people concerned both a fair standard of living, and freedom from aggression from any quarter.[2]

Nevertheless, there was a significant difference in emphasis given by the two parties to the relative speeds of political and economic advance. The Labour Party sought to maintain a concurrency in their development and was prepared to accept delay in constitutional advance until adequate standards of living had been achieved: the Conservative Party regarded political development as the pace-setter. The leaders of both parties were over-sanguine about their own abilities to control the speed of change because they were aware that governors of many colonial territories had reached agreements with their local political leaders not to make public demands for independence before their people were ready for it.[3] Such promises were easier to make than keep in the anti-colonial state of world opinion in the 1950s.

The focus of anti-colonial pressure, which undermined the good sense of such agreements, lay in the United Nations and was reinforced from time to time by the Afro-Asian conferences originally sponsored by Pandit Nehru. Despite economic difficulties Britain poured millions of pounds into post-war colonial development schemes. Some of the money was spent unwisely in over-hastily conceived projects like the East African Ground-Nut Scheme, but most of it was used judiciously. Britain received scant acknowledgement of her efforts in the United Nations where the colonial powers were heavily out-numbered by the 40 or so 'have nots' and newly independent states. The atmosphere is well described in the *British Official History of Colonial Development*:

The prevailing notion was that there was something inherently reprehensible about the existence of non-self-governing territories as such and a complete failure to admit that most of the problems which arose in these territories were manifestations of the same problems which arose in the critics' own territories, but about which their sovereign status enabled them to preserve a discreet silence. It augured ill for the future. The 'Colonial Question' of the 1930s, which the Hitler Government had raised and which American prodding during war time had kept alive, thus became part and parcel of the politics of the United Nations from the beginning of that Organisation's existence.

Three chapters of the United Nations Charter dealt with colonial matters. Chapters XII and XIII replaced the League of Nations Mandates with the International Trusteeship system. As far as Britain was concerned only Tanganika, Togoland and the Cameroons came in this category: Iraq and Transjordan had been given their independence in 1946 and the Palestine Mandate had been surrendered in 1947. The majority of her colonial territories came under Chapter XI, which covered non self-governing dependencies. Article 73 of this chapter laid a number of unexceptional and unobjectionable responsibilities upon the colonial powers. It also called for annual reports to be sent to the Secretary General *for information purposes* on economic, social and educational conditions in each territory. Political, security and constitutional matters were specifically excluded from the regional reports. Such exclusions were not to the liking of many of the anti-colonial lobby, who sought the right to debate the whole spectrum of a colonial power's performance. Matters came to a head with a proposal for regional conferences of representatives of the people of non-self-governing territories at which their wishes could be expressed. The United States, hitherto having stood aloof from lobbying on colonial affairs, suddenly realized that such a proposal could lead to meetings of representativs of the people of Alaska, Puerto Rico and Hawaii behind the US government's back, probably on US soil. Thenceforth the Americans were more willing to consider the points of view of the older colonial powers.

There were other reasons why British confidence in being able to control the speed of colonial development was misplaced. The oft-repeated statement of the British government's intention to lead its dependent people to independence created internal struggles for succession. Political leaders, as they emerged, were bound to seek the 'promised land' in their own lifetime rather than in that of their grandchildren, as would often have been the case if Britain had stuck to her principles of not granting independence until a colony was politically, economically and socially mature enough to stand on its own feet. The spur of personal ambition was sharpened by the precedents of the Indian Subcontinent, and in some cases by the knowledge that there were alternative sources of power and aid behind the Iron and Bamboo curtains.

Britain's defeat by the Japanese in 1942 had broken the colonial mould in Southeast Asia. Paradoxically it was Britain's victory over the Axis powers in Abyssinia, the Western Desert and Burma that helped to break it in Africa. Both East and West African troops had taken part in these campaigns and had not been impressed by the social conditions that they saw in independent countries outside Africa. On their return home they began to question why their own countries were politically so backward and why Africans played so small a part in African affairs. General Sir Alan Cunningham (later British High Commissioner in Palestine), who drove the Italians out of Ethiopia and the Horn of Africa in 1941, warned at the end of his campaign that his askaris would not be content to remain junior partners in their own countries after the war. TANU, the Tanganika Africa National Union, which eventually led Tanganika to independence, was originally formed by East African troops waiting in a transit camp in India for shipment back to Africa at the end of the war.

Though the same wartime seeds of political ambition had been sown in the minds of men from both sides of Africa, they were to germinate in very different soils. In West Africa, the climate held few attractions for Europeans. Colonial officials and businessmen came and went on relatively short tours and put down no roots. There were no European farmers. In East Africa, the opposite occurred. The climate, the farming conditions and the emptiness of the land at the turn of the twentieth century attracted European settlers much as Australia and New Zealand had done in the latter half of the nineteenth century. West Africa's march to independence was thus the easier of the two: only British business interests were at risk. In East Africa the interests of the European settlers could not be ignored, and strategically the area was of some importance to Britain as a support area for the British military position in the Middle East and the Indian Ocean.

In the immediate post-war period most of Britain's colonies, which were producers of primary products, suffered from successive sterling crises. Dollar earnings had to be increased and dollar expenditure cut, so colonial production was increased and higher wages were paid, but there was a lack of consumer goods on which the extra money could be spent. Britain was unable to satisfy the demand and yet was reluctant to allow her colonial governments to buy outside the sterling area. Rising prices generated a feeling in the colonies that British commercial interests were manipulating colonial economies for their own ends. In East and West Africa an atmosphere of suspicion was generated despite the generous disbursement of development and welfare funds and improvements in standards of living and economic expectations. Disenchantment was most marked in the Gold Coast and Kenya, and was exploited to the full by a small number of Europe-educated and personally ambitious young men, who were nationalist at heart but were also flirting with Communism.

Trouble first flared in the Gold Coast. Serious rioting broke out in February 1948 in Accra and lasted four days, during which time the police had to open fire to restore order. The subsequent Commission of Enquiry under Mr Aitken Watson KC set the pattern for African constitutional development. It laid the blame for the unrest upon political, social and economic factors in equal proportions, and recommended that the remedy lay in greater African participation in government. British ministers were prepared to implement Aitken Watson's recommendations, provided they were shown to be acceptable to African opinion. A local committee under the Chairmanship of an eminent African Judge, Sir James Coussey, composed entirely of Africans of all shades of political opinion, endorsed and elaborated Aitken Watson's constitutional proposals for a phased advance to fully responsible internal self-government, based upon universal suffrage, and with independence within the Commonwealth as the ultimate goal.

Coussey's proposals were accepted by the British government, but a fundamental difference of opinion arose amongst the local African political leaders. Doctor Danquah's United Gold Coast Convention accepted that British rule had not been despotic and advocated gradual constitutional change on the Coussey lines: Doctor Nkrumah, at the head of the extremist Convention People's Party denounced Danquah as too pro-British, out of date and over-cautious. Taking a leaf from the Indian Congress Party's book, Nkrumah demanded 'Self-government now'. His call for 'positive action', and his organization of a series of illegal strikes, landed him in prison with a two-year sentence for sedition. At no time did the internal security situation deteriorate enough to warrant the intervention of Imperial troops to slow the rate of political change. Moderation amongst the majority of the population enabled the police to contain the extremists.

The Gold Coast general election of 1951 was a milestone in the history of British colonial development in Africa. For the first time a British African colony went to the polls to elect a parliament with an unrestricted African majority. Doctor Nkrumah's party swept the poll and he was summoned from prison by the Governor, Sir Charles Arden-Clarke, to become the 'Leader of Government Business', virtually Prime Minister in all but name. For the next six years the two men worked closely together constructing the foundations upon which the new nation of Ghana was to be built. Independence within the Commonwealth was granted in March 1957.

Ghana's march to independence set the pattern for the rest of Africa and the West Indies. In most cases moderation, spurred on but not overtaken by extremism, prevailed. The presence of the Royal Navy's frigates in the Caribbean was generally sufficient military backing for the local police forces, but on several occasions battalions were flown out from England at short notice to deal with difficult internal security situations, none of which resulted in serious fighting.[5] In Kenya, and later in Rhodesia, black and white extremists dominated the struggles for succession, which led to civil wars in both countries.

The Mau Mau rebellion amongst the Kikuyu tribe in Kenya broke out with surprising suddenness in mid-1952, but there was a long history of unrest amongst the Kikuyu, stretching back to the arrival of the Europeans in Kenya in the last few decades of the nineteenth century. Colonel Meinertzhagen of the King's African Rifles wrote in 1902:

But the Kikuyu are ripe for trouble and when they get educated and the medicine men are replaced by political agitators, there will be a general rising.[6]

The Colonel was proved right over the rebellion but wrong over its methods: agitators combined with rather than replaced medicine men to bring it about. The Kikuyu were the largest, most intelligent and, in European eyes, the least warlike of the Kenyan tribes. They nursed a deep-seated grievance about the supposed theft of their land by European settlers. Their claim could be and was dismissed in legal argument, but not from their minds. Looking across at the European farms, on which many of them worked, the fields were certainly greener, and so were the psychological pastures of education, political representation and social status. The earliest Kikuyu political organization, the Kikuyu Association, formed in the 1920s had as its aims:

to stimulate enmity between black and white and to get the people to consider that they are in a state of slavery which has been imposed upon them.[7]

In the 1930s Kikuyu aspirations were articulated by the moderate Kikuyu Provincial Association and by the extremist Kikuyu Central Association (KCA) whose General Secretary was Jomo Kenyatta and whose battle cry was 'Get back our land'. During the war the latter was declared illegal for proven connections with Italian agents. Jomo Kenyatta escaped arrest because he was living in England, ostensibly representing the KCA and misrepresenting Kenya to left-wing bodies such as the 'Congress of peoples against Imperialism'. During his sojourn in Britain, which lasted 15 years, he joined the Communist Party and visited the Soviet Union in 1929 and 1933.

In September 1946 Kenyatta returned to Kenya and joined his old KCA colleagues in revitalizing the extremist movement. They used the moderate Kikuyu parties as a front, behind which they organized their Mau Mau secret terrorist society, dedicated to the expulsion by murder and fear of murder of Europeans and Asians from Kenya, and to eventual Kikuyu sovereignty over East Africa.[8] They harped on the long standing Kikuyu grievances about land and education, and they exploited their primitive beliefs in black magic and witchcraft. The Mau Mau initiation rituals copied traditional Kikuyu oath-taking, binding its recruits to secrecy and obedience. Once the rebellion started the rituals became more bestial and obscene, and the oaths more sadistic. Fear of the supernatural turned men and women into fanatics, who delighted in the most gruesome ways of killing. Each section of the oaths ended with the phrase 'if I fail, may this oath kill me'.

Although Jomo Kenyatta was the inspiration and driving force behind the creation of Mau Mau, he was but one of a small number of ambitious

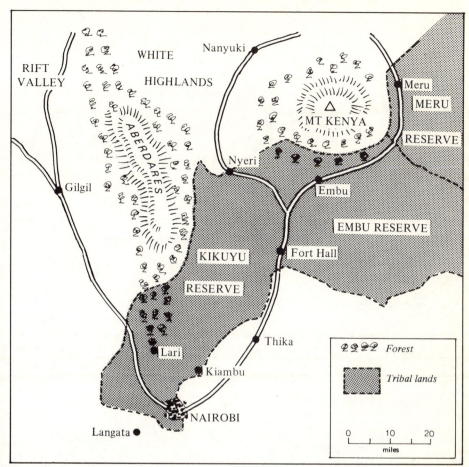

6. The Mau Mau area of Kenya, 1952–6.

educated Kikuyu bent upon African emancipation by violent means. The organization of the society followed the time-honoured Kikuyu custom of decision by committee and the avoidance of personal aggrandizement.[9] Mau Mau committees were established in Nairobi for each district, division and location in the Kikuyu reserves and linked with corresponding committees in the reserves themselves. This complex interlocking network gave the society a Hydra-like strength and resilience. It was divided also into military and passive wings, the latter being responsible for recruiting for the terrorist gangs and for their supply. Before the British had stopped the Masai tribesmen raiding the Kikuyu lands at the beginning of the century, the forests of the Aberdare mountains and Mount Kenya, north of Nairobi, had offered sanctuary for the Kikuyu. These forests now provided the safe bases for the gangs of the Mau Mau military wing.

Throughout 1950 and 1951 Kenyatta and his colleagues played an overt part in the political activities of the moderate Kenya African Union in pressing for African constitutional advance. Covertly they were subverting the loyalty of the Kikuyu from their Chiefs and making them the enemies of the government. Kenyatta was guided by three tactical principles: hoodwinking British justice by never committing anything to paper; ensuring that all witnesses were 'our own people'; and always using the word 'democracy' in public speeches because it was so dear to British liberal minds. He was so successful in this that Sir Philip Mitchell, who had been Governor for nine years, told his successor, Sir Evelyn Baring, in June 1952 'there really is a genuine feeling of desire to co-operate and be friendly at the present time'.[10]

Mitchell's belief was surprising. There was no lack of Intelligence pointing in the opposite direction, if he and his senior officials had wanted to look for it. As early as December 1947 the District Commissioner of Fort Hall had reported secret meetings and oath taking, saying:

There is a very strong rumour circulating that all the wrongs of the Kikuyu will be simultaneously righted by the murder of all Europeans.[11]

By August 1950 enough was known about the Mau Mau society for it to be declared illegal. During 1951 and early 1952 the tide of subversion grew, despite many successful prosecutions, and so did the flow of Intelligence reports of Kikuyu disaffection. In January 1952 a campaign of arson was begun on European farms, which was clearly Mau Mau-inspired. The first full assessment of the Mau Mau threat was made by the Director of Intelligence at the end of April 1952. His report rang no alarm bells. He concluded:

Mau Mau is likely, therefore, to continue, although there is no indication that any widespread overt, subversive action is planned ... Its cure is education, the emergence of a reputable African political organisation which can present political views sanely to the Government ..., and, most of all, the solving of the land question on a reasonably permanent and long-term basis.[12]

These conclusions chimed in well with Sir Philip Mitchell's views. He was imbued, like many British colonial governors with, to use his own words, 'a determination to persevere in the task to which we have set our minds—to civilize a great mass of human beings who are in a very primitive moral and social state'. Mau Mau was just one of those burdens which he and his colleagues had to carry until they could wean the people away from such puerile activities by good administration. After all, only one African tribe was involved.

May 1952 brought the start of the Mau Mau murders and mutilation of loyal Kikuyu, and of those who were thought to have broken their oaths. Oathing ceremonies were reported to be on the increase and more barbaric, with mandatory murder of Europeans added to secrecy and obedience. Sir Philip Mitchell left in June, but such was the lack of concern about the internal security situation both in Nairobi and Whitehall that Sir

Evelyn Baring was not sworn in as his successor until 30 September. By then the situation could no longer be disguised however rosy the idealist spectacles of the observer. After a tour of the disaffected areas and full consultation with local opinion Sir Evelyn recommended to the Colonial Office that a state of emergency should be declared and the full panoply of Malayan-style emergency regulations introduced. Since June 59 Kikuyu, including Chief Waruhu, had been murdered.

In 1952 the only infantry units available to support the police in Kenya were the local King's African Rifle (KAR) battalions. Fortunately, the Kikuyu were not considered a martial tribe and had not been enlisted as askaris. In making his recommendations to Whitehall, Sir Evelyn asked for a British battalion to be flown in and for authority to arrest Kenyatta and his indentified henchmen. If Kenyatta was not removed, he feared that more Kikuyu loyalists would be killed, other more warlike tribes might be infected, and there could be a European backlash.

On 20 October, the day before the state of emergency was proclaimed, 1st Lancashire Fusiliers started to arrive in Nairobi from Egypt in RAF Hastings' transport aircraft. Movement of military reserves by air was still in its infancy, the move of 450 men taking four days. The Governor signed the proclamation in the evening of 21 October. One hundred and eighty three known Mau Mau leaders, including Kenyatta were arrested. The Association had been beheaded, but by then it had acquired a momentum of its own. Its decimated committees were soon reformed with younger and even more militant men. The unpalatable fact was that the Mau Mau were more feared than the security forces.

The area in which the anti-Mau Mau campaign was to be fought was no larger than an average-sized Malay state. It was triangular in shape, its corners marked by the northern end of the Aberdare Range, Mount Kenya and Nairobi. The sides of the triangle were about 100 miles long, and it contained the three districts of the Kikuyu Reserves (Kiambu, Fort Hall and Nyeri) and was bordered by the Aberdare forests to the west and those of Mt Kenya to the northeast. The whole area was surrounded by the European settled areas except to the east where the Embu and Meru lived in their respective reserves south and east of Mount Kenya. The thick forests encircled both mountain masses beginning at the 8,000 foot contour and giving way at about 10,000 feet to belts of dense bamboo before opening out into moorland which covered summits.[13] The Kikuyu lived in scattered family settlements rather than villages, and farmed the ridges running down from the Aberdares and Mount Kenya.

The Mau Mau were primitive only in their oathing system and their military equipment. Having no foreign backers to run guns and ammunition to them, they had to rely on theft. There were no large dumps of surrendered British or Japanese arms ready to be pilfered as there had been in Malaya. The only sources were the laxly-guarded Ordnance Depot at Gilgil and the sparsely-armed police and settlers. It is doubtful whether they had more than 1,500 modernish small arms at the beginning of the emergency with which to arm the 8,000 to 12,000 men who joined the forest gangs. The majority had to be equipped only with *simis* (broadbladed machetes, used for slashing undergrowth and reaping crops), and locally-made guns, which were a greater hazard to the owners than to their targets. Lack of equipment was compensated for by the determination and natural sense of fieldcraft of their leaders and by the standard of their Intelligence system which was very high. Many Kikuyu were employed as clerks and in junior management posts in Nairobi and the settled areas with access to valuable information. Their oaths of secrecy enabled them to live double lives, undetected, in the city and on European farms.

The British East Africa Command with its headquarters in Nairobi has been justifiably described as a military back-water. Lieutenant General Sir Alexander Cameron was subordinate to the C-in-C Middle East in Cairo, and was responsible for all British East African dependencies except Southern Rhodesia. He took a lofty view of his responsibilities and left the military affairs of Kenya to the Brigadier commanding the 70th East African Brigade which had three KAR battalions. The small military Intelligence effort of East Africa Command was beamed on the strategic problems of East Africa as a support area for Britain's position in the Middle East and Indian Ocean. The 70th Brigade itself was more interested in sending two KAR battalions to fight in Malaya than in local internal security. Even the Kenyan territorial army unit, the European-manned Kenya Regiment, was organized and trained as an officer producing unit for general war overseas rather than to combat internal rebellion. The only other military units in Kenya were the locally-raised East African Heavy Anti-aircraft Battery and Armoured Car Squadron. Air support was available from the RAF base at Eastleigh.

The police, whom the Lancashire Fusiliers came to support, had been slightly expanded as the crime rate rose in 1950 and 1951, but were quite inadequate to contain the upsurge of lawlessness in 1952. The regular colony police only operated in the larger towns and the settled areas: the reserves were policed by the irregular tribal police working under the District Officers. The Kenya Police Reserve was a source of European police reinforcements, but any large scale expansion of the police required the recruitment of officers from outside Kenya and took time. The greatest police weakness lay in its Special Branch, which was small, confined to Nairobi and subordinate to the CID so that crime detection took priority over political Intelligence. The Special Branch weakness was compounded by the governmental system which placed responsibility for internal security under the Attorney General, who was the Executive Council Member for Law and Order. As the government's senior law officer, the Attorney General was hardly best suited by training, experience or psychology to directing the Intelligence organization and assessing its reports. Much of the blame for the tardiness of Sir Philip Mitchell's reactions to the growing crisis lay in this organizational defect, which was put right by a visit from Sir Percy Sillitoe, Director General of the British

Security Services, in November 1952 after much of the damage had been done. Internal security was handed back to the Chief Secretary, whose responsibility it should have been in the first place and was in most other colonies.

The proclamation of the state of emergency and the arrival of British troops in Kenya was treated by many organs of the world press as another manifestation of British Imperialism trampling on the legitimate aspirations of the East African peoples. Some went as far as portraying Mau Mau as a figment of the Kenyan government's imagination. In Kenya itself there was a general feeling of relief amongst all communities that action was, at last, being taken to stamp out lawlessness. There were high hopes that raising the stick would be enough. Measures were taken to expand the regular and tribal police, and to create a Kikuyu home guard under the Chiefs for the protection of the majority of the tribe, particularly the older generations, who remained loyal to the government.

At the turn of the year, hopes that the worst was over were shattered by a series of brutal murders and attempted murders of European farmers and their families, and of loyalist Kikuyu. The settlers vented their feelings with a march on Government House and were only dispersed by the courage and eloquence of the two European elected members of the Legislative Council, Michael Blundell and Humphrey Slade.

The learning curve in Kenya was steeper and shorter than in Malaya thanks to the experience gained there. Nevertheless, the government made a very shaky start in gearing itself to the emergency. Instead of appointing a Director of Operations straight away and establishing the emergency committee system on Malayan lines, Brigadier R. W. N. Hinde was appointed Chief of Staff to the Governor and a cumbersome colony emergency committee was formed, which was far too large for effective development of policy and executive action. Hinde's worst hurdle in trying to co-ordinate the police, military and administrative effort was the attitude of the Provincial Commissioners and District Officers on the one hand, and of the settlers on the other. The former had always been allowed to run the reserves in their own way without outside interference and were reluctant to share responsibility with anyone, let alone a British Army officer based in Nairobi; and the latter demanded tougher government action, but were quite unwilling to tolerate any diminution of their pleasant carefree lives and were determined to maintain the status quo in racial relations despite HMG's oft-stated intent to lead its East African territories to independence.

Hinde was a cavalry officer, who had acquired the nickname 'Looney' in his youth. It was the antithesis of his character and abilities. He had relations farming in Kenya so he was not entirely free of settler prejudices, but he was an able, energetic soldier who had the knack of getting the best out of difficult people: he needed it. Fortunately, the CIGS, General Sir John Harding, who had been instrumental in the despatch of Briggs to Malaya when he was C-in-C Far East in 1950, visited Kenya in February just after Hinde had taken over as Chief of Staff to the Governor. He sensed all the malaise from which Malaya had suffered in the early days of its emergency and the difficulty of Hinde's position. When he got back to London he persuaded Churchill that a Briggs was needed in Kenya and that the security forces should be reinforced with an experienced British brigade. General Sir George Erskine, a strong personality and a soldier with wide operational experience, was appointed C-in-C and Director of Operations. Harding would have liked him to take over the Governorship, but this was not accepted because Oliver Lyttelton was a strong supporter of Baring. At Baring's request Hinde stayed on as Deputy Director of Operations, amply justifying Baring's confidence in him by his performance as tactical commander under Erskine of most of the major military operations undertaken in Kenya.

The brigade nominated was Brigadier J. W. Tweedie's 39th Brigade with 1st Devons and 1st Buffs, the former having recently done well in Malaya. Before Erskine or Tweedie could arrive the security situation deteriorated alarmingly and loyalist confidence was sapped by two hideously successful Mau Mau attacks. The first was deliberately aimed at undermining the formation of an effective Kikuyu Home Guard. The Lari area at the southern end of the Aberdare forest was chosen by the Mau Mau leadership because of its strong loyalist character and successful home guard. A gang of about a thousand strong left the forest at dusk on 26 March and in a carefully pre-planned operation surrounded the huts of the known loyalists. Cables were tied round them so that the doors could not be opened. Petrol was then poured on them and fired. Members of the gang were positioned to hack down anyone who escaped. The home guard, 150 strong, were away at the time patrolling the nearby forest. By the time they got back and the tribal police had arrived 200 huts had been destroyed and 84 Kikuyu, mostly women and children, had been killed and another 31 grievously mutilated. The other attack was carried out the same night on the fortified police post at Naivasha, just south of Gilgil. It was over-run and all the police garrison were killed. One hundred and seventy-three prisoners held there were released. Settler pressure on the government intensified with demands for the introduction of martial law to put an end to the slow and ponderous working of the civil courts.

The 39th Brigade arrived by air in April and took the Lancashire Fusiliers under command. After a short period of acclimatization and training they started operations in the Aberdares, leaving 70th Brigade with its KAR battalions, which had been increased to six by withdrawing battalions from Tanganika, Uganda and Mauritius, to support the police in the reserves. Officers and NCOs of the Kenya Regiment were attached to British battalions to advise on Kikuyu customs and methods. Pilots of the Kenya Police Reserve, mostly ex-RAF, provided a light aircraft service for reconnaissance, liaison, supply and casualty evacuation. Possibly the greatest help came from a special emergency regulation that declared the forests prohibited zones where the security forces could open fire without challenge. All other operational areas became special zones where troops could halt and question suspects, but only open fire if a challenge was defied or a curfew broken.

The 'needle in a haystack' problems of searching the forests were similar to those in Malaya with two obvious differences: the weather was cooler and far less humid, and, in place of malaria-carrying mosquitos and typhus-bearing ticks, herds of large game animals like rhino, buffalo and elephant could be dangerous. Contacts with the Mau Mau gangs were as fleeting as in Malaya. They were just as intent as the CTs on avoiding contact with Army patrols and were concentrating upon terrorizing their own people in the reserves. Lack of any real military success in the forests and continuing Mau Mau intimidation on the farms led to settler demands for greater protection and hence the dispersal of Army and police resources on static defensive tasks. As in Malaya, these pressures were resisted by the Army. Success could not be expected until Intelligence improved. Initially it had to be fought for by harassing the gangs even if contacts were infrequent.

Erskine arrived in June 1953 intent on pursuing an offensive strategy aimed at wresting the initiative from the forest gangs with British troops while the KAR, police and home guards built up a security framework in the reserves and the settled areas around the Kikuyu lands. He had to fend off further demands for a declaration of martial law. He refused consistently to countenance its imposition because the government of Kenya had not broken down and the rebellion, in any case, affected only a small part of Kenya. The Army did not have the resources to take over the administration of the country. He was far from popular with the settlers for rejecting their demands and for insisting that the security forces must always act within the law. He was satisfied that the emergency regulations gave him all the powers needed to crush the rebellion.

Erskine, like Briggs, decided to tackle the worst areas first where contact was most likely. He organized three striking forces: 39th Brigade and the Kenya Regiment were to operate in the forests; a mobile force, based on the East African Armoured Car Squadron with troops of the Heavy Anti-aircraft Battery acting as infantry in its support, would operate in the more open areas of the Embu and Meru Reserves and the settled areas of the Rift Valley; and the RAF, the third force, would support both using slow Harvard training aircraft fitted to drop 20-pound bombs (later reinforced with Lincolns with 1,000-pounders). Specific areas were taken on in succession with search operations lasting two to three weeks. The RAF exerted pressure on areas where the troops were not operating by bombing likely camp areas to harass the gangs and also provided air transport for both mobility and supply.

The results of these early operations were not encouraging. Intelligence was still too sparse for accurate planning but it was through them that the scale of the problem was identified and the Intelligence picture was gradually built up. While this had been going on the police and home guard units were being strengthened and were improving in efficiency, enabling Erskine to free more troops for offensive operations. The gangs did take some hard knocks, as did their suppliers, but their recruiting was being boosted by the farmers shedding Kikuyu labourers in favour of other tribes. These unemployed men were easily swept into the Mau Mau fold.

At the beginning of August Erskine reviewed the situation and came to four conclusions: operations were taking far longer than he had anticipated; he needed more troops; the best method of contacting the gangs was to drive tracks deep into the forests where infantry company bases could be established to dominate the forests from within; and the time was ripe to offer an amnesty since the hostile element amongst the Kikuyu could be under no illusions about British determination to crush the Mau Mau. His request for more troops was met by the dispatch by air in September of Brigadier G. Taylor's 49th Brigade with the 1st Northumberland Fusiliers and the 1st Royal Inniskilling Fusiliers, the former with Korean experience and the latter Malayan. The construction of forest tracks, which was initially carried out by the Kenya Public Works Department, was speeded up by the arrival, also by air, of the 39th Engineer Regiment. An amnesty was announced by the government, but the hold of the Mau Mau oaths was still too strong to produce significant numbers of defections.

By the end of 1953 there was a general feeling that the rebellion had been contained. It had not spread to other tribes and the Mau Mau incident rate had flattened out. Even more encouraging was the increasing flow of Intelligence and the improvements in its assessment. Erskine planned to make 1954 a decisive year.

The fuller Intelligence picture showed that the core of the rebellion was in fact in Nairobi rather than in the forests. The complex network of secret Mau Mau committees in the city was not only organizing recruitment and supply for the gangs but was also carrying on a major campaign of political subversion. A Mau Mau reign of terror and intimidation had been established; crime and general lawlessness were rife; and strikes and boycotts, designed to damage European and Asian commercial interests, were making life intolerable. Erskine decided he had three main tasks: clean up Nairobi; continue to improve the security of the settled areas and the reserves; and, only when these two tasks had been accomplished, a general offensive against the forest gangs.

Clearing Mau Mau supporters from Nairobi was no mean task. The only precedent was the 6th Airborne Division's clearance of Tel Aviv in July 1946 after the bombing of the King David Hotel. Eighteen major units had been used for that operation which had lasted 48 hours. Erskine could only risk withdrawing the 49th Brigade with five battalions (four British and one KAR) for the much larger task of clearing Nairobi, which was expected to take several weeks. To have used more troops would have weakened his grip on the disaffected areas outside the city.

The simplest way of dealing with the Kikuyu in Nairobi would have been to return them all to their reserves, but this would have brought the municipal services and economic life of Nairobi to a stand-still. It would also have filled the reserves with more disgruntled unemployed who would have been ready recruits for the Mau Mau gangs. Winning back Kikuyu loyalty would have become all the harder. Erskine, with Baring's full approval, decided instead upon selective screening of the African population of the city. He estimated that he would need camps for some 50,000 detainees, which were to be erected at MacKinnon Road and Manyani on the railway to Mombasa, 250 miles east of Nairobi, with a temporary holding camp for 10,000 at Langata, five miles from the city centre. These camps could not be completed before the beginning of April and their construction could certainly not be kept secret. Erskine hoped, however, to conceal the date of the operation and its scope.

While preparations went ahead for 'Anvil'—the Nairobi operation— two quite different but important events occurred. The first had its origins in the continuing European dissatisfaction with the handling of the emergency. The settlers claimed that neither Baring nor Erskine understood Africa and they demanded greater participation in the Kenyan government. In their criticism of military policies they overlooked what had, in fact, been achieved. In the 15 months since the emergency began only 16 Europeans had been killed and five wounded, whereas 613 loyal Kikuyu had been slaughtered and 359 maimed. The Mau Mau had suffered a loss of 3,000 men, 1,000 more were captured, and 157,000 suspects had been arrested and screened, of whom 64,000 had been brought to trial. This had all been achieved by the security forces from a standing start. The political criticisms and attitudes of the settlers were more serious. They refused to face up to the need for a political as well as a military solution to the rebellion. Britain would not and could not put the constitutional clock back for their benefit, and it was not possible to give the Europeans a greater say in government without a corresponding increase in African and Asian participation, a course totally unacceptable to the white extremists.

Oliver Lyttelton, accompanied by General Sir John Harding, visited Kenya in February: the former had draft proposals for a new constitution in his brief case, and the latter came with ideas for sharpening up operational control. The Lyttelton Constitution was far from the settlers' liking: local representation was to be increased by the introduction of six elected ministers (three European, two Asian and one Arab) and five nominated Africans were to be appointed as under-secretaries. It was a small start in widening the government's base to other races and was bitterly opposed by the Europeans. Operational control was to be improved by the abolition of the cumbersome Colony Emergency Committee and the introduction of a much leaner war council, backed by a council of ministers. The former was to consist of the Governor, Deputy Governor, C-in-C and the European Member without portfolio, Mr Blundell; the Minister of Defence, and Minister for Native Affairs were also to attend. A Cabinet Secretariat under George Mallaby from the Cabinet Office in London was to serve the War Council and the Council of Ministers. An emergency joint staff drawn from the administration, police and Army was to carry out the forward planning and to co-ordinate operational policy. Further thought was to be given to replacing Baring with Erskine as Governor and Director of Operations, but, in the end, the idea was not pursued.

The second event was the surrender of 'General China', who was one of the principal gang leaders in the Mt Kenya forests, to Superintendent Ian Henderson in a highly secret Special Branch operation. China agreed to try, with the help of other captured gang leaders, to arrange the surrender of the gangs he had formerly controlled. After two abortive attempts, a meeting took place between representatives of the government and the Mau Mau on 30 March at which a five point agreement was reached: no terrorist, who surrendered, would be executed but hard core Mau Mau would be detained; the security forces would cease all operations in the prohibited areas until 10 April to allow the gangs to consult each other; a further meeting would be held on 10 April at which the details of surrender would be agreed; the gang leaders would do their best to prevent incidents in the reserves and settled areas; and the cease-fire would only apply to the forests.

The security forces honoured their side of the bargain, but the Mau Mau leaders were unable to control their men in the reserves. On 7 April a large gang, which had left the forest, was cornered and 25 of its men were killed; so were the chances of success in the surrender negotiations. It happened that there was a gang meeting to discuss the China agreement being held in the forest within earshot of the engagement. The sound of firing gave those opposed to surrender the upper hand in the argument and the peace initiative collapsed. Two of China's henchmen also escaped and Erskine came under further settler criticism for his handling of the operation. Unknown to his critics the information gleaned during the negotations helped both 'Anvil' and subsequent operations. Over a thousand Passive Wing members were identified and picked up.

'Anvil' started on 24 April and was more successful than had been expected. Rumours of a major security force operation in Nairobi had been circulating for some months and nothing had happened. When it came, surprise was complete: few of the Mau Mau dissidents had left the city; and everyone—African, Asian and Europeans alike—was taken unawares by the scale and thoroughness of the operation. It was controlled from a joint Army, police and administration headquarters set up in Nairobi. The Army provided the cordons and escorts; the police and Special Branch did searching and screening; and the administration gave out the necessary instructions to the inhabitants in each area as it was cordoned off and searched, and arranged for the removal and storage of property of those detained. Two thousand five hundred troops and 600 police took part.

At dawn on 24 April the Army's covering screen was in position around the city and the first African quarter was being cordoned off. Within 48 hours 11,600 Africans had been screened of whom 8,000 had been removed to Langata for further screening. The operation continued for nearly two weeks; the total eventually detained was 16,538 and 2,416 dependent relatives were sent back to the reserves. In an attempt to keep Nairobi 'clean' a new passbook system was introduced, which was both an identity document and residence permit. A second phase screening of the city was continued up to the end of May, but the issued passbooks took until the end of October.

The first result of 'Anvil' obvious to the people of Nairobi was the dramatic drop in the crime rate. Prior to the emergency there had been an average of 450 serious crimes per month; at the beginning of 'Anvil' this was up to 950; and after 'Anvil' it fell to 152 for May. The effect on the Mau Mau organization was devastating. Not only were most of its committees shattered, but information about Mau Mau also began to flow more freely, enabling Special Branch to make them difficult to rebuild. The security forces were, at last, more feared than the Mau Mau. The time had come to consider making another amnesty offer.

The announcement of a renewed amnesty was complicated by indiscipline amongst the home guards, some of whom were implicated in counter-Mau Mau atrocities and paying off old scores which had nothing to do with the Mau Mau. It was feared that attempts to reorganize the home guards on a more regular basis would lead to mass desertions with arms to the forest gangs. The Kenya War Council deemed it sensible to announce an amnesty for home guard crimes and their reorganization in the same policy statement which renewed the amnesty offer to the terrorists. This was made on 1 January 1955. The subsequent home guard reorganization was carried through without undue difficulty. The most reliable men were enrolled in the tribal police and the rest were turned into a 'Watch and Ward' for the local defence of villages. The terrorist amnesty on the other hand, had little identifiable effect on the gangs, but it infuriated the settlers.

As soon as 'Anvil' was over Erskine concentrated his efforts upon securing the reserves and settled areas, and upon setting up the infra-structure for the major offensive against the forest gangs which he had decided to make the main feature of the 1955 campaign. A line of police posts was established along the forest edge and the prohibited zones were extended to include a mile-wide cleared no-man's land around the forests to make food-running and contact with the gangs more difficult for the passive wing. In many sectors a wide ditch was dug and filled with sharpened bamboo stakes to block routes to and from the forests. The 39th Engineer Regiment and the Public Works Department pressed on with building access tracks into the forests.

It was during this period that Captain Frank Kitson (now General Sir Frank Kitson) developed his idea of using pseudo-gangs to contact and trap the real gangs. He was one of the military Intelligence officers sent out to Kenya to help Special Branch with the acquisition of tactical military

Intelligence. Using Swahili speaking NCOs of the Kenya Regiment and 'turned' terrorists, he proved it practicable, though highly dangerous, to form and operate such gangs successfully. As most pseudo-gang operations were by night it was possible to disguise the European leaders sufficiently well to deceive the genuine Mau Mau, provided the talking was left to the 'turned' terrorists. Kitson won Erskine's support and the techniques, which he developed, became battle-winners in the later stages of the emergency when the main gangs had splintered and become weaker but more difficult to find.

The year 1954 also saw the RAF helping to keep the pressure on the forest gangs while the Army's preparations were going ahead. Using various photographic techniques to identify camps in the forests and radar to give bombing accuracy in all weathers, the RAF flew 1,118 Lincoln and 3,376 Harvard offensive sorties. How much damage was done to the gangs and how great was the psychological effect on them is uncertain. Kenya's wild-life certainly suffered the most. More definable benefits accrued from the RAF's Valletta transport aircraft and the Kenya Police Reserves' light aircraft in providing air supply, reconnaissance and communication sorties.

Erskine's major operations against the forest gangs started at the turn of the year. Their timing was dictated by the completion of the forest tracks in December and by the onset of the rains in April. He decided to tackle the Aberdares first and then Mt Kenya. The general tactical concept was to push patrols through to the moorland summits and to work downwards to a line of stops on the lower edge of the forest, manned by police and home guards with some military backing. RAF and the East Africa Anti-aircraft battery, using 3.7 inch AA guns with their long range, harassed areas not under pressure from the Army. Erskine appreciated that he had too few troops to eliminate the gangs entirely so he set three objectives for the operations: to bring home to the Mau Mau that the forests were no longer a secure haven: to break up the larger gangs, making it easier for the weaker members of them to desert; and to continue the build up of Intelligence. It was thought that there were still about 1,700 men in the Aberdares and about 1,000 on Mt Kenya.

The Aberdare operations lasted until mid-February with a final elimination figure of 161 terrorists killed, captured or surrendered. The Mt Kenya operation followed immediately and, by its end on 7 April 1955, a further 277 terrorists had been eliminated. Statistically the monthly elimination rate outside the forests was equally encouraging: 39 in 1953, 49 in 1954 and 66 in the early months of 1955. The number of Mau Mau incidents also showed a corresponding decline. Erskine judged that he could risk withdrawing troops from the Fort Hall and Thika districts to increase pressure on the active gangs. The back of the rebellion had, in fact, been broken.

Erskine left Kenya in May 1955. In his final report he summed up what had been achieved during his time as Director of Operations and what was yet to be done:

Mau Mau has been halted and driven back on its heels. Many of the leaders had been killed, captured or surrendered. The rank and file are now of poorer quality, much reduced in numbers and mostly concerned with personal survival. The tribal areas were well administered, the Police and Tribal Police efficiently organised and led. The Army is experienced at operating in some of the most difficult country in the world. In many parts of the Colony the situation is not much different to what it was before the Emergency. In some, particularly Nairobi, it is better. Nevertheless, there are still some determined leaders in the field. Their objective is probably to keep the fighting going on as long as possible in the hope that they will outlast Government. It will take a long time to eliminate the last terrorists from the forests, but I am sure that this is within the capacity of the Security Forces and meanwhile a large part of the Colony will be able to return to peaceful development.[15]

Erskine was right in his final assessment. General Sir Gerald Lathbury, who succeeded him, was faced with the task of rounding up the scattered groups of hardened ruthless men intent upon survival. Some 50 gang leaders were still at large. But the Kikuyu people now knew who was winning, and so Intelligence was much easier to acquire and support for the government was more readily forthcoming. Only one more major forest operation was mounted. In July 1955 Operation 'Dante' took place at the southern end of the Aberdares. The results were meagre for the resources used. Thereafter, Lathbury relied on smaller Army and police operations aimed at specific gangs when information as to their whereabouts was good enough. The organization and training of pseudo-gangs were centralized under Super- intendent Henderson, who had captured 'China', and they became the terriers of the Mau Mau hunt. Sweeps of the forest and the reserves were left to the tribal police, often supported by lines of *simi*-wielding women, who cleared the undergrowth methodically around areas in which gangs were thought to have gone to ground. Those who were trapped were sometimes hacked to pieces by the women before they could be stopped.

The military campaign came to an end with the wounding and capture of the Mau Mau 'C-in-C' Dedan Kimathi, in October 1956. The withdrawal of British battalions on emergency tours had already begun in August 1956 and was completed in November. A small residual British garrison was retained as a reassurance for the settlers in the subsequent period of rapid political change, and as an assurance to the Africans that Whitehall's writ would run until independence within the Commonwealth became a reality. British troops did not intervene again in East African affairs until after Independence in December 1963 when three KAR battalions mutinied in quick succession in Tanganika, Kenya and Uganda. The unrest was quickly quelled and the last British troops withdrew in 1965.

The final statistics for the Kenyan Emergency were:

Mau Mau

Killed	10,527
Captured	2,633
Surrendered	2,714
	————
	15,874

Government and civilian population

Security forces killed

British Troops	12	(5 officers)
Police and KAR	578	(63 Europeans)

Civilians killed

European	32
Asian	26
Loyal Africans	1,817
	————
	2,465

Some 75,000 Mau Mau supporters were passed through the system of detention and rehabilitation camps, but it is doubtful whether the effort expended on retraining them produced any real change of heart. The military defeat of Mau Mau and the progressive constitutional advances made thereafter were decisive in giving Kenya renewed peace and prosperity. The realization that emancipation was more likely to be achieved by non-violent means turned the energies of the African political parties towards the internal electoral struggle to become the inheritors of British power. The British Army had prevented the simi replacing the ballot box as the arbiter of Kenya's affairs.

Small and successful though the anti-Mau Mau campaign had been in military terms, it made an important impact on British political thought. It had taken 10,000 British and African troops, 21,000 police, 25,000 home guards and four years to defeat one determined, but not particularly warlike African tribe, which had no external political sponsor or arms supplier. It confirmed that Britain could only rule in Africa, as elsewhere, by consent and that consent depended upon the credibility of her policy of leading her dependent peoples initially to internal self-government and ultimately to complete independence. The Mau Mau rebellion also showed that the time scale for the process was likely to be much shorter than most British politicians had previously envisaged: it would not be possible to create another Australia or New Zealand anywhere in Africa.

We left the Malayan emergency at the end of 1951, with public confidence in the government's ability to master the Communist threat at a low ebb. Three of the four principal officers had gone: Gurney, Briggs and

Jenkin, and no replacements had been appointed. Gray was still Commissioner of Police, but police morale was low and public confidence in them even lower. Malay antipathy towards the Chinese was not easing and there was no sign of the Chinese population sliding off the fence onto the government side. Worst of all, the average monthly civilian and military casualty rates were not dropping.

On the Communist side things were no better. The new directive, changing emphasis to political activity and military survival, was just reaching the lower levels of the Party. Losses were higher than ever (942 in 1950, 1,401 in 1951) and were now outstripping the Party's ability to find suitable new recruits. Stalemate stared both sides in the face. The only winner was the Malayan climate, which sapped the energies of the Europeans in the government service and the health of the CTs in the jungle.

Oliver Lyttelton carried out an exhaustive and exhausting three week familiarization tour of Malaya in November 1951 with instructions from Churchill to revitalize the political and military campaigns. He was appalled by what he found. In his view the malaise stemmed from constitutional and administrative muddle, lack of clarity in the division of responsibility, and the enervating effects of the climate on government officers. In his public statements he rejected the slogan 'Malaya for the Malays' and insisted that Britain wanted to hand over to a united Malayan nation. The road to self-government was being blocked, he said by the Communist rebellion, which could only be defeated by the joint efforts of all races, especially the Malays and Chinese. A Malay/Chinese coalition could open the way to constitutional advance. In his report to the British Cabinet he put his finger on the three key appointments of High Commissioner, Director of Operations and the Commissioner of Police. He recommended that one man should combine the first two to end the split personality of the Federation government, and the third should be given to a man who could rebuild the public's confidence in the police and the police in themselves.

Finding one man to replace Gurney and Briggs was not easy; nor was the selection of a successor for Gray, whose resignation Lyttelton obtained. General Sir Gerald Templer was not the first choice for the job of 'Supremo'. There were several successful wartime commanders, who had shown political acumen in the immediate post-war period of military governments. Field Marshal Sir William Slim and General Sir Brian Robertson were both approached. Templer, though unknown outside the Army, had been Director of the British military government in Germany and had sacked Doctor Conrad Adenauer, the *Burgomeister* of Cologne and later West German Chancellor, for idleness and inefficiency! In 1946 he had become Director of Military Intelligence at the War Office, then Vice-Chief of Imperial General Staff and he was C-in-C Eastern Command when he was summoned to meet Churchill, who was in Ottawa at the time, to receive very comprehensive riding instructions. He was to have two immediate subordinates to help him straddle the political and military horses: Donald MacGillivary was brought from the West Indies to become his Deputy Governor and General Sir Robert Lockhart became Deputy Director of Operations.

Templer reached Kuala Lumpur in February 1952. His appointment filled many politicians and officials with misgivings. Malcolm Macdonald, for one, made it known that he did not welcome a General in the political appointment of High Commissioner. The local press feared a military dictatorship. Parallels drawn between Templer and De Latre de Tassigny in Indo-China were hardly flattering. The Army, knowing his irascible style, had its doubts too.

Templer himself was always the first to acknowledge how much he owed to his predecessors. His greatest contribution to winning the Malayan campaign was the way in which he energized the government, the security forces and Malayan peoples in putting Gurney's and Briggs' policies into effect and driving them to their successful conclusions. While this is certainly true, he also made a large number of original contributions of his own that brought victory nearer.

First, and perhaps most important of all, he broke the prevailing idea that somehow government administration and prosecution of the war were two entirely separate things. In his view, the emergency affected every aspect of the peoples' lives and it just could not be dealt with by different people, working to different priorities and at differing levels of urgency. One of his first acts was to amalgamate the war council with the executive council to bring the two sides of the government's brain together within one skull. This had the additional advantages of widening the base of advice tendered to him, and of involving a larger cross-section of Malaya's political leaders in the struggle against the Communists.

Lyttelton had articulated the British requirement to hand over to a Malayan rather than a Malay successor: it was Templer who made it practicable to do so. Only three months after he arrived he grasped the nettle of Malayan nationality and successfully argued an amendment to the Federation Agreement through the legislative council, which would confer citizenship upon considerable numbers of Malayan-born Chinese He followed this remarkable achievement by pushing the Village Council Bill, which enfranchised some 400,000 Chinese already in the resettlement villages. Elected village councils would administer their villages, collect their own rates and taxes, employ their own staff and be responsible for the village budget and education. The Bill brought criticism from the Malay members of the council that more was being done for the New Villages, as they were now called, than for the existing Malay *Kampongs*. There was a lot of truth in this as there was in the Malay view that they were being cajoled into sharing Malaya with other races.

By the time these bills were passed at the end of May Sir Gerald had visited every State and town of any importance. He was accompanied by Lady Templer on most of his non-military trips so that she could mirror his work amongst the Malay, Chinese and Indian women's associations and clubs. They both paid particular attention to education, encouraging an emphasis upon the creation of a Malayan nation with a pride in its own way of life and its own social ethics instead of clinging to the dogmas of China and India.

The same theme lay behind his creation of the Federation army, based initially on the greatly expanded Malay Regiment, which was exclusively Malay. He formed the multi-racial Federation Regiment and all races were recruited to form the technical arms and services of the army. Its commanders, senior officers and warrant officers were initially British, but a process of Malayanization of the command and staff structure was put in hand from the very start of the army's formation.

Sir Gerald and Lady Templer would have been blowing in the wind had it not been for a perceptible swing in public opinion away from the racial prejudices of the past, brought about by the experiences of the first four years of the emergency. This political trend, and that is all that it was in 1952, was reflected in the Kuala Lumpur municipal elections that took place as the Templers were arriving. The principal Malay political leader, Dato Onn, had resigned the leadership of the dominant United Malay National Organization (UMNO) to form the Independence for Malaya Party (IMP). Tunku Abdul Rahman succeeded him as the leader of UMNO and formed an *ad hoc* alliance with the Malayan Chinese Association (MCA), which Gurney had done so much to foster. The motive behind the coalition was narrowly tactical: the defeat of Dato Onn. At the election the Tunku won nine out of the 11 elected council seats. Realizing that they had struck a political chord of some significance the two parties accepted formal linkage and were joined a year later by the Indian National Congress to form the Alliance Party under the Tunku's leadership, which was to carry Malaya to independence and to form its government for the first 15 years of its statehood.

In the military field Templer also built on the foundations laid by his predecessors and upon the ever-widening experience gained by the Army and police in fighting the CTs. His own contributions were no less significant than in the political field. His whirlwind tours and acid, though constructive, comments galvanized all ranks. He visited every major unit and headquarters and, like all good commanders, sensed where and when his presence was needed most. There was, at first, very little change of tactics. Food denial was tightened and new village defences were strengthened progressively as experience was gained and resources became available. Having been Vice-Chief of General Staff he was able to extract more and better weapons, radio equipment, armoured vehicles and, above all, helicopters out of Whitehall.

Templer was initially shocked by the SWEC and DWEC system of committees, which seemed to him to be the antithesis of a decisive command. He quickly realized that it was the easiest way of getting the best out of the complex political environment in which the Malay state governments jealously guarded their entrenched rights. It also helped his policy of involving the widest possible cross-section of politicians and officials in the emergency. He tightened the command system by forming a joint emergency planning staff, comprising officers of the Malayan civil service, the police and the Army; by co-locating the policy staffs of the security forces in a joint headquarters in Kuala Lumpur; and by concentrating all the Intelligence agencies under a Director of Intelligence with a central Intelligence staff to assess, at the highest level, the information collected by Special Branch and other agencies.

Major operations involving brigade-sized formations continued during Templer's time as Director of Operations with the aim of bringing unrelenting pressure to bear on the CTs and to keep them moving. With greater experience, better training and improving intelligence they became more closely related to the framework operations. The RAF played its full part in harassing the CTs and giving the Army and police greater mobility. The value of RAF bombing and Army shelling of the jungle remained controversial. The clandestine introduction of homing devices into CT radios, repaired by 'turned' Min Yuen, produced spectacular kills on the few occasions it and similar ruses were carried out successfully. The impact of most of the bombing and shelling could never be properly assessed. The same could not be said of the growing use of the helicopter, which gave the jungle battlefield a genuine third dimension. By 1953 the first helicopter wing was formed with one RAF squadron of the small S51s and an RN squadron of the larger S55s. The latter lifted some 14,000 troops during the year, which marked the beginning of the helicopter era for the Army. Patrols could penetrate the jungle deeper, quicker and for longer with helicopter support, and reinforcements could be flown in and casualties evacuated when necessary. A whole new field of military technology began to open up in exploiting the use of these machines in the jungle, including new techniques for clearing landing pads and guiding the pilots onto them.

The Order of Battle during Templer's time remained as it had been since 1950, fluctuating around 24 to 26 infantry battalions and two armoured car regiments, but it had become a Commonwealth force with the arrival of the King's African Rifle battalions, a Fijian battalion and later, after his time, of Australians and New Zealanders. The 22nd SAS came back into existence for work amongst the aborigine tribes in the deepest jungle and a sixth battalion was raised for the Malay Regiment. The heaviest concentration of troops was in the south, commanded by the reformed 17th Gurkha Division at Seremban with four brigades: the 26th and 99th in Johore, the 48th in Pahang and the 63rd in Negri Sembilan. The 18th British Brigade remained independent in the centre of Malaya covering parts of Selangor, Pahang and Perak. The North Malaya District at Ipoh acted as a divisional headquarters for the six Malay, one Gurkha and two East African battalions covering the north. Most of the 24 or so battalions were responsible for sectors of the military framework and were only moved away temporarily for specific major operations.

Templer placed his emphasis on a trio of principles which formed an interdependent triangle. He sought to restore the public's confidence in the police; to develop the information services to give the public greater confidence in the government's will to win and conversely to sap the morale of the CTs; and to gear operations to the flow of Intelligence generated by public confidence. When asked in June 1952 whether he had sufficient powers and resources he gave his well-known reply at the head of this chapter. It was winning the hearts and minds of the people that mattered and not more power and resources. The words 'hearts and minds' had originated with Mao Tse Tung: Templer made it his maxim and its appropriateness turned it into the touch-stone of British military thinking for the rest of the withdrawal from Empire.

The reorganization of the police was carried through by Gray's successor, Colonel Arthur Young, the Commissioner of Police in the City of London, who was seconded to Malaya for one year. The Malayan police by force of circumstances had become a para-military organization. Young's genius lay, as Malaya's official historian puts it:

in presenting the image of the ideal London Bobby, and in transforming that ideal into a Malayan reality.[15]

The seven-fold expansion of the police in four years had so diluted the original trained cadre that the principles of service to and within the community had been submerged by needs of counter-terrorist operations. Young's aim, wholly supported by Templer, was to recreate a police service out of the force which it had become. There were enough troops to carry on the jungle war: the police began to concentrate upon winning the respect and co-operation of all communities through their efficiency, tolerance and understanding at local level. A clear distinction was made between the regular police and the various auxiliary bodies: the former was a fully-trained service with obligations to the public; the latter were armed guards enlisted primarily to protect the public and vulnerable installations during the emergency.

Nowhere was Templer's energy, colourful language, and obvious genuineness of purpose to have a greater impact than upon Hugh Carlton Green's Emergency Information Service. It had three distinct purposes: to raise the confidence of the public; to attack the morale of the CTs and the Min Yuen; and to create an awareness of the values of a democratic life in the Malayan nation which was threatened by international Communism. Templer's activities provided the Service with much of its straight news. Most of its operational successes came from the work of its psychological warfare section, beaming both 'white' and 'black' propaganda at the Communists and their supporters. A high proportion of the output was the work of a brilliant Chinese information officer, C. C. Too, who was head of the section and made the fullest possible use of surrendered terrorists to impress on their erstwhile colleagues, still in the jungle, of the futility of the struggle.

Growing public confidence and its corollary, better Intelligence, led to the development in Templer's time of the concept of the Federal Priority Operation that was to be used with decisive effect by his successors and became standard practice. It was first used in its crudest form in Operation 'Hive' by Brigadier Sir Mark Henniker in the latter half of 1952 to destroy the terrorist organization in the Seremban District of Negri Sembilan. The first step in a Federal Priority Operation was the selection by the central Intelligence staff of the next Communist district to be attacked. The choice was governed by the degree of penetration of the Communist organization achieved by Special Branch and the likelihood of success leading to the undermining of neighbouring Communist districts so that a snowball effect could be achieved.

The Federal Priority Operation itself had three phases. *Phase 1*, which might last for up to four months, was a systematic survey by Special Branch of the target district, during which an accurate Intelligence picture was built up of the character, strengths and weakness of all the personalities thought to have connections with the CTs or the Min Yuen; of the ways of life, interests and daily routine of the inhabitants; and of the topographical peculiarities of the area. From this survey a plan was made to tighten food denial and to sever the CTs from their main suppliers. Specific areas were then selected as killing zones in which the CTs would be encouraged to forage for food when their stocks began to dwindle.

Phase 2 began with the drafting in of additional troops, police and specialist food denial teams to impose the most rigorous controls on the civilian population, including in many cases communal cooking of rice because once cooked it would not keep. Simultaneously there would be a selective pick up of known Communist supporters and suppliers: selective because some were 'turned' by Special Branch into double agents. As the weeks of tight food control went by the weaker members of the CT gangs tended to surrender and many were 'turned'. More often than not *Phase 2* faded into *Phase 3*, the decisive killing stage, in which the hard-core terrorists were forced by hunger and security force pressure to forage in the killing zones where ambushes awaited them, or they were rooted out from their jungle hides by Army patrols often led by surrendered members from their own gangs.

Unlike the French operations in Indo-China and later the American war with the Viet Cong, there were no big battles. Eliminations by killing, capture or surrender were in ones and twos. Each minor success led the security forces nearer to the hard core in each district, and districts were crumpled one by one. It seemed surprising that so many dedicated Communists were willing, like the Mau Mau, to turn against their former colleagues. The elimination of the gang leaders was, however, the best insurance policy for the terrorist rank and file who deserted. Some of the rewards collected for treachery to the Communist cause were very large indeed and ensured that the recipients could start new lives with some capital to help them open businesses. Few suffered from local reprisals; most became accepted Malayan citizens.

The rigours of food control and the other restrictions on personal freedom legislated for in the emergency regulations became more and more irksome to the civilian population as terrorist incidents lessened and the need for them became less apparent. Templer decided to risk lifting restrictions selectively. In the autumn of 1953 he started to declare areas 'white' where the central Intelligence staff were satisfied that the Communist hard core had been eliminated. In these areas most restrictions were relaxed and the civilian population could return to their normal way of life. The threat of re-imposition of restrictions acted as an incentive to keep an area 'white', and the chance of achieving 'white' status was a carrot that drew the information from the inhabitants of areas which were still 'black'. The system was an undoubted success.

One of the effects of the growing pressure exerted by the security forces was the withdrawal of many of the gangs deeper into the inaccessible jungles on the eastern side of Malaya's mountain spine. There they depended largely upon the aborigine tribes for food. Early attempts to grapple with this problem by re-settling the aborigines under government supervision were a failure: many of those moved into camps just died from the psychological effect of leaving their nomadic way of life and their jungle fastnesses. The 22nd SAS was tasked to help the Aborigine Department and the police to bring the government to the tribes rather than vice versa. This was done by establishing some ten jungle forts in the remotest areas to which the aborigines could come for supplies and medical help instead of depending upon and thus supporting the CT gangs. The forts were maintained by helicopter initially and later by light aircraft as soon as landing strips could be cleared.

The same policy but a different method of bringing the government to the people was used in the Thai border areas of Kedah. Roads were driven forward through the jungle by Royal, Malayan and Gurkha Engineers which drew people to settle along them as had happened in the development of most British colonial territories.

Templer seized and held the initiative as Director of Operations: as High Commissioner he forced the political pace. Since his initial speech to the Legislative Council in March 1952, when he reiterated HMG's intention that Malaya should become a fully responsible self-governing and Malayan nation, he had accelerated the constitutional reform process without much help but little obstruction either from the political leaders. A national convention of state *Mentri Besars* (Chief Executives) was set to work framing the future constitution; an official committee looked at electoral procedures and another planned the Malayanization of the public services; and Templer handed over the chair of the Legislative Council to a Malayan Speaker. Tunku Abdul Rahman caught the tide of opinion running in Whitehall and, indeed, in Malaya. His demand for immediate internal self-government with election to 60 per cent of the Legislative Council seats was well timed and met no British opposition. Templer was able to announce three months before he left Malaya that HMG had agreed to 52 of the 98 seats being elective. When the elections took place a year later, in July 1955, the Tunku's Alliance Party swept to victory, winning 51 of the 52 seats. Malaya was on its way to independence within the Commonwealth as a multi-racial state far earlier and with much less acrimony than would have been the case had it not been for Templer's energy and political acumen.

Templer left Malaya in July 1954 as the effects of the climate and his killing, self-imposed personal regime began to take toll of his health. During his two and a half years in the Federation, two thirds of the CTs had been eliminated; the incident rate had fallen from 500 to less than 100 per month; and the average monthly civilian and military casualty rate from 200 to less than 40. Chin Peng had withdrawn his Politbureau to the safety of southern Thailand, leaving a satellite, Southern Bureau, under Hor Lung, in Johore to continue the fight in South Malaya. The Templers had carried Malaya over the broad crest of the Emergency where it had been stalled when they arrived. By the time they left the governments' political and military success were gathering momentum and defeat was staring the Communists in the face.

No attempt was made to find a successor to Templer as 'Supremo'. There was no need to run any further risk of creating a military dictatorship or a police state as some critics accused Templer of doing. Donald MacGillivary moved up to take over as High Commissioner. General Sir Geoffrey Bourne came out from England as Director of Operations, and was succeeded in due course by a succession of eminent generals: Sir Roger Bower, Sir James Cassels, Frank Brooke and Sir Rodney Moore.

In 1955 world events began to impact on the Malayan scene. Despite the Communist victory over the French in Indo-China (Bien Dien Phu fell in May 1952) and their success in imposing a stalemate in Korea, the 'Armed Struggle' was losing popularity in Peking. Chou En-Lai, the Chinese Prime Minister, took a surprisingly conciliatory line at the Afro-Asian Conference at Bandung in April that year. Chin Peng's Malayan Politbureau appreciated that the time had come to re-enter the political arena to lay the foundations for a Communist take-over after the Federation had been granted independence. The Tunku had made these thoughts credible by proposing a new amnesty in his election manifesto. A Communist peace offensive was launched on 1 May 1955 in an attempt to identify the Party with the cause of Malayan idependence. This led, tortuously, to a meeting between the Tunku and Chin Peng at Baling on the Thai border in December 1955.

The talks lasted for eight hours spread over two days. Chin Peng sought recognition for the Malayan Communist Party in the future independent Malayan State. The Tunku insisted that recognition could only be given to those who were genuinely loyal to the freely-elected government of Malaya and to Malaya as their permanent home: membership of the Communist Party with its external links to Moscow and Peking was inconsistent with that loyalty. No compromise was possible and Chin Peng went back to the jungle to await for another political opportunity.

During the Baling period from September to the end of December 1955 the pressure of military operations was reduced to avoid jeopardizing the talks. Once they were out of the way the four year mopping-up phase of the campaign began. Briggs had tried to roll up the gangs from south to north, but the Communist roots in Johore had proved too deep. Templer's methodical framework operations had shown greatest success in central Malaya. Bourne decided to exploit this by building up a band of 'white' areas across the Peninsula from which he could crumble the Communist districts northwards and southwards. His policy had the added advantage of severing Communist communications between Chin Peng over the Thai border and Hor Lung in Johore.

When Sir Roger Bower took over in May 1956 the 'white' band had been established and he was able to start the crumbling process with Federal priority operations designed to root out the Communist infra-structure and gangs in their strongest areas in Johore and Perak. Six major operations were mounted in succession (three in each direction), the first phases of each taking an average of six months before the decisive third phase was reached.

In the southern thrust the Segamat District was tackled in July 1956, Yong Peng/Labis in January 1957, and Kulai/Pontian, close to Singapore, in December 1957. In April 1958 Hor Lung surrendered and was 'turned'. With his help most of the hard core were rooted out or induced to surrender. The last 70 CTs in Johore were eliminated in 1959.

The Perak hard core was more difficult to crack because of their closer links with Chin Peng's base camps in Thailand. Southern Perak was cleared with the help of a Communist Regional Political Commissar who surrendered in October 1957. *Phase 2* of the last federal operation of the emergency, Operation 'Ginger', started in the middle of January 1958. Seven battalions were deployed and took 15 months to eliminate the last 170 CTs and Min Yuen from northern Perak. One hundred and twelve surrendered, 50 were killed and the rest escaped over the border. The end of the emergency was declared on 31 July 1960.

By then Malaya had been independent for almost three years during which British forces had been operating under the Anglo-Malayan Defence Agreement. The final casualty balance sheet was:

Communist Terrorists

Killed	6,711
Captured	1,289
Surrendered	2,704
	10,704

Government and civilian population
Security forces killed
Army	519
Police	1,336
Civilians	
Killed	2,473
Missing	810
	————
Total	5,138[16]

Two other interesting statistics were that, on average, it took 1,000 patrol hours to effect a capture and 1,600 for a kill.

Chin Peng stayed over the Thai border with about 700 men, always hoping that the tide would turn in his favour. It never did. The captured and surrendered terrorists were offered repatriation to China or resettlement. The majority opted for the latter and were re-absorbed into the community. Britain had successfully handed over a prosperous Malaya to a stable multi-racial government. The Malayan campaign was a classic in counter-insurgency operations of which the British services have every right to be proud. The key to success was Intelligence, which initially had to be fought for with apparently blind and blundering jungle sweeps. As the public gained confidence, the information began to flow and operations could be mounted with increasing precision. Resettlement in the new villages and food control were important steps, but, as Templer forecast, the battle was won in the hearts and minds of the Malayan people.

By the beginning of 1956, the Baling talks had shown that the Malayan campaign was already won though it took another five years to end the emergency. Malaya had given Britain no cause to question her policy of converting Empire to Commonwealth at a speed of her own choosing. Events in the Middle East that year were to suggest otherwise.

6 Failure in the Middle East

The Canal Zone, Cyprus and Suez: 1955–1957

The political constellation was not characterised by the old opposition of three (America, France and Britain) against one (Russia), but by a new formula ... the two biggest (America and Russia) against the two less big, and it is from that fact that the quashing of the Suez action occurred.

Mendez-France to the French National
Assembly on 18 December 1956[1]

By 1955 Britain's attempt to rebuild her post-war position in the world using the idiom of Commonwealth rather than Empire seemed to be succeeding. In the Far East, the Communist threat to Malaya had been defeated by harnessing Malayan nationalism. In Africa and the West Indies, the process of transition was moving faster than Britain would have wished or deemed sensible, but fighting had been confined to Kenya where the Mau Mau rebellion had been mastered by a combination of military action and constitutional progress. In Europe, the security of British Isles had been strengthened by the creation of NATO. Only in the Middle East was there the continuing failure that had started with the British withdrawal from Palestine under American and Jewish duress.

Successive post-war American administrations had tried to adopt a neutralist stance in Middle Eastern politics. With their hands full in the Pacific and Far East they were content to let Britain take the lead in the Middle East, acting themselves as 'honest brokers' in disputes as they arose. But neutralism did not last. Congressional pressures generated by the oil and Zionist lobbies and by Cold War considerations (including the effects of McCarthyism) led to growing involvements. By the mid-1950s the United States was playing a major, if 'stand-offish', role in the area.

The emergencies in Malaya and Kenya could be fairly called colonial wars. In the Middle East the struggle was essentially strategic, but was dubbed colonial by the Americans and the non-aligned states led by Nehru's India. The area had always been the gateway in the arch of British imperial pretentions. Through it ran her main sea and air communications and, latterly, it contained her main sources of cheap oil. She had fought successfully in the two world wars to control it. Few people in Britain doubted the need for Britain to provide the gate-keepers: where they should live was more controversial. Under the Anglo-Egyptian Treaty of 1936 they could only remain in the Suez Canal Zone until 1956 unless some new treaty could be negotiated. The majority view was that such a treaty was strategically essential to British and Western interests.

Two of Britain's political leaders took a different view: Hugh Dalton, Chancellor of the Exchequer, naturally wished to cut the cost of Britain's overseas commitments wherever there was doubt about their validity; and Clement Attlee was sceptical about the importance of the Middle East to Britain. In Attlee's view it was no use pretending that Britain could keep the Mediterranean open in general war; nor could she defend Turkey, Iraq and Persia against the Russian armies. With India and Pakistan independent there was little sense in spending vast sums on the defence of imperial lines of communication which were neither essential nor tenable. In war, the Cape route would have to be used to the Far East and Australasia. Establishing minimal bases south of the Sahara, in West Africa and Kenya, would make more strategic sense than continuing to maintain the large sprawling installations of the Suez Canal Zone amongst a potentially hostile population. In a paper to the Defence Committee in 1946 he went further:

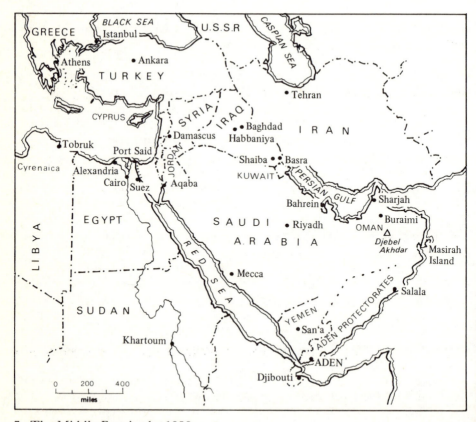

7. The Middle East in the 1950s.

We must not for sentimental reasons based on the past give hostages to fortune. It may be we shall have to consider the British Isles as an easterly extension of a strategic area the centre of which is the American continent rather than as a power looking eastwards through the Mediterranean to India and the East.[2]

Ernest Bevin, Foreign Secretary, did not agree with either Attlee or Dalton: nor did the Chiefs of Staff. In Bevin's view, the post-war decline in British power was only temporary. He was opposed to any withdrawal that would leave a political vacuum in the Middle East ready for Russia to fill. As late as August 1949, after his bitter experiences in handling the Palestine issues, he could still advise the Cabinet.

In peace and war, the Middle East is an area of cardinal importance to the U.K., second only to the U.K. itself. Strategically, the Middle East is a focal point of communications, a source of oil, a shield to Africa and the Indian Ocean, and an irreplaceable offensive base. Economically it is, owing to oil and cotton, essential to United Kingdom recovery.[3]

The Chiefs of Staff fully supported this view and added a further factor. British air bases in Iraq and Jordan were essential to the defence of the United Kingdom: they were the only airfields from which RAF deterrent counter-strikes could be launched to reach the Soviet heartland. The range from the British Isles was too great for the bombers of the 1950s.

Bevin and the Chiefs of Staff were not as one on method. Bevin believed:

The benefits of partnership between Great Britain and the countries of the Middle East have never reached the ordinary people, and so our foreign policy has rested on too narrow a footing, mainly on the personalities of kings, princes or pashas. There is thus no vested interest among the people to remain with us . . .[4]

In his view the existing treaties, which enabled Britain to impose on local people, were out of keeping with the post-war era and should be replaced by regional defence pacts with arrangements for joint defence boards and training teams to raise the standards of indigenous defence forces. He sought genuine partnerships embracing economic, technological and military co-operation.

The Chiefs of Staff did not oppose Bevin's ideas about partnership. It was clearly more sensible to harmonize rather than antagonize Arab nationalism. The idea of moving British bases south of the Sahara was quite another matter. The British Isles were nearer to the Suez Canal than, say, Lagos or Mombasa, and they also lacked the skilled labour needed for efficient bases. Furthermore, it was fanciful to suggest that money could be found in the Defence vote to reprovide new and expensive military facilities overseas. The services would have to do with what existed: the left-overs of the war in the Mediterranean. Bevin's concept of partnership might well enable them to do so if it could be successfully carried through. But, like enduring marriages, it takes two to make a viable political partnership. The alternatives to King Farouk and his pashas were the Arab nationalists of Nasser's clandestine 'Free Officers' movement or the Muslim

Brotherhood, both bent on the eviction of the British rather than partnership with them.

Bevin had perforce to deal with kings and pashas. In October 1946 he came near to success in drafting a new Anglo-Egyptian treaty whereby Britain would leave Egypt by September 1949 in exchange for an Anglo-Egyptian defence agreement. Farouk's ambition to become King of the Sudan as well as Egypt ruined his efforts. He had already announced publicly that the Sudan was to be given responsible internal self-government as a prelude to self-determination. He could not let the Sudanese down. Nevertheless, with agreement apparently so near, all British troops and RAF units were withdrawn from Cairo and Alexandria into the Canal Zone to demonstrate Britain's good faith. The evacuation was completed in March 1947 with GHQ and Air HQ Middle East moving into makeshift accommodation at Fayid on the shores of the Great Bitter Lake.

Two significant events led to Bevin's Conservative successor having to deal with Nasser rather than Farouk's corrupt regime. The humiliating defeat in 1949 of the Arab League armies, which had tried to over-run the new state of Israel, gave Nasser and his colleagues the spur to revolution. The overthrow of Farouk was added to their aim of evicting the British. Two years later Doctor Mossadeq's successful nationalization of the Anglo-Iranian Oil Company made the unthinkable thinkable to a wider circle outside the 'Free Officers' movement. If the Iranians could tweak the British lion's tail, why not the Egyptians? Not to be outdone in nationalist fervour, King Farouk's government abrogated the Anglo-Egyptian Treaty of 1936 and laid economic siege to the British held Canal Zone, triggering the series of events which led to his own downfall.

General Sir George Erskine, who, as we saw in the last chapter, was later Director of Operations against the Mau Mau in Kenya, was GOC British Troops, Egypt in 1951. There were only two infantry brigades and an artillery group in the Zone when Egyptain 'non-cooperation' started. These were quickly reinforced by two more brigades from Britain, and civilian labour and pioneer units were brought in from Cyprus and Mauritius to replace the Egyptians who had been coerced into leaving British employment. Erskin had two trump cards: the ability to cut off the Egyptian army in the Sinai, facing Israel, and to close the oil pipeline from Suez to Cairo, upon which the life of the city depended. Neither was used because the Egyptians held the ace of trumps: they could stop the flow of fresh water from the Nile into the Sweet Water Canal needed by the towns and garrison of the Canal Zone. The crisis came in a different way.

Constant attacks on British targets by Egyptian snipers and terrorists, who were under covert control of the Egyptian police, led Erskine to take a number of reprisals, including bull-dozing flat a village notorious for these attacks. At the end of January 1952 he decided to disarm the Egyptian police in the Canal Zone. On Cairo's instructions the police fought back. Tanks had to be used to quell resistance in one police barracks where the

Lancashire Fusiliers lost five men killed and nine wounded storming the building. The Egyptians lost 50 and over 100 were wounded. The popular reaction in Cairo was horrific. The Cairo mob, swollen by unemployed from the Canal Zone, surged through the city, looting in the wake of organized gangs, who set fire to British commercial buildings and institutions. Venerated establishments like the Turf Club and Shepheard's Hotel went up in flames. A great pall of smoke brought premature darkness to the city. The date 26 January 1952 earned its name 'Black Saturday'.

Anthony Eden, then Foreign Secretary, authorized Erskine to march on Cairo if the British community was in danger. The 1st Division and 16th Parachute Brigade stood to, ready to advance, but no call came from the British Embassy. The residential areas had not been attacked. It was the Egyptian and not the British Army that quelled the disturbances that night. King Farouk, like Nero, fiddled while Cairo burnt, celebrating the birth of a son. From the embers of the Cairo riots came Nasser's determination to rid Egypt of Farouk and his pashas as soon as possible. The military coup, staged by his 'Free Officers' in July 1952, brought Eden face to face with Arab nationalism.

No tears were shed in London or Washington for Farouk. On the contrary, there was some optimism that Egypt could be brought more easily into the Western camp as the 'Free Officers' were known to be ardently anti-Communist. Their twin aims of ending imperialism and feudalism in Egypt should not be too difficult to accommodate. The door was ajar for the departure of British troops from Egyptian soil and could be fully opened if the new regime was prepared to join in the collective defence of the Middle East against Soviet penetration and would accept self-determination for the Sudanese. Ending feudalism was an internal matter, in which Britain and the United States would not wish to interfere, though both applauded the concept and were prepared to offer generous economic aid to help the Egyptians solve the pressing problems of their exploding birthrate and the miserable standard of living of the Egyptian peasantry.

Nasser cleared the Sudanese problem out of the way by persuading the Revolutionary Command Council, headed by General Neguib, that getting rid of British troops was more important than opposing Sudanese self-determination. By supporting pro-Egyptian elements in the Sudan it should not be difficult to engineer a vote in favour of Egypt: evicting the British troops from Egypt would not be so easy.

Anglo-Egyptian negotiations were resumed in April 1953 with Nasser leading the Egyptian delegation. Agreement seemed near at times but two obstacles stood in the way. Churchill insisted that the British technicians, who were to maintain the Canal Zone base after British troops had left, must wear uniform: Nasser held that this would be an affront to the dignity of a free Egypt. The analogy of US servicemen wearing uniform at American bases in Britain cut no ice: Britain, the Egyptians claimed with some justification, was not having to prove her independence.

The second unresolved difficulty was agreement on conditions for reactivating the base in time of war. The Egyptians were prepared to accept attacks on other Arab states as justifiable triggers, but not attacks on Turkey and Iran, the 'northern tier' states, which Britain and the United States were keen to incorporate in the future Baghdad Pact to extend NATO's southern flank eastwards from the Bosphorus to the Himalayas. The new Egyptian leaders were determined to avoid involvement in the Cold War. The real enemy, in their eyes, was Israel and not the Soviet Union. Negotiations broke down in October 1953 because Britain was not prepared to evacuate the Canal Zone without adequate arrangements being made for the protection of the Canal itself, and for the strategic defence of the Middle East as a whole. The Egyptians resumed their blockade of the Canal Zone, making the life of the large British garrison and its families as uncomfortable as possible.

In theory British and American policies in the Middle East were convergent. Both governments were intent on preventing Soviet penetration to the Persian Gulf and to the Suez Canal; both believed that this could best be achieved by partnership with the Arab states; and both appreciated that the Israelis must not be allowed to upset that partnership. In practice their policies diverged. Britain had close treaty relations, including defence commitments, with the Hashemite Kingdoms of Iraq and Jordan, which she had helped to create after the First World War, and with the Gulf States. The RAF had major air bases at Amman in Jordan and at Habbanyia in Iraq as well as in Egypt, and smaller ones in most of the Gulf States: indeed, the RAF was responsible for providing the British military presence in the Middle East outside Egypt. America's major oil interests in Saudi Arabia and the US military air base at Dharan brought her closest to the Saudis and their allies, the Egyptians. In Middle East politics Baghdad and Cairo were rivals for the leadership of the Arab world. Britain naturally backed the Anglophile, Nuri es-Said, Prime Minister of Iraq, against the Anglophobic ambitions of Nasser. The Egyptians, for their part, tended to court the Americans who, in their turn, advised and helped them covertly in their struggle with the British. Two successive US ambassadors in Cairo, Jefferson Caffrey (1949–1953), an Irish American, and Henry Byroade (1953–6) served American national interests well, but were, by personal inclination, anti-British and anti-colonial. They were both confidants of Nasser and were distrusted by their British diplomatic colleagues in Cairo. Eden records his personal antipathy to both men in his memoirs.

These tactical differences of approach tore two significant rifts in the fabric of Anglo-American Middle East co-operation at strategic level. The Americans did not support the British view that they could not leave the Canal Zone until adequate arrangements for safe-guarding the Suez area had been enshrined in a new Anglo-Egyptian treaty. They believed that only a British withdrawal without strings would bring Egypt wholeheartedly into the Western camp. They, the Americans, had strong enough economic and military levers to influence Egyptian policy once the irritant of the British presence on Egyptian soil was removed. The British could not agree and were proved right by events all too soon.

The second rift occurred in the Anglo-American attempt to extend NATO's eastern flank through the 'northern tier' states. Britain led the negotiations with the founder members of the Baghdad Pact—Turkey, Iran, Iraq and Pakistan—with full American support. The Pact was signed in Baghdad in February 1955 and immediately aroused great hostility in Cairo where it was seen both as a British device to maintain control of the Middle East and as a step towards Iraq assuming the leadership of the Arab world. In Nasser's view, the only political organization that Arab states should join was the Arab League with its headquarters in Cairo, its bankers in the oil-rich Saudi capital of Riyadh, and its target: Israel. The vehemence of Egyptian and Saudi opposition to the Pact and its possible extension southwards to embrace Jordan and then themselves, was such that the Americans pulled back and found every excuse to delay joining it. Britain was left holding the unpopular brain child of John Foster Dulles, the US Secretary of State, whose policy was to encircle the Soviet Union with a belt of collective security organizations.

A year earlier in the first half of 1954 pressure had built up in Cairo, London and Washington for a resumption of Anglo-Egyptian negotiations. In Cairo, the internal struggle for power within the Revolutionary Command Council was reaching its climax. Nasser unseated General Neguib and became the dictator of Egypt in February. He needed a startling success to consolidate his power. In London, the politico-military debate on the implications of warfare in the nuclear era, which will be looked at more fully in the next chapter, was beginning to influence military thinking and strategy. The Chiefs of Staff advised the Cabinet that, while the Suez Canal had not lost any of its strategic importance, the military base in the Canal Zone was a declining asset. Smaller, more widely dispersed bases, established well away from the major nuclear targets like the Canal, would make more sense. Moreover, the sprawling complex of Canal Zone depots and workshops, which covered an area about half the size of Wales, with the roads and railways to serve them, were far larger than would be needed to sustain forces likely to be deployed in the Middle East in any future war. Its maintenance was not only a heavy burden on the defence budget, but the stocks held there and the machinery in the workshops were becoming obsolete and too costly to replace. They were not worth keeping for more than another decade: time which could be best used setting up less elaborate and cheaper alternatives elsewhere. Greece and Turkey were Britain's allies in NATO and could provide base facilities for defence of the 'northern tier'. GHQ, Middle East and HQ Middle East Air Forces should move to Cyprus where limited British advanced base facilities could also be established, provided improvements were made to the ports of Limasol and Famagusta which were, at that time, little more than lighter-served anchorages. A further factor considered by the Chiefs of Staff was the adverse effects that service in the Canal Zone was having on recruiting regular soldiers for the Army. Both political and military thinking was already turning towards the abolition of National Service which would only be practicable if enough regulars could be recruited.

In Washington, Cold War considerations were generating additional pressure on London and Cairo to end what the Eisenhower administration saw as 'a colonial situation' in Egypt. The continued impasse could only be to the advantage of the Soviets, giving them propaganda leverage and an opportunity to infiltrate the area with offers of political and military aid. There was undoubted force in the American arguments.

The British government, on Chiefs of Staff advice, authorized the future transfer of GHQ Middle East to Cyprus and voted the money for preliminary work to be carried out in the 1954 defence budget. Eden, in his memoirs, deplores the government's failure to fund the development of a deep water port as well. It would have been costly, but not as costly as lack of such a port in Cyprus was to prove during the Suez crisis of 1956.

The last round of Anglo-Egyptian negotiations started in July 1954. The British government was under American pressure to take risks in order to win Egyptian friendship; and the Egyptians were being encouraged to be reasonable by American promises of generous economic and military aid. The heads of agreement were signed before the end of the month. British troops would leave Egypt 20 months after the new agreement was signed; the base would be taken over and run by British civilian contractors for an initial period of seven years; the trigger for military reactivation of the base would be an attack on any Arab state and Turkey by an 'outside power' other than Israel. The agreement was gilded by Egypt extending over-flying rights and landing facilities to the RAF, and by an Egyptian re-affirmation of the 1888 Constantinople Convention, guaranteeing freedom of transit through the Suez Canal to all nations in peace time. It was tarnished by Egypt's refusal to join any Western-orientated defensive alliance to resist Soviet penetration of the Middle East, and by her continued embargo on Israel-bound ships and cargoes using the Canal. Egypt claimed that the Arab League was still at war with Israel.

The final agreement was signed on 19 October 1954. The handover of the base to the consortium of British contractors, employing 1,200 technicians, went quicker than expected. On 13 June 1956 the last British unit, 2nd Grenadier Guards, sailed quietly away from Port Said without ceremony, just 74 years after their forebears had taken part in the Tel-el-Kebir campaign, which brought Egypt under British protection in 1882. GHQ with its communications and Intelligence gathering systems was already established in Cyprus. The RAF were using Nicosia airfield and a new strategic airfield was nearing completion at Akrotiri near Limasol at the south-west corner of the island. In the House of Commons doubts were being expressed about the wisdom of moving from one unstable area to another. Both Greece and Turkey had long-standing claims to the island.

There was some irony in the British move to Cyprus from Egypt. The island had been acquired from the Ottoman Empire in 1878 as a British military base in the Levant, but it had not been developed because the Battle of Tel-el-Kebir gave Britain far better base facilities in Egypt. At that time the Greek and Turkish populations on the island were not too unequal. The Turks, as the sovereign power, provided the administration. The Greek Orthodox Church looked after both the religious and temporal needs of the Greek population, as had been the case during the Turkish period in Greece itself. The head of the Church was both archbishop and ethnarch or political leader of the Greeks. Greece's successful war of independence against Turkey in the 1820s and 1830s was mirrored in Cyprus where the ethnarchy espoused the concept of 'Greater Greece' and the return of all 'unredeemed' Greek communities to the mother country. The *Enosis* (re-union with Greece) Movement was well established in Cyprus by the mid-nineteenth century. The Greek attempt after the First World War to 'redeem' the Greek populations on the Turkish mainland and amongst the Turkish-held Aegean islands led to their disastrous war with Turkey of 1920–21 in which Greece was humiliated. Greek refugees fled from Smyrna and other cities in Anatolia to Cyprus where they were allowed to settle by the British authorities out of sympathy for Greece. By the end of the Second World War the Greek population of Cyprus, swollen to some extent by these refugees, had so far outstripped the Turks numerically that Enosis was no longer an emotional ideal: it had become the political platform of both the conservative ethnarchy and the Cyprus Communist Party. When, in 1946, the Attlee government offered the island a new constitution that provided a measure of responsible internal self-government, both the Greek Right and Left turned it down with the slogan 'No constitution without self-determination'. With the Greeks by then in a four to one majority over the Turks, self-determination meant transfer of sovereignty to Greece.

Between 1946 and 1954 agitation for Enosis gathered momentum in Cyprus and Greece. Preparation of barracks for British troops withdrawn from Palestine and rumours that Cyprus might take the place of the Canal Zone as the main British base in the Middle East pointed to an increase in Cyprus's strategic importance. The Greeks were not slow to realize that this could be used as a lever to persuade Britain to accept Enosis. With the implementation of the Truman doctrine Greece had become a client of the United States and so was less dependent upon Britain for economic aid and external security. It would be easier than it had been for some years for the Greek government to risk offending Britain. King Paul put the Greek case in a speech that he made in 1948:

Greece certainly desires and will continue to desire the union of Cyprus with the rest of Greece ... The argument that this might interfere with British security positions is not valid. Were Cyprus given to Greece, as the vast majority of its population desires, this would in no way interfere with any military or other bases

Britain has established there. Furthermore, if it could be arranged under the United Nations, Greece would be prepared to offer further base facilities to Britain and the United States in Crete or elsewhere . . .[5]

King Paul's words encapsulated the Greek government's case as it stood throughout the struggle for Enosis. The Turkish reaction was, at first, slow to generate and gave a false impression of probable acquiescence, provided the Turkish Cypriots were given acceptable constitutional safeguards.

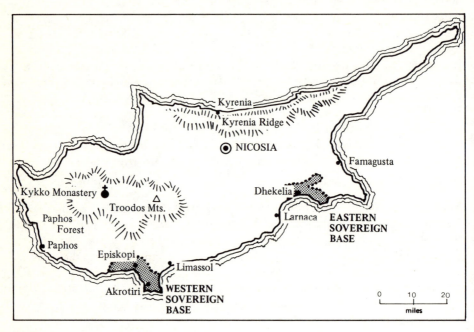

8. Cyprus, 1954–1960.

Two men fanned the glowing embers of Enosis into the EOKA[6] rebellion, which started on 1 April 1955; Archbishop and Ethnarch Makarios and Colonel George Grivas. Makarios was a firm anti-Communist and an even firmer advocate of Enosis. Grivas was Cypriot by birth, but had joined the Greek regular army before the Second World War. When Greece was overrun by the Germans in 1941, he formed the nucleus of the extreme right-wing terrorist organization 'X', dedicated to the elimination of Communists and to the concept of 'Greater Greece'. Soviet domination of the southern Balkans made success in 'redeeming' Greek communities in Bulgaria and Albania unlikely; Turkish hostility barred 'X's' efforts in Turkish Thrace, Anatolia and the Aegean Islands; but there was Cyprus. The British withdrawal from the Indian Subcontinent and the surrender of the Palestine Mandate suggested to Grivas that he might have some success in his own homeland.

The two men were opposites in everything except their determination to achieve Enosis. Makarios, clever and politically devious, believed he could win by using international political pressure and was, at first, sceptical about the terrorist methods advocated by Grivas, a military fanatic, who was looking for a cause. Makarios did not give Grivas much support in building up his EOKA terrorist organization until he found his political campaign for Enosis frustrated by the Greek government's failure to have the Cyprus issue inscribed on the United Nations' agenda for its 1954 session. Terrorism offered an alternative way of bringing Enosis to the attention of the world.

Grivas was under no illusions about the unsuitability of Cyprus for a successful guerrilla campaign. The island was too small; the remoter areas in the Paphos Forest, the Troodos Mountains and the Kyrenia ridge, which might offer some cover for guerrilla bases, could all be reached too easily by British security forces; and the people were, on the whole, too submissive and apathetic to provide the ruthless killers he would need. Makarios had once told him bluntly 'Not 50 men will be found to follow you'.

Makarios was not far wrong, but he under-estimated Grivas's immense energy, personal dedication and organizational skill. Grivas also had the essential ingredient for most successful rebellions: almost total support within the Greek Cypriot population for his cause, Enosis. Moreover, he had, with Makarios's eventual blessing, the help of the Greek Orthodox Church and its Ethnarchy Council to organize psychological and logistic support for his EOKA terrorists. His aim was not to defeat the British militarily. He deemed that to be impossible. He intended to add weight to Makarios's international political campaign by demonstrating the Greek Cypriot's determination to win Enosis and the British government's inability to quench their ardour. One of the principles beloved by the British was honouring the wishes of the people: his bombs and ambushes would show the world that they were not doing so in Cyprus.

Grivas visited Cyprus quite openly with a British visa in his passport in 1951 and 1952 to reconnoitre the island and to prepare his campaign. By 1954 British suspicions had been aroused and he was refused another visa. He returned to the island clandestinely after a rough sea voyage in a small caique, which sailed from Rhodes in November 1954. He was almost captured when a second caique, carrying arms and explosive, was intercepted. He had intended to supervise its unloading in a remote cove but, at the last moment, was by chance prevented from doing so. The rest of the reception party was arrested and provided the first hard evidence of the existence of EOKA. In setting up his organization, Grivas did not recruit widely because he envisaged only a short spring and summer campaign to create an impression before the next United Nations Assembly in the autumn of 1955. He set up five small gangs in the mountains, several sabotage groups in the main towns and supply groups in the villages. These were backed by a handful of execution squads, who were to kill Cypriots considered hostile to Enosis, and by several Intelligence centres established amongst Greek Cypriots in government service and amongst employees of the British military headquarters and the garrison. He supplemented his preparations by infiltrating the Greek schools and educational institutions. Many of the teachers were mainland Greeks and needed little persuasion to become active EOKA leaders of impressionable teenagers and even younger children.

In Greece, the succession of right-wing governments of the 1950s found themselves on the horns of a dilemma. Such was the popular support, which Makarios had managed to generate in Greece for Enosis, that no Greek political party could risk not paying at least lip-service to it; and yet for a Greek government to give it overt international support could jeopardize Greece's security by alienating her NATO allies, Britain and Turkey. Covert support was the most that Makarios and Grivas could expect initially and this was forthcoming after Anthony Eden snubbed Field Marshal Papagos, the Greek Prime Minister, over the Cyprus issue when the two men met during Eden's convalescent holiday in Greece in the autumn of 1954. By March 1955 Makarios considered that he had received enough encouragement from the Greek government to authorize Grivas to open his terrorist campaign on 1 April that year.

The British authorities were not caught unawares when, on All Fool's Day 1955, several bombs exploded in different parts of the island and leaflets appeared in the streets signed 'The Leader, Dighenis' (after a Byzantine warrior of the twelfth century). Political agitation for Enosis had so intensified during the winter of 1954–5 both in Cyprus and Greece that an outburst of some kind was anticipated, but, as Grivas's organization was still rudimentary and not seen as posing a major threat, there had been no strengthening of the Cyprus security forces. EOKA's first efforts were pathetic and mortifying to Grivas. Only one bomb, planted at the Cyprus broadcasting station, caused any serious damage: the rest were either thrown from too far away or failed to explode. Public reaction was tepid. There was a general revulsion against terrorism amongst Greek Cypriots and the usually strident Athens Radio came out in favour of passive resistance. Makarios judged Grivas's efforts to be politically counter-productive and ordered him to cease fire on the valid grounds that EOKA needed more time for training. Grivas did not agree and relations between the two men became strained and continued thereafter to be so throughout the EOKA campaigns. Nevertheless, there was a pause in violence while he tried to improve his organization. In its place he organized rowdyism by students and school children, which was orchestrated with the trials of the EOKA men captured when the first arms smuggling caique was intercepted. Dealing with rioting youths and children was to become the stock in trade of both the police and army as the campaigns developed and a difficult task it proved to be. Any over-reaction by the security forces provided instant EOKA propaganda material for the world press.

The Cyprus police were a mixed British, Greek and Turkish force with a small Special Branch of only 37 men whose attention had been focused hitherto upon the Communists rather than the Ethnarchy. When the EOKA rebellion started there were two British infantry battalions garrisoning Nicosia and Larnica, a Gunner regiment training near Famagusta, and an Engineer regiment working on the construction of the two new British base areas at Episkopi, near the RAF airfield at Akrotiri in the southwest, and Dhekelia in the southeast. GHQ Middle East was temporarily housed in Nicosia, waiting for its headquarters buildings to be completed at Episkopi. A small District HQ administered the Cyprus garrison.

Grivas could not have attacked at a worse time from his own point of view. Britain was not short of troops. The backs of the Malayan and Kenya emergencies had been broken and the withdrawal from Egypt had started. British units were still full of inexperienced National Servicemen, but the regular cadres had all taken part in plenty of internal security and counter-guerrilla operations. Consequently they started well up the learning curve when first called upon to support the police in dealing with EOKA inspired rioting and in tracking down Grivas's mountain gangs. Their two main problems were handling rioting school children with sufficient firmness to disperse them without ugly incidents, and 'needle in haystack' searches for terrorists hidden amongst the increasingly hostile Greek population.

Grivas opened the second phase of his campaign on 19 June 1955, aiming to demoralise the police. His mountain gangs started ambushing security force vehicles and attacking police stations. Again the results disappointed Grivas. A new element in the situation was created when a bomb at the Central Police Station in Nicosia killed a Greek bystander, but also injured 13 Turks. The anger of the Turkish community brought it squarely behind the British administration and added inter-communal bitterness to the corrosive brew already concocted by EOKA and the Ethnarchy. At the end of the month Grivas called his men off for a second time at the Archbishop's behest because there seemed to be political movement in London and Athens.

In London, Eden had replaced Churchill as Prime Minister and Harold Macmillan had succeeded him as Foreign Secretary. The new brooms started to sweep clean with firm political and military strokes. Macmillan concluded that the Cyprus problem was international rather than colonial. In his view the Greek Cypriots were fighting not for independence but for a change of yoke: Greek instead of British or Turkish. They could demonstrate their feelings on the island, but any decisions on change of sovereignty could be made only at international level in London, Athens and Ankara. On 30 June 1955, Eden invited the Greek and Turkish governments to a conference 'in London at an early date on political and defence questions which affect the Eastern Mediterranean, including Cyprus'.[7]

The Turkish government accepted straight away: the Greeks were hesitant. Makarios rushed to Athens to denounce the British invitation as a trap. He maintained that Cyprus was an issue between Britain and the people of Cyprus and no-one else. The Turks should not be allowed to interfere. The Greek government's dilemma was magnified by a visit by the Soviet leader, Marshal Bulganin, to Yugoslavia in May 1955. Retention of British friendship was clearly more important to Greece in the Cold War than supporting Greek Cypriot ambitions. On the other hand, Field Marshal Papagos was ailing. With an election in the offing no Greek political party could be seen to be softening on Enosis. After much diplomatic effort the conference was fixed for August, but the Greek government then accused the British of engineering the delay to forestall the autumn session of the United Nations.

In the interval before the conference could begin, the Colonial Secretary, Lennox Boyd, and the CIGS, General Sir John Harding, visited the island and put in hand measures to strengthen the security forces. A state of emergency was not declared to avoid jeopardizing the Tripartite Conference or to make it any easier for the Greek government to have Cyprus inscribed on the agenda of the autumn meeting of the United Nations. The headquarters of 50th and 51st Brigades and two infantry battalions arrived from the Canal Zone. The two brigades took over control of Nicosia and Famagusta respectively, and 3rd Commando Brigade with two Commandos was sent from Malta to cover the Limasol area and the Troodos Mountains. There were thus seven major operational units, excluding the engineer regiment, establishing a security framework in conjunction with the police when the Tripartite Cyprus Conference began at Lancaster House in London on 29 August 1955.

At the Conference, each national delegation gave its views in turn. There was no division of opinion on the strategic importance of Cyprus, the vital contribution Britain was making to the security of NATO's southern flank, or her need to establish and operate Army and RAF bases on the island with their specialized facilities like the new airfield at Akrotiri, the long-range surveillance radar on the top of the Troodos and the special communications centre near Famagusta. But there was no meeting of minds over sovereignty.

Britain's sovereignty had been reaffirmed by both Greece and Turkey in the 1923 Treaty of Lausanne. Her military installations were so widespread in the island, so dependent upon the population for local labour and so vulnerable to any threat, either internal or external, to the security of the island that transfer of sovereignty was unthinkable. The Greeks could not agree. They pointed out that the bases would be much safer amongst a friendly rather than a hostile population. Granting Enosis would be a great act of statesmanship in keeping with Britain's historical support of Greece and would earn her the eternal gratitude of the Greek people, who were willing to give the Turkish minority any reasonable safeguards that the Turkish government might require. The Turkish delegation was uncompromising. Cyprus was essentially part of Anatolia and it guarded the backdoor to the Turkish mainland. In war, Turkey could only be supplied through her southern ports, which could be threatened if Cyprus fell into unfriendly hands. If Britain ever contemplated surrendering sovereignty over the island, it must be handed back to Turkey from whom it was originally leased. In the back of British and Turkish minds there were unspoken doubts about the stability of the Greek state: would it go Communist and leave NATO before long?

At the end of the conference, Macmillan put forward British ideas for solving the crisis. He proposed a new constitution, giving fully responsible internal self-government to the island with entrenched safeguards for the Turkish minority. The Governor would only retain responsibility for foreign affairs, defence and internal security. He added the novel proposal that a tripartite commission of British, Greek and Turkish representatives should be set up to supervise the development of the new constitution. There would also be Greek and Turkish representatives resident in Nicosia with special access to the Governor. It was all to no avail. Greece would only accept the new constitution as a step towards self-determination which meant Enosis: Turkey would only agree to internal self-government if the Greeks dropped their demand for self-determination.

The Tripartite Cyprus Conference cleared the air, but, in so doing, gave wider publicity to the issues which divided the three governments. Vicious anti-Greek rioting broke out in Greek and Turkish towns where there were large minorities of the other race; and, in Cyprus, the gulf widened between the Greek Cypriots on the one hand and the British and the Turks on the other. Greek support for EOKA and inter-communal rioting increased. The deteriorating internal security situation was highlighted by the burning of the British Institution in Nicosia on 17 September 1955 by rioting youths, and by the escape of 16 captured EOKA men from Kyrenia Castle.

Sweeping changes were clearly needed with the breakdown of the Tripartite Cyprus Conference. They came with the announcement on 25 September that Field Marshal Sir John Harding had been appointed Governor in view of the island's strategic importance. Four years of British experience in Malaya were telescoped into one in Cyprus. Harding arrived on 3 October 1955 with supreme political and military authority combined in his hands in the Templer fashion. His brief was to restore order whilst pressing on with social and economic development, and with encouraging local Cypriot acceptance of the proposals for the new constitution, which were to be developed further by a commission chaired by the eminent constitutional lawyer, Lord Radcliffe, who had presided over the Indo-Pakistan Boundary Commission in 1947. Harding was given Brigadier George Baker (later to become C.G.S. and a Field Marshal) as his Director of Operations and George Sinclair of the Colonial Service from the Gold Coast as his Deputy Governor and political adviser.

Makarios, somewhat disillusioned by the ham-fistedness of the EOKA campaign, decided to give priority to the political struggle. He surprised everyone by agreeing, in conciliatory terms, to meet the new Governor. Grivas, not to be outdone, stepped up violence to show that he was undaunted by the appointment of a field marshal as Governor. He was able to do so because, through his own personal efforts, EOKA had expanded and was becoming a more cohesive organization with the experience it had gained during the spring and summer months. Its weaker leaders had been weeded out and those who had shown courage and ingenuity had taken their places. The number of mountain gangs had been increased to 15 and were operating directly under Grivas's command. Every town and village had its EOKA group made up of separate cells with specific but limited tasks: murder squads, bomb throwers, surveillance teams, propagandists and women's squads. Few of the membership were over 25: many were still in their teens. The deliberate corruption of youth by Grivas was one of the tragic aspects of the EOKA campaign. It did lasting damage to relations between the Greek and Turkish communities on the island.

After exploratory meetings with Makarios, which started on the day after his arrival, Harding reported to London that:

... the alternatives confronting the island were sharp. Either he would reach a basis of co-operation with the Archbishop, or a full scale conflict would break out.[8]

Four extra battalions were sent out from the United Kingdom in October and eight Malayan-style district security committees were established to co-ordinate the action of the administration, police and Army. The police force was reinforced with 300 extra British policemen and its morale and efficiency were restored by the inspired leadership of Colonel Geoffrey White, who had been Chief Constable of Warwickshire.

Harding's efforts to reach a basis for co-operation with Makarios went on intermittently for six months against a background of EOKA-inspired rioting and general unrest. The count of terrorist incidents rose so steeply during the autumn that on 26 November Harding, with HMG's concurrence, declared a state of emergency. This helped Brigadier Baker to lay the foundations for a major military offensive that would be launched if no political progress could be made. He was faced with the usual military difficulties in such a situation: lack of hard Intelligence about EOKA activity and divided loyalties amongst the Greek Cypriot element of the government service and the police. The former could only be overcome by the Army working to build up its own Intelligence until the police expansion began to pay dividends. The latter helped EOKA to anticipate the Army's operations and to heighten its propaganda. The leaks in the government offices could only be sealed by confining operational planning to British army and police officers. Even so, Grivas received many a useful tip-off that aborted some carefully planned security force operations such as the simultaneous search of 24 monasteries carried out in December. Little was found and, despite the presence of Army padres during the searches to ensure no sacrilege, EOKA propaganda gave lurid and totally false reports of supposed desecration of holy shrines by British troops.

In his political negotiations Harding found Makarios devious and insincere, conceding ground only to take up new positions of intransigence on other issues. Between November 1955 and February 1956 there was intense diplomatic activity between London, Athens, Ankara and Washington. A formula was devised that was just acceptable to the Greeks and the Turks, and had the backing of the Americans, whose Consul in Nicosia, Mr Courtney, unlike their ambassadors in Cairo, was extremely helpful. The key phrases were couched in an ingenious double negative:

Her Majesty's Government adhere to the principles embodied in the Charter of the United Nations, the Potomac Charter and the Pacific Charter, to which they have subscribed. It is not, therefore, their position that the principle of self-determination can never be applicable to Cyprus. It is their position that it is not now a practical proposition both on account of the present strategic situation and on account of the consequences on relations between NATO powers in the eastern Mediterranean.

Her Majesty's Government have offered a wide measure of self-government now. If the people of Cyprus will participate in the constitutional development, it is the intention of Her Majesty's Government to work for a final solution consistent with the treaty obligations and strategic interests of Her Majesty's Government and its allies, which will satisfy the wishes of the people of Cyprus.

Her Majesty's Government will be prepared to discuss the future of the island with representatives of the people of Cyprus when self-government has proved itself a workable proposition and capable of safeguarding the interests of all sections of the community.[9]

The Ethnarchy Council was split on the issue. Makarios and the moderates appreciated that continued rejection of the constitution would alienate international opinion: the extremists, echoing Grivas, would have none of it. In the end the moderates won conditional acceptance as a step towards Enosis, but with a number of extremist provisos. Makarios asked Harding to spell out more clearly various sections of the British proposals and made two specific demands: an amnesty for EOKA and the transfer of responsibility for internal security to the local ministers when the constitution came into effect. The British government was willing to grant the former provided violence ceased, but it was not prepared to consider the question of internal security until the Governor, at some future date, recommended that its transfer would no longer endanger the security of the British military installations on the islands, the sole reason for Britain's retaining sovereignty in the first place.

In spite of the efforts of Lennox Boyd, of the Labour MP and well-known philhellenist, Francis Noel-Baker, and of the Greek government, Makarios, with Grivas' pistol in his back, would not compromise further, nor would he condemn violence. Grivas ended negotiations by opening another phase of his terrorist campaign on 29 February with 19 bomb explosions while Lennox Boyd was still in Nicosia. On 3 March a bomb was discovered and defused in an RAF Hermes transport aircraft just before wives and children of British servicemen were to be embarked on it. Six days later the Archbishop and his right-hand man, the Bishop of Kyrenia, were arrested as they were about to fly to Athens to seek further support from the Greek government. They were flown into exile on the Seychelles.

Makarios's arrest was not a sudden decision. Ample evidence had been piling up linking him with EOKA. There was some controversy as to who was leading whom. The Americans, Greeks and most Cypriots believed the Archbishop was in the hands of Grivas and the extremists: Harding was not so sure. In his dealings with Makarios he found the Archbishop's negotiating ploys too closely linked with terrorist incidents for mere coincidence. Makarios was certainly not speaking from someone else's brief. As soon as Harding realized that agreement was no longer possible he advised Whitehall that the influence of both Makarios and Grivas must be removed: the former by deportation and the latter by military defeat. The gloves came off.

During the winter the 16th Parachute Brigade with two parachute battalions had been brought to Cyprus to form Britain's Middle East Strategic Reserve, but was available to Harding for specific operations in Cyprus. In addition, another infantry battalion and an amoured car regiment arrived to join the garrison. By the time Makarios was arrested, Harding had 15 operational units available to mount a major offensive against EOKA based upon Intelligence gathered through the hard work of the troops and police in the five months since he took over as Governor.

Brigadier George Baker in his account of military operations during the Cyprus emergency described the island as an unsurpassed training area for junior leaders, who had to be able to lead their men in anti-riot duties in the towns, in cordon and search of villages, and in large-scale search and ambush operations in the mountains and forests. As the spring of 1956 warmed into the glaring heat of summer, the growing strength and efficiency of the police reduced the calls on troops for riot control. The riots, when they occurred, were becoming increasingly inter-communal as the Turks fought for greater political consideration. Troops were still needed to help the police to impose curfews and to collect fines levied on towns, villages or country districts where acts of terrorism had taken place and evidence withheld by the local community. For instance, after 21 incidents had occurred in Metaxos Square in Nicosia a four day curfew was imposed while the houses surrounding the Square were methodically searched one by one. Another particularly brutal murder led to the closure of Nicosia's bars, restaurants and cinemas for a week. In country districts farmers usually paid collective fines quickly rather than face indefinite curfews that stopped them tending their crops and livestock.

Grivas became seriously worried about the effects of the British counter-measures on endurance of the Greek Cypriot population, who were not renowned for courage. He became obsessed with the need for spectacular coups to keep them loyal to Enosis. In this he was not entirely unsuccessful, although an ingenious attempt on Harding's life failed. One of the Greek Cypriot members of the Government House staff placed a bomb under his bed with a delay action mechanism in it. The bomb-maker forgot the

14. Colonel George Grivas, the EOKA
leader, in the Paphos Forest

15. A parachute battalion patrol in the
    Troodos Mountains

16. An RAF fighter burnt out by an
    EOKA incendiary device

17. A parachute battalion corporal covering the entrance to an EOKA hide underneath a farmhouse used by six terrorists

18. The British commanders at Port Said: General Sir Charles Keightley, C-in-C Middle East (right), and Lieutenant General Sir Hugh Stockwell, commander of the British forces landed in Egypt (left)

19. Royal Navy Sea Hawks attacking an Egyptian tank park

20. The parachute battalion landing at Gamil Airfield

21. The first flight of Royal Navy helicopters flying-in Royal Marine commandos at Port Said

22. The aircraft carrier *Victorious* (left) and commando carrier *Bulwark* (right) off Kuwait in June 1961

23. Brigadier DGT Horsford (right), Commander of British troops landed at Kuwait, talking to Rear Admiral Talbot at a command post

24. The Mutlah Ridge, north of Kuwait City

25. 1st/2nd Gurkha Rifles emplaning in an RAF Britannia at Changi on 9 December 1962 to intervene in the Brunei rebellion

26. 1st Queen's Own Highlanders emplaning in an RAF Beverley to retake the Shell installations at Seria

27. Shell Company staff hostages at Seria after their release by the Queen's Own Highlanders

28. A police and Special Branch follow-up after the Brunei rebellion

English habit of opening the windows at night. The drop in temperature probably saved Harding's life.

In May, Brigadier Baker launched his offensive with a series of major operations to destroy Grivas and his mountain gangs. Brigadier 'Tubby' Butler with his 16th Parachute Brigade HQ controlled the offensive, using his own 1st and 3rd Parachute Battalions, 40th and 45th Royal Marine Commandos, and the Gordons, KOYLI and Royal Norfolks. The plot of terrorist incidents showed an area within about a ten-mile radius of the Kykko Monastery on the northern side of the Troodos had been suspiciously free of incidents though there were plenty on its periphery. This seemed to indicate the location of Grivas's main base. Using tactical Intelligence gleaned by the Commandos during the winter, Brigadier Butler planned a two-phase operation to comb the area with converging patrols, ambushes on escape routes and surprise infiltrations by helicopter. Helicopters and light aircraft were also to be used extensively for surveillance and for command and control of the operation. In the first phase, Operation 'Pepper Pot', the northern slopes of the Troodos around the Kykko Monastery were to be cleared; in the second phase, Operation 'Lucky Alphonse', the Paphos Forest on the south-western slopes was to be similarly treated.

Grivas soon realized that major operations were afoot and did his best to disperse his gangs and to keep them mobile. He also arranged for his people in the towns and villages to stage diversionary incidents to tie down as many troops as possible. 'Pepper Pot' lasted from 17 to 28 May and was unusually successful for sweeps of this kind, based upon general rather than specific Intelligence. Seventeen hard-core terrorists were captured of whom several turned informer almost immediately. Four gangs had been broken up, and 52 weapons and several caches of ammunition were recovered. 'Lucky Alphonse' began after a ten day pause and lasted from 8 to 23 June. Though even more successful in the number of gangs splintered or destroyed, the prime target, Grivas, escaped through poor shooting by a parachute battalion patrol, which surprised him and five companions resting in a stream bed. Brigadier Baker later recorded of the campaign as a whole 'the standard of shooting in all types of unit was deplorable ... the proportion of hits to contacts was disgracefully small'. This was understandable with the troops spending so much time on riot and curfew duties in support of the police. The standard of snap shooting needed in anti-terrorist operations takes many long hours of practice that must be continuous. National Servicemen did not have the time to acquire the necessary skills. Brigadier Baker also remarked of the National Servicemen:

The problem ... is to convert the gormless young man ... from a comic-strip reading callow youth into a self-reliant, tough, useful member of military society—a fascinating and difficult task, but far from being impossible of achievement, as experience over recent years in many parts of the world has shown.[10]

'Lucky Alphonse' was marred by loss of 21 officers and men, mostly from the Gordons, in a forest fire which was probably started by mortar bombs that set the tinder-dry mountain sides alight. There were also seven other deaths in shooting mistakes and road accidents. Nevertheless, the mountain gangs had been routed out and, though they continued to exist, they never presented any real threat thereafter. Grivas found a safe house in Limasol and left the mountains for good. His main force became the EOKA cells in the towns, which were much more difficult to uncover within the mass of the hostile Greek Cypriot population than the gangs in the sparsely peopled mountains.

The Suez crisis started to affect anti-EOKA operations in July 1956 when the Parachute and Commando Brigades had to be withdrawn for training. British military and police pressure, however, remained unrelenting. Athens Radio was successfully jammed and Intelligence started to flow more freely as people began to feel that Harding had won the military initiative. The public, as Grivas feared, had grown weary of curfews, searches and fines, made all the more tiresome by the summer heat. EOKA needed a breather to reorganize after three disastrous months. Grivas also knew that the Greek government had begun to work up its case for another approach to the United Nations in the autumn. On 16 August he reluctantly announced 'a suspension of operations' to create a better atmosphere for resumed negotiations.

Grivas's cease-fire lasted barely a fortnight. On 23 August leaflets were distributed by the government offering an amnesty: EOKA terrorists, who surrendered, could leave for Greece, if that country would accept them, or could stay in Cyprus and would only be prosecuted 'for crimes of violence against the person'. At the same time it was announced that the Radcliffe consultations on the new constitution would be speeded up. Grivas rejected the amnesty terms and announced that he would resume 'his freedom of action' if genuine negotiations were not begun by 27 August. The British response was to publish extracts from his diaries, which had been unearthed during a search by British troops a week earlier. These showed the deep involvement of Makarios and the Ethnarchy Council with EOKA terrorism. Attempts were made in London, Athens, and Cyprus to prove that the extracts were forgeries but without success. Subsequent extracts left even less doubt about the Archbishop's complicity in violence and wholly justified his deportation.

On 29 August, Grivas did 'resume his freedom of action', but sympathy for the Greek Cypriot cause was on the wane, particularly in the United States when the Suez crisis came to the boil in the autumn of 1956. Cyprus remained on the front pages of the world press not as an international bone of contention, but as the advanced base for the Anglo-French 'police action' in Port Said.

Tome upon tome has been and will continue to be written about the Suez crisis of 1956; and rightly so because it was a turning point in British and

World history. It was the moment when, for better or for worse, the United States and Soviet Union combined to elbow their wartime allies and the former leaders of the old world off the twentieth century's stage. There was nothing surprising about the Soviet actions: it was the Americans' disloyalty to their friends which changed the course of history.

The Suez crisis was a Greek tragedy entirely of American making from start to finish. It was written by two men, who were doubly religious, being deeply committed Christians as well as devotees of the United Nations as the hope of the world: President Eisenhower and his Secretary of State, John Foster Dulles. There were three acts in the drama, each with several interlocking scenes: the initial 'tit-for-tat', which ended in Nasser nationalizing the Canal; the search for a peaceful and just solution by negotiation; and, finally, the burst of frustration that drove Britain and France to their ill-judged attempt to overthrow Nasser by force. In each act American policy was ambivalent as the Eisenhower administration tried, in the presidential election year, to reconcile a number of irreconcilables: the need to support their NATO allies, the wish to win Third World support for Cold War purposes, and the fear of triggering a third world war over an issue which, though vital to Britain and France, was only of marginal importance to the United States. The theme of Eisenhower's re-election campaign was a 'a man of peace': not until it was far too late did he or his Secretary of State, make it clear in London and Paris to what lengths they would go to preserve that image. While Eden and his Foreign Secretary, Selwyn Lloyd, strove to avoid a repetition of Munich, Eisenhower played Chamberlain to the Egyptian dictator.

Act I: 'Tit for Tat'

The first act began as soon as the ink was dry on the Anglo-Egyptian Agreement of 1954. Having bowed to American pressure for the evacuation of the Canal Zone, Britain had good reason to hope for better relations with Egypt and a closer alignment of Anglo-American policies for the Middle East. Neither hope was fulfilled. As soon as Nasser had achieved his primary aim of evicting British troops from Egyptian soil with American help, he looked for further American help in his plan to unite the Arab world under his leadership for the destruction of Israel. Under the Tripartite Declaration of 1950 the United States, Britain and France had agreed to limit the probable Arab/Israeli arms race by restricting and balancing the sale of arms to both sides. Whilst the three Western powers were willing to supply generous economic aid to Egypt, they were sparing with military equipment. Nasser was forced to look elsewhere for arms.

Nasser's quest for arms was given urgency in February 1955 when Israeli forces destroyed the Egyptian military headquarters in the Gaza Strip in reprisal for Egyptian Fedayeen commando raids into Israel. Two months later he found an answer to his military equipment problem at the Bandung Conference of non-aligned states where he rubbed shoulders with

Afro-Asian leaders like Nehru, Chou En-Lai and Sukarno for the first time. He came away convinced of the merits of Nehru's 'positive neutralism' in the Cold War. Smaller powers could exploit the fears and rivalries of the superpowers by playing off one against the other to secure maximum help from each with minimum commitment to either. Nasser was to prove an apt pupil in the art of the neutralist double-cross.

During the conference Chou En-Lai advised Nasser to forget his Muslim allergy to Communism and to seek arms from behind the Iron Curtain. The Russians were not slow to pick up the scent. The Egyptian Communist Party and the Soviet press, which had both been fulminating against Nasser's regime as bourgeois reactionaries, turned turtle and came out in his support. The Soviet Ambassador in Cairo, Daniel Solod, made a point-blank offer of Eastern Bloc arms in May 1955. A secret deal was signed in July during the visit to Cairo of Demitri Shipilov, who was soon to become Soviet Foreign Minister. The deal was not made public until September 1955 when Nasser announced that he had signed a barter agreement with Czechoslavakia to supply Egypt with MIG fighters, Ilyushin bombers, Joseph Stalin Mk III tanks (the most advanced in the world at that time) and the lighter T34 tanks in exchange for Egyptian cotton. Unlike previous arms deals with the West, there were no political strings attached.

The Western Allies accepted that they had been outmanoeuvred by Moscow. In one simple stride, the Russians had stepped over the 'northern tier' and placed their feet on the most vulnerable choke point on the West's strategic highway as well as amongst the Arab states, on whose oil production most Western economies had come to depend. It was tempting to respond by cutting economic aid to Egypt, but the double-cross came into play. To have done so would, it was feared in Western capitals, accelerate Egypt's drift into the Eastern bloc. It was thought wiser to counter Soviet influence with continued Western economic aid. The jewel in the aid programme was finance for Egypt's Aswan Dam which, when completed, would add a third to Egypt's agricultural land and multiply her generation of electric power by a factor of eight. In December 1955 Dulles announced that the US and Britain would finance the project in conjunction with the World Bank.

In negotiating the Aswan deal, the World Bank insisted on a number of unexceptional financial conditions to secure the loan. Nasser objected. The economic strings attached to the deal reminded him of the Anglo-French exploitation of Khedive Ismail's bankruptcy in 1875 and its sequel, the Battle of Tel-el-Kebir and Britain's 'temporary' occupation of Egypt, which had lasted until 1956. He saw any conditions, whether financial or political, as an affront to the dignity of Egypt. The United States Congress was equally exercised by Nasser's recognition of Communist China in May 1956. Fears of the American cotton growers and objections by the Zionist lobby brought further pressure to bear on the administration to reconsider the loan for which money was already set aside in the federal budget. Nasser, fearing that the double-cross was failing this time, sent the

Egyptian Ambassador post-haste to Washington to clinch the deal, strings and all. The Ambassador called on Dulles on 19 July 1956. Sensing that the American Secretary of State was about to tell him that the deal was off, he blurted out 'don't please say you are going to withdraw the offer because . . . we have the Russian offer to finance the Dam right here in my pocket.' Dulles is said to have replied 'Well, as you have the money already you don't need any from us. My offer is withdrawn.'[11]

In the official State Department announcement terminating negotiations, derogatory remarks about Egypt's financial viability hurt Nasser's dignity more than the actual withdrawal of the money. Eden had no reason to quarrel with Dulles' decision except for lack of consultation before the final break. He had already concluded that there was an Arab Hitler in the making in Cairo. Anglo-Egyptian relations had been further soured by Egyptian political intrigues in Jordan. Field Marshal Sir Gerald Templer had been snubbed when he visited Amman in December 1955 to encourage Jordan to join the Baghdad Pact; and then in March 1956 Glubb Pasha, the British commander of the Arab Legion, was sacked to the accompaniment of Cairo Radio's 'Voice of the Arabs' blaring out anti-British and anti-Baghdad Pact sentiments in tones all too reminiscent of Doctor Goebbels' Nazi propaganda machine.

The French Prime Minister, Guy Mollet, was equally hostile to Nasser for aiding and abetting the Nationalist rebellion in Algeria. French hostility found expression in support of Israel. After Nasser's arms deal with Czechoslovakia, France became Israel's principal supplier of aircraft and military hardware, overtly within the quotas allowed by the Tripartite Agreement, but covertly far in excess. Franco-Israeli diplomatic and military relations had always been close since the United States and Britain had manoeuvred France out of Syria and the Lebanon immediately after the war. Just before Dulles withdrew the Aswan Dam offer, Couve de Merville, French Ambassador in Washington, who had also been Ambassador in Cairo, warned the State Department that refusal of the Aswan loan could result in the seizure of the Suez Canal now that there were no British troops there to pre-empt such action. He was proved right within a week.

Nasser's nationalization of the Canal was not entirely unpremeditated. The existence of the internationally based Suez Canal Company had long been a source of irritation to Egyptian nationalist opinion. Soon after Farouk's abdication, the Revolutionary Command Council had opened negotiations with the Company for increased Egyptian participation and a larger share in the profits. The Company was willing, provided its lease, which was due to end in 1968, was extended. This was a price Egypt was not prepared to pay. Instead a commission was set up to examine alternatives, including the precedent of nationalization set by the Attlee government in Britain after the war. The commission concluded that the cost of compensation would be too high and prudently recommended patience until 1968. During its deliberations the workings of the Company and its operation of the Canal had been thoroughly examined. The wave of nationalist emotion that surged through Egypt when the Aswan loan was withdrawn swept caution aside. On 26 July the curtain fell on the first act of the Suez drama as Nasser harangued a vast crowd of his supporters in Alexandria, announcing Egypt's nationalization of the Canal to pay for the Dam and to rid Egypt of the indignity of foreign control of part of her territory and of her greatest asset.

Act II: Peace with Justice

The second act began in Downing Street that night, 26 July. The strings attached to the Aswan loan may have reminded Nasser of his unfortunate predecessor, the Khedive Ismail: his nationalization of the Canal was seen by Eden as a re-run of Hitler's march into the Rhineland in 1936. When the Cabinet met next day, with the Chiefs of Staff present, there was general determination that a new Munich crisis must not be allowed to develop. The policy agreed at the meeting was well expressed in Eden's first letters on the subject to Eisenhower:

We ought in the first instance to bring the maximum political pressure to bear on Egypt. For this, apart from our own action, we should invoke the support of all the interested powers. My colleagues and I are convinced that we must be ready, in the last resort, to use force to bring Nasser to his senses. For our part we are prepared to do so. I have, this morning, instructed our Chiefs of Staff to prepare a military plan accordingly.[12]

Eden's letter also reflected the public mood in Britain at that time. Gaitskell, leader of the opposition in the House of Commons, led Labour party opinion when he said:

It is all very familiar. It is exactly the same that we encountered from Mussolini and Hitler in those years before the war . . . I believe we were right to react sharply to his move.[13]

The French were equally determined to take decisive action and so it appeared were the Americans. By the time Dulles arrived in London at the end of the month the three powers—Britain, France and the United States—had agreed to call a conference of the 22 Maritime powers most closely concerned with the operation of the Canal. These included Soviet Russia and Eastern Bloc countries. On 1 August, at their first meeting, the three Foreign Secretaries—Selwyn Lloyd, Pineau and Dulles—agreed a five point negotiating position:

(1) It was intolerable that the Canal should be under the domination of any single country without any international control;
(2) We should use the 1888 Convention as a basis for discussion in order to avoid complications with the Panama Canal;
(3) Force was the last method to be tried, but the United States did not exclude the use of force if all other methods failed;

(4) We should mobilize world opinion in favour of international operation of the Canal;

(5) We should attempt to get our tripartite views accepted by at least a two-thirds majority of the conference that was to be called.[14]

There was little divergence of view between America and her European allies at the beginning of the second act. The difference lay hidden in the length of negotiating time fuse that each power envisaged as reasonable before resorting to the use of force. The American fuse was measured in months, if not years: their vital interests were not at stake and it was election year. Weeks rather than months were the British and French criteria: demonstration of a determination to use force was part of their negotiating position.

Throughout the second act military preparations and political negotiations unfolded on separate halves of the stage, but were closely inter-related. The first 'off-the-cuff' idea for military action had been given during the first evening of the crisis to the Prime Minister by Admiral Mountbatten, then First Sea Lord, who was acting as Chairman of the Chiefs of Staff in the absence, due to illness, of Marshal of the Royal Air Force, Sir William Dickson. According to Mountbatten's biographer, Philip Ziegler,[15] he suggested that the Mediterranean fleet, then assembled around Malta, should pick up the Royal Marine Commandos in Cyprus and land them within a few days at Port Said to seize the entrance and the first 25 miles of the Canal. Military surprise would undoubtedly have been achieved, the political impact of which might have been decisive. The risks, however, were all too obvious. If the Egyptians were not thrown off balance and decided to resist, using their recently acquired Soviet tanks, guns and aircraft, the landing force of little more than 1,200 marines would have been hard-pressed to hold Port Said even though supported by the fleet with its aircraft carriers off-shore. The idea was set aside as the Chiefs of Staff went about planning a sounder and less risky operation to bring Nasser to his senses as called for by the Cabinet on 27 July.

The first fully considered estimates given to the government by the Chiefs of Staff set out the broad parameters of time and resources needed for success. It would take six weeks to assemble and deploy adequate forces to unseat Nasser and to deal with the aftermath of the operation, which might involve the reoccupation of most of Egypt by Anglo-French forces. D-day, therefore, could not be before mid-September. The weather would begin to deteriorate by mid-October, making airborne and amphibious operations increasingly hazardous as winter approached. If possible, political negotiations should be brought to a head early in September. As regards resources, the Chiefs of Staff warned that the operation could not be mounted without a limited recall of some 20,000 reservists to the colours, particularly to mobilize logistic units of the Reserve Army that would be needed to sustain the forces on shore. Merchant shipping would also have to be requisitioned. For economic as well as political reasons the men and ships should be held for as short a time as possible: another reason for keeping negotiations short.

Immediately available Anglo-French military resources and the facts of geography dictated the first contingency plan for the use of force: Operation 'Musketeer'. Ideally, the initial phases of the operation should have been carried out by airborne troops, using Cyprus as their base. Unfortunately, although there were enough British and French parachute troops, the necessary numbers of transport aircraft were not available. Most of the wartime troop carriers had been American. The French had developed the robust Nord-Atlas troop transport and cargo-carrying aircraft as a result of their experience in Indo-China. The Nord-Atlas was in operational service in Algeria, but there were not enough of them to mount a major air borne operation. The British Army had paid little attention to the development of its airborne forces since the war and Transport Command was still the Cinderella of the RAF. While the

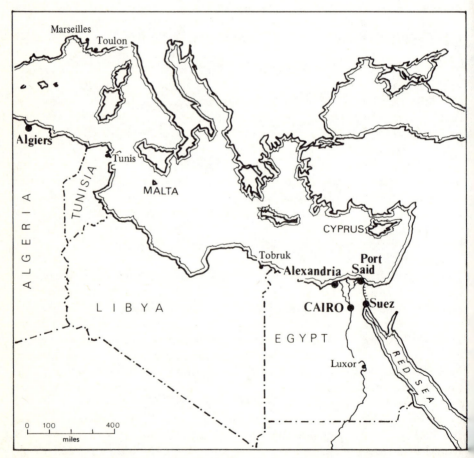

9. The facts of geography in planning the Suez Operations in 1956.

French believed that an airborne descent on the Canal would have been practicable even with the limited forces available, the British General Staff deemed the risks too great. While it was accepted that the large numbers of Soviet tanks and aircraft in Egyptian hands would not present a significant threat if they were manned by Egyptians, planning had to be based on the assumption that the six week negotiating period would allow time for at least some of these key equipments to be manned by Russian technicians already in Egypt or by Eastern Bloc volunteers. Airborne forces might need the help of more heavily equipped units early in the operation and these could only come by sea from Malta, the nearest British naval base (six days sailing for the slower landing ships), or across the Western Desert of Egypt along Rommel's old axis of advance from Tobruk to the Nile Delta (if the Libyan government would sanction the use of 10th Armoured Division, stationed in Cyrenaica, to invade Muslim Egypt from its territory). Cyprus could not be used for amphibious forces because its port facilities had not been developed as Eden had suggested in 1954, and they were wholly inadequate for major naval concentrations.

The availability of amphibious ships and craft was only slightly better than that of transport aircraft. In the decade since the end of the Second World War, age, obsolescence and financial stringency had eroded the vast

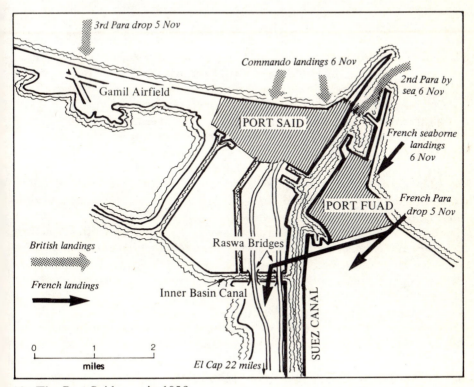

10. The Port Said area in 1956.

resources used for the invasion of Normandy. There were only enough British and French landing ships and craft to mount one very modest amphibious landing. There were two practicable landing areas: Port Said at the northern entrance of the Canal or Alexandria on the western edge of the Nile Delta, just over 100 miles from Cairo by the shortest route across the desert. Port Said was obviously preferable from the political point of view because it was nearest to the Canal, the most likely *casus belli*. It was, however, a port only in name. It was mainly lighter operated with a few deep-water berths, and it was virtually an island connected to the rest of Egypt by causeways formed by the Canal banks, which could easily be blocked by demolition of the two Raswa bridges over the Inner Basin Canal. From the military point of view a landing at Port Said would be slow and rapid exploitation difficult. Alexandria, on the other hand, was a deep-water port, through which troops, tanks and vehicles, carried in merchant shipping, could be landed quickly, and from which there were no obstacles to a rapid advance on Cairo. The immediate aim of enforcing international control of the Canal could be achieved by toppling Nasser through the rapid defeat of Egyptian forces defending their capital, hopefully in a decisive battle on the Alexandria–Cairo road.

Eden did not like this plan because it might be politically hard to justify when the time came, but he accepted the military reasoning and so detailed contingency planning and preparation went ahead with Alexandria and Cairo as the targets. General Sir Charles Keightley GOC-in-C Middle East with his GHQ in Cyprus, was made responsible for the combined Anglo-French forces with Admiral Barjot, C-in-C French Mediterranean Fleet as his deputy. General Sir Hugh Stockwell, Commander 1st (British) Corps in Germany, was brought back to London as Land Force Commander with General André Beaufre from Algeria as his French deputy. The naval forces were to be led by Vice Admiral Durnford-Slater with the French Admiral Lancelot as deputy, and the air forces were under Air Marshal Sir Denis Barnett with French Brigadier Brohon as deputy.

The British and French task force commanders met for the first time on 10 August in the claustrophobic atmosphere of the underground offices beneath the old War Office building in Whitehall, which were to serve as their headquarters until they moved to Algiers, Malta and Cyprus early in September. The British land forces at their disposal were 16th Parachute Brigade in Cyprus, 3rd Commando Brigade now back in Malta, 3rd Infantry Division in England and the skeletal 10th Armoured Division in Libya. The French made two divisions stationed in Algeria available: General Massu's 10th Colonial Parachute Division and General Huet's 7th Mechanized Division. The bulk of the logistic troops needed to handle the force of almost 80,000 troops (45,000 British and 34,000 French) through Alexandria together with 12,000 British and 9,000 French vehicles were to be British. General Beaufre was critical of the joint nature of the force and its entirely British logistic tail because he appreciated that, at some time, the French might wish to go it alone. Plans were also prepared to ship follow up divisions from BAOR and from metropolitan France via Toulon and Marseilles.

The operational plan envisaged British and French airborne troops flying from Cyprus to Alexandria where the British would drop to secure the port and its defences, while the French landed on the southern exit routes from the city to ensure rapid exploitation southwards towards Cairo when sufficient forces had been landed. The amphibious forces were to be sailed from Malta and Algiers on timings that would allow them to land as soon as the airborne troops had captured the coast defence guns, which were covering the seaward approaches. The 10th Armoured Division would make best speed across the Western Desert from Tobruk, and the balance of the 3rd British and 7th French Divisions would land from merchant ships in the port itself. The build up in Alexandria was expected to take just under a week. The timings issued for planning purposes were:

2 September:	decision could be taken to mount 'Musketeer'.
3 September:	British transports leave English ports.
11 September:	French transports leave Algiers.
15 September:	air action to subdue the Egyptian air force begins.
17 September:	simultaneous airborne and amphibious landings.
24 September:	build up complete and force ready to advance on Cairo.
Beginning of October:	Second Battle of Pyramids?

For once the British military habit of first committing a battalion to do a brigade's job and, having received a bloody nose, despatching a division, was reversed: no less than four British divisions were to be echeloned back from Cyprus to Britain and BAOR with full logistic backing. Nothing was being left to chance on the military side of the stage. Eden's determination to have no Munich was matched by the Chiefs of Staff resolve to risk no Dunkirk.

On the political side of the stage the representatives of the 22 Maritime powers met for the first London Conference on 14 August under the chairmanship of Selwyn Lloyd. By the end of the month 18 delegations had agreed to the six principles that should guide them in negotiating a fair and just solution with Nasser:[16] freedom of international use of the Canal; respect for the sovereignty of Egypt; isolation of the Canal from the politics of any country; an equitable level of tolls; a fair proportion of profits to Egypt and for the future development of the Canal; and disputes to be settled by international arbitration. The conference adjourned on 23 August to allow a delegation from the 18 nations to go to Cairo to start working out a new Canal convention with Nasser which would replace the 1888 Convention.

Dulles had played the leading role during the Conference and it was his ideas that had accepted by the 18 users. He was the obvious choice to lead the delegation but he declined to do so. He said he had been away from Washington far too long as it was: in truth the United States had begun to distance itself from its allies. World reaction to the crisis had shown that the non-aligned Afro-Asian states led by Nehru, and the Eastern Bloc countries, were forming up behind Nasser and were doing their utmost to change the international complexion of the dispute in an anti-colonial crusade. Dulles talked about paving the way for economic sanctions against Egypt, but took no action to introduce them. He would not even instruct US ship owners to pay their canal dues to the old Canal Company as most of the other 18 users were doing. He also made capital out of the qualms being expressed across the political spectrum in Britain about the possible use of force to settle an international dispute without recourse to the United Nations, although it was he who had advised the British government against such an approach in view of the likelihood of a Soviet veto. The precedent, which might be set, for the continued American control of the Panama Canal was a factor in his thinking.

Australia's Prime Minister, Sir Robert Menzies, agreed to lead the delegation to Cairo instead of Dulles. Careful preparations of his case took some days and he did not leave for Cairo until 3 September, the day the British ships could have left English ports on the original 'Musketeer' schedule. They remained at anchor, fully loaded with only the ships' crew and maintenance men on board to keep the tanks and vehicles serviced.

The pause gave time for political and military second thoughts. The Cabinet had to decide what should be done if the Menzies mission failed. It was clear that an appeal must be made to the Security Council, despite US opposition, before there was a resort to force. This would take time and the summer weeks were slipping by, and sufficient was known in political circles of the readiness of the 'Musketeer' forces for the Labour Party, the trades unions and, indeed, many of the government's own supporters to begin expressing anxiety about what they saw as the possibility of Britain going to war in breach of her own principles of liberal morality and against the general trend of Commonwealth and world opinion. Mountbatten, for example, stressed the longer term effects of such action in his opposition to the use of force:

If we were fighting a visible enemy who was trying to dominate the Middle East by force of arms I should back you to the limit . . . The Middle East conflict is about ideas, emotions and loyalties . . .
    You cannot, I suggest, fight ideas with troops and weapons. The ideas and problems they create are still there when you withdraw the troops . . . Can the British way of life, which you and I believe must be preserved at all costs, survive if we use our young men to repudiate one of its basic principles—the right to self-determination—as permanent occupation troops?[17]

The text of a British approach to the Security Council was drafted and sent to the State Department for Dulles' comments; support of Britain's NATO allies in Europe was also sought and largely given.

    There were a number of other reasons for disquiet. Was Alexandria the right target? If the aim was to topple Nasser, fine, but Nasser would have to make some aggressive move or fail to keep the Canal traffic flowing before war with Egypt could be justified. Thanks to the advice of the American Embassy in Cairo, Nasser had not put a foot wrong and showed no sign of doing so. The London Conference had narrowed the issues down to the establishment of an international authority to control the affairs of the Canal in a way acceptable to Egypt. The *casus belli*, if one appeared, was likely to be closely related to the Canal rather than to Egypt as a whole. The political attractions of Port Said instead of Alexandria as the target for 'Musketeer' were becoming more compelling as the weeks passed.

There were doubts too about the plan itself. Was it really necessary to mount a Normandy-type landing at all? Could Egypt not be brought to her senses in some way which did not risk high civilian and military casualties? It would be possible to shift the 'Musketeer' objective to Port Said, if it were not for the difficulty of landing large numbers of troops, tanks and vehicles through its inadequate port facilities at the speed required to beat an Egyptian attempt to bottle up the force in its bridgehead. But was so large a force really necessary? The Chiefs of Staff began to look for an alternative. Their Chairman, Marshal of the Royal Air Force Sir William Dickson, was back in office and quite naturally reflected the RAF's latent ambition to prove that it could settle affairs on land more cheaply and effectively than the older services. It should be possible, nay desirable, he advised, to bring Nasser to his senses by air action. The 'Musketeer' forces would still be needed but only for follow-up purposes and for temporary occupation of Egypt while a settlement was worked out. The airborne and amphibious assault forces should be retained in case the air action did not prove decisive.

And so the concept of an eight to ten day 'aero-psychological' campaign to break the Egyptian political will to fight was born. It had obvious political attractions. Civilian casualties could be minimized by careful selection of targets; timing and weight of attack could be orchestrated to respond to political requirements; and the main objection to landing at Port Said was overcome because speed of build-up would no longer be a critical factor. There were military advantages as well. The Royal Navy had, from the start, been anxious about sailing the assault convoys within range of the Egyptian Iluyshin bombers before the Egyptian air force had been neutralized. Under the new concept they need not be sailed east of Malta before the air action began. The air plan was to destroy the Egyptian air force, as previously, in the first 48 hours, and then turn to Egyptian army and economic targets, including the vulnerable Suez to Cairo oil pipeline and other oil targets upon which the life of Cairo depended. In all probability the 'Musketeer' forces would be able to land at Port Said and re-occupy the Canal Zone unopposed. The fact that all the ships were loaded for discharge at a deep-water port had to be accepted: there was no time to reload. As a 'belt and braces' measure the airborne and amphibious forces would be retasked to seize a Port Said bridgehead: the British would take Port Said itself and the French would seize Port Fuad and the Raswa bridges. Both would then advance rapidly down the Canal to Ismailia and the Suez. When sufficient follow-up forces were ashore an advance on Cairo could be made if it proved politically necessary.

The French had other reasons to support the new concept. They had never liked the militarily sound but ponderous nature of 'Musketeer'. While they were not enamoured with the 'aero-psychological' concept, they were keen to move the target area from Alexandria to Port Said for essentially French reasons. Their supply of arms to Israel had brought the French and Israeli General Staffs into close liaison. The possibility of an Israeli winter offensive against Egypt had been self-evident for some time. Nasser's constant harping on the theme of the coming destruction of Israel; the build up of Soviet equipped Egyptian troops in the Sinai opposite Israel's southern frontier; the continuous Fedayeen raids into Israel from the Gaza Strip and from Jordan; the refusal to allow Israel's ships and cargoes through the Suez Canal in direct contravention of United Nations resolutions; and the siting of Egyptian coastal artillery at Sharm-el-Sheikh at the tip of the Sinai peninsula to close the Gulf of Akaba to Israeli shipping all added up to a growing threat that Israel could not ignore. It did not take much imagination to see that the launching of 'Musketeer' would provide an ideal opportunity for a pre-emptive strike by Israel. The French General Staff appreciated that Israel's main weakness lay in the vulnerability of Tel Aviv to Egyptian bombers. The greatest military contribution that France could make to her Israeli allies' operational plans was the provision of air and naval support. This could be given more easily if the 'Musketeer' target was Port Said and not Alexandria.

The Menzies mission did fail. Nasser knew he had Russian and Afro-Asian support. It was Eisenhower, however, who unintentionally torpedoed Menzies' chances of success by stating in an answer to an impromptu question at a White House press conference—'We are committed to a peaceful settlement of this dispute, nothing else!'[18] The trump card of the possible use of force was knocked from Menzies' negotiating hand. Nasser had nothing to fear in rebuffing him. On 7 September the talks ended and two days later Menzies flew back to Australia. The British government decided to appeal to the Security Council at once. Dulles stepped in with his proposal for a 'Suez Canal Users' Association'—SCUA for short—which would operate the Canal with Egyptian co-operation. Until a diplomatic minuet had been danced around this impracticable proposal, Dulles insisted there should be no approach to the United Nations.

Replanning 'Musketeer' started on 8 September. The new target date was set for 1 October. A decision to go ahead would have to be taken by 21 September to sail those ships that were still in British ports. The French parachute troops had already arrived in Cyprus and the amphibious shipping was standing by in Malta and Algiers with equipment loaded and troops ready to embark.

The SCUA negotiations, which included the second London Conference of Canal Users, dragged on until 26 September when, in desperation and in opposition to American wishes, Britain and France took their case to the Security Council. Dulles had undermined his own SCUA brainchild by stating publicly that 'we did not intend to shoot our way through'. The only 'tooth' left in his scheme was the non-payment of Canal dues to Egypt, but he extracted it himself by refusing to instruct US shipowners to pay their dues to SCUA. He added insult to injury by not preventing American citizens from replacing the British and French canal pilots when they left Egypt in mid-September. Encouraged by Dulles's refusal 'to gang up' as he put it with the 'colonial powers', and by Soviet determination to reap its Egyptian political harvest, the Afro-Asian world united to humiliate Britain and France. In Britain, the Opposition tended to forget that the United Nations Charter for *peace with justice*: peace was all that mattered to them. Eden and Mollet were still intent on winning a modicum of justice as well.

With the decision to go to the Security Council went the further postponement of 'Musketeer' until 8 October. Shortly afterwards the Chiefs of Staff were instructed to prepare a 'Winter Plan', the main feature of which was the replacement of requisitioned shipping by 'Grey Funnel' ships taken out of mothballs during the summer. The transfer of cargoes was to be done by sailing the ships to the military port of Cairn Ryan in Scotland where all equipment was to be unloaded, refurbished and reloaded as a major exercise for the 'Musketeer' logistic units, port and docks operating squadrons, and the logistic staffs. The curtain came down on the second act as the ships started sailing north and the members of the Security Council made ready to debate the crisis on 5 October. In London there was a deep disillusion and bewilderment about American policy, but in Paris attitudes were hardening. A Franco-Israeli attack on Egypt was becoming thinkable preferably with, but if necessary without, Anglo-American support.

Act III: Misjudgements

The third and final act of the Suez drama was brought to its climax by the interplay of the misjudgements of three of the leading actors who were all sick men: Eisenhower was just recovering from an operation for ileitis; Dulles was to be operated on for cancer on 3 November; and Eden was suffering a recurrence of his abdominal complaint that had laid him low in 1953.

The Security Council debates followed a predictable pattern. The United States delegation under Cabot Lodge continued to avoid any possibility of a charge of 'ganging up' with the colonial powers, but did oppose the arguments of the Soviets and their Eastern Bloc satellites. India led the non-aligned on Nasser's side. A consensus was articulated in a two-part resolution: the six principles agreed by the 18 users at the first London Conference were set out in their latest form in the first part; and, in the second, the management proposals carried by Menzies to Cairo were confirmed as a just solution and the governments of Egypt, France and the United Kingdom were requested to continue negotiations for their implementation. The first part was passed unanimously on 13 October; the second was vetoed by the Soviet Union and Yugoslavia. Nasser's 'march into the Rhineland' had succeeded. Eden now feared that he would be forced by the United States government and British public opinion into another Munich to end the immediate crisis, leaving Nasser stronger and more ambitious than ever. The French with fewer inhibitions about their national self-interest decided that Nasser should be toppled in collaboration with Israel whatever the Anglo-Americans might do.

Franco-Israeli outline military planning had started in mid-September. Israel planned to launch her three available divisions in succession against the Egyptian garrisons of the Sinai, amounting to the equivalent of two divisions: one Egyptian and one Palestinian. There were to be three axes of advance towards the Canal. The Egyptians would be thrown off balance by a surprise outflanking thrust along the southern axis that ran through Nakl to the Mitla Pass only 40 miles east of Suez, which was to be secured by a parachute drop. The main attacks would follow on the central axis through Abu Agheila and along the northern axis based on the Mediterranean coast road. The final manoeuvres would be the clearance of the Gaza Strip in the north and an advance southwards to seize Sharm-el-Sheik at the entrance to the Gulf of Aqaba. The plan assumed French naval and air support and a landing by French troops at Port Said to neutralize the bulk of the Egyptian army concentrated to the west of the Canal. British co-operation would be a bonus: benevolent neutrality was all that was expected. The greatest service Britain could render the Franco-Israeli cause would be to keep the United States neutral as well.

On 12 October, as the Security Council debate was drawing to its close in New York, Admiral Barjot and General Beaufre were directed to carry out detailed contingency planning to provide Israel with naval and air support and to seize Port Said 'as a hostage'. Beaufre in his memoirs claims that he suggested the ploy of intervening on behalf of the United Nations to safeguard the Canal after an act of aggression by Israel. In an appreciation written for General Ely, French Chief of General Staff, he said:

This solution would turn us into a UNO advanced guard and might lead with equal certainty to the political results at which we aim.[19]

It was an ingenious idea but not one that could be played with much credibility in the heated anti-colonial atmosphere that had been generated at the United Nations.

After the stalemate in New York, Eden was in honour bound to try to align his policies with the French Prime Minister, Guy Mollet, while the UN Secretary General, Dag Hammarskjold, went about seeking a negotiated settlement. On 16 October Eden flew with Selwyn Lloyd to Paris

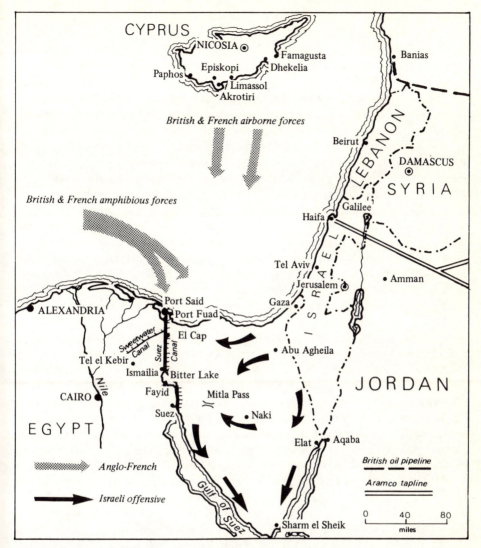

11. The Anglo-French and Israeli attacks on Egypt in November 1956.

where they had a long private meeting with Mollet and Pineau, the French Foreign Minister, with no staff present. There was a lot to discuss besides the continuing development of SCUA, which, though dying, was not yet dead. After the Russian veto in the Security Council Nasser had turned his attention to his campaign against Israel; Fedayeen raids were being stepped up; Cairo Radio was blaring anti-Israeli slogans; and a joint Egyptian/Syrian military command was being negotiated with Israel as its target. Israeli counter-action was also obviously in the making.

The Israeli army had already launched a reprisal raid on Jordan,

Britain's ally, on 10 October. If Jordan were to be seriously invaded, both Britain and Iraq had treaty obligations to go to Jordan's assistance: France would be on the other side, supporting Israel. The situation was fraught with the type of inflammable ingredients which could lead remorselessly to the third world war. It seems inconceivable that Eden and Selwyn Lloyd were not told, perhaps only in the broadest outline, about the Franco-Israeli military staff discussions. Selwyn Lloyd confirms in his personal account that there was a full discussion of the political effects of an Israeli attack and of the plan to safeguard the Canal in that eventuality.[20] But with Anglo-Israeli relations so cool and Britain's wish to avoid antagonizing the Arabs so strong, the French were left to handle collaboration with Israel, freeing Britain from the incubus of collusion with the Israelis.

The question of whether there was direct British collusion with Israel fades into insignificance against the three glaring errors of judgement made by Eden and his closest ministerial colleagues which led to the Suez débâcle. They failed to inform, let alone carry, their American allies with them; they chose a *casus belli* which lacked international credibility; and they stopped short of their objectives.

On 17 October a diplomatic and military blackout was imposed in London and Paris. Washington was totally excluded as were all but the most senior military officers in Whitehall. The 'winter plan' was stopped. Ships already on their way to Cairn Ryan were turned about and all 'Musketeer' forces were brought to immediate readiness. The final positioning of Naval and Air units at Malta and Cyprus was completed. On 20 October the French forces started their embarkation in Algiers. Three days later the world's attention was distracted by the Hungarian revolt and its subsequent suppression by Soviet tanks. On the same day, 23 October, Nasser announced the formation of the Joint Egyptian/Syrian military command, which Jordan joined two days later. The 26 October brought news of an Israeli mobilization and on 29 October Israel invaded the Sinai. Next day Britain and France issued their ultimatum as a 'request' to Egypt and Israel, demanding a cease-fire, a withdrawal of all troops ten miles back from the Canal, and the acceptance of a temporary re-occupation of the Canal Zone by British and French forces. An answer was required within 12 hours. To highlight Anglo-French determination, the British amphibious forces were sailed from Malta: the French were already at sea. The combined amphibious force could not reach Port Said before 6 November: election day in the United States.

Israel accepted the Anglo-French 'request'; Egypt, with Soviet backing, did not. 'Musketeer', modified to meet the actual situation prevailing at the time, started at 4.15 p.m. on 31 October when RAF Valiant and Canberra bombers took off to start the neutralization of the Egyptian air force and the unnerving of Nasser's regime. The timings envisaged were: capture of Port Said 6 November, Ismailia 11 November and Suez 12 November. There was nothing unsound about the military plan. Under normal circumstances six days of increasing military pressure would have allowed time for decisive diplomatic efforts to produce results. But the circumstances were not normal. The high-handed Anglo-French international 'police' action smacked too much of their gunboat diplomacy of the nineteenth century and united most of the world and a good half of Britain against them. At least tacit American support was essential to success and was expected by Eden, but outright hostility took its place.

The British and French Cabinets totally misjudged the effect of their actions on Eisenhower and Dulles. Harold Macmillan, who was Chancellor of the Exchequer, had been a colleague and close friend of Eisenhower during the North African campaign and the invasions of Sicily and Italy when he was British political adviser at Eisenhower's headquarters in Algiers in 1943. As Foreign Secretary in Eden's government he had had a close association with Dulles. In his memoirs Macmillan takes full responsibility for the underestimation of the wave of resentment that swept through the minds of the two American leaders when they heard of their allies' unilateral action. He believed they would protest vigorously in public but in private would be relieved that decisive action was being taken without involving the United States directly in the conflict.[21]

The United States government's reaction was as emotionally illogical as it was unexpected. It had consistently opposed an Anglo-French approach to the United Nations and had refused to enforce the simplest of economic sanctions against Egypt such as withholding Canal tolls and discouraging Americans from enlisting as Canal pilots. And yet, when British, French and Israeli patience ran out, they rushed to the Security Council to impeach their allies and imposed on them the most vicious economic sanctions they could devise: refusal to allow Britain to withdraw money from the IMF to support the pound; deliberate selling of sterling by the Federal Reserve Bank; and refusal to make up Europe's loss of Middle East oil with supplies from the western hemisphere at a reasonable price. It was if the United States had to complete some unfinished business of the Great American Rebellion of 1776 by humiliating their erstwhile enemy as well as their ally of those earlier days.

The course of 'Musketeer' is too well known to need elaboration. The Egyptian air force was destroyed in the estimated 48 hours, its surviving aircraft being flown off to safety at Luxor and to Saudi airfields, well out of range of the amphibious convoys. The Fleet Air Arm and French air force then switched to Egyptian army targets such as tank and artillery parks. Cairo Radio was forced off the air temporarily but, to avoid raising the political temperature any more than necessary, the oil targets were not attacked. On 3 November, however, the Syrians blew up the British pipeline from Iraq to the Mediterranean coast: the American Aramco Tap Line was left intact. At the same time the Egyptians blocked the Canal in an orgy of scuttling ships, some filled with concrete to make clearance more difficult. On 5 November the 3rd Parachute Battalion dropped on and took Gamil airfield just west of Port Said and the French dropped on Port Fuad and the Raswa bridges, securing them with equal success. Next day the amphibious landings began. On neither day was opposition negligible, but it was easily swept aside. All regular resistance had ceased when, at 5 p.m., 6 November, General Stockwell was instructed to cease fire at midnight. An *ad hoc* force made up of 2nd Parachute Battalion with tanks from 6th Royal Tank Regiment was rushed down the west bank of the Canal against no opposition. By midnight they had reached El Cap 23 miles to the south but still some 78 miles from Suez.

The political crunch had come during 5 November when Bulganin sent letters to Eden, Mollet and Ben Gurion threatening to intervene with 'volunteers' and, if need be, atomic weapons. This blatent threat to start the third world war frightened Washington much more than London or Paris where the Russian *démarche* was seen for what it was: a cynical attempt to widen the rift between the United States and her NATO allies and to consolidate the Soviet advance into the Middle East. Eisenhower, who was about to be re-elected President on the 'man of peace' ticket, phoned Eden during the morning of 6 November and presented him with a brutally phrased ultimatum: ceasefire by midnight or forfeit Anglo-American friendship and solidarity. Hoping that compliance would lead to a more constructive and realistic US policy, Eden accepted the ultimatum in good faith without waiting until Ismailia and Suez had been occupied. His hopes were not to be realized.

In the six days of 'Musketeer' the Israeli army had driven the Egyptians out of the Sinai, had cleared the Gaza Strip and taken Sharm-el-Sheik, but during that time intolerable internal and external pressures had built up against Eden and his policy of avoiding another Munich. Internally, Britain was split asunder between those who found the use of force without United Nations' authority repugnant and those who were equally sure that Britain should not follow Chamberlain's fatal policy of appeasement now that the United Nations had failed in much the same way as the League of Nations had done over the Abyssinian crisis in 1935. The Commonwealth also divided, the old dominions generally on Britain's side and the new following India's lead in Afro-Asian opposition. Canada made the most constructive attempt to bring commonsense to bear in the United Nations by proposing the introduction of a United Nations Emergency Force to take over policing the ceasefire while new attempts were made to find a just solution to the crisis. The United States opposed Britain and France at almost every point and in every phase in the United Nations debates, branding them and Israel as the aggressors, totally ignoring Egypt's breach of international treaties and intolerable Egyptian pressure on Israel that had triggered the Anglo-French 'police' action.

A Churchill or a de Gaulle perhaps would not have stopped until the whole of the Canal Zone had been re-occupied. Even Dulles was surprised that Eden had done so. Talking to Selwyn Lloyd on 17 November, while still in hospital, he is reported to have asked 'Well, once you started, why didn't you go through with it and get Nasser down?' Lloyd replied 'Foster, why didn't you give us a wink?' Dulles answered 'Oh! I couldn't do anything like that'.[22] But American policy did not soften in the aftermath of the ceasefire. By not occupying the whole Canal Britain and France could not clear it of the 17 sunken ships and two demolished bridges which blocked it, and so could not restore the flow of Persian Gulf oil to Western Europe. By refusing to allow the clearance of the Canal until all British, French and Israeli troops had withdrawn from its territory, Egypt with United States and Soviet support in the United Nations, was able to enforce withdrawal. The United Nations Emergency Force (UNEF) began to arrive in the Canal Zone on 19 November; Britain and France under US pressure, which included oil sanctions, started their evacuation on 3 December and completed it just before Christmas. The Israelis hung on until 8 March and the Canal was re-opened to traffic on 25 March. International control of the Canal had not been established; Israel's security had not been improved; and though, to the world at large, Dag Hammerskjold had succeeded in demonstrating that aggression did not pay, Nasser had survived not only unscathed but with his reputation and ambitions further enhanced. In American eyes their dream of a world fashioned in their own image with the United Nations as the final arbiter of its affairs seemed one step nearer fulfilment. For the older colonial powers, the writing was on the wall, written in an Afro-Asian script.

The black cloud of Britain's withdrawal from Port Said had one small thread of silver in it. The 16th Parachute Brigade and several other 'Musketeer' units returned to Cyprus, bringing Harding's force level up to 18 major fighting units. During November EOKA had avoided antagonizing the French troops in Cyprus, but had taken every opportunity to attack British targets, perpetrating over 400 terrorist incidents. In January the tables were turned. In a series of well-planned and executed operations during the first two months of 1957 Grivas was forced to confess 'Harding has rounded up the majority of our guerrilla bands in the mountains'. Many of his most trusted and active leaders had been killed or captured. He himself led a charmed life in his hide-out in Limasol, and he still had control of his people in the towns and villages, who were more difficult to identify, but EOKA, for the time being was a spent force.

Complimentary progress was being made on the political front. Lord Radcliffe's constitutional proposals had been published in December 1956 and were favourably received by the British and Turkish governments. Neither the Greek government nor the Greek Cypriots were willing to accept them without reference to Makarios. The Archbishop, quite reasonably, said he was too far away and out of touch with Cypriot opinion to be able to give his agreement. In February, Cyprus was debated in the United Nations. A consensus resolution acceptable to the three powers was passed calling for renewed negotiations. Grivas took the opportunity to disguise his military defeat by offering a ceasefire as soon as the Archbishop was released. The British Cabinet, with the exception of Lord Salisbury who resigned, was prepared to release the Archbishop in order to make progress on the Radcliffe proposals, but hoped to persuade him to renounce terrorism as part of the price for his release. Makarios' reply fell well short of outright condemnation of EOKA violence, but, as an act of conciliation, the government agreed to release him, provided he did not return to Cyprus. Grivas was also offered safe-conduct off the island, which he refused.

The release of Makarios was greeted with jubilation by the mainland Greeks and Greek Cypriots which, though natural, did little to encourage reconciliation with the Turks. The Archbishop made matters worse by trying to exclude them from all negotiations except when their minority rights were to be discussed. Turkish resistance increased and once more partition, the panacea of most of Britain's post-imperial problems, became the paramount issue.

At the end of 1957, Harding handed over to a civilian Governor, Sir Hugh Foot, who was renowned for his liberal views. There were high hopes that his diplomatic skill might soon lead to a generally acceptable solution. The first anti-terrorist campaign in Cyprus was over, but the Enosis concept and Grivas' EOKA were still alive. A further military effort would be needed as Sir Hugh Foot's political efforts drained away into the sands of Greek and Turkish nationalism.

PART II

THE DECISION TO GO

The tumult and the shouting dies;
  The captains and the kings depart:
Still stands thine ancient sacrifice,
  An humble and a contrite heart.
Lord God of Hosts, be with us yet,
  Lest we forget—lest we forget.

Rudyard Kipling's *Recessional*, 1897, Verse 2

7 FIVE WINDS OF CHANGE
The post-Suez era: 1957–1962

Ever since the break up of the Roman Empire one of the constant factors in political life . . . has been the emergence of independent nations . . . The wind of change is blowing through this Continent [of Africa], and whether we like it or not, this growth of national consciousness is a political fact. We must all accept it as a fact, and our national policies must take account of it.

Harold Macmillan, Cape Town, 8 February 1960[1]

The Suez crisis in 1956 is rightly judged by many historians to be the moment when Britain, at last, abandoned her attempt to regain super-power status in the post-war world and began the final phases of her withdrawal from Empire. At the time it was seen as nothing of the sort: Britain was reacting sensibly to the 'winds of change'. When Harold Macmillan made his 'wind of change' speeches in Accra and Cape Town three years after the Suez débâcle, he was talking specifically about Africa. Looking back on the immediate post-Suez years from 1957 to 1962, they can now be seen as a period of transition in which there was not just one but at least five 'winds of change' blowing: changes in Anglo-American relations; in defence policy; in colonial policy; in Britain's approach to Europe; and in Sino-Soviet relations. All of them had been blowing fitfully long before Suez: the events of 1956 acted like a wind tunnel, accelerating them and creating new politico-military patterns for Britain's policy-makers. A chronology of the final phases of the withdrawal from Empire (1957–1972) is to be found on the front papers of this book.

The 'wind of change' in Anglo-American relations was the warmest and most favourable to Britain of the five. Before Suez there had been the family rivalry between a still active father and his up-and-coming son: after Suez, rivalry declined as the Anglo-American relationship changed to that of retiring father and successful son who had taken over the chairmanship of the family business. Advice from London was welcome, but the major decisions affecting the Western alliance were taken in Washington.

The transition in Anglo-American relations was helped by the close personal friendship between Harold Macmillan, who succeeded Eden in January 1957, and Eisenhower, who was just starting his second term as President. Macmillan had an American mother and so was mentally attuned, as Churchill had been, to American thought processes and prejudices. He made it his primary task on assuming office to mend the Anglo-American fences broken by Suez and in this he was met half-way by Eisenhower.

The most urgent fence mending was needed in the Middle East and was made easier by Nasser's Soviet-inspired policies which alienated the US administration. The era of American backseat driving in the Middle East came to an end in March 1957 when Congress accepted the Eisenhower doctrine, which he himself described as:

The U.S. resolve to block the Soviet Union's march to the Mediterranean, to the Suez Canal and the pipelines; and to the underground lake of oil which fuels the homes and factories of Western Europe.[2]

The change in American attitudes in the Middle East was put to the test in 1958. Nasser had succeeded in creating his United Arab Republic, embracing Egypt, Syria and later the Yemen. The UAR was Eastern Bloc orientated and had the Hashemite kingdoms of Jordan and Iraq and the Christian-dominated Lebanon on its 'hit list'. On 14 July 1958 the Iraqi royal family and Iraq's pro-British Prime Minister, Nuri es-Said, were brutally murdered in a Nasser inspired military coup, during which the British Embassy was sacked. Similar coups were being fermented in Lebanon and Jordan. Lebanon's call for help was answered next day by the United States landing Marines from the US Sixth Fleet at Beirut. Jordan's cry was answered on 17 July by Britain flying in 16th Parachute Brigade and a force of RAF Hunters from Cyprus to Amman, the Jordanian capital. Both operations momentarily checked the pro-Nasser tide of opinion in the Middle East. Macmillan, commenting in his memoirs on the marked change in American policy since Suez, described it as:

Not merely in words but deeds, a recantation—an act of penitence—unparalleled in history.[3]

America's assumption of Western leadership in the Middle East was confirmed when the United States belatedly accepted the full responsibilities of membership of the Baghdad Pact at the end of July 1958, which, a year later, became the Central Treaty Organisation (CENTO), linking NATO in the West with the Southeast Asian Treaty Organisation (SEATO) in the East.

Longer term fence-mending had started when Eisenhower and Macmillan met in Bermuda in March 1957. The Anglo-American special relationship was fully restored and indeed strengthened at their subsequent meeting in Washington in October that year. 'Interdependence' became the name of the game. Powerful though the United States had become, both men recognized that even the Americans could not go it alone against the combined pressures of Russian and Chinese Communism. Britain would provide active support where and whenever she was well enough placed to do so.

'Interdependence' was most needed in the grossly expensive development of nuclear weapons. Although Britain, the United States and Canada had been partners in the original atomic bomb programme, the British security scandals soon after the war had led the US Congress to pass the McMahon Act of 1946 which forbade continued exchange of nuclear know-how across the Atlantic. There were a number of cogent arguments, which led Eisenhower to seek its repeal in 1957, but they were given a decisive emotional boost in Congress by the Russians landing their Sputnik on the Moon in October 1957. Hitherto the West, when contemplating the Warsaw Pact's numerical superiority in conventional force had found comfort in the assumption of Soviet technological backwardness. The Sputnik destroyed this illusion and made inter-Allied co-operation more attractive in Washington. Britain had two things to offer: complementary nuclear and delivery system know-how, British scientists having developed their own H-bomb and missiles single-handed; and a geographic position that could provide a platform for US aircraft and Intermediate Range Missiles, bases in Scotland for US Polaris submarines, and sites for early-warning radar installations like Fylingdales. The McMahon Act was amended in July 1958, making nuclear interdependence possible. The Anglo-American special relationship became as close as it had ever been.

The defence 'wind of change' had started blowing the year before Suez. After the general election of 1955 Eden had set in hand a series of major reappraisals of British defence policy in the light of the build up of nuclear weapons and delivery systems on both sides of the Iron Curtain. It was realized that within a few years the two sides would have enough to obliterate each other. War in Europe in the nuclear era was becoming incredible if not unthinkable in Moscow, London and Washington. Eden saw that the Soviet Union would find it more profitable to turn NATO's flanks by exploiting opportunities that arose in the Middle and Far East than to mount a direct attack on Western Europe. He also believed that the successive economic crises, which had plagued Britain since 1945, were caused by trying to do 'too much, in too many spheres of defence'. He set out what he called 'three pointers for the defence reappraisals': the main threat to Britain's position and influence in the world was to be seen as political and economic rather than military; ways must be found to improve Britain's balance of payments; and

3. In our defence programmes generally we are doing too much to guard against the least likely risk, viz. the risk of major war; and we are spending too much on forces of types which are no longer of primary importance.[4]

Large conventional forces had been the sword and shield of Western European defence. Nuclear weapons would provide the sword in future. Their destructive power should make a reduction in conventional forces possible as only a 'trip-wire' would be needed instead of a shield. It might thus be practicable to do away with National Service.

A special committee was set up under General Sir Richard Hull (later to become CIGS and Chief of Defence Staff) to probe the National Service issue and to establish the size and shape of a future all regular army. The Hull Committee concluded that an army of 200,000 to 220,000 would be about right with a figure of 185,000 as the irreducible minimum. The Suez crisis occurred before any far-reaching decisions could be taken on its report. Suez certainly confirmed Eden's thesis that the main Soviet threat was around the flanks, but it also suggested that Britain would never go it alone again and, therefore, need not maintain large forces for limited war operations outside the NATO area.

On 12 January 1957 Macmillan appointed Duncan Sandys Minister of Defence with a brief to pull together all the many strands of defence thinking and to recommend a twin-barrelled post-Suez defence policy based upon nuclear deterrence to prevent war in Europe, and upon speed of reaction to snuff out lesser threats to British interests elsewhere. Maximum use was to be made of advancing weapon technology to reduce manpower and so make it practicable to end National Service; missiles should replace manned combat aircraft; and transport aircraft and helicopters should give a smaller Army the strategic and tactical mobility, speed and flexibility so conspicuously lacking during the Suez operations.

Only 11 weeks after taking office Sandys published his controversial 1957 Defence White Paper on 4 April, setting out a five-year defence programme. It was a dogmatic document built around dependence upon nuclear weapons and abolition of National Service. The economic health of the nation was to dictate the level of military expenditure and manpower allocations: the former was to be reduced from ten per cent to seven per cent of the gross national product, and the latter from 600,000 to 375,000 men over the five years of the programme. National Service would be ended with no further call-up after the end of 1960 rather than first adopting a transitional period of selective service.

Though Sandys paid lip-service to the defence of Britain's overseas commitments, he reversed Eden's thesis that the main threat to British interests was around the flanks rather than Europe. In his re-roling of the three services he gave priority to Western European defence and made the RAF responsible for Britain's independent nuclear deterrent with a force of 180 V-bombers carrying British 'A' and 'H' bombs. In due course these were to be replaced by the British Blue Streak ballistic missiles.[5] The RAF, however, did not emerge unscathed. Sandys acknowledged that, if nuclear deterrence did fail, there was no way of stopping at least a few Soviet nuclear armed bombers penetrating Britain's air defences. Fighter Command was to be reduced to the few squadrons needed to protect the V-bombers until they were airborne. The fighters themselves were to be replaced as soon as possible by surface to air missiles.

In the Sandys plan the Royal Navy found itself for the first time in its long history without a major war role. No-one could envisage nuclear war lasting more than a few days: a repeat of the Battle of the Atlantic seemed most unlikely. Moreover, the extraordinary build up of the Soviet surface and submarine fleets had not, as yet, become apparent, and so the Royal Navy's plea for increased anti-submarine forces fell on deaf ears. The White Paper suggested that the Navy had a rather ill-defined role of 'bringing power rapidly to bear in peace-time emergencies or limited war'.[6] The process of arming the fleet with guided missiles was to be put in hand, and a number of task forces were to be formed around its existing aircraft carriers which would serve as mobile air bases. One carrier group was to be deployed most of the time in the Indian Ocean.

The Army bore the brunt of the Sandys cuts. The Hull Committee figure of 200,000 was trimmed to 165,000, not because anyone believed its commitments could be proportionately reduced without risk, but because the demographers maintained that this was the largest number of volunteers the all regular Army was likely to recruit even with higher pay and better conditions of service. The Army was to lose 46 major fighting units (17 infantry battalions, eight armoured and 21 artillery regiments), the equivalent of twice the size of force deployed in Malaya at the height of the jungle war. Balancing the manpower books was to be done in three ways: by reducing the large training organization and administrative overheads associated with National Service; by pruning BAOR from 80,000 to 50,000 as the new West German *Bundeswehr* took over sectors of the NATO front in Germany; and by building up an air mobile strategic reserve in the United Kingdom so that overseas bases and garrisons could be cut back as well.

Sandys' defence policy had been constructed too quickly to stand the test of time. It over-emphasized Britain's commitment to the defence of Western Europe at a time when Britain's military obligations overseas were expanding rather than contracting. The philosophy adopted by Whitehall officials became 'if a proposal contributed to the enhancement of the deterrent well and good; if not, don't make it'. In consequence the second barrel of the Sandys policy, strategic mobility and speed of reaction, received scant attention. The Transport force was at a disadvantage in competing for resources against the V-bombers. As long as the RAF was responsible for building and manning Britain's independent nuclear deterrent there was little enthusiasm amongst the Air Staff for the role of taxi driver to the Army. The few new transport aircraft and helicopters, which were included in the Air vote, were bought primarily to increase the RAF's own strategic mobility rather than that of the Army.

Two crises in the Middle East soon highlighted difficulties in implementing an air mobile strategy, upon which the reductions in overseas garrisons depended. The first was the despatch of 16th Parachute Brigade from Cyprus to Jordan in July 1958, which had already been mentioned in connection with the American 'wind of change'. One of the consequences of Britain's failure to unseat Nasser was the imposition of an air as well as sea barrier across the Middle East, stretching from the southern borders of Turkey to the northern borders of Kenya. The only way to reach Jordan by air was over Israel. Through a diplomatic lapse, clearance was not sought from the Israeli government before the first aircraft took off from Cyprus for Amman. The operation had to be stopped almost before it had started. Fortunately, the Israelis agreed to over-flying within a few hours and the air-lift went ahead. Two parachute battalions, a gunner regiment and an engineer squadron were flown into Amman, but supply of the force was expensive in air effort. This could only be reduced by ferrying a battalion north from Kenya in HMS *Bulwark* to establish a sea-head at Aqaba, through which the force at Amman could be supplied overland.

The second crisis also occurred on the far side of the Middle East air barrier. Until the Yemen joined Egypt and Syria in the United Arab Republic, Aden, the Aden Protectorates and the Persian Gulf States under British protection had been relatively quiet backwaters in which the RAF had been able to enjoy demonstrating the effectiveness of their air policing theories. Keeping the peace amongst tribes had been the task of British political officers, supported by the locally-raised levies commanded by RAF officers and with RAF aircraft readily available to wield the big stick whenever it was needed. Nasserite propaganda and supply of arms to dissidents through the Yemen and Saudi Arabia (still at loggerheads with Britain over the Buraimi Oasis) transformed the situation.[7]

The same month that British and American forces landed in Jordan and the Lebanon a Saudi-inspired rebellion, that had been simmering for some time, broke out in central Oman. The Sultan's forces lost control and he appealed for British help. This time punitive air action did not work against the better armed, trained and disciplined rebels. Troops had again to be flown up from Kenya so that a properly co-ordinated army/air operation could be mounted at the beginning of August. By the end of October the Sultan's writ had been re-established except in the mountain fastnesses of the Djebel Akhdar to which the rebels had withdrawn. In January 1959 the Djebel was cleared with the help of 22nd SAS, who were on their way back from Malaya, faced with disbandment as part of the Sandys cuts. Their remarkable feat of scaling the Djebel Akhdar and forcing the rebels to surrender probably saved the SAS from extinction. Primary responsibility for military security in the Aden Protectorate and Gulf States passed to the Army.

The British intervention in Jordan, the small Omani campaign and the effects of the loss of the British air bases at Habbaniya and Shaiba[7] after the Iraqi military coup, showed that air mobility alone was not the panacea which would reduce overseas garrisons. The limitations in range and load capacity of aircraft in the 1950s meant that heavy equipment would still have to be stockpiled in or near a theatre of operations or possibly stored afloat. The Oman campaign had also highlighted the need for acclimatization of troops. They could be flown out from the United Kingdom quite quickly, but it took weeks rather than days for them to get used to heat or humidity. Furthermore, it was found impracticable to command military operations east of the Middle East air barrier from Cyprus. These facts of military life led to the stationing of part of the

Strategic Reserve on the far side of the air barrier in Kenya and Malaya, and the establishment of Tri-Service command headquarters in Aden and Singapore. Aden had little to commend it other than its geographic location. Its climate was inhospitable; and Britain's security of tenure there in the face of growing Arab nationalism could only be described as tenuous. Efforts were to be made to ensure that Aden did not become yet another vulnerable British base, but its strategic position drew more and more essential command and logistic units to its black rocks and dirty silver sand as the months of the post-Suez period rolled by: there was simply nowhere else to put them. The garrisons and numbers of stationed aircraft at Aden, and at Bahrein and Sharjah on the Persian Gulf, also grew instead of diminishing.

The Royal Navy under Mountbatten's leadership was not slow to appreciate that it had an important role to play in filling the gaps in the concept of strategic mobility opened up by the limitations of air transport and the imposition of the air barrier by the Arab States. In the Jordan operation the Amman airfield was in friendly hands, and in the Oman British forces were already on the spot. In future emergencies it might be necessary to seize points of entry before the air mobile units of the Strategic Reserve could be landed. The success of the Royal Marines landing by helicopter from the aircraft carriers *Ocean* and *Theseus* during the Suez operation, and the experience of the US Marine Corps, pointed to the way ahead. The conversion of two carriers, *Bulwark* and *Albion*, to the commando/helicopter-carrying role was proposed, and the plans were begun to replace the ageing ships of the Amphibious Warfare Squadron with the assault ships, *Fearless* and *Intrepid*, and four Army-owned logistic ships. Once these units were available the Royal Navy was confident it could seize points of entry with the added advantage of being able to lie unseen over the horizon during the periods of tension. The very presence of a carrier task force with accompanying amphibious ships might, on occasion, deter trouble. Such forces did not have the speed of deployment enjoyed by air portable units, but with intelligent anticipation they could be positioned off a potentially troublesome area in plenty of time. Though many of the crises involving British forces in the 1960s were to appear totally unexpected, it was remarkable how often the Naval Staff had made far-sighted anticipatory deployments and had appropriate forces in the right place at the right time.

Progress in the development of the amphibious element in the strategic mobility concept was slow until Duncan Sandys was moved on by Macmillan to be Minister of Supply in October 1959. He was replaced by the less flamboyant Harold Watkinson, who was an able administrator rather than an innovator. Three months earlier Mountbatten had moved up from the First Sea Lord to be Chief of Defence Staff with clear views on inter-service co-operation and the need to harmonize the work of sea, land and air forces to create a truly Maritime capability (using the word to embrace air and sea mobility) for the defence of British interests world-wide. The conversion of *Bulwark* and *Albion* and the construction of the new amphibious ships were finally authorized and the work was put in hand. The emphasis in British defence policy began to swing away from its over-simplistic concentration on nuclear deterrence in Europe to grappling with the more immediate threats which were growing outside the NATO area. The rebound was accelerated by events in the Middle East.

Before the Watkinson/Mountbatten modifications to the Sandys policy could take effect the concept of maritime as opposed to solely air-transported strategic mobility was given a dress rehearsal. On 25 June 1961 the military regime in Iraq laid claim to the small oil-rich state of Kuwait at the head of the Persian Gulf on the grounds that it had once been part of the Ottoman province of Basra. A series of contingency plans had been drawn up to honour Britain's pledge to go to the assistance of the ruler of Kuwait at his request. The Iraqi threat was given substance on 27 June when the British Embassy in Baghdad reported the movement of Iraqi troops and tanks from the capital to Basra with the evident intention of invading Kuwait. At the time there were three British frigates on patrol in the Gulf and the Amphibious Squadron was at Bahrein. Fortuitously, the tank-landing ship carrying half a squadron of Centurion tanks was being relieved by another so there was a complete squadron available afloat in the Gulf. There was a further half-squadron stockpiled in Kuwait itself. The 3rd Carbiniers, who were responsible for manning the tanks, were in Aden, as were 45th Royal Marine Commando and the 11th Hussars equipped with armoured cars. HMS *Bulwark* had finished her conversion to the commando carrier role and was at Karachi with 42nd RM Commando embarked and about to carry out hot weather trials. The Royal Air Force had a striking force of two fighter squadrons of Hunters and four Shackleton bombers available at Aden, and a transport force of 12 Beverleys and six Vallettas split between Aden and Kenya. The 24th Brigade of the Strategic Reserve was in Kenya with two battalions. Arrangements had been made to charter civil aircraft for its move to Kuwait if it become necessary. One parachute battalion was also earmarked in Cyprus to fly to Kuwait in RAF aircraft.

On 28 June, before an actual request for military assistance from the ruler had been received, precautionary measures were authorized by the Ministry of Defence in London. *Bulwark* was ordered from Karachi to the Gulf; the Amphibious Squadron left Bahrein for Kuwait with orders to stay out of sight of land; the Hunters and Shackletons were flown up to Bahrein; a Canberra squadron was flown out from Germany to Sharja; and 24th Brigade was alerted in Kenya. The request for help did come on the evening of 30 June, but then Turkey and the Sudan refused British requests for permission to over-fly. Diplomatic action reversed both these decisions, but they did cause some delay in the air movements from Britain and Germany. *Bulwark* was first to arrive off Kuwait. During the morning of 1 July her marines landed by helicopter on the Kuwait airfield, followed almost immediately by the RAF Hunters. The Amphibious Squadron arrived and off-loaded its tanks. By the end of the first day elements of 45th Commando from Aden and two companies of Coldstream Guards from Bahrein had been landed by air, giving Brigadier Horsfield, Commander 24th Brigade, the equivalent of half a brigade with tank and air support with which to reinforce the Kuwaiti army deployed in defensive positions on the Mutlah ridge north of the city. By the end of the first week there were five British battalions with artillery, tank, air and naval gunfire support ready to meet any Iraqi invasion. Iraq did not attack, but a useful exercise had taken place which gave confidence that Britain's all regular forces were being developed on the right lines. The operation had not gone without hitches because the necessary air transport and amphibious ships were not yet available and improvization had been the order of the day. Nevertheless, it was a far cry from Suez and an encouraging start in the development of the Maritime element of Britain's strategy for the 1960s.

The defence 'wind of change' fortuitously opened up a door through which a solution could be found to the intractable Cyprus problem. There was no longer any need to station part of the Strategic Reserve there because any crisis points west of the Middle East air barrier could be reached just as quickly from the United Kingdom where the majority of the transport aircraft were based. All that the Army needed in Cyprus was an air staging post with minimal logistic installations and the command facilities of HQ Near-East Land Forces at Episkopi. The RAF's strategic air base at Akrotiri, the long-range radars on the top of the Troodos and the communications monitoring installation near Famagusta were important to the defence of NATO's southern flank and the CENTO area. Suez had, however, shown that lack of a deep-water port and protected anchorages made the island of little use to the Royal Navy. In consequence, Britain's military requirements in Cyprus could be met by retaining sovereignty only over two small enclaves: the western, comprising the air base at Akrotiri and the adjacent headquarters site at Episkopi; and the eastern covering the Army's small logistic installations around Dhekelia and the communications centre nearby. Special rights of access would be needed to the Troodos radar station and one or two other installations scattered about the island which it would be too expensive to move into the enclaves. Macmillan proposed a tri-dominion solution whereby the island would become self-governing on the lines of the Radcliffe constitution, and representatives of the Greek and Turkish governments would sit on the Governor's Executive Council. Britain would only maintain unfettered sovereignty over the two enclaves deemed vital to Britain's defence requirements, which became known as the British Sovereign Base Areas or in Macmillan's words 'two Gibraltars on the Cyprus coast'. It was to be the task of Field Marshal Harding's successor, Sir Hugh Foot, to work towards this solution.

The substitution of an able colonial administrator with such well-known liberal views for a field marshal, who had brought military but not political stability to the island, was to prove premature. EOKA had been beaten militarily but none of the parties involved in the dispute had had any real change of heart. Grivas used the 1957 cease-fire to rebuild and to widen his EOKA organization. Continuing support for Enosis amongst the Greeks was matched by a new Turkish determination to impose partition on the island. And EOKA was no longer the only terrorist organization trying to influence opinion and events: the Turks had formed their own, called TMT,[8] and had begun to act with greater confidence, knowing that the Turkish army could intervene more quickly than the Greek if civil war broke out.

Foot arrived at an awkward time. The usual publicity-seeking incidents were taking place in the run-up to the 1957–8 United Nations General Assembly. Rioting, both inter-communal and anti-British, was the worst for 18 months. The two sides were intent on impressing upon the new Governor, as well as the United Nations, their determination to refuse compromise. Foot misread the situation. In trying to substitute conciliation for confrontation he alienated the Turks without gaining anything substantial from the Greeks. The Greek government and Makarios gave him the benefit of the doubt, but Grivas saw him as a man sent to trap the Greeks with soft words. Furthermore, he lost the confidence of the senior officers of the security forces by premature relaxation of the emergency regulations and a Christmas release of some detainees.

Foot produced his formula for reconciliation in January 1958, which abandoned Harding's concentration on achieving an internationally acceptable solution, which excluded both Enosis and partition, before trying to implement internal self-government. Instead he sought to shelve the sovereignty issue while developing his own plan for self-government based on the theme of 'partnership'. Here too he misjudged the depth of communal antipathy within the island and the width of the gap which separated Athens from Ankara. He failed to win anyone's agreement and by the end of February 1958 Grivas decided to make full use of his revitalized EOKA in a bid to win Enosis from a softer British governor than Harding.

Grivas' second EOKA campaign started with passive resistance. On 2 March he declared a boycott of all British goods and services which, in fact, did more harm to the Greek traders than to British commercial interests. It had to be enforced by intimidation. A fortnight later he re-opened his terrorist campaign with 50 bombing incidents throughout the island, but on this occasion he was up against fully alert and experienced security forces operating under Major General Joe Kendrew, who later became Governor of Western Australia. But there was one new wild card in the pack. It was British election year and Grivas had high hopes that the Labour Party, if returned to power as was confidently predicted, would agree to self-determination in Cyprus and hence open the door to Enosis. In his view, it was well worth making the British hold on Cyprus as uncomfortable and expensive as possible even though the chances of military success were negligible.

The second EOKA campaign differed from the first in that it became viciously inter-communal and anti-Communist. Murders of Turks by EOKA and Greeks by TMT invariably triggered racial rioting in mixed towns and villages. It was worst along the green line, dividing the two communities in Nicosia. The bitter feud between Grivas' right-wing extremists and the Communists complicated the scene and reflected the contemporary political struggle in Greece itself. Both the Cyprus police and the British Army were more involved in damping down Greek and Turkish hatred for each other than in dealing with EOKA attacks, which were largely road mining and ambushes. The inter-communal vendettas reached their peak on 17 July 1958 when five Turks were murdered by EOKA. Faced with the growing probability of civil war. Foot dropped his conciliatory policies. On 22 July he authorized the arrest of some 1,500 suspects, many of whom he had only recently released. He was too late to stop many Greeks and Turks fleeing from their homes and migrating to safer areas.

Realizing that disaster faced both communities in Cyprus, the Greek and Turkish Prime Ministers joined Harold Macmillan in appealing for an end to violence. Pressure for a compromise settlement was also being exerted upon Makarios by prominent Greek Cypriots, who could see no future in continuing the struggle for Enosis. On 4 August 1958 Grivas responded by ordering a five day ceasefire. The TMT replied with orders to its members to stop reprisals against Greeks, provided there were no further direct attacks on Turks and their property. The inter-communal strife died away and was not resumed during the rest of the British period in Cyprus. Migration stopped as well and partition was seen, even by the Turks, as an unhappy solution.

The alarm, which brought some sense to the Greek and Turkish Cypriots, spread to the NATO Council in Brussels. War between Greece and Turkey could only weaken the defence of the southern flank of NATO. Paul-Henri Spaak, the Secretary General, held informal discussions with both countries, while Harold Macmillan visited Athens, Ankara and Cyprus during August seeking an agreement to a modified version of his tri-dominion plan. It was well received by everyone except the Greeks. Grivas could see international support for Enosis slipping away and redoubled his efforts to grab world press headlines by stepping up his attacks on the British and on Greek 'traitors' to Enosis. On 3 October two wives of British soldiers were shot down while out shopping near Famagusta: one died instantly, the other was seriously wounded. The discipline of the units in the Famagusta area held—only just. The follow-up searches were undoubtedly rough, but Grivas did not manage to engineer the counter-atrocity by British troops for which he had been hoping. Instead Enosis lost more international support.

Makarios, in Athens, could also see his chances of achieving Enosis were fading. In spite of opposition by Grivas, he agreed with the Greek government that the only alternative was to work for independence rather than accept British ideas on partnership or Turkish partition. He tried with no success to persuade Grivas that independence under United Nations' guarantees would be a useful half-way house on the road to Enosis which should become their long term rather than immediate aim. Grivas just intensified his campaign. A series of attempts to place explosive devices on RAF aircraft, some of which were successful, led to the dismissal of 3,000 Greek Cypriot workers in NAAFI canteens. Seventeen thousand people in Britain volunteered to take their places. Economic distress amongst the Greek population, which was still being forced at pistol point to maintain the anti-British boycott, was mounting. EOKA's popularity, if not its power, was declining within Cyprus as well as abroad.

Throughout the autumn the diplomatic quest for an internationally acceptable solution went ahead. The United Nations Assembly of 1958 proved a further disappointment to the Greeks. The breakthrough occurred at the December NATO meeting in Brussels when the Greek and Turkish Foreign Ministers agreed, with British encouragement, to meet in Zurich to find a mutually acceptable solution as an alternative to Enosis or partition. Thereafter the slide to peace accelerated. It was agreed that Cyprus should become independent with a Greek Cypriot President and a Turkish Vice-President; the organs of government were to be split on a 70/30 basis; and Britain would retain the two sovereign base areas with access to specified sites elsewhere in the island. The Zurich Agreement was ratified in London on 17 February 1959 and Makarios was allowed to return to the island on 1 March. Grivas, whose whereabouts had by then become known to the security forces, was given safe-conduct back to Greece.

Unfortunately, the Cyprus problem had not been finally resolved. The two EOKA military campaigns had been small compared to the political noise that they had generated. One hundred and fifty-six members of the security forces had been killed, and, out of the 238 civilian deaths, 203 were EOKA murders of suspected Greek Cypriot collaborators. EOKA set off some 1,400 devices and lost 51 men, 27 more were imprisoned and 1,500 were detained. But they had tied down, at times, up to 25 major units of the British Army. Grivas was less concerned with military confrontation than with the impact of his attacks upon opinion outside Cyprus. He had the determination not to be deflected from his objectives, but he lacked humanity and personal warmth. He held his organization together through his own unrelenting efforts and meticulous planning. His departure from Cyprus on 9 March 1959 was forced upon him: he did not give up the Enosis idea, nor did his more fervent followers.

After months of tortuous negotiations with Makarios over the exact boundaries of the British sovereign bases, Cyprus became a republic within the Commonwealth under his presidency in August 1960. Foolishly the Greeks would not leave well alone. Both sides, Greek and Turk, stockpiled arms and prepared for another round. In December 1963 the Greeks attacked the Turks in Nicosia. Makarios appealed for help. The two British garrison battalions in the sovereign bases were inadequate to part the two sides and most of the 3rd Division of the Strategic Reserve was flown out by stages to hold the ring in Cyprus until it could be relieved by a United Nations force in March 1964. Ten years later the Greek National Guard staged the coup that ousted Makarios. Turkish patience ran out and the Turkish army invaded the island in September 1974, imposing *de facto* partition. Cyprus remains a United Nations problem, but the British sovereign bases continue to serve the interests of Western defence without undue hindrance.

The third, colonial 'wind of change' had been blowing strongly, but controllably, since the Second World War. Individual leaders of outstanding ability, like Nkrumah in Ghana, had accelerated the transfer of power in their territories and had set precedents for others. Nevertheless, the British colonial policy-makers in Whitehall had kept a firm hold on the brake and accelerator until Suez. Experience in the late 1940s and in the 1950s had taught them to favour the accelerator. By the 1960s their view was that most colonies needed at least another two decades for their political leaders and locally-recruited officials to gain enough experience to make a success of independence. On the other hand, they saw that in that time many of the ablest men, capable of assuming power, would have been lost to the indigenous nationalist movements and would be generating hatred amongst their kith and kin rather than gaining a sense of responsibility in government. It says much for the British Colonial Service that a reasonably sensible balance was maintained between brake and accelerator despite the uncertainties of the road ahead.

In one respect the British colonial judgement was clearly at fault. The desire to hand over prosperous colonies led to an over-emphasis upon economic factors. In an age when bigger was invariably considered better, the temptation to organize economically advantageous federations was hard to resist. Federations were put together in the West Indies, East Africa, Central Africa and Nigeria, in spite of the political lessons of the partition of India. In the same way that Indian Muslims saw no advantage in exchanging the British for a Hindu Raj, the weaker members of the new federations preferred political independence to the economic advantage of joining a stronger neighbour. None of the artificially created groupings survived the strains of approaching independence. Only the disparate provinces of Nigeria held together for a time without civil war because they had been centrally administered throughout their British colonial period, and still do so today.

After Suez, other feet and hands tried to grasp the controls of the independence band-wagon. During Suez the Afro-Asians had found their voice and had achieved a degree of cohesion and co-ordinated political effort that could not be denied, especially in the United Nations, which became their principal forum. At the 15th General Assembly in December 1960, the Afro-Asian block forced through the Decolonisation Resolution

1514 (XV), and the following year the Special Committee of Twenty Four was set up to monitor progress. The US government had to choose between her European allies and the Third World; this time it stood by the former and with them abstained when the vote was taken. The Soviet Union tried to make political capital by supporting the Afro-Asian lobby, but failed to win the necessary number of votes for its own resolution that demanded the dismantling of military bases in all colonial territories.

By this time Harold Macmillan had won his second term as Prime Minister in the general election of 1959 and the United Nations were pushing at an open door as far as Britain was concerned. All her Asian family had flown or were about to fly the nest for the nearby Commonwealth tree. Malaya had become independent in August 1957; Singapore was granted responsible internal self-government in June 1959; and thoughts were already turning to the creation of an independent Greater Malaysia, incorporating Malaya, Singapore and the three British territories in Borneo—Sarawak, Brunei and North Borneo (later called Sabah). In the Caribbean, the Federation of The West Indies broke up in 1961 as Jamaica and Trinidad and Tobago approached independence, which they were granted in August 1962. In West Africa, the Gold Coast had become independent as Ghana in March 1957; Nigeria followed in October 1960; and Sierra Leone in April 1961. The picture was very different in East, Central and South Africa where the surge of African nationalism was meeting resistance from the white settler regimes. It was with the problems of Africa in mind that Macmillan appointed Iain Macleod, a man steeped in the traditions of British liberal-morality as Colonial Secretary in his post-election government, and set off to see for himself on a tour of Africa during which he made his 'wind of change' speech first in Accra, where it was hardly noticed, and then in Cape Town on 8 February 1960 where its aptness was lost on no-one. Britain was faced with two stark choices: to continue to work for a Commonwealth based upon multi-racial partnership, which meant speeding up the devolution of power to a pace that was acceptable to moderate African opinion; or to slam on the brakes in order to slow constitutional change to the speed and format recommended by the white minority governments, using force, if need be, to do so. Macmillan's speech made it clear which course Britain would adopt.

In opting for a multi-racial policy in Africa, Macmillan was maintaining continuity with the past and was reflecting the majority view in both the Tory and Labour Parties. The only point of difference between the two was, as ever, the actual speed of change. The Tories tended to be the more worried about Macleod pressing the accelerator too hard. Even if there had been the political will to grab the brake, the means of doing so had disappeared with the ending of National Service. Large numbers of infantry battalions and not nuclear weapons would have been required. The 60 battalions left after the Sandys defence revolution were all to be needed on the interface with the Communist powers in Europe, the Middle

East and Far East, and too few could have been spared to impose white minority government in Africa.

Under Iain Macleod's leadership the rate of constitutional change was indeed accelerated. Target dates for the grant of independence to East African territories were brought forward by a decade: Tanganika from 1970 to December 1961, Uganda 1973 to October 1962, and Kenya from 1975 to December 1963. All three target dates were met without recourse to military action, though in January 1964 British forces had to intervene to crush the mutinies in the former King's African Rifle battalions in Tanganika, Kenya and Uganda, as will be described in the next chapter.

In Central Africa he had much more difficulty. Southern Rhodesia had been a self-governing colony since 1923, but Britain's determination to maintain a multi-racial policy made the grant of complete independence unthinkable without adequate guarantees for the black majority. The consequences of failure to entrench such guarantees when the Union of South Africa was given dominion status in 1910 was being clearly demonstrated by the development of the South African Nationalist government's apartheid policies. False hopes had been placed on economic benefits holding together the Central African Federation of the two Rhodesias and Nyasaland. The reality was that both Northern Rhodesia and Nyasaland saw the partnership in terms of rider and horse, and they had no desire to go on being ridden by the white dominated federal government in Salisbury. Despite the efforts of the Monkton Commission to find an acceptable formula for partnership, the Federation broke up at the end of 1960 with the three territories going their separate ways: Southern Rhodesia accepted a new constitution at the end of 1961 with a promise of independence as soon as its governmental institutions were considered by the British government to be sufficiently representative; Nyasaland became the independent state of Malawi in July 1964; and Northern Rhodesia followed as Zambia in October the same year. The civil war in the Congo, which blazed in the wake of Belgium's over-precipitate withdrawal in 1960, had hardened white opinion in Southern Rhodesia. By the end of 1962 the swing to the right in Rhodesian politics had begun to make a unilateral declaration of independence from Britain a growing possibility. The chances of having to use force in Central and, possibly, southern Africa were increasing: so was the unpalatability of such a possibility to most of the British electorate.

If there had ever been any doubts about Britain's determination to pursue a multi-racial policy in Africa they were set at rest during the South African constitutional crisis of 1960–61. In March 1960, the Sharpville massacre occurred, reminiscent of Amritsar in the 1920s. At Sharpville, 67 Africans died and 180 were wounded when the South African police opened fire on an African crowd demonstrating against the pass laws. In the subsequent Security Council debate at the United Nations Britain was faced with a dilemma over the resolution deploring apartheid. The old

Commonwealth countries and the Southern Rhodesian government hoped Britain would veto it on the grounds that it constituted interference in the internal affairs of a member state and was, therefore, *ultra vires*: the new Commonwealth would never have forgiven Britain had she done so. Harold Macmillan placed the unity of the Commonwealth first and Britain abstained, thus allowing the resolution to be carried. In October, Doctor Verwoerd's Nationalist government held its referendum on whether the Union should become a republic within the Commonwealth. The Republicans won by the narrowest of majorities: nevertheless, Verwoerd went ahead with his plans and made his request for South Africa's readmission to the Commonwealth as a republic at a specially called meeting of Commonwealth Prime Ministers in March 1961. Britain could no longer abstain: a choice had to be made. Doctor Verwoerd made it easier for Britain to side with the new Commonwealth countries by his dogmatic inflexibility over apartheid. He added insult to injury by insisting that even the High Commissioners and their staffs from new Commonwealth countries would be subject to its indignities. Having heard the views of Macmillan and the other Commonwealth Prime Ministers, Doctor Verwoerd withdrew South Africa's application and South Africa became a republic outside the Commonwealth in May 1961. In effect the Dutch settlers had won the second round of the Boer War. The third round is now being fought. Britain's policy has remained multi-racial.

The fourth, European, 'wind of change' had also been blowing strongly since the Second World War, but it was the signing of the Treaty of Rome in March 1957 rather than the Suez crisis which made the greater impact on British European policy. Britain had played a leading role in developing Western European collective security through the Brussels Treaty, but her strong links with her Commonwealth and Empire and her special relationship with the United States, had made it difficult for her to lead the way towards political and economic co-operation within Europe. British public opinion was as divided over Europe as it had been in Queen Anne's day. Until Suez, those who looked upon Europe with suspicion, if not actual dislike, were in the majority. After the Treaty of Rome had been signed the economic dangers of being left out of the Common Market started to moderate anti-European attitudes. Disillusion caused by the Suez failure helped to swing opinion towards finding ways of co-operating more closely with Europe without damaging Commonwealth and US links.

Macmillan's government took this post-Suez political surge at its flood, first, by creating the seven-member European Free Trade Association at the end of 1959, and then by applying to join the EEC in August 1961. It was no fault of his that his efforts failed. De Gaulle had been swept back to power in May 1958 by French failure to master the Algerian nationalist rebellion that had been embarrassing France since 1954.

Like the post-war conflict in Indo-China, French operations in Algeria were on a far larger scale than any of the British counter-insurgency campaigns. They were fought to keep Algeria part of metropolitan France. The French army won most of the battles, which cost the lives of 21,000 on their side and 140,000 on the rebels', but the succession of weak French governments could find no political solution which would satisfy both the French colonists and the French army on the one hand and the Algerian leaders on the other. De Gaulle grasped the twin nettles of French and Algerian nationalism, but could only solve the problem by bringing the French army to heel after conceding self-determination to Algeria in September 1959.

The fighting in Algeria made little impact on British policy other than confirming the wisdom of the decision to guide rather than oppose nationalist forces in Africa. De Gaulle's return to power, however, was as fatal to Britain's application to join the EEC as it was to the Algerian ambitions of the French Army. By the autumn of 1961 the six original signatories of the Treaty of Rome were gaining confidence in the working of their embryonic institutions, and so they had no wish to endanger their success by widening their club to include Britain and her EFTA partners. However, they might not have refused Britain's application had it not been for de Gaulle's personal dislike of what he called 'the Anglo-Saxons', who had, in his view, treated him so churlishly during the war. In announcing his veto in January 1962 he suggested Britain had not yet lost enough of her Empire to be truly European and was bent on becoming an American Trojan horse within the EEC. There was some truth in both suggestions.

The fifth, Sino-Soviet, 'wind of change' was as unexpected as it was welcome to the West. Kruschev's policy of 'peaceful co-existence' between the Communist and non-Communist worlds did not appeal to the rigidly orthodox Chinese Communist regime of Mao Tse Tung. Nor did Moscow and Peking find it easy to harmonize their territorial ambitions in Eastern and Central Asia. All had been well in the early 1950s because Mao was busy consolidating the Communist system within China's own borders. In 1958 he turned his attention to re-establishing Communist control over all those neighbouring states which had paid tribute to Peking in the past. The Chinese Communist bombardment of Quemoy and Matsu, the Nationalist-held off-shore islands, brought them into conflict with the United States in August 1958. Their occupation of Tibet in 1959 fouled their relations with India and led in October 1962 to their punitive invasion of India with its humiliation of Pandit Nehru. The Russians for their part became increasingly irritated by Chinese arrogance and border incidents in Mongolia. The supposedly monolithic Communist world fell apart when the Chinese delegation walked out of the 22nd Communist Party Conference in Moscow in October 1961.

While the Sino-Soviet split was clearly to the advantage of the West, the road to *détente* with Russia was far from straightforward. Eisenhower and Macmillan should have joined Khrushchev for a summit meeting in May 1960. At the last moment the shooting down of Gary Power's U2 spy aircraft over the Soviet Union aborted the meeting. Then, in the first days of John Kennedy's presidency, Khrushchev engineered the twin crises of the Berlin Wall and Soviet nuclear missiles in Cuba. Thanks to close Anglo-American co-operation over Berlin and to Kennedy's tough crisis management over Cuba in October 1962, Khrushchev was forced to back down: the missiles were withdrawn from Cuba, though the Berlin Wall remains to this day. The prospects of stability being achieved in Europe through the nuclear balance of terror looked encouraging.

Elsewhere in the world, particularly in areas where the US and Soviet nuclear writs did not run and Chinese influence was increasing, there were fewer grounds for optimism, but enough to encourage America to oppose the growing Chinese influence in Indo-China. In November 1961 the US Military Assistance Group was set up in Saigon. By February 1962 there were 4,000 US servicemen in Vietnam and that figure was steadily rising. The United States was following France down the slippery slope into the quagmire of Asian Nationalism driven on by Chinese-inspired Communism.

By the beginning of 1962, five years after Suez, the new politico-military patterns created by the 'winds of change' were discernible: the Anglo-American special relationship had been reforged with the United States taking the lead everywhere except in the Indian Ocean and Persian Gulf which remained British spheres of influence; British defence expenditure had been reined back from ten per cent to seven per cent of GNP, a level that it was thought the British economy could bear; National Service had ended and Sandys' over-emphasis on nuclear weapons had been softened by greater attention to Maritime strategy, which was proving successful despite the Middle East air barrier; the decisions to persevere with the creation of a multi-racial Commonwealth and to speed up grants of independence had been taken; Britain's European aspirations had been cooled by de Gaulle's rebuff; the nuclear balance had made war in Europe less likely; and the Sino-Soviet split was increasing instability elsewhere. Field Marshal Montgomery, in a speech to the House of Lords in March 1962, gave a generally accepted view of the world situation when he said:

The Atlantic is safe; Europe is safe; the Mediterranean is safe; the potential danger spots lie elsewhere, in the Near East, the Middle East and the Far East and in Africa. It is to those areas that we should direct our gaze ...[9]

Instead of adopting a 'Little England' posture after Suez as many people had predicted, Britain retained and revitalized her world roll by accelerating the transition of Empire to multi-racial Commonwealth and by accepting the need to play a full part in curbing the ambitions of the Communist powers along the interface between East and West. There were two major anxieties: could the final phase of the withdrawal from Empire be carried through in Central and Southern Africa without white rebellion and intervention by British forces to prevent a repetition of the civil war in the Congo; and would the smaller but more mobile British regular forces be able to maintain their share of the defence of Western Europe while, at the same time, handling the unexpected crises which were bound to occur from time to time in other parts of the world? The end of National Service foreshadowed a clash between Britain's commitment to the defence of the NATO area and the defence of her interests beyond NATO's boundaries. No hard choice had to be made as yet because both major political parties accepted the validity of Britain's overseas commitments and her need to retain her world-wide military capability.

NOTE: The dates, on which all Britain's dependent territories gained their independence within or outside the Commonwealth, are set out in the Appendix at the end of this book.

8 FIGHTING FOR PEACEFUL CHANGE

Borneo, the Radfan, the East African Mutinees and Southern Rhodesian UDI: 1962–1965

The need for garrisons of British troops to support the civil power in internal security emergencies has demonstrably diminished already and may be expected to diminish still further. At the same time, we may suffer restrictions on our freedom to use some territories for military purposes, and we must accordingly adapt our strategy. We must ensure against possible loss of fixed installations overseas by keeping men and heavy equipment afloat, and by increasing the air and sea portability of the Strategic Reserve.

Harold Watkinson, Statement on Defence 1962[1]

The acceleration of Britain's withdrawal from Empire and the final phase of its conversion to the multi-racial Commonwealth could not be carried through without paying a military price. This was recognized in Harold Watkinson's 1962 Defence White Paper which covered the second five-year period after Duncan Sandys' military revolution. Plans were already laid for all Britain's larger colonies to complete their passage to independence within its time span. Where, when and how trouble might arise could not be foreseen with any certainty. Nevertheless, it did not require strategic genius to predict growing instability around the shores of the Indian Ocean as Afro-Asia shook off its colonial past and sought its own new order; nor to foresee Soviet and Chinese Communist efforts to draw the new states into their orbits. There was little dissent on either side of the House of Commons when Harold Watkinson paid but lip service to Britain's Continental commitments and, instead, laid greater stress on the dangers to British interests east of Suez. The only difference between Government and Opposition lay in the Labour Party's emphasis on Britain's moral obligation to ensure orderly transition of power, during which the terrorist bullet should not be allowed to replace the ballot box in the early days of each country's independent existence.

The military views of Mountbatten and the Chiefs of Staff were well reflected in the 1962 Defence White Paper. They sought balanced general purpose forces, which could react to the unforeseen in the last delicate years of withdrawal from Empire. Britain's contribution to the Western nuclear deterrent and to the collective defence of Western Europe were still top of the list of Britain's military priorities, but they were no longer accorded absolute ascendancy. More emphasis was to be placed than hitherto on achieving a sensible amalgam of Britain's Continental and

Maritime strategies in which forces assigned to the former could support the latter and vice versa. Under Mountbatten's leadership a supreme effort was also made to improve joint service co-operation so that the strengths of each service could be used to offset the inherent weaknesses of the other two in maintaining a British military presence east of Suez as the British governors departed and the Union flags were hauled down.

The strength of the Royal Navy in the east of Suez context lay in its ability to provide an immediate British military presence anywhere around the great crescent of the Indian Ocean's shore line from Simonstown in the south west to Singapore in the south east. With two commando carriers *Albion* and *Bulwark* in commission and the assault ships *Fearless* and *Intrepid* under construction the Royal Navy would have the ability to seize points of entry for larger forces flown in by air as had been done in the Kuwaiti crisis. Air defence and air support would also be available from the Navy's aircraft carriers although these were ageing and would soon have to be replaced. Design work on the first of four replacement carriers, CVA 01, was authorized by Harold Watkinson in 1962 and its construction was approved by his successor, Peter Thorneycroft, the following year. There were doubts, however, in many minds as to whether using costly and valuable carriers would be the right way to deploy air power in the 1970s, when operating ranges of aircraft would have been greatly increased and it could be assumed that most of Britain's overseas commitments would have been liquidated. The four new carriers were expected to cost £1,400m at 1962 prices; no mean sum which would be in direct competition with other important Army and RAF projects.

In the five years since Duncan Sandys' 1957 White Paper, strategic and tactical air mobility had improved significantly. Cynics attributed this to the Air Staff's concern about their possible loss of responsibility for Britain's nuclear deterrent if *Skybolt* was cancelled and the Royal Navy took over with Polaris submarines. To be fair, *Skybolt* was not cancelled until the end of 1962: by then there had already been major improvements in Transport Command's fleet with the introduction of Comet 4Cs, VC10s and Belfast freighters for strategic movement, and the Argosies for intra-theatre work. Any RAF reluctance to purchase enough Whirlwind, Wessex and Belvedere helicopters was offset by the Royal Navy's enthusiasm for these machines in the anti-submarine and commando-carrying roles. By 1962 Transport Command could lift a brigade of 4,000 men with 60 vehicles and 170 tons of stores to Aden in four to five days and to Singapore in nine: a far cry from the Mau Mau days of the early 1950s when it took four days to lift a single battalion over the relatively short distance from Cairo to Nairobi.

The range of aircraft, although greatly increased, and the availability of staging airfields worried the Air Staff. Several ambitious schemes were put forward in the early 1960s for a chain of island air bases to enable strike aircraft and troop transports to reach the Far East on an all Red route, avoiding the Middle East air barrier and the Congo: Sal in the Cape Verde

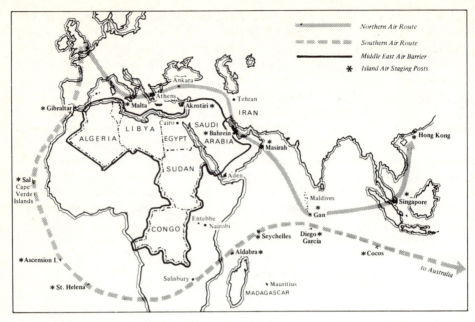

12. Air reinforcement routes in the early 1960s.

Islands, Ascension, Aldabra, Gan, Diego Garcia and the Cocos were all studied. Only Gan, which had been in use since the 1950s, was fully developed in the 1960s because Bahrein and Masirah were available in the Persian Gulf area, so the northern route via Turkey and Iran to Gan and Singapore became the air line of communication to the Indian Ocean and Southeast Asia. In Whitehall, the island air base concept was seen to be in direct competition for resources with the Royal Navy's carrier programme.

While the Naval and Air Staff policies tended to be in competition with each other, the Army's requirements were decisive in settling the strategy for the 1960s. Great naval and air battles were unthinkable as long as the nuclear deterrent limited major wars; it would be the Army which would bear the brunt of military actions fought to maintain stability east of Suez. The dress rehearsal of the Kuwaiti operation had reconfirmed the Army's twin needs of acclimatization of troops and the stock-piling of their heavy equipment near possible areas of operations. Although the Iraqis did not attack Kuwait, there were significant numbers of heat casualties amongst the British troops on the Mutlah ridge; and it was a godsend that tanks had been stockpiled in Kuwait and were available in the Amphibious Squadron. Troops could not fight with any efficiency if they were pitch-forked from the temperate English climate into the scorching, arid heat of Arabia, or into the hot, clammy humidity of Southeast Asia. Nor could they gain decisive tactical superiority without training under desert, jungle and mountain conditions. The Army still required enough troops stationed east of Suez to handle the initial phases of any emergency. Rather than depend entirely upon sea and air mobility, the Chiefs of Staff had earlier accepted the need to keep three bases east of Suez: Kenya, Aden and Singapore. Kenya, however, had been lost when its newly independent government decided to grant only training and air staging facilities for British forces: to have agreed to the continuing presence of 24th Brigade of the Strategic Reserve would have laid it open to the charge of neo-colonialism in Afro-Asian circles.

The Foreign Office estimate of Britain's likely security of tenure in Singapore and Aden was a minimum of seven and four years respectively. There was plenty of good barrack accommodation and equipment storage in Singapore, but little in Aden. The shortages in Aden could have been overcome with temporary buildings, but both the Foreign Office and Ministry of Defence objected: the former argued that hutting would suggest an early British departure; and the latter that regular recruiting would suffer if troops and airmen were not accompanied by their families. In consequence, large sums were spent on permanent buildings that would have been better used for equipment such as helicopters, which were to prove themselves the battle winners in the last phases of the withdrawal from Empire.

The Chiefs of Staff policy of deploying Britain's armed forces so that they could help maintain the credibility of the deterrent in Europe while being able to react to unforeseen crises elsewhere in the world, with only the United Kingdom, Aden and Singapore as major military bases, was soon to be tested and vindicated. Two alarms occurred in 1962. The Communist Pathet Lao forces came near to invading Thailand, thus involving the SEATO powers. The RAF despatched six Hunters and a Canberra to Thailand in token support and a Royal Engineer Squadron assisted in airfield construction. As the Thai crisis faded the Chinese invasion of India in October 1962 seized the headlines. Britain came to India's aid with immediate supplies of military equipment and later 12 RAF Javelins took part in Anglo-American exercises in the air defence of India's largest cities. Then three rebellions occurred in successive years which drew more and more of Britain's military resources east of Suez: the confrontation with Indonesia over the formation of an independent Malaysia began in 1963; the Radfan rebellion in the Aden Protectorate and the subsequent terrorist campaign in Aden itself started in 1964; and the Rhodesian Front government of Ian Smith declared UDI in 1965. In addition there was the flare-up in Cyprus in December 1963, already mentioned in Chapter 7, which drew British troops back to the island where they eventually became part of the United Nations' force. The elastic of Britain's new all-regular army was stretched to the limit as it fought for peaceful transition of power, but it never broke. The three major attempts at revolutionary change were not interconnected so it is easiest to look at each separately. There were also the minor East African mutinies at the beginning of 1964 which will also be looked at briefly.

The Indonesian confrontation was triggered by the small and almost Gilbertian rebellion in the oil-rich and autocratically-ruled Sultanate of Brunei on the north coast of Borneo in December 1962. Eighteen months earlier the Prime Minister of Malaya, Tunku Abdul Rahman, had made the first public reference to the possibility of a political merger between Malaya, Singapore and Britain's three North Borneo territories. Such a merger had long been attractive to Lee Kuan Yew, Chief Minister of Singapore, as a way of accelerating Singapore's independence and of opening up Malaya to Singapore's dynamic manufacturers and traders. The Tunku had been reluctant to agree to a merger with Singapore alone because this would have upset the delicate Malay/Chinese ethnic balance to the advantage of the Chinese. However, the addition of the North Borneo territories would keep the balance in favour of the Malays. Harold Macmillan had been suspicious of the proposal because it looked like yet another of those apparently sensible federations that past experience had shown could so easily fall apart with embarrassing consequences. Nevertheless, he was persuaded to support the Tunku's proposal because it provided a short cut in the constitutional advance of the backward North Borneo territories, the political development of which could thereby be handled by their Malay kith and kin in Kuala Lumpur rather than through continuing British tutelage in an area where charges of neo-colonialism were being wielded with particular venom by the Afro-Asian block. The Tunku's ideas thus fell on relatively fertile soil and took root remarkably quickly. The terms of the merger with Singapore were agreed by August 1961 and in November the Tunku won Macmillan's final agreement, subject to a test of North Borneo opinion, which was to be carried out by the Cobbold Commission. Lord Cobbold, the Deputy Governor of the Bank of England, did his work equally quickly and reported favourably on the merger. The 31 August 1962 was set as the target date for the inauguration of the Federation of Malaysia.

But it was all too good to be true: other people had very different plans for the development of Southeast Asia in the wake of a British withdrawal. First and foremost were the Indonesian geo-politicians and religious leaders, supported by President Sukarno, who saw the whole of the island of Borneo (Kalimantan to them) as part of Greater Indonesia, which it was the Indonesian government's sacred duty to recover from the British. Then there was President Macapagal of the Philippines, who had a tenuous claim to Sabah (British North Borneo) and grandiose dreams of a great confederation of states with Malay origins, which he called Maphilindo (Malaya, Philippines and Indonesia). In 1961 neither Sukarno nor Macapagal were in any hurry. The former was still deeply committed to confrontation with the Dutch over West Irian and the latter's ideas were still embryonic. Furthermore, both countries' need for western economic aid made it undesirable to add Britain to their enemies. Doctor Subandrio,

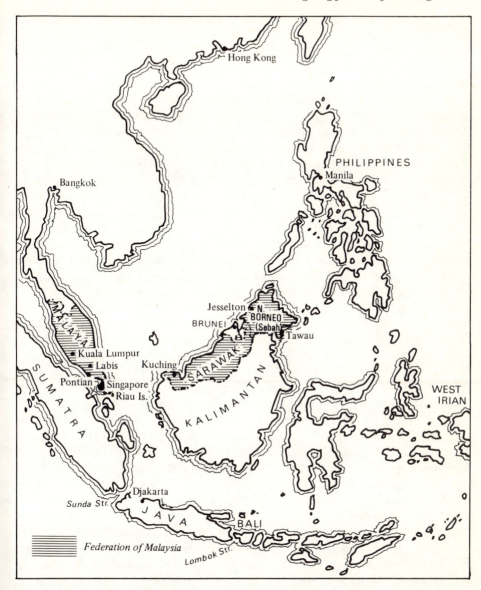

13. Southeast Asia in the 1960s.

Indonesia's Foreign Minister, was studiously moderate when he declared in the United Nations in the autumn of 1961:

Naturally, ethnologically and geographically speaking this British part [of Borneo] is closer to Indonesia than, let us say, to Malaya. But we still told Malaya that we had no objections to such a merger, based upon the will for freedom of the people concerned.[2]

The sting lay camouflaged in the last ten words. The Indonesian government had every confidence that it would be able to win the votes of the people of North Kalimantan when the time came, and it was already making preparations to subvert the loyalties not only of the Sarawak, Brunei and Sabah, but also of Malaya and Singapore. Indonesian intelligence agents were active in preparing pro-Indonesian fifth columns in all five territories. The most publicized effort was the recruiting of Malay and Chinese volunteers in Malaya and Singapore to fight the Dutch in West Irian. Three thousand five hundred volunteers came forward, but only 124 were selected and sent to Djakarta for training. None were sent to West Irian: instead they were secretly indoctrinated as Indonesian agents and sent back to Malaya and Singapore to bide their time.

Within the three North Borneo territories there were those who believed that their states should be given independence before being asked to choose whether to join Malaysia or not. The Sultan of Brunei was also particularly ambivalent. He wanted close association with Kuala Lumpur, but he had no wish to share his oil wealth with anyone; nor was he keen to become a constitutional monarch like the other Malayan rulers. It was only with some difficulty that he was persuaded by Britain to accept elected members on his council.

Then there were the Chinese in North Borneo, many of whom were Communist. They held most of the economic strings and wished to take full advantage of any weakening in British power. The idea of having to accept Malayan instead of British rule held no attractions for them. They had already built up a secret subversive organization with some 24,000 members, known to the security forces as the Clandestine Communist Organisation (CCO). It had close links with the Communist Party of Indonesia, which had Sukarno's tacit support but not his membership. He was too great a nationalist to be an orthodox Communist as well.

The most active opposition to the Malaysian concept came from a small number of pro-Indonesian political activists in Brunei led by Sheikh Azahari and his two brothers. They dreamed of a United States of North Borneo under the leadership of the Sultan of Brunei, whose ancestors had ruled much the same area at various times in pre-British days. He and his political party had little faith in British-inspired constitutional progress and began to recruit, train and organize their own clandestine North Borneo National Army (TNKU) with Indonesian help and encouragement. Its strength reached about 4,000 in the kampongs in and around Brunei town and in the Fifth Division of Sarawak. Only about 150 were well armed; another 2,000 had shot-guns; and the rest were unarmed supporters. They had nothing like the drive and military efficiency of the Malayan Communist Terrorists.

Rumours of the TNKU's existence were circulating by May 1962, but hard evidence of Indonesian involvement was lacking and Special Branch attention was focused more on the CCO, which was considered the greater threat. Azahari and his Partai Ra'yat won a sweeping victory in Brunei's first elections to the Sultan's council, but they soon found themselves with less power than they had hoped for: they could be out-voted by the nominated members of the council on critical issues. Rebellion seemed the only way to stop the creation of Malaysia and to get rid of the British.

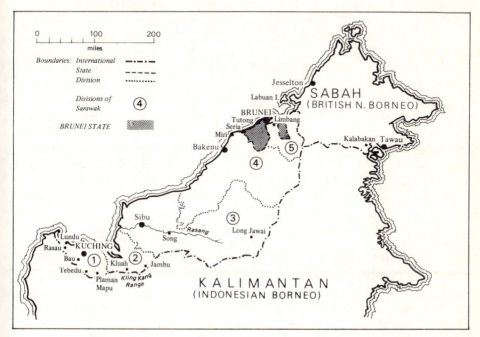

14. Eastern Malaysia during the Indonesian Confrontation, 1962–6.

The first positive warning of trouble was gleaned by the newly arrived British Resident at Limbang in the Fifth Division of Sarawak, Richard Morris, an Australian. Sir Claude Fenner, the Inspector General of the Malayan police, flew to Brunei to assess the situation. On his return, the C-in-C Far East, Admiral Sir David Luce, ordered a contingency plan to be drawn up for military support of the Brunei police in an emergency. Two companies of 1st/2nd Gurkha Rifles were nominated, one earmarked for Brunei town and the other for the Shell company oil centre at Seria, 80 miles along the coast to the west. The oilfield at Miri, still further west, was not thought to be in danger. The Singapore 'stand-by' battalion, the Queen's Own Highlanders, would be available in support as would 42nd Commando in *Albion*. The 40th Commando battalion was also stationed in Singapore. There was still too little evidence, however, on which to prepare an operational plan.

On 6 December the British Residents in both the Fourth and Fifth

Divisions of Sarawak heard from reliable sources that a rebellion was expected on 8 December. When the TNKU struck at 2 a.m. that day the police were on full alert. The main police station in Brunei town, the British residency and the Sultan's palace were all attacked. The only power station was taken and that only for a short time; the Acting British High Commissioner had to be rescued from the rebels by the Commissioner of Police. Outside Brunei town the TNKU had more success. Most of the coastal and riverine towns like Tutong and Limbang were in their hands by dawn as were the Shell installations at Seria where company employees were being held hostage. The rebels, however, had made one fundamental mistake: they failed to secure and block the airfields and airstrips through which British reinforcements could arrive.

Within 12 hours the two companies of 1st/2nd GR took off from Singapore and after a 750 mile flight in three Beverleys and a Britannia they were deplaning at Brunei airfield and at the RAF station on Labuan Island in the Bay of Brunei. Clearing the town was left until daylight on 9 December, but two platoons were despatched in requisitioned transport towards Seria. Exchanging fire with rebel-held centres on the way they reached Tutong where they were stopped short of their objective by more efficient rebel resistance. They set about clearing the town when daylight came. Seven rebels were killed, 20 wounded and 100 captured. One Gurkha officer and seven Gurkhas were wounded.

Government control was re-established in Brunei town by 9 a.m. Soon afterwards Brigadier Jack Glennie arrived from Singapore with an *ad hoc* Joint Force HQ to co-ordinate land, sea and air operations. He called for the Queen's Own Highlanders to recapture Seria and for the 42nd Commandos to rescue Richard Morris and his wife who were in rebel hands in Limbang. As more of 1st/2nd GR arrived he despatched one company by air to secure the Miri oilfield, 40 miles west of Seria in the Fourth Division of Sarawak. He also asked for a force to retake the towns in the Bekenu area, a further 40 miles to the south west. The 1st Royal Green Jackets were embarked in the cruiser *Tiger* for this purpose.

Three small epic actions at Seria, Limbang and Bekenu crushed Azahari's rebellion. The Commanding Officer of the Queen's Own Highlanders, Lt Col W. G. McHardy, reconnoitred Seria from the air during the morning of 10 December while his battalion was arriving from Singapore by air and sea. His plan was straightforward and effective. He decided to land his battalion on two small airstrips ten miles apart on the coast either side of Seria and then work inwards to encircle the rebels. A Beverly carried an initial lift of 90 men into Anduki to the east and five Twin Pioneers landed another 60 men at Panaga to the west. There was some opposition at Anduki, which was quickly silenced, and none at Panaga. It took most of 11 December to complete the fly in and the encirclement of the rebel hard core of 200 who were found to be holding the Seria police station and the nearby bazaar. Realizing that the hostages would be endangered if the rebels could see no escape, McHardy left them an obvious way out to the south and placed a concealed ambush further away to trap those rebels who tried to use it. During his main assault on the police station during the afternoon of 12 December RAF Hunters buzzed the area to keep the rebels' head down. The defenders did not stay to fight. Forty-six hostages were released unharmed from the police armoury and station cells where they had been held by the rebels. The Highlanders had completed their task without a casualty to themselves. Most of the rebels did escape southwards but were rounded up over the next few days.

The only way in which 42nd Commando could reach Limbang was by river, using two civilian ramped lighters found locally and manned by Royal Naval crews from the minesweepers *Fiskerton* and *Chawton*. There was no protection for the company embarked as the assault force. To minimize the risk of casualties the approach to Limbang was made before dawn on 12 December with one craft covering the other. Two Marines were killed and a coxswain wounded in the landings, and three more Marines were killed and several wounded in the subsequent fighting. The Morrises were rescued unharmed. Fifteen rebels were killed and another 20 were reported to have died of wounds in the jungle. Two days later the Marines retook Bangor, five miles further up-stream.

In the third action two companies of 1st Royal Green Jackets were disembarked at the Shell installations at Miri and were ferried on westwards in Shell company craft to retake Bekenu and other towns up the nearby rivers. They accomplished their task in close co-operation with loyal tribesmen, who had been gathered together by the local Shell and Borneo Company managers. They suffered no casualties, killed five rebels, wounded six and rounded up 328 from whom they took 327 shot-guns. Their successful co-operation with the tribal people was to bear fruit in the days ahead.

By 14th December all organized resistance in Brunei was over and the difficult business of mopping up was begun. Precautions had also to be taken to make sure that no smouldering embers of the rebellion could burst into flames again to spread the fire into three western divisions of Sarawak or into Sabah. Kuching, the capital of Sarawak, was potentially the most vulnerable because it was only 30 miles from the Indonesian frontier and was known to be a centre of CCO activity. One battery of 20th Field Regiment RA, acting as infantry, arrived there on 13 December. Next day 40th Commando was disembarked from *Albion* and Brigadier F. C. Barton, the Commander of 3rd Commando Brigade, took over responsibility for security in the First, Second and Third Divisions of Sarawak and was appointed military adviser to the Governor of Sarawak. With *Albion* came two squadrons of naval helicopters. The RHQ and one squadron of the Queen's Royal Irish Hussars also arrived with their armoured cars. In Brunei, HQ 99 Gurkha Brigade commanded by Brigadier A. G. (Pat) Patterson, took over the security of Brunei, the Fourth and Fifth Divisions of Sarawak and the whole of Sabah. On 19 December Major General Walter Walker, commander 17th Gurkha Division, arrived to take over from Brigadier Glennie as Commander British Forces Borneo with his Joint Force HQ on Labuan Island.

Walter Walker was a Gurkha officer with a wealth of experience in jungle warfare, culled fighting in Burma during the Second World War and throughout the Malayan emergency. He was a strong, rather austere personality, who would only accept the highest professional standards and did not suffer fools gladly. He held crystal clear views on the policies to be pursued in North Borneo about which he left no one in any doubt. From the moment of his arrival he saw that he had two tasks: to round up the rebels so that they would not become a running sore, tying down troops searching for them in the kampongs and jungle; and to be ready to meet an Indonesian attack if it came. There was no lack of Intelligence about the latter. Supported by Admiral Sir Varyl Begg, who had taken over from Admiral Sir David Luce as C-in-C Far East, he insisted on maintaining the force levels in Borneo though the Azahari rebellion was clearly over. 40th Commando, however, was returned to Singapore and a contingency plan was made for its quick return. Lt Col J. M. Strawson, commanding officer of the Queen's Royal Irish Hussars, took over in Kuching.

Walker started in Borneo where Templer left off in Malaya. He insisted from the very start on unity and joint planning between government, police and the three services at every level. In his first directives he stressed six principles: joint operations; timely and accurate Intelligence; speed, mobility and flexibility; security of bases; the domination of the jungle; and finally, and most important of all, winning and keeping the confidence of the indigenous people. The defeat of Azahari's rebellion gave him a flying start in the battle for hearts and minds, but he did not under-estimate the dangers of Indonesian infiltration across the 1,000 mile jungle covered frontier or of internal CCO subversion in the cosmopolitan coastal towns.

Mopping up the rebels went faster than expected but was hampered by torrential rain. Many more troops were used rescuing people from the floods than in helping the police round up the dissidents. By the beginning of January, 3,500 rebels had been detained of whom 1,500 were sent back to their kampongs with a warning. Only the hard-core leadership was still at large. Azahari himself had slipped off to Manila before the rebellion began so that he could set up a government in exile. On 9 December he had foolishly proclaimed that the North Borneo National Army of 20,000 had attacked the main towns and that the Sultan had thrown off the British yoke. His credibility was irreparably damaged as the truth emerged. He had left his two brothers and Yassin Affendi, the military commander of the TNKU, to manage the revolt. They were not tracked down until April when one brother was killed and the other captured. Affendi stayed free for another month but was caught with three of his aides in mid-May. Both operations were carried out by 2nd/7th GR in conjunction with Special Branch.

The speed of the British military reaction to Azhari's challenge had an equal and opposite effect in Malaysia and Indonesia. In Malaysia, most of the political fence-sitters jumped down on the Tunku's side and the CCO went underground. In Indonesia Sukarno saw it as a blatant neo-colonialist challenge to his 'continuing Indonesian revolution' and to his theories about the strength and historical inevitability of the victory of 'the new emergent forces in Asia'. He had just brought his confrontation with the Dutch over West Irian to a successful conclusion so he was free to turn on the British. Despite his earlier relaxed attitude to the Tunku's ideas, his propagandists now dubbed the Malaysian merger as a creation of the British and their puppets in Kuala Lumpur and Singapore. The first reference to 'confrontation' came in a speech made by the Subandrio towards the end of January 1963. In it he said:

We cannot but adopt a policy of confrontation against Malaya because at present they represent themselves as accomplices of the neo-colonialists and neo-imperialists pursuing a hostile policy towards Indonesia.[3]

He did not spell out what was meant by 'confrontation', but it was assumed to be a blending of political, economic and military pressures just short of war.

Indonesia's confrontation with Malaysia was to last three and a half years. It was a six-round contest between Sukarno as the self-styled leader of the 'new emergent forces of Asia' and the Tunku, who was bitterly anti-Communist and had no wish to substitute Indonesian for British influence in Malaysia. The Tunku, with the help of his British seconds, won the first five rounds conclusively on points. In the sixth round Sukarno's seconds fell out amongst themselves and threw in the towel as Indonesia's economy spun out of control in the latter half of 1965, leaving the Tunku the undisputed victor. Sukarno's political power depended upon his ability to balance the ambitions of his two principal groups of supporters: the anti-Communists, led by Western orientated senior officers of the Army, and the powerful Indonesian Communist Party (the PKI) who looked for and found support from Communist China. As each round was lost Sukarno lent more heavily upon left-wing support until the PKI became over-confident and risked a *coup d'état* in October 1965. The Army's reaction led to the defeat of the PKI and the horrific massacre of the Communists and their supporters throughout Indonesia. Confrontation ended as Sukarno's successor, General Suharto, re-established relations with the West. Such was the broad political outline of the North Borneo campaign. We will look briefly at each round in turn.

Sukarno's aim in the first round was to stop the creation of the Federation of Malaysia by political pressure, but to do so he needed to demonstrate that, although Azahari's rebellion had been crushed, the majority of the local people were still opposed to the Federation and were prepared to fight for their right to join their kith and kin in Indonesian Kalimantan. In the early hours of 12 April 1963 the police post at Tebedu, three miles inside the Sarawak frontier, due south of Kuching, was surprised by a 30-strong raiding party, who killed two policemen and went on to loot the nearby bazaar. At first it was uncertain whether the raid was an 'inside job' by the CCO or a cross-border raid. Documents left by the raiders purported to show that they were TNKU, but later evidence revealed that they were Indonesian-trained local volunteers led by Indonesian regular soldiers from a special raiding unit. Almost simultaneously with the Tebedu raid Sarawak police Special Branch uncovered evidence of CCO preparations for military action. The Governor's Sarawak Emergency Committee called for military assistance to help the police confiscate the 8,514 licensed shot-guns held by the inhabitants of the First and Second Divisions. 40th Commando returned to Kuching from Singapore and 2nd/10th GR were sent to Sibu, the principal town of the Second Division. With their support the police recovered 8,000 of the shot-guns without much difficulty.

The hallmark of the Borneo campaign, which was just beginning, was anticipation of Indonesian and CCO intentions and speed of British reaction. The former depended upon Intelligence and the latter upon helicopter mobility and good radio communications. Although the Indonesians, as the aggressors, held the initiative until the fifth and sixth rounds, the British command was always two or three steps ahead of them with its defensive measures. Nowhere was this more apparent than in the development of the irregular Border Scouts. Soon after the Azahari rebellion broke out several of the British managers in such firms as Shell and the North Borneo Company had organized bodies of the indigenous peoples—Dyaks, Ibans and other tribes—to protect their commercial operations. Walker decided to form them into a recognized military force. The initial spade work was done by Tom Harrison, Curator of the Sarawak Museum, who had been dropped into the Borneo jungle during the Second World War to help organize tribal resistance to the Japanese. He knew the tribes and the tribes knew and trusted him. His creation of the Border Scouts is a saga all of its own. Suffice it to say that, with the help of 22nd SAS and the Gurkha Independent Parachute Company, they became 'one thousand pairs of eyes' watching the tracks across the frontier. Their first military commander was Major John Cross who had come to Walker's attention during the Malayan campaign. They lived in the long houses and villages along the frontier, which few Indonesian raiding parties managed to cross undetected by them.

Sukarno opened his political offensive with an invitation to the Tunku to meet him in Tokyo in May 1965. The meeting was cordial and it was agreed that they should settle their differences 'in a spirit of neighbourliness and goodwill'. Their foreign ministers met in Manila in June under Philippine auspices. The Malayan government accepted the resulting 'Manila Accord', the crucial paragraph of which read:

10. The Ministers re-affirm their countries' adherence to the principle of self-determination for the people of non-self-governing territories. In this context, Indonesia and the Philippines stated that they would welcome the formation of Malaysia, provided the support of the people of the Borneo Territories is

ascertained by an indepedent and impartial authority, the Secretary General of the United Nations or his representative.[4]

The Manila meetings did not stop parallel negotiations between Whitehall and Kuala Lumpur on the final details of the Malaysian merger. The Sultan of Brunei decided not to join the Federation but to remain under British protection. The Tunku flew to London on 5 July and, much to Sukarno's fury, signed the London Agreement which would bring the merger into effect on or soon after 31 August 1963. In spite of Sukarno's threats to 'crush Malaysia' the Tunku still attended the Philippines-inspired Maphilindo summit meeting at the end of July in Manila and there agreed to Sukarno's demand for a United Nations test of opinion in the North Borneo territories although this meant delaying Malaysia's vesting day until 16 September 1963.

While these political events had been unfolding 'volunteers' continued to raid across the Sarawak frontier in support of Sukarno's thesis that the people of the British territories were discontented with their lot and were still in a state of open rebellion. None of the raiders had any real success and proved more a nuisance than a real threat. Nevertheless, no time was wasted in getting ready to meet more serious attacks if they materialized. Police posts were strengthened and the Border Scouts began to provide useful Intelligence. The British and Gurkha units gained acclimatization and experience of the operational conditions in Borneo. They also began the development of new techniques for using helicopters effectively to land and retrieve ambush parties and to supply the remoter frontier posts.

The first round of confrontation, which was little more than a preliminary political and military sparring match, came to an end when the Secretary General of the United Nations, U Thant, announced on 13 September the result of his mission's test of opinion:

There is no doubt about the wishes of a sizeable majority of the people of these territories to join the Federation of Malaysia.[5]

Sukarno had lost the first round. The second opened with his angry rejection of U Thant's ruling and refusal to recognize the new Federation of Malaysia when it was proclaimed on 16 September 1963. In Djakarta the British Embassy was attacked on 16 December and sacked two days later, and British businesses were taken over by Communist mobs. Kuala Lumpur severed diplomatic relations with Djakarta and Manila, but Britain did not do so on the assurance from the Indonesian government that it had not condoned the violence and would return British businesses which had been seized. A week later Sukarno added economic pressure to political confrontation. He severed all trading links with Singapore and Malaya, and over the next few months tried to break the hold of the Singapore and Penang merchants on the rubber and tin trades. Singapore did suffer some loss of trade and consequent unemployment, but the Indonesian economy was harder hit by the curtailment of Western economic aid. As the months went by Sukarno had to seek financial help elsewhere. Moscow's doors were shut to him because Indonesia's debt repayment to the Soviet Union was behind schedule. Doors were, however, ajar in Peking so Sukarno began to pay more attention to the advice of his Communist seconds.

In Borneo, Indonesian military tactics became more ambitious and aggressive. Instead of contenting themselves with terrorizing the frontier villages and long houses, they started the Maoist revolutionary war tactic of trying to establish 'liberated' areas deep inside British territory. They went on using 'volunteers' led by Indonesian regulars to maintain the fiction of a continuing TNKU rebellion. The country lent itself to such tactics. The 1,000 mile long frontier lay unmarked along the top of the mountain spine dividing British from Indonesian Borneo. The whole area was covered by dense rain forest. Much of the range was between 5000–8000 feet high, though it was lower at the eastern and western ends. There were relatively few tracks over the frontier used by the jungle people, and these usually led to primitive boat stations on the upper reaches of the rivers from which long boats could be used to reach the villages further down-stream. As it was impossible to stop infiltration, Walker's tactics during the second round were to hold his troops well back and to depend upon the SAS and Border Scouts for news of infiltrators. Helicopters were then used to place ambushes behind the raiders on their anticipated withdrawal routes, while others were placed to block and destroy the raiders if they pushed on towards their target.

Placing patrols in the jungle by helicopter was not easy. It involved difficult flying techniques and a variety of ways of finding and creating landing zones. Gravel banks in river beds were favourite sites. When no clearing could be found, roping down had to be used to land the men and chain saws were lowered to enable them to clear their own landing pad. In spite of the helicopters' noise, surprise could often be achieved by careful selection of approach routes and low level contour flying. Walker often said a battalion with six Wessex helicopters was more value to him than a brigade without. There were never more than 70 helicopters available in Borneo: in Vietnam the Americans had 2,700.

The first Indonesian deep penetration raid started towards the end of September 1963. A force of 150 regular led 'volunteers' crossed the border of the Third Division undetected and managed to reach the village of Long Jawai, 30 miles inside Sarawak. There they surprised and over-ran the small Border Scout post, killing two Gurkhas of the 1st/2nd GR, a policeman and a Border Scout. 1st/2nd GR's reaction was swift and effective. Cut off parties were flown in by Royal Naval helicopters and ambushes were set on the raiders' probable withdrawal routes. Twenty-six raiders were soon killed when two of the long boats which they were using were ambushed. Hard tracking carried out by the battalion during October led to the deaths of another dozen or so, and by the end of the month the disheartened survivors struggled back over the frontier. The news of the security forces' speed of reaction and relentless follow-up spread on both sides of the border.

The first Indonesian attempt to establish a liberated area had failed. They did not give up. Their next target was the Tawau district at the northeast corner of Sabah. It was a prosperous area with tea, rubber, palm oil and cocoa estates, and it was an important logging centre for the timber trade. Two factors made it an attractive target: it was close to the Indonesian border and there was a large Indonesian contingent in its labour force who could be subverted relatively easily. A third factor may or may not have been taken into account by the Indonesian commanders. With the creation of Malaysia General Walker became responsible to the Malaysian National Operations Council, chaired by the Tunku in Kuala Lumpur. The 3rd and 5th Battalions of the Royal Malay Regiment and a squadron of the Federation Reconnaissance Regiment were placed under his command for operations in Borneo. He deployed the 3rd Battalion to the Tawau Residency and the 5th to the First Division of Sarawak. Although there was a company of the King's Own Yorkshire Light Infantry in the Tawau area as well, any Indonesian attempt to infiltrate the estate would be met largely by the less experienced Malayan troops. There was no lack of Intelligence about Indonesian interest in the area, and there was a Royal Naval frigate on anti-piracy patrol off the coast.

Towards the end of December an Indonesian commando force of 128 men, of whom 35 were regular Marines, started their infiltration. On 29 December they attacked the Bombay-Burma Company's logging centre at Kalabakan, some 40 miles west of Tawau. A company of 3rd Royal Malay Regiment was surprised and lost eight men, including the company commander, and 19 others were wounded. Fortunately, the Indonesian commander did not press on to Tawau quickly enough to maintain the momentum of the surprise he had achieved. 1st/10th GR were flown in to intercept and soon had the raiders encircled and on the run. It took some weeks of patient tracking and ambush work to account for most of them. Only about 20 escaped back across the border.

Three other attempts were made during January to establish pro-Indonesian enclaves. In the First Division 40th Commando repelled a company-sized force; in the Fifth Division, almost on the border with Sabah, 1st Royal Leicesters frustrated a similar effort; and in the Fifth Division 1st/7th GR intercepted a party, which arrived by sea with the intention of building up local CCO support along the Rajang River.

The Indonesians were no more successful in establishing liberated areas in North Borneo than the Communist terrorists had been during the Malayan emergency or Grivas in Cyprus. Sukarno's political propaganda, however, was having an effect in Washington, where the American government saw the conflict as another potential source of Communist expansion; and in New York, where U Thant was conscious that his ruling on Malaysian opinion was being flaunted by Indonesia. President Johnson despatched Senator Robert Kennedy to Djakarta with a brief 'to get the war out of the jungle and back to the conference table'; and U Thant appealed to both sides to bring hostilities to an end. These combined political initiatives brought about a cease-fire on 23 January as a prelude to peace negotiations under Thai auspices in Bangkok. The second round ended with Malaysia again winning on points.

The third round started with a political interlude and ended with a major change in Indonesian military policy. Sukarno's acceptance of the cease-fire was a tactical ploy. He could not stop the cross border raids because they were, in theory, inspired by internal discontent within Eastern Malaysia and were carried out by local 'volunteers'. When the Foreign Ministers met in Bangkok on 5 February 1964 it soon transpired that the two sides interpreted the cease-fire agreement quite differently. Subandrio took it to be a stand-still order allowing such Indonesian troops as were inside Malaysia to stay there until there was a peace settlement. Tun Razak, representing Malaysia, insisted that all infiltrators must be withdrawn before substantive negotiations could start. The whole argument was political rather than military because there were few, if any, Indonesians on the Malaysian side of the frontier, but Subandrio could not be expected to admit this publically. During the Bangkok negotiations, which went on fitfully for the whole of February and the first week of March, three substantial raids by parties of from 30 to 50 men each were made across the frontier of the First Division: at Lundu at the end of January; at Bau on 21 February; and at Rassau on 6 March. On each such occasion they were trapped by 42nd Commando and 1st/2nd GR and suffered severely before escaping back across the border.

The Bangkok talks finally broke down in mutual recrimination over the cease-fire on 4 March. Two days later the major change in Indonesian military policy became discernible. Two attempts were made in quick succession to push back the recognized frontier by *de facto* occupation of commanding hill features just inside Sarawak. On 6 March 2nd/10th GR detected an unusually large force of some 200 men holding a prominent ridge in the Kling Kang Range in the Second Division. Their positions were skilfully outflanked by the Gurkhas and the Indonesians withdrew equally skilfully, demonstrating a much higher standard of training than the raiders had displayed hitherto. They were also equipped with heavier infantry weapons, including mortars. Documents left behind identified them as the 328th Raider Battalion of the Indonesian regular army. A radio message intercepted during the withdrawal said, 'We have a lot of dead and wounded and are in great difficulty'. The reply from their headquarters was curt, 'Get on with it: there are plenty more where they came from'.[6]

Within a few days of this action another large force was reported in a similar position 24 miles to the east still in 2nd/10th GR's sector. The Indonesian commander was at pains to impress on the people of the nearby long houses at Kluah that his men were there to stay. Lt Col J. A. I.

Fillingham, CO 2nd/10th, decided to use a greater weight of fire power to deal with this second invasion. There was a passable track from which two Saladin armoured cars with 76mm guns could support his attack. In addition he had a troop of 105mm guns in range and two Royal Naval Wessex helicopters each armed with two French SS11 missiles. One Gurkha company climbed the hill while the Wessex, guns and armoured cars gave fire support. Three camps were attacked and cleared and a lot of abandoned equipment was found. Only two Indonesians were seen, one of whom was killed. The Indonesian regulars had once more shown considerable tactical skill. Confrontation had taken a significant step towards regular warfare with the use of heavier weapons by both sides.

Infiltration was not entirely abandoned by the Indonesians. While the Kling Kang operations were in progress a 36 man raiding force from 'The Black Cobra Battalion' slipped over the Second Division border and headed for Jambu. They were located by 2nd/10th GR at the beginning of April. Fillingham switched his battalion's effort to this new target. Helicopters were used both to place real ambushes and to sell dummies. After a week of constant harassment the Black Cobras had had enough. As they tried to withdraw they were caught in ambush, losing three men killed and a number wounded, and lost all their packs and food. Using quick helicopter lifts, the party was gradually encircled by 2nd/10th GR: four contacts were made in the next three days and seven more were killed. The rest tried to find food in a cultivated area and were trapped. Only one was thought to have escaped and he probably died of starvation in the jungle. The key to the Gurkhas' success was excellent shooting. In the Black Cobra hunt they had the remarkable record of one hundred per cent hits on every fleeting target engaged. The Cyprus emergency might have ended more quickly had the British battalions achieved the same standard against EOKA.

The third round ended with a further flurry of political activity. The Tunku won a sweeping victory in the first Malaysian elections in April 1964 which gave him a renewed mandate to oppose Indonesian ambitions. He demonstrated the Federation's determination to defend itself by announcing the introduction of selective National Service with a call-up of 100,000 men. Sukarno responded with a flamboyant proclamation of the creation of a 'Volunteer Command' to which, he claimed, 21 million Indonesians, pledged to crush Malaysia, already belonged. Both were empty gestures. Malaysia could not expand its small army quickly enough to absorb 100,000 men, and so the brunt of military operations in Borneo continued to be borne by British and Gurkha troops. Sukarno's Volunteer Command was only useful for internal propaganda and raising national morale at a time when necessarily harsh trading regulations and lack of Western financial support were destroying the Indonesian economy.

The tone of the fourth round was set up by Sukarno in a speech on the Indonesian National Resurrection Day on 20 May 1964. In it he boasted that he would crush Malaysia by the time 'the sun rises on 1 January 1965'.

While this threat could be interpreted as heady rhetoric for internal consumption, Intelligence sources had been reporting that not all Sukarno's bluster was hot air. A steady build-up of Marine commandos and parachute troops was detected in camps on the Indonesian side of the Borneo frontier, on the Sumatra coast opposite Malaya, and in the Riau Archipelago south of Singapore. General Walker called for reinforcements to pre-empt a major Indonesian offensive. The 51st Brigade of the Strategic Reserve was despatched to the Far East Command with one Gurkha and two British battalions, which were to be used in Borneo and to help in the relief programme. British and Gurkha battalions were being rotated between Borneo and their permanent stations in Malaya, Singapore and Hong Kong where their families lived.

The arrival of the three extra battalions eased the tightness of the rotational programme. HQ 51st Brigade's arrival enabled Walker to strengthen his command structure and improve the balance of his deployment. He established three brigade sectors: 99th Gurkha Brigade (having relieved 3rd Commando Brigade) became West Brigade with five battalions holding Kuching and the three western divisions of Sarawak; 51st Brigade took over as Central Brigade with two battalions holding the rest of Sarawak and Brunei; and 5th Malaysian Brigade, based at Tawau, had three battalions holding Sabah. The SAS and Border Scouts still watched long sectors of the frontier which were not covered by military or police posts.

Analysis of the new Indonesian tactics of trying to push the frontier back, and of using a higher proportion of regulars to 'volunteers', persuaded General Walker to make a major change in his own tactics. It was no longer enough to hold his main forces well back from the frontier and to depend upon destroying infiltrators within the first 30 miles or so by heliborne cut offs. The frontier itself had to be defended, but Walker was determined to do this by offensive action rather than see his troops pinned down in defensive posts as the French had been in Indo-China. He moved the company bases forward to the frontier area and strongly fortified them, but insisted that each must be defensible by only a quarter to a third of the company's strength: the rest of the company was to be on offensive patrols or in ambush, dominating the jungle in its sector. He stressed that the jungle must belong to the British, Gurkha and Malay battalions and not to the Indonesians: and in this he was entirely successful.

The great distances involved forced him to make another major change in tactical policy. Contrary to well-established military principles, he had to insist upon the decentralization of both artillery and air power to improve speed of reaction. Guns were deployed to company bases singly or in pairs. One gun per battery was held in reserve to be flown forward in emergency, slung under the Belvedere or Wessex helicopters, or in pieces inside the smaller Whirlwinds. The only troop with 5.5 inch medium guns available in Borneo moved its guns singly along the tracks in the West Brigade's sector where they came to be highly respected by the Indonesians. One of their large rounds would silence Indonesian mortars within 500 yards. In decentralizing air resources, helicopter bases were pushed as far forward as it was practicable to do so to save dead flying time. Construction of forward landing pads and light airstrips was a continuous and never-ending task of the British and Gurkha sappers who were also heavily committed in strengthening the defences of the company bases which became mini-fortresses.

In diplomatic circles there was a growing body of opinion that Sukarno was looking for a face-saving formula to scale down confrontation, and was increasing military pressure only to gain as much as he could in further peace negotiations that President Macapagal was hoping to engineer for June in Tokyo. To give Macapagal's peace initiative a chance and to let Sukarno off his confrontation hook, the Tunku agreed reluctantly that any Indonesian raiders inside Malaysia should be allowed to withdraw step by step as negotiations progressed. After much wrangling about numbers of check points, it was agreed that the Thais should supervise the withdrawal through one checkpoint only, which would be at Tebedu. On 18 June 34 Indonesian raiders were ceremoniously withdrawn through Tebedu so that the Tokyo talks could begin between the Tunku, Sukarno and Macapagal that day. The condition of the raiders was such that it was clear that they had been infiltrated into the Tebedu area only a few days before: they were too clean to have been there long or to have carried out any jungle operations!

The Tokyo Summit was little more than a charade. If Sukarno had ever wished to slip off the confrontation hook, he showed no sign of doing so. Instead he made it abundantly clear that he believed that the Tunku had tricked him over the original Manila Accord, probably with British advice, and that he still intended 'to crush Malaysia' if the Tunku did not join the new emergent forces and give up his connections with the British. Subandrio declared 'we are not aggressors since Malaysia is not in existence'. Such obtuseness could only mean one thing: Indonesia's military preparations for an offensive were complete. In the fifth round, Sukarno was intent on a knock-out.

Indeed, the fifth round did start ominously for Malaysia, but not from any Indonesian action. During the Malaysian elections in April Lee Kuan Yew's People's Action Party (PAP) in Singapore had tried to win the support of the Chinese in Malaya, and to draw them away from the Tunku's Alliance Party. This was considered by the Malays to be a political foul. They viewed the new Federation as a 'Malay Malaysia' in which the Chinese were the junior partners: the PAP sought a 'Malaysian Malaysia' in which all races would have an equal share.

On 21 July serious inter-racial rioting broke out in Singapore and lasted several days. Twenty-two people were killed and nearly 500 injured. There appears to have been no Indonesian involvement, but the Indonesian naval staff, who were responsible for the build up of forces in Sumatra and the Riau Islands, decided to profit by them. On 17 August 1964 they landed a force of 64 regulars and 34 Malayan Communists and Indonesian 'volunteers' on three beaches near Pontian in southwest Johore (see Map 13). They were instructed to push quickly inland and to set up secret training centres and guerrilla bases in the jungle in preparation for an airborne force, which would be dropped near the old Communist stronghold of Labis in central Johore. They were told to expect whole-hearted support from the local population.

The landings at Pontian were a fiasco. Far from welcoming the raiders, the local people raised the alarm. Most of the raiders were killed or captured in the first few days after the landing. The leader and a handful of men found a safe hide-out and were not tracked down until mid-October when the leader was killed. A few survived until mid-1965.

The airborne landing at Labis went wrong as well. It was timed to take place simultaneously with a second bout of inter-racial rioting in Singapore, this time inspired by Indonesian agents. Four aircraft were due to take off from Djakarta on the evening of 1 September, each carrying 48 paratroopers and supply containers: of the 192 men, 151 were regulars and 41 Malayan Communists. One aircraft went unserviceable before take off; another disappeared without trace in the China Sea; a third failed to find the Dropping Zone (DZ) and spread its men over a five-mile stretch of partially cleared jungle; and only one dropped its load near the actual DZ and that had been chosen in thick jungle where several men and all the containers were lost. 1st/10th GR and the 1st Royal New Zealand Regiment spent the rest of September tracking down the survivors. The inter-racial rioting, which did start on 2 September, fizzled out by 7 September.

Over the next six months ten further attempts were made to land small parties of saboteurs on Singapore Island and in South Johore, mainly from the Riau Islands. In each case they were rounded up by the local security forces as soon as they were detected: they never received the support they had been told to expect from the coastal towns and villages.

In Borneo the Indonesian army had taken off what gloves it might have been wearing hitherto and in June had started to mount prepared assaults on British company bases along the frontier. 'Volunteers' were left behind and regular raiding battalions attacked, using the full array of conventional support weapons. They had an early success against a base held by the rear party of a 1st/6th GR company. They attacked the post five times during the night of 21 June, killing five Gurkhas and wounding another five. As the weeks slipped by attacks became more frequent and were pressed with greater determination as the Indonesian army tried to honour Sukarno's boast that he would have crushed Malaysia by the end of the year. They had no successes.

The Indonesian raids on Malaya and Singapore, combined with the much larger attacks on company bases in Borneo, brought Sukarno's confrontation dangerously close to the brink of all-out war. The British and Malaysian governments decided to try to damp down the escalation

29. A 1st Green Jackets patrol on the
river near Bekenu

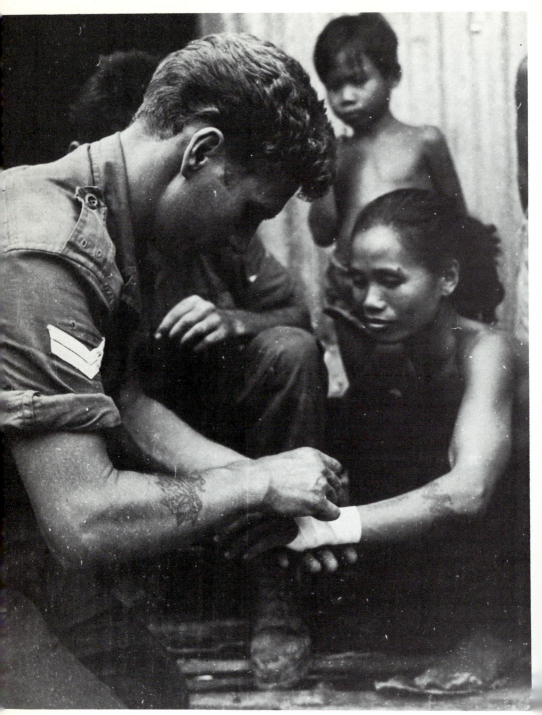

30. 'Hearts and Minds' in Borneo: an
Army medical team visiting a long
house

31. Gurkhas deplaning in a jungle
    clearing

32. A company base near the Indonesian frontier

33. The Radfan commanders: Brigadier James Lunt (left in Arab headgear), Lieutenant General Sir Charles Harington, C-in-C Middle East (centre) and Major General JH Cubbon, Chief of Staff (right)

34. Men of the 3rd Parachute Battalion in the Radfan

35. The Rabwa Pass, showing the
    sapper-built road
36. A Royal Navy Buccaneer over Aden:
    Isthmus (left), Maalla (foreground)
    and Cratar (right)

37. The last British officer to leave Aden,
    Lt Col 'Dai' Morgan, CO 42nd
    Royal Marine Commando, landing
    back on *Albion*, 29 November 1967

38. ZANU guerrillas showing the variety
of Eastern Bloc small arms carried by
them

with an appeal to the Security Council and by a show of British military power and political commitment to the defence of Malaysia. The Security Council and deterrent approaches were subtly orchestrated to Indonesia's disadvantage by the Malaysian government complaining to the United Nations about Indonesian aggression, while Britain started an overt build up of RAF V Bombers and Royal Navy warships within striking distance of the principal Indonesian air and naval bases.

The Tunku called on the Security Council to condemn Indonesian aggression soon after the Labis parachute drop. The Indonesians did not dispute the facts: instead they accused Malaysia of causing the fighting by its neo-colonial policies and by its sabotage of the Bangkok and Tokyo negotiations. This line of argument might have succeeded in the Afro-Asian dominated General Assembly, but it won only two of the 11 Security Council votes. As one of the two votes was Russia's, the Malaysian resolution 'deploring Indonesian military action' was vetoed. Nevertheless, Sukarno took this adverse vote with ill grace and began a campaign against the United Nations as a neo-colonialist organization that needed 'retooling to meet the needs of the post-colonial era'. He was irked all the more by the knowledge that Malaysia would take one of the rotational seats on the Security Council in the New Year. Insult was added to injury when he failed in his further efforts to isolate Malaysia politically at the autumn conferences of the non-aligned and the Afro-Asian states.

The British deterrent moves were more forthright than they might otherwise have been because the Labour Party had just won the 1964 general election and the new Wilson government was determined to honour Britain's moral obligations to new Commonwealth countries which might be in trouble with aggressive neighbours. No secret was made of the despatch of V Bombers, Javelin fighters and Bloodhound air defence missiles to the Far East; nor of the reinforcement of the Far East fleet, which, with some 80 warships, was stronger than at any time since the Korean War. It included the carriers *Victorious* and *Centaur*, the commando carrier *Bulwark* and the guided missile destroyer *Kent*. The British military challenge to Indonesia was demonstrated by the movements of *Victorious*, which was brought back from Australia to Singapore. She should have come through the Sunda Strait between Java and Sumatra, but the Indonesians, acting within their international rights, declared the Straits a temporary naval exercise area. *Victorious* sailed instead through the Lombok Strait, east of Bali, trailing the British coat. There was no Indonesian reaction: Sukarno had no wish to give Britain the excuse to destroy his air force and navy. The US had made a similar demonstration of its determination to retaliate against North Vietnam in the Gulf of Tonkin in August. The incident had led to direct American military involvement in Vietnam. The risks of a similar British reaction to an attack on *Victorious* were deemed by the Indonesians to be too high.

From Borneo Walker warned that he might need more British troops if the Indonesian offensive continued. He also asked for authority to operate across the frontier to ambush the Indonesian raiders and to hit their base camps. Reinforcements were sent out early in 1965: 1st Scots Guards, 2nd Parachute Battalion and 3rd Royal Green Jackets joined the Far-Eastern order of battle. The Australian and New Zealand governments also agreed that their troops in the Commonwealth Brigade at Malacca could take their turn in the rotation of units between western and eastern Malaysia. 3rd Commando Brigade HQ returned to Borneo, and the front was then divided into four brigade sectors so that 99th Brigade could concentrate on the defence of Kuching and the First Division of Sarawak only since this was where the main Indonesian regular army threat lay. 3rd Commando Brigade took over Second and Third Divisions as the Mid-west Brigade. The Central and Eastern Brigade sectors were unchanged. In all there were 13 British, Gurkha and Malay battalions in Borneo for the fifth round with a further five British and Gurkha battalions in western Malaysia and Hong Kong providing the rotational reliefs in Borneo.

As long as the United Nations was seized with the Malaysian complaint against Indonesia, no authority could be given for cross-border action. After the favourable outcome of the debate in the Security Council, Walker was allowed to penetrate Indonesian territory up to 5,000 yards, provided incursions were kept secret and each raid was specificaly authorized by himself as Director of Operations. A special war room was set up to handle these clandestine operations, which were so successful and the secret so well kept that permission was given for penetration by largish bodies of troops up to 20,000 yards, or about 11 miles. The ambushes laid lowered the morale of the Indonesian soldiers, but Sukarno gave no publicity to these actions as he was not prepared to admit to the world that more fighting in the fifth round was taking place on his side of the frontier than in Malaysia. There were few large scale battles: just an extension of patient patrolling and ambushes based on an increasing flow of Intelligence from many sources. Walker's own description of the fighting painted the picture well:

In late 1964, Indonesia stepped up her campaign and trebled her regular garrisons in the border area, particularly in West Sarawak. In 1965 and 1966, we were, therefore, dealing with the regular Indonesian Army in a real war, akin to fighting the Japanese in Burma. It was long range patrolling, often in company strength, ambushing and attacking relatively large bodies of enemy, often dug in. It had become a company commanders' war. The enemy fought with tenacity and skill. He had mortars and guns and used them efficiently. Gone were the days when the immediate reaction to contact was to charge the enemy. During 1965 and 1966, only the highest standards of patrolling, battle-craft, fire and movement, and the fullest use of our artillery and mortar support, could win the day.[7]

Some idea of the air's contribution was shown by the figures he gave for the period November 1964 to October 1965. The *monthly* averages were: 19,000 troops air lifted, mostly by helicopters: 1,900,000 lb of supplies air landed; and 2,000,000 lb air dropped.

Half-way through the battle with the Indonesian regular army, Sukarno brought the fifth round to an abrupt end by leaving the United Nations early in January before Malaysia could take her seat on the Security Council. At the same time he swung Indonesia firmly into the Chinese Communist orbit, seeking political and economic aid from Peking. The right-wing army leaders lost much of their influence and the disintegration of the Indonesian economy accelerated, but he was confident that with China's help he could salvage something from the wreck of his policies.

The sixth and last round was dominated by Sukarno's own internal political and economic problems, which came to a head in October 1965. In Borneo the war went on with no apparent relaxation on the Indonesian side and no let up by the British and Malaysian security forces. General Walker's tour as Director of Operations came to an end in March 1965 and he was succeeded by Major General George Lea, a former commander of 22nd SAS and no stranger to jungle warfare. Though a less controversial character than Walker, George Lea was a worthy successor, who maintained the pressure on the Indonesians without allowing the fighting to escalate in an embarrassing way for either the Tunku or the Wilson government.

Shortly after Lea's arrival the Indonesian army showed that it was still able to bite. On 27 April one of the company bases of the recently arrived 2nd Parachute Battalion at Palaman Mapu in the southwest corner of the First Division was attacked by an Indonesian battalion. Most of the company were out on patrol and only a weak rear party under C.S.M. Williams was in the base when the attack came in at 5 a.m. A fierce battle ensued, which Field Marshal Carver had described as another 'defence of Rorke's Drift' in the Zulu War of 1879. Though Williams was wounded early on, he and his paratroopers fought off three attacks in an hour and a half, losing two men killed and eight wounded. The Indonesian force was harassed by the rest of the battalion as it withdrew. Villagers reported that the raiders were seen carrying off about 30 casualties: only two bodies were recovered. The battalion had their revenge in subsequent ambushes, accounting for at least 35 more of their Indonesian opponents.

As many of the actions at this later stage of the campaign were fought on the Indonesian side of the frontier no publicity could be given to them. One of the hardest fought actions was by 2nd/10th Gurkhas in August 1965 south of Bau, in which Corporal Rambahadur Limbu won the only VC awarded during the campaign, and his company and platoon commanders won MCs. An enemy camp was located and destroyed after a day long battle in which 24 Indonesians were killed and three Gurkhas lost their lives.

In August 1965 Indonesian fortunes suddenly changed. It looked as if Sukarno's dream of destroying Malaysia might come true, though not through his own efforts. The incompatabilities of Chinese Singapore and Malay Malaya became intolerable to both states. The Tunku asked Lea to withdraw Singapore from the Federation and he did so with great regret but without animosity. Ironically it was Sukarno who suffered most from fatal internal political disorder. The PKI misjudged its own strength and launched its *coup d'état* in Djakarta on 1 October. The whole affair was botched and easily crushed by the Indonesian army. In the popular anti-Communist upsurge that followed, many thousands of Communists and their supporters were massacred throughout Indonesia as Sukarno's right-wing seconds regained political ascendency in Djakarta. Such was Sukarno's pre-eminence as the 'Father of the Indonesian Revolution' that the Army leaders did not move against him personally. He was only gradually shorn of his powers. His confrontation with Malaysia became as irrelevant as his attempts to re-assert himself. Nevertheless, it took until May 1966 before the two sides met again in Bangkok to seek a new *modus vivendi* in Southeast Asia. On 4 August 1966 General Suharto, Sukarno's *de facto* successor, declared confrontation to be at an end. Diplomatic links and trading relations were restored and Britain began to wind down her military commitments in Southeast Asia.

At its peak 17,000 Commonwealth servicemen had been engaged in Borneo with another 10,000 stationed in Malaya, Singapore and Hong Kong, providing reliefs. One hundred and fourteen had been killed and 181 wounded, a high proportion being Gurkhas. It was estimated that the Indonesians lost about 1,600 (600 killed, 200 wounded and 800 captured). For once, Britain had not reacted with too little, too late. The British Far East Command was always a step ahead of its opponents. Joint service co-operation was at its best, giving a speed of reaction and a sustained effort far beyond anything achieved before. The services have every right to be proud of their victory. The battle for hearts and minds in Borneo was never lost: in Vietnam and in Aden it was never won. Denis Healey paid the forces a special tribute in the House of Commons on 27 November 1967:

When the House thinks of the tragedy that could have fallen on a whole corner of a Continent if we had not been able to hold the situation and bring it to a successful termination, it will appreciate that in history books it will be recorded as one of the most efficient uses of military force in the history of the world.[8]

An exaggeration, but a worthy expression of the feeling at the time.

The North Borneo and Aden campaigns had one obvious similarity. They were both confrontations with Afro-Asian nationalism in which the Communist powers played a relatively small part though they were always in the wings encouraging the 'progressive' forces. Of the two, Nasser's Arab nationalism held far greater attractions for the people of Southern Arabia than Sukarno's pan-Malayanism ever had for the people of Southeast Asia. But, until Egyptian troops entered the Yemen in the autumn of 1962 to support the revolution of General Sallal, Nasser's threat was the more distant and the less immediate of the two.

There was one important difference. In Borneo, British troops were supporting an established independent Commonwealth government under a leader of international stature, the Tunku Abdul Rahman. In southern

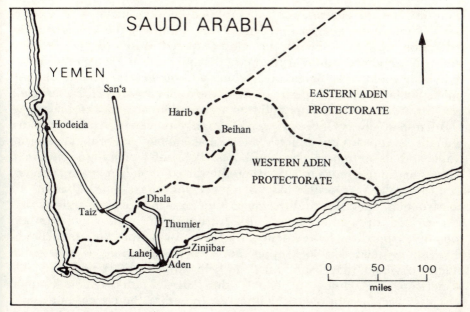

15. Southern Arabia in the 1960s.

Arabia, Britain was still trying to encourage the formation of a viable government to which power could be transferred without jeopardizing the security of the Aden base. When independence would be granted to South Arabia and whether the base would be secured by a defence treaty as in Singapore or as a sovereign base enclave as in Cyprus, were still undecided at the end of 1963 when fighting started in the arid, inhospitable mountains of the Radfan 60 miles north of Aden, just to the east of Thumier.

Though Aden had been a Crown colony since the middle of the nineteenth century, no attempt had been made to impose British sovereignty over the fiercely independent tribes of the hinterland. A cordon sanitaire had been created around Aden by negotiating treaties of protection or advice with individual sultans and sheiks, forming what became known as the Eastern and Western Aden Protectorates. The establishment of a South Arabian Federation had been suggested by the British Colonial authorities in Aden in the early 1950s to counter the growing agitation of the Imam of the Yemen for the restoration of his sovereignty over the Protectorates and over Aden. The proposal found no favour with the tribal rulers until Egypt federated with Syria and the Yemen to form the United Arab Republic early in 1958. A year later the Federation of South Arabia was established at the request of the majority of the rulers. Each state nominated six representatives to the federal council because there were no political parties as such spanning all the sultanates and sheikdoms. To ensure that power was, in fact, transferred from the states to the federal government the rulers themselves became its ministers and the chairmanship was rotated between them on a monthly basis. Those states nearest the Yemen were naturally the keenest on the federation. All but one of the most exposed states of the Western Protectorate joined: those in the more distant Eastern Protectorate never did. Aden colony, like Singapore, did not join the Federation initially but, unlike Singapore, had no desire to do so: the differences in political attitude between Aden and the hinterland were too great for an amicable marriage.

Aden had always been a cosmopolitan city where Arabs, Indians, Somalis, Europeans and others came to make money out of the bunkering trade and its entrepreneurial offshoots. Political activity was minimal. Things began to change in 1954 when BP started to build a new oil refinery at Little Aden across the bay to replace the one lost at Abadan. Its construction, operation and the general increase in economic activity that it generated, drew in a flow of workers from the Yemen, whose numbers soon outstripped the local Adeni work-force. Away from their homelands, the Yeminis tended to look upon the Aden trades unions as their tribal elders to whom they could turn for help and advice. Under the able leadership of Abdullah al Asnag, the Aden Trades Union Council (ATUC) became not only a political force within the colony but also a Yemeni Trojan horse inside it as well. Asnag made no secret of his aim of freeing 'occupied South Yemen' from British rule and of carrying both Aden and the two Protectorates into the Yemen under his political leadership. As 'the progressive forces of the Arab revolution in Aden' Asnag's ATUC and its political arm, the People's Socialist Party (PSP), had nothing but contempt for the autocratic rulers and their nascent federal government, which was being set up at Al Ittihad, a small village on the road round the bay between Aden and Little Aden. They viewed the Federation as little more than a neo-colonialist facade for the perpetuation of British rule, much as Sukarno viewed Malaysia. Until the Egyptians intervened in the Yemen, however, their ideas of supplanting British with Yemeni sovereignty were but pipe dreams.

The events of 1962 in the Yemen spurred the development of the Federal government while, at the same time, encouraging anti-British agitation in Aden. On 19 September 1962 the Imam Ahmed of the Yemen died and was succeeded by his son al Badr. A week later he was overthrown by an Egyptian-inspired republican revolution led by General Sallal. The revolution was enthusiastically acclaimed by al Asnag and the pro-Yemeni elements in Aden, particularly the PSP, who demanded the union of Aden with the 'new' Yemen. Sallal was not slow to reciprocate calling 'on our brothers in the occupied south to be ready for revolution'. Unfortunately for Sallal, al Badr had not been killed during the coup as was at first reported. He had escaped and with Saudi help raised the Yemeni mountain tribes loyal to him in a counter-revolution. Nasser intervened on Sallal's side, despatching some 20,000 Egyptian troops to the Yemen. The American government wished to recognize Sallal's government at once on the grounds that it was preferable to the autocratic regime of the Imam.

Harold Macmillan fortunately heeded the advice of Aden's Governor, Sir Charles Johnston, that British recognition would be taken very badly by the rulers in the Federal government because it would imply political support for Sallal, who was more hostile to them than the ramshackle regime of the Imam had been. Despite continuing British objections, the US government recognized Sallal in December 1962 in return for categoric Egyptian assurances that they would withdraw their troops from the Yemen. They did just the opposite, reinforcing Sallal with more troops and air support. The strength of the Egyptian forces in the Yemen during the five-year civil war reached 70,000 men at its peak—half the strength of the Egyptian army.

Although Nasser met his Vietnam in the Yemen, the presence of Egyptian forces there gave him a useful base from which to squeeze the British out of South Arabia. It was not long before Egyptian and Yemeni agents were crossing the border to offer arms and training to dissident tribesmen in the Federation and political support to pro-Yemeni elements in Aden itself. Egypt's own failures in the Yemen were masked by the screams of revolutionary and anti-British propaganda broadcast from Radio Sana'a and Radio Taiz in the Yemen, which faithfully reflected and embroidered for local consumption the out-pourings of Radio Cairo. Throughout 1963 general unrest grew in the states of the Western Aden Protectorate, and in Aden the PSP and Aden TUC became more aggressive and confident in their opposition to all things British and to the Federal government.

Surprisingly, Aden did join the Federation as an internally self-governing state. It was, however, a shot-gun marriage made possible by the British government's insistence that further constitutional advance in Aden would be dependent upon the city joining the Federation. In spite of anti-federal strikes and demonstrations by the PSP and the trades unions, the moderate members of the Aden Legislative Council ratified the merger in September 1962 before the effects of the Yemeni revolution could complicate the issues still further. The marriage ceremony in January 1963 was a close run thing: consummation was to prove much more difficult.

In the view of Sir Kennedy Trevaskis, who became High Commissioner for the Federation in August 1963 after long years of service in the Western Aden Protectorate, political stability would only be achieved in an atmosphere of independence, in which the Arabs could manage affairs in their own way with British help but without British interference. There was the recent precedent of the grant of independence to Malaya which had been decisive in winning the fight against the Communist Terrorists. He persuaded Duncan Sandys, who had become Colonial Secretary, to adopt a similar policy towards the Federation, so that a genuinely independent South Arabia could emerge, commanding the loyalty of all its people and making the Yemeni alternative abhorrent to them. It was agreed that the way ahead should be thrashed out at a further constitutional conference in London in December 1963. As the High Commissioner and his party of federal ministers were boarding their aircraft to fly back to London for the conference on 10 December a grenade was lobbed amongst them. One Indian lady was killed and 53 other people were injured. George Henderson, Trevaskis' assistant who had deliberately shielded him from the blast, died in hospital shortly afterwards.[9] A state of emergency was declared by the Federal government: the Yemen frontier was closed; 280 Yemeni undesirables were deported; and 57 members of the PSP were detained. The constitutional conference also became a casualty. The battle for southern Arabia had begun.

As in most pre-independence struggles for power, Aden spawned a complex tangle of rival political factions, some of which sought power through the ballot box while others were keener on the bomb and bullet. Apart from the rulers in the Federal government, whose aim was an independent South Arabia, two pro-Yemeni groups emerged: al Asnag's trades unions supported by the PSP, who favoured strikes and rioting as their main weapons, and the Yemen-based National Liberation Front (NLF) led by Qahtan as Shaabi, which was only formed in September 1963 and was dedicated to guerrilla warfare and urban terrorism. Both had the support of Egypt initially, but the NLF eventually struck out on its own, its leaders not wishing to exchange British for Egyptian over-lordship in their 'promised land' of a Greater Yemen. It was the NLF that posed the greatest military threat to the Federation. The PSP collaborated by generating political unrest in Aden.

Though the first bomb had gone off in Aden, the NLF's main objective at the end of 1963 was to raise a rebellion amongst the Radfan tribes, who, over the centuries, had levied their own tolls on people and caravans using the road from Aden to Dhala, a major trading centre 6,000 feet up in the mountains on the Yemen frontier. They had been bought off by the Federal authorities with financial subsidies in the style of the North West Frontier of India. This took much of the enjoyment out of life for the tribesmen and was seen by them as an encroachment into their prized independence. It was not difficult for Egyptian-paid agents to incite and excite them about the iniquities of the Federal government and the inadequacy of its subsidies; nor was there much to stop parties of NLF guerrillas, trained and armed in the Yemen, from infiltrating across the long unmarked frontier to help in kindling tribal rebellion. No tribesman worth his salt could resist an offer of a new rifle whatever the cause in which he was asked to use it. British Mark VII anti-tank mines from the abandoned Canal Zone bases were another attractive item on offer: easy to lay in roads and tracks and deadly in their destructive effect.

Until the state of emergency was declared on 10 December 1963 the Federal security forces had been deployed defensively to limit cross border infiltration and to snuff out potential dissidence in the sultanates and sheikdoms. They consisted of two elements: the Federal Regular Army (FRA) formed from the old Aden Protectorate Levies; and the Federal and Tribal Guards. The FRA had four battalions, whose British officers were being replaced by Arabs as and when suitable men with sufficient training and experience became available. The National Guard was a local gendarmerie for internal security within each state of the Federation. In Aden there were two British battalions, one of which was a Royal Marine Commando, with small supporting detachments of tanks, armoured cars, gunners and sappers from 24th Brigade in Kenya. The British units were in support of the Federal Regular Army and were responsible for internal security in Aden State. The main fire support for operations up country came from RAF Hunters and Shackletons used as bombers, based at RAF Khormaksar on the isthmus between Aden and the mainland.

The chances of the Federation of South Arabia becoming an independent state in the face of Egyptian and Yemeni opposition depended on the degree of confidence that could be instilled in Federal ministers, and on the efficiency with which they could be seen to handle the affairs of South Arabia. In a land where the philosophy of an eye for an eye was the principal ingredient of politics, British prestige was an important element in the balance between success and failure. In the eyes of the rulers it had been seriously eroded by the failure to topple Nasser during the Suez crisis. The Federation would never have been launched if it had not been for the success of the British interventions in Jordan, the Oman and Kuwait and for successive assurances by British ministers that Britain would not let down her friends either in Southern Arabia or the Persian Gulf. The Egyptian/Yemeni infiltration of the Radfan in the autumn of 1963 put these assurances to the test. Had energetic action not been taken, the Federation might have collapsed during 1964 or 1965—a far cry from the situation in Malaysia.

Several methods were considered for bringing the dissidents amongst the Radfan tribes to heel. The RAF's favourite method of air proscription was ruled out because it was too like the Egyptian use of air power in the Yemen civil war, which had been badly received by world opinion. An intensified 'hearts and minds' campaign would take too long to sway tribal opinion and, in any case, would require military action to make the initial penetration into the remote tribal fastnesses. As a military operation of some kind would have to be undertaken the Federal government decided to mount a demonstration of its ability and will to enter the Radfan when and wherever it chose. Brigadier James Lunt, the British Commander of the FRA, had reservations about this plan. He was in the throes of 'Arabizing', re-equipping and retraining his force, so it was hardly an appropriate time to mount a major military operation. What he feared most, however, was the open-endedness of such a commitment. He would have preferred to mount a series of more limited operations to secure the Dhala road from direct attack without having to occupy the Radfan itself. His objections were set aside and he was directed to mount a show of force.

Brigadier Lunt decided that the most important tactical objective in the Radfan was the cultivated basin of the Wadi Taym. He proposed to force an entry into it by an advance up the Wadi Rabwa from Thumier, 60 miles

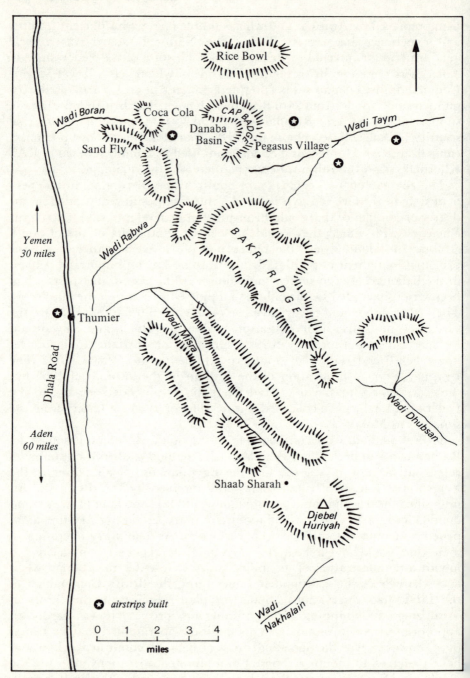

16. The Radfan in 1964.

north of Aden on the Dhala Road. For the operation, code-named *Nutcracker*, he concentrated three of his four FRA battalions and the Federal Armoured Car Squadron. He was given in support a troop of Centurion tanks from 16th/5th Lancers, a battery of 105mm pack howitzers from 3rd Royal Horse Artillery, and a troop of British sappers. The RAF provided its available Hunters and Shackletons and two heavy lift Belvedere helicopers. The aircraft carrier *Centaur* sent up six Wessex helicopters. There was remarkably little Intelligence about the dissidents' locations or intentions: topographical features and logistics were the main considerations.

Brigadier Lunt's plan for his advance up the Wadi Rabwa was based on picquetting the heights on either side with two battalions while the third advanced up the valley in true North West Frontier style, but with one important difference: the picquets would be placed by helicopter. *Nutcracker* started on 4 January 1964. The first Belvedere placed its picquet successfully, but the second was shot at with rifles and was hit several times though not seriously damaged. The RAF officer in charge stopped all further flying and consulted the Air Commander back in Aden. By the time he was told to go ahead again the picquetting battalions had reached their picquet positions on foot. During the day they were attacked by numerically stronger groups of tribesmen, but were withdrawn successfully once the attacking battalion had reached its objective at the head of the pass overlooking the Wadi Taym. They had had five men wounded. The sappers started to construct a road up the Wadi Rabwa, which was completed at the end of January. Much of the labour was drawn from the local tribesmen, some of whom had most probably been opposing the initial advance.

Lunt did not wait for the completion of the road before pushing on with circumspect Belvedere and Wessex support to the dominant Bakri Ridge. The 105mm guns were flown forward by the Belvederes, and a firm base was established deep in the Radfan from which he could control not only the Wadi Taym but also the Danaba Basin and the Wadi Dhubsan. The operation was highly successful as a demonstration of British and Federal government determination to stamp out NLF-inspired dissidence. The morale of the rulers improved. Lunt was presented with a sword inscribed 'Hero of the Radfan' by the grateful Emir of Dhala. The FRA had gained valuable experience operating with helicopter support at a total cost of five killed and 12 wounded.

By March, however, it was clear that the FRA could not be left indefinitely in the Radfan without prejudicing the defence of the rest of the frontier. The dissident Radfan tribes had been taught their lesson as intended, so the force was withdrawn, though the base at Thumier was retained and its airstrip improved to take medium-range transport aircraft. The decision to pull the FRA out was as unfortunate as it was inevitable. Radios Cairo, Sana'a and Taiz blared out fabricated stories of the great victory of 'the Wolves of the Radfan' and their heroic efforts in the cause of 'the liberation of occupied South Yemen'. The tribesmen were soon encouraged 'to have another go at the Dhala road'.

One form of encouragement for the dissidents was over flights by Yemeni aircraft. On 13 March 1964 they did more than just over-fly: they bombed and straffed a frontier village in the State of Beihan. The Sultan of Beihan, who was a firm believer in an eye for an eye, complained bitterly about lack of British air retaliation. On 19 March the Federal government officially envoked their defence treaty with Britain, demanding air protection. Not to have met with their wishes would have been to destroy all the new-found confidence of the rulers, generated by *Nutcracker*. On 28 March the Yemeni fort at Harib, from which it was suspected the air incursions were being controlled, was attacked by RAF Hunters with bombs and rockets after due warning had been given to the local inhabitants. The Egyptian and Yemeni governments immediately screamed 'unprovoked aggression' in the United Nations. Even the British press was hostile, seeing the attack as an unnecessary escalation of a war, about which they had their doubts in any case. The *Economist*, in an earlier context, had written:

The pieces are falling into a wearily familiar pattern: on the one side, Russia, Egypt and 'progress'; on the other, the Arab monarchies, Britain and 'reaction'.[10]

Unlike operations in North Borneo, which generally had a good Press, there was latent disquiet about British policy and actions in South Arabia which was never dispelled. The shadows of failure in Palestine, the Canal Zone and Suez still fell across the British view of the Middle East and not just in Fleet Street. There was a cleavage of view in Whitehall as well. One school of thought believed that Britain's interest would be best served by supporting Arab nationalism as the United States was doing. The Iraq coup had shown how pointless it was to put too much faith in Arab monarchies; British military presence was more an irritant than a help in Arab lands; oil supplies were best secured by commercial deals—the Arabs after all could not eat their oil, they had to sell it; and who would willingly become involved in the deviousness of Arab politics if it could be avoided? The other school believed that Britain had a moral obligation to stand by her Arab friends; to lead the people of South Arabia to an independence of their own choosing; and to maintain stability in the Persian Gulf until the Arab states there were able to look after themselves. In its view, Nasser was not to be trusted nor was the Soviet Union, which was poised to fill the political and military vacuum that would be created if Britain reneged on her treaty obligations. The Persian Gulf oil would only go on flowing as long as British prestige was maintained in lands where strength and loyalty were cardinal virtues. The oscillations between these two schools of thought gave British policy in South Arabia a damaging ring of uncertainty.

Attacks on the Dhala Road started all over again in April 1964 and Yemeni over-flights did not stop. Intelligence sources suggested that there were about 500 hard-core dissidents operating in the Radfan of whom 200 were Egyptian trained. There were some 6,000 to 7,000 tribesmen on whom the hard core would call for support. A second military operation to pacify the Radfan could not be avoided; nor was it possible to concentrate more than two FRA battalions without prejudicing security elsewhere. An *ad hoc* force of British and FRA battalions was, therefore, assembled on 14 April under Brigadier R. L. Hargroves, commander of the Aden garrison, to meet Britain's defence obligations to the Federal government. *Radforce* consisted of 45th Royal Marine Commando which had just returned from Dar-es-Salam having completed an operation described later in this chapter, one company of 3rd Parachute Battalion from its parent unit in Bahrein, 1st East Anglians of the Aden garrison, and two FRA battalions. In support were a squadron of armoured cars (4th Royal Tank Regiment), a battery of 105mm Pack Hows (3rd RHA) and a troop of sappers. The RAF allocated two squadrons of Hunters, one of Shackletons, four (later six) Belvederes and a squadron of Twin Pioneers. The Army Air Corps provided two Scout helicopters and a mixed bag of light aircraft.

Hargroves was given three political objectives: to prevent the tribal revolt spreading; to reassert the Federal government's authority; and to stop attacks on the Dhala Road. He was to reduce the risks to women and children by issuing warnings before bombing or shelling inhabited areas. The operation would not start until the end of April so Hargroves had to take full account of daytime temperatures of 120°F. The troops would need an average of two gallons of water per man per day: a major logistic problem. The nights would be cold and would be the best time for movement. Apart from the normal tactical advantages of night operations, the tribesmen rarely fought at night so surprise was easier to achieve.

There was still remarkably little hard Intelligence about which areas the dissidents were keen to hold or about their actual whereabouts. Detailed reconnaissance convinced Hargroves that the most important tactical features were the escarpment north of the Wadi Taym, code-named *Rice Bowl*, and the mountain mass at the head of the Wadi Taym, called *Cap Badge*. The only practicable route to them from Thumier was up the Wadi Boran. The *Nutcracker* road up the Wadi Rabwa had been destroyed by the tribesmen and was, in any case, too obvious an approach, though useful for a diversionary thrust.

In his first plan Hargroves envisaged landing 45th Commando on *Rice Bowl* by helicopter and opening a supply route to them up the Wadi Boran, but the helicopter lift was found to be inadequate so he had to think again. His final plan was equally ambitious. While a diversionary attack was being made up the old Wadi Rabwa approach, 45th Commando was to advance by night on foot up the Wadi Boran on a seven-mile trek over atrocious terrain to secure *Rice Bowl* before dawn. Around midnight B Company 3rd Parachute Battalion was to land on a dropping zone marked by a patrol from 22nd SAS, from which they were to penetrate the

Danaba Basin at first light. The FRA battalions were to follow up along the Wadi Boran to secure a firm base at the head of the Wadi on hill features named *Coca Cola* and *Sand Fly*.

The operation started on 30 April and began to go wrong almost at once. The ten-man SAS patrol, led by Captain Robin Edwards, was landed successfully by Scout helicopters, but when daylight came was still short of the DZ. They lay up in a hillside sangar, but were discovered around midday by a shepherd, who gave the alarm. They were soon under attack by about 50 tribesmen whom they held at bay until dusk with the help of Hunter air strikes. As the light faded one of the dissidents managed to lob a grenade into the sangar which killed Sapper Warburton, the radio operator, and wounded Edwards and two other men. Unfortunately, Warburton's radio was also put out of action. Unable to call for further fire support Edwards decided to fight his way out when it was dark enough. He was shot dead leading the break-out, but the rest of the patrol fought their way back to Thumier, having had to leave the bodies of Edwards and Warburton behind. When they were eventually recovered some weeks later, they were found to have been decapitated, confirming rumours circulating at the time that their heads had been displayed on stakes in a Yemeni town.

A second DZ marker patrol was flown forward at once but this time the Scouts were met with sustained rifle fire and had to turn back. The Parachute Company volunteered to drop blind, but the GOC rightly refused to allow them to do so. The 45th Commandos were by this time well on their way to *Rice Bowl*. Radio communications were difficult due to screening in the Wadi, but a message was eventually got to them ordering them to seize *Coca Cola* and *Sand Fly* and to go firm there. B Company 3rd Para were trucked forward from Aden, arriving at Thumier at about 2 a.m. on 1 May.

From *Coca Cola* the Danaba basin and Wadi Taym were in full view, but so was the massive bulk of *Cap Badge*, which clearly dominated the area and would have to be taken before control could be established over the cultivated areas and the dissident held villages. Hargroves decided to relieve 45th Commando with 1st East Anglians on *Coca Cola* and *Sand Fly* so that they and the Parachute Company could attack *Cap Badge* on foot during the night 4–5 May. Thanks to the hard work of the sapper troop, the RHA's pack hows were moved up the Wadi Boran to just within the range of *Cap Badge*. Though Hunters could not be used at night, Shackletons were to circle slowly overhead to drown any noise of the troops moving across the hard, rocky ground, and to drop flares if required.

There were only two practicable routes up *Cap Badge*: from the southwest or from due east. The 45th Commando used the former and reached the top before daylight. The Parachute Company was ordered to use the latter. They had a long detour to make and the going was worse than expected. In consequence they were caught still in the low ground where the sun came up. They were soon under fire from a cluster of buildings and forts on the lower slopes of *Cap Badge*. The RHA's guns were at extreme range and could not give close fire support, but the RAF Hunters were soon in action. Nevertheless, casualties began to mount and ammunition and water were running low. Two Army Air Corps' Beavers did a successful ammunition drop which helped, but the scales were not turned until about midday when 45th Commando's reserve company was landed behind the dissidents by helicopter. This proved too much for them. They disengaged, leaving behind six dead: the Parachute Company had lost two men killed and six were wounded. With *Cap Badge* secure a start could be made in pacifying the tribes of the Danaba Basin and Wadi Taym. A better Intelligence picture could also be built up of the Wadis stretching southwards parallel to the Bakri Ridge. Their pacification would need more troops.

Hargroves' *Radforce* HQ had always been seen as a stopgap until a regular brigade HQ could be sent from the United Kingdom with reinforcing battalions. Such was the Army's over-stretch in 1964 that it was not easy to find either a brigade headquarters or extra battalions. With four emergencies on its hands—Cyprus, Aden, East Africa (see later in this chapter) and North Borneo—calls had to be made on BAOR HQ. 5th Brigade was withdrawn to England to re-equip and re-train in the strategic reserve role; two BAOR battalions were taken for emergency tours; and most of BAOR's fighting and logistic units were under-posted to provide overseas reinforcements. Britain's NATO allies accepted these reductions with good grace principally because it was US policy to encourage Britain to continue her role east of Suez.

Until 5th Brigade could be reconstituted, the strategic reserve cupboard was bare. The only brigade HQ which could conceivably be sent to Aden was 39th Brigade commanded by Brigadier 'Monkey' Blacker in Northern Ireland. A calculated risk was taken with Ulster security and it was despatched to Aden where it took over operations in the Radfan on 10 May. Extra battalions with some acclimatization were equally difficult to find. The rest of 3rd Parachute Battalion was flown down from Bahrein; 1st King's Own Scottish Borderers, who had only returned to Engand from Aden three months earlier, were sent back; and 1st Royal Scots were flown out as well though they would need acclimatization in the Aden garrison before moving up to the Radfan. The Far East was asked to send one troop of 5.5 inch guns in *Centaur* because it was found that the 105mm shell was not heavy enough to damage some of the stronger stone forts in the Radfan: more range was also needed.

With the equivalent of five British and two FRA battalions under command Brigadier Blacker started the twin tasks of pacifying the Danaba Basin and Wadi Taym, which had been penetrated by *Radforce*, and of opening up the Radfan in a southeasterly direction. The former was carried out by patrolling, the construction of airstrips to ease supply, and a rudimentary 'hearts and minds' campaign. For the latter, Brigadier Blacker decided that the key feature was Brigadier Lunt's six-mile long Bakri Ridge, which led into the important but inaccessible Wadi Dhubsan.

Of secondary importance was the Wadi Misra, running parallel to and six miles southwest of the Bakri Ridge, which in its turn ran up to the Djebel Huriyah, the highest mountain in the Radfan and, as such, of some psychological significance to the tribes.

Before tackling the Bakri Ridge Blacker launched an unfortunate diversionary tank and armoured car thrust up the Wadi Misra. The going was difficult and made worse by unexpected heavy rain. The force had to withdraw prematurely to avoid being cut off by floods. Radio Cairo made the best of 'this victory for the wolves of the Radfan'. On the night 18–19 May 3rd Parachute Battalion with a company of 45th Commando scaled the Bakri Ridge and cleared it in four days with the help of the RAF Hunters and of the 105mm pack hows, which were hauled forward as fast as the sappers could build a track for them. Though helicopters were re-supplying the force, there were not enough of them and so much of the ammunition, water and supplies had to be humped on men's backs. On 26 May 3rd Para carried out their epic descent into the canyon-like Wadi Dhubsan. Assuming that the recognized approaches would be heavily defended, the CO, Lt Col Farrar-Hockley, decided to use a precipitous track which involved, at one point, roping down a 30-foot drop. Surprise was complete when the battalion entered the Wadi by this route. Caught off balance, the tribesmen put up brisk but ineffective resistance and by early afternoon were melting away. During the action a Scout helicopter, carrying the CO, was forced down by hostile fire. The pilot managed to land near enough to the forward troops for them to rescue the occupants and to cover it while fitters, flown up from Aden, repaired it. Nevertheless, the battalion had to stay in the Wadi all night while repairs went on. Next day it was successfully flown out and the troops withdrew to a firm base up on the Bakri Ridge.

Heavy rain forced the postponement of the Wadi Misra operation until 1 June. In the interval a series of armoured feints were delivered up the Wadi Nakhalain on the south side of Djebel Huriyah, which met little opposition but led to nowhere. 1st East Anglians carried out the advance up the Wadi Misra with 2nd FRA picquetting the heights either side. By 7 June they had reached the head of the Wadi where surprisingly the tribesmen decided to abandon their normal guerrilla methods and to stand and fight near the village of Shaab Sharah on the northern slopes of Djebel Huriyah. Brigadier Blacker was able to concentrate the punishing fire of Hunters, 5.5 inch and 105mm guns, and the battalion weapons of 1st East Anglians and 2nd FRA. The battle raged all day. During the night preparations were made for a set-piece attack, but when dawn came the enemy positions were found deserted. Djebel Huriyah was occupied unopposed. The decisive battle of the Radfan campaign had been fought and won: pacification with an energetic 'hearts and minds' campaign was begun. Airstrips and rudimentary camps were built in the disaffected areas and battalions were rotated between Aden and the Radfan on a six-weekly cycle. Most of the tribes had given up by the end of October. Their actual submission to the Federal government was not formally recognized until March 1965. By then, 24th Brigade had arrived from Kenya and had taken over responsibility for the Radfan, allowing 39th Brigade to return to Ulster.

In May 1964, Duncan Sandys had visited Aden and the Radfan at the height of the row over the bombing of Harib. He agreed to reconvene the constitutional conference that had been postponed after the Aden airport bomb incident in December 1963. The conference took place in London in June 1964. The outcome was a further constitutional advance for the Federation and an announcement that the Federation would be granted its independence not later than 1968. The Aden base would be retained to support the British position in the Persian Gulf and, more importantly, from the Federation's point of view, to counter any continuing Yemeni ambitions. The future status of the Aden base was left to be decided after the forthcoming Aden state elections.

In Malaya the announcement of the date for independence had drawn all parties and races together in a concerted effort to end the Communist insurgency. In Aden the opposite happened: it was taken as a further sign of British weakness, and it encouraged pro-Egyptian, pro-Yemeni and anti-Federal groups to redouble their efforts to undermine the Federal government and to speed the British on their way. Further heat was applied to the conflict between the 'progressives' in Aden and the Federal rulers by the Labour Party's victory in the British general election of October 1964. While the Federation of Malaysia received whole-hearted support from Harold Wilson's new British government in the confrontation with Sukarno, the Federation of South Arabia was not so well supported in its fight for survival. The ambivalence of British policy towards Arab nationalism ensured that this would be so.

The Labour Party's victory came at a fortunate moment for the NLF, who needed to revise their strategy after their defeat in the Radfan. They decided to switch to urban terrorism in Aden where they had the support of the unions and the PSP at this time. They chose the visit of Anthony Greenwood, the new Colonial Secretary, in November 1964, as the appropriate moment to launch their campaign. It was, at first, poorly executed, but like most terrorist campaigns was able to snatch press headlines from time to time with attacks like the grenade thrown into a service children's Christmas dance at Khormacksar, which killed one girl and wounded four other teenagers. Officer's messes became favourite targets, but the most dangerous and effective element of the NLF terrorist campaign was the deliberate attack on the police Special Branch, whose original members were eliminated one by one. In the whole of 1965 there were just under 300 incidents in which 35 people were killed (19 in the security forces and 16 civilians).

While the NLF concentrated upon improving their terrorist techniques, the PSP endeavoured to make the local Aden government unworkable and its relations with the Federal government impossible. Sir Kennedy Trevaskis found himself out of sympathy with Anthony Greenwood, who saw the PSP and the Aden TUC as direct reflections of Britain's Labour Party and TUC with the good of the workers at heart, instead of the Yemeni Trojan horses, which they were, bent on the overthrow of the Federal government. He was replaced by Sir Richard Turnbull, who had co-operated with Julius Nyerere in leading Tanganyika to independence. In pursuing Greenwood's policy of trying to come to terms with the nationalists, Turnbull appointed Abdul Mackawee, the Leader of the Opposition in the Aden Legislative Council, as Chief Minister when the moderate Bahroon resigned in February 1965 after an argument with the Federal government. Mackawee was a militantly pro-Yemeni nationalist, who made no secret of his aim to free 'occupied South Yemen'. Like Makarios in Cyprus, he refused to condemn terrorism and set about obstructing all measures taken by the new High Commissioner to stamp it out. By the end of September, Turnbull, like Foot, had had enough and with HMG's full support dissolved the Aden government and imposed direct rule. Mackawee fled to Cairo where he complained publicly about British 'oppression'. In Aden, the FRA was deployed for the first time to quell disturbances in Crater, the Arab city, and was remarkably effective, thus confirming the Federal government's ability to maintain order in Aden as well as up-country, if allowed to do so. The Labour Party's honeymoon with the 'progressives' in Aden was over. The NLF's campaign up-country had been neutralized; its challenge in Aden itself had yet to be mastered. There was little doubt that it could be, provided there was the political will to do so. At the end of 1965 there was no reason to believe that the political and military successes won in Borneo would be not repeated in South Arabia.

The Joint Service C-in-C Middle East Command in Aden, Lieutenant General Sir Charles Harington, had more to think about than just South Arabia and the Persian Gulf. He was responsible for the protection of British interests on the eastern side of the African continent. In June 1963 he had sent 1st Gordons by air from Kenya to Swaziland to deal with political unrest. More serious trouble started in East Africa soon after Kenya's independence celebrations in December 1963 as African extremists sought greater power. On 12 January the African population of Zanzibar rose against their Arab sultan. Arab and Asian property was attacked and the safety of the British community was put at risk. A company of 1st Staffords from 24th Brigade in Kenya was embarked in a frigate, HMS *Rhyll*, at Mombasa, but did not have to intervene. The Sultan escaped the coup and was given sanctuary by Julius Nyerere in Tanganyika. On 20 January Nyerere himself was in trouble. The 1st Tanganyika Rifles in Dar-es-Salaam mutinied, locked up their British officers, seized the airport and arrested the British High Commissioner. Nyerere called for British help. With the airport in the hands of the mutineers troops of 24th Brigade in Kenya could not be flown in. The aircraft carrier, HMS *Centaur*, was sailed from Aden with 45th Commando embarked. She was off Dar-es-Salaam by 24 January. At first light on 25 January the Commandos landed by helicopter. With weapons blazing they stormed the mutineers' barracks. An anti-tank rocket fired into the guardroom ended the affair at the cost of three askaris killed and six wounded. Nyerere's authority was re-established.

But mutiny is infectious. On 23 January, President Obote of Uganda called for help to deal with the 1st Uganda Rifles, who were refusing the orders of their British officers and NCOs in their barracks at Jinja, 70 miles from the Uganda airport at Entebbe. 1st Staffords with a Scots Guards company under command were flown north from Nairobi on 24 January. Leaving the Scots Guards to hold Entebbe airport, they reached Jinja in the early hours of 25 January in civilian trucks. The leading vehicles drove straight in and seized the guardroom before the mutineers realized what was happening. At first light they surrendered when they saw they were surrounded by the Staffords.

Almost simultaneously the 3rd Kenya Rifles mutinied at Nanyuki, only 20 miles from 3rd RHA's barracks at Gilgil. They put up more of a fight when the Gunners arrived that evening to disarm them. They had already cleared the battalion armoury of arms and ammunition and opened fire. The CO, Lt Col 'Paddy' Victory, decided to wait until daylight before attacking. When he did so next morning the mutineers agreed to surrender their arms but only to their African officers. This was agreed and all seemed to be going well when a group of askaris changed their minds and tried to repossess their weapons. The gunners reacted quickly, using the machine-guns of their Scout cars to stop a break out. The affair ended quickly after that.

There were fears that further mutinies might occur, but news of the British reaction travelled fast enough to deter any more. The East African governments were grateful for this effective support. No change, however, was made in the planned withdrawal of 24th Brigade to Aden. The last British unit to leave Kenya was 1st Staffords, who flew back to England in October 1964.

The third major rebellion—Southern Rhodesia's Unilateral Declaration of Independence—was the most serious of the three and yet involved the British armed forces least of all. The threat of UDI was neither new or unexpected when Ian Smith announced it in November 1965. Several events in the late 1950s and early 1960s had swung the white electorate away from the moderate policies of Sir Edgar Whitehead's United Party, which had led Southern Rhodesia under various labels since 1923, and had followed a policy of gradual development of a multi-racial partnership. The philosophy of 'separate development' on South African *apartheid* lines proposed, in modified form, by the Rhodesian Front, led initially by Winston Field and later by Ian Smith, became increasingly attractive. Success breeds success, but the reverse is also true. Britain's failure at Suez left a sour taste: Macmillan's 'wind of change' speech in Cape Town made

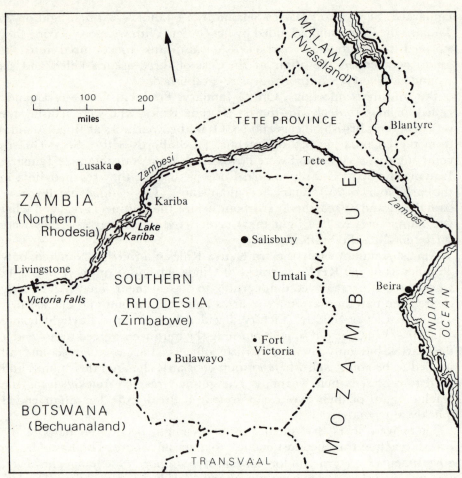

17. Southern Rhodesia/Zimbabwe, 1965–1979.

white nerves tingle; and the blood bath in the Congo, so near to Southern Rhodesia's borders, set them on edge. It was not just the descendants of the original pioneers, who feared for the future. Many of the white population, who arrived in the country after the Second World War, were artisans and white-collar workers. They had left the United Kingdom to find a new life away from the egalitarianism of post-war Britain and had no wish to see white supremacy in Rhodesia eroded. They were joined by others, who had found Kenya uncongenial after Mau Mau or who had to leave Egypt and other places when the Union Jack had been hauled down.

The decisive swing towards the Rhodesia Front started with the break up of the Central African Federation in 1961 and the consequential grants of independence to Northern Rhodesia as Zambia and to Nyasaland as Malawi. The British government's refusal to hand over its residual powers in Southern Rhodesia was seen by the white community as unfair, obtuse and unfriendly. On the other hand, the failure to entrench the rights of the black majority in the South African Constitution of 1909 imposed a moral obligation on all British governments—Conservative and Labour—to see that such a thing did not happen again. Five principles were laid down by successive British governments for the final transfer of sovereignty to Southern Rhodesia: unimpeded progress to majority rule; guarantees against retrospective amendment of the Constitution; improvement in the political status of Africans; progress towards ending racial discrimination; and finally, and most difficult of all, satisfying the British government that any basis proposed for independence was acceptable to the people of Southern Rhodesia as a whole.

The Rhodesian Front swept the Southern Rhodesian election in December 1962 and set about trying to prove to the British government that independence was what both white and black Rhodesians wanted. There was no doubt about the former. The calling of an *indaba*, or meeting of chiefs, in October 1964 to prove the latter cut no ice with British or world opinion. The chiefs were virtually government employees and it would have been more than surprising if they had not confirmed the government's contention. The two main African political parties, the Shona people's Zimbabwe African National Union (ZANU) and the Ndebele people's Zimbabwe African People's Union (ZAPU) had been banned and their leaders were either in detention or had fled the country. Subsequently, a referendum was held on 5 November 1964, which also gave the answer 'yes', but as those African, Asian and coloured people, who had the vote, refused to use it, the result only confirmed white opinion and did not satisfy the fifth principle.

The October 1964 general election in Britain brought the Labour Party to power just before the Rhodesian Front decided to bring matters to a head. With a mere three seat majority in the House of Commons the Wilson government was in no position to take political risks. Military intervention in Rhodesia would have divided the country more deeply than Suez, and would have been logistically more difficult, though not impossible, to mount. Wilson chose to seek a negotiated settlement, but tied his own hands by stating publicly that Britain would not use military force. When Ian Smith declared UDI on 11 November 1965, sanctions and mobilization of world opinion were the only weapons left in Wilson's hands, neither of which were likely to produce results very quickly in spite of his claim that the former would prove effective in weeks rather than months.

Only the Royal Navy and the RAF were involved in any way in the Rhodesian crisis. They maintained a patrol of frigates supported by Shackletons off the Mozambique port of Beira to stop oil shipments to Rhodesia, but it was a futile exercise as adequate supplies were sent by rail from South Africa. Apart from oil, Southern Rhodesia was, or could make herself, self-sufficient within a siege economy. Zambia was the Achilles heel of the British blockade. Apart from the British need for Zambian copper,

Zambia needed coal, oil and electric power from Southern Rhodesia for its copper mines. Southern Rhodesian hands controlled the switches of the Kariba Dam power-station which supplied both countries. To make matters worse, when the Federation broke up, most of its defence forces, including the air force, became Southern Rhodesian. The Zambian government appealed to Britain for military help. Reluctantly, the British government sent out a squadron of RAF Javelins with associated radars and an RAF Regiment detachment for their immediate protection, but refused to provide ground forces. The maintenance of the Beira patrol, the occasional presence of a carrier off Mozambique and the air defence of Zambia were the only British military contributions to the quest for a negotiated settlement.

It is interesting to speculate what would have happened if the Wilson government had not ruled out the use of force. There were suggestions at the time that another Curragh incident might occur in the Army if a force was sent to Rhodesia.[11] Some officers, who felt strongly about coercing their 'kith and kin' in Rhodesia, might have resigned but the Army's long tradition of political neutrality would, in all probability, have been maintained. Though over-stretched, it was seasoned and experienced in quick intervention operations and had BAOR as a reserve upon which to draw if the over-stretch became too serious. The loyalty of the Rhodesian security forces to the Smith regime was much more questionable. Smith took the precaution of retiring its GOC, Major-General John Anderson, who was known to be hostile to any treasonable act against the Crown, but his successor and most of the Rhodesian army, air force and police officers had similar reservations. The preparatory deployment of British forces might well have been sufficient to compel the negotiated settlement which Wilson sought. But the political will was not there. The defection of just two or three right-wing Labour MPs could have brought the government down. Moreover, the risks of escalation into a major war in southern Africa were incalculable. Nevertheless, quick military intervention in December 1965 might have saved Rhodesia from the later agony of the long guerrilla war.

9 THE FINAL DISENGAGEMENT

The 1967 devaluation of sterling and withdrawal
from East of Suez: 1966–1971

Britain's defence effort will in future be concentrated mainly in Europe and the North Atlantic area. We shall accelerate the withdrawal of our forces from Malaysia and Singapore and complete it by the end of 1971. We shall also withdraw from the Persian Gulf by the same date.

Statement on Defence Estimates, 1968[1]

The withdrawal from Empire was to end as it began with a decision by a Labour government to fix a date for disengagement in order to concentrate the minds of factions fighting for the succession. In India the outcome had been partition and massacre: in Aden it was to be anarchy with some bloodshed.

When Harold Wilson won the 1964 general election neither he nor his Defence Secretary, Denis Healey, had any intention of abandoning Britain's commitments east of Suez, or of forsaking her role as a world power. On the contrary, they were both as intuitively pro-Commonwealth and anti-European as Attlee and Bevin had been in the immediate post-war years. They believed they could restore British prosperity by more efficient economic management and make the new Commonwealth a force in world affairs with a progressive foreign policy: left could speak to left. While Wilson, the economist, led the way in developing the new Labour government's 'National Plan', Healey set about seeking a defence policy that would give greater value for money. His philosophy was set out in the introduction to the Defence Review, which started soon after his arrival in the Ministry of Defence:

Military strength is of little value if it is achieved at the expense of economic health. The defence plans of the previous Government would have imposed an excessive burden both in resources and in foreign exchange. As we emphasised in the National Plan ... to continue spending over 7 per cent of the Gross National Product on defence would be seriously damaging to Britain's economy, at a time when we need a rapid increase in production so that we can export more and import less; when industry must be re-equipped and modernised; and when we are running into a shortage of manpower.[2]

Healey's task was to reduce Defence spending from £2,400m to £2,000m (at 1964 prices) by the end of the decade, thus lowering Defence's share of the national cake from seven to six per cent. He set about it in two ways: seeking immediate short term savings in the equipment votes by demanding greater 'cost-effectiveness'; and by pressing the political departments, principally the Foreign Office, to reduce overseas military commitments.

Healey worked fast in the equipment jungle. His philosophy of cost-effectiveness, encouraged by Robert McNamara US Secretary for Defence, led to the logic of buying American in specific fields. The British armament industry had not been able to compete with the Americans in terms of scale and hence price for many years: British production runs were too short. The British taxpayer had made up the difference, but, by the time Healey came to office, the gap had widened so much that it could no longer be ignored. The Pentagon's research and development funds alone exceeded the whole of the British Defence budget. Britain had already become a middle power, if for no other reason, because she did not have a big enough industrial base to compete with the superpowers, nor the resources to develop military equipment across the whole range of advancing technology at reasonable cost. The decline in the British armament industry had been made worse by the loss of the captive imperial arms markets after the Second World War. Indeed, a vicious circle of declining sales and increasing costs had set in, destroying Britain's competitiveness in arms sales. The older Commonwealth countries had gained a taste for American military equipment through wartime US lend-lease policies; the newer members, like India, and the former protectorates, like Egypt, sought arms elsewhere to underline their independence and non-aligned postures; and the consequent drop in sales increased British prices and gave former customers this additional reason for changing suppliers. The British services suffered most because their budgets bought less and less as long as they maintained a buy British policy, which they wished to do in order to retain a British armament industry.

Healey gave the retention of a sound military industrial base just as much emphasis as the Chiefs of Staff, but he was quicker to accept the hard fact that Britain could no longer cover the whole spectrum of war and must be selective in the types of equipment British industry should be invited to develop and produce. Each of the three services suffered from his analysis of their programmes and budgets. The RAF had four major projects on its books: the P1154 supersonic vertical/short take-off and landing (VSTOL) interceptor, the HS 681 military transport, the TSR 2 advanced strike and reconnaissance aircraft, and the P1127 (VSTOL) ground attack aircraft. Only the fourth survived Healey's scrutiny and became the famous Harrier of the Falklands War. American phantoms, Hercules and F 111s were to replace the other three, the foreign exchange costs being covered by US purchases of British defence equipment agreed between Healey and McNamara.

The Army lost its swollen and outdated Territorial Army, the divisions of which could never have been mobilized in time to take part in a nuclear war in Europe. It was rightly replaced with the very much smaller TA and VR, raised and trained for the rapid reinforcement of BAOR's existing formations.

It was in the Navy where the fiercest controversy raged which, in the end, resulted in the resignation of the Navy minister, Christopher Mayhew, and the First Sea Lord, Admiral Sir David Luce. It was, in effect, a battle between the Royal Navy and the RAF for longer-term survival, fought over the future of the aircraft carriers with Healey as the intellectual and non-military referee. The RAF managed to show that carriers were only supplementary to land-based air power. Even if the new carrier, CVA 01, was followed by two more of her class, which was the most that the defence budget could have accommodated, it would only have been possible to station one east of Suez where carriers were most likely to be needed. Its air striking power, however, would not have been greater than that of three shore-based F 111s. The Navy refused to concede, at this stage, that the unique element of the carrier's job—providing air cover in the early stages of an intervention operation—could be done by smaller and hence cheaper ships. They lost the battle on military cost-effectiveness arguments.

Healey's equipment measures provided about half the defence savings demanded by the National Plan. The rest had to be wrung from the Foreign Office in reductions in overseas commitments. The successful defeat of Sukarno's confrontation was already sufficiently obvious for credit to be taken for a substantial reduction in force levels in the Far East. Paradoxically failure to establish a credible successor government in South Arabia did much the same in Aden. The recent fighting in the Radfan and the start of terrorism in Aden itself strengthened the Whitehall school of thought that believed the presence of British troops in Arab lands endangered rather than protected British interests, and that it was perverse to go on keeping military bases in areas where the local people were hostile. Moreover, there was the deep-seated dislike amongst the Labour Party of giving support to unrepresentative governments of sultans and sheiks. The axe fell on Aden in terms of political cost-effectiveness.

The results of the first phase, of what was to become a rolling Defence Review that went on throughout Denis Healey's tenure as Defence Secretary, were announced in February 1966. They were just as revolutionary as Duncan Sandys' review a decade earlier. There was, at last, public acknowledgement that Britain had declined into middle power status. Three principles were laid down: Britain would not undertake major military operations without allies; military obligations would not be accepted unless the country concerned provided the base facilities to make military assistance effective in time; and no attempt would be made in future to maintain bases in an independent country against its wishes.[3] The British services would only stay in Malaysia and Singapore for as long as their governments agreed to their presence 'on acceptable conditions'. Discussions had begun with the Australian government on the possibility of establishing alternative base facilities on its territory. In the Middle East, the Aden base would be given up when South Arabia became independent in 1968. There would be a small increase in the British military presence in the Persian Gulf. The garrisons of Gibraltar, Malta and Cyprus would be pruned.[4]

The vigour with which Denis Healey drove his cost-effectiveness policies in the Defence field was not matched by the economic departments pursuit of the National Plan. A revolution in working practices was needed to create the 'British economic miracle' that the Labour government sought, but it was far too hag-ridden by its retrogressive trades union paymasters to push through the radical changes which were needed. For the moment, however, there was some confidence that, with government and unions on the same side, a miracle could be achieved. The electorate seemed to think so when it gave Wilson a working majority in the general election in March 1966.

When Parliament reassembled in April 1966 there was a marked change in tone, reflecting public opinion revealed during the election campaign. Britain's continuing presence east of Suez was more generally questioned. The days of Empire were clearly drawing to their close. Britain should from now on seek her future in Europe. Wilson caught the mood of the country by resisting President Johnson's pressure for at least a token force of British troops to join the Australian and New Zealand contingents in Vietnam. Instead he tried to don Eden's mantle as peace-maker in Indo-China, and set in hand a fresh look at 'the pros and cons' of renewing Britain's application to join the EEC.

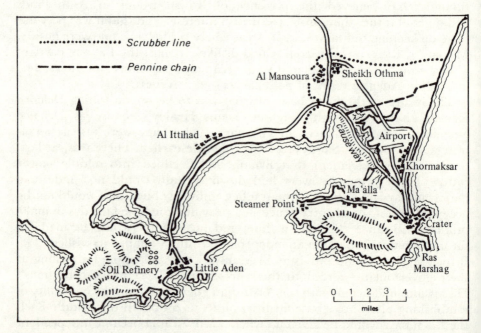

18. The Aden area in the 1960s.

Events in Aden were soon lending support to the anti-east of Suez and pro-European lobbies. The announcement of the ending of the Aden base had equal and opposite effects in Cairo and the Yemen on the one hand, and in South Arabia on the other. The naïve assumption in Whitehall that Britain's military withdrawal would usher in a new era of Anglo-Arab goodwill was quickly disproved. Nasser, for whom the civil war in the Yemen had been going so badly that he was on the point of evacuating his troops, quickly reversed his decision and proclaimed they would stay until all British troops were out of Aden. Arab nationalists hailed the British decision as a victory for their cause and another sign of British weakness, which should be exploited to the full by redoubling efforts to prove their own virility in Arab eyes and to hasten the British departure. In Al Ittihad a wave of bitterness engulfed the Federal government. The rulers had been encouraged by successive British governments to give up some of their prized independence to form the Federation of South Arabia, which they were promised would be under-pinned by British military power until it was strong enough to stand on its own feet. As long as Egyptian troops stayed in the Yemen the Federation's security would be in jeopardy without a countervailing British military presence. Security apart, their own personal positions were being undermined. They knew that they were seen as anachronistic in London; as unrepresentative in the United Nations in New York; and as British stooges in the Arab world. From the rulers at the top down to the workers in Aden and the tribesmen in the hinterland, all began to re-insure with the nationalist faction that each individual thought most likely to come out on top when the British left.

In the immediate post-announcement euphoria in the Arab world, Nasser managed to unite Qahtan as Shaabi's Djebel-based NLF and Mackawee's and Al Asnag's Adeni parties in the 'Front for the Liberation of Occupied South Yemen', FLOSY for short. It was another uncomfortable shot-gun marriage. The members of the NLF were largely dissident tribesmen from the old protectorate states who had a liking for independent military action and objected to Egyptian interference. The non-NLF elements of FLOSY were Adeni townsmen, who favoured less violent means and were prepared to accept Egyptian help and Yemeni sovereignty. FLOSY had as little chance of staying united as the Federal government had of surviving Nasserite revolutionary pressures when the British had gone.

In Aden the internal security situation deteriorated rapidly. Intelligence dried up as supporting the British was seen to be a lost cause; the terrorists gained confidence and local support; and intimidation of the local pro-British establishment became more blatant and successful. An attempt to broaden the Federal government soon failed. Out of the 24 seats alloted to Aden State only six men could be found brave enough to risk murder by accepting them. Up country the story was rather different. Minor military actions with NLF infiltrators, sporadic ambushes and intermittent mining of the Dhala road, were the daily fare of 24th Brigade's battalions operating in support of the Federal Regular Army. The vigorous 'hearts and minds' campaign launched after the Radfan campaign was having some success. New schools were being provided; agricultural schemes opened; irrigation projects started; and Army and RAF helicopter-borne teams brought medical help to the remoter villages, while the sappers opened up roads to them. The tribes remained loyal to their sultans and sheiks, not so much out of gratitude, but because they were waiting to see who was going to win the crucial battle for power in Aden.

In December 1966, the FLOSY marriage broke up under the strains of its incompatibilities. The NLF decided to go it alone without Egyptian support. The rest retained the name FLOSY and built up their own terrorist group called PORF, the hard core of which was Egyptian-trained. FLOSY probably enjoyed the greater political support in Aden both amongst the professional classes and the workers, but the NLF was the most feared as it had the better terrorist organization.

Until the beginning of 1967 British troops had been operating in the support of the police, dealing with 'normal' internal security problems all too familiar to them: provocative strikes, grenade throwing, hostile local reaction to follow up operations after terrorist incidents, and intimidatory assassination of prominent people. There were three main trouble spots: Crater (the old Arab city), Maalla (the more modern area round the port), and the twin townships of Sheikh Othman and Al Mansoura, which sprawled across the main road running northwards out of Aden State. During 1966 the Scrubber Line, a wire fence patrolled by armoured cars and helicopters, had been built across the desert north of Sheikh Othman in an attempt to stop gun-running. It reduced the flow of arms and ammunition but did not stop it.

As ever, the British soldiers rose to the challenge which faced them. They were mostly young men in their late teens and early twenties, who accepted the discomfort of the heat and squalor of the Arab back streets, the dangers of ambush and sniping, and the frustration of applying the principle of minimum force against an unseen enemy, who observed no such rules. Loyalty to the reputations of their regiments played a greater part in their minds than any sense of political purpose in Aden. They kept the lid on the powder-keg while diplomatic and political efforts were made to find an acceptable successor government.

In January 1967 there were unmistakable signs of civil war developing between the NLF and FLOSY. On 19 January, the NLF, despite FLOSY opposition, started two days of anti-British disturbances. These were handled ineffectively by the police who let them get out of control. There was evidence that the police had been penetrated by the NLF and were no longer reliable. There was also suspicion that arms were being smuggled through the Scrubber Line with police connivance. Sir Richard Turnbull, the High Commissioner, took three important decisions: British troops would take over responsibility for internal security in Aden State; they would deploy before rather than after demonstrations started; and all passenger-carrying traffic would be halted during periods of public disorder.

The success of the 19–20 January demonstrations emboldened the NLF, who called for 'A day of the Volcano' for 11 February when there were to be outbreaks of mass violence throughout Aden and the hinterland. They were in for a nasty shock. Instead of meeting irresolute Arab police they found four British battalions already deployed and dominating the key areas in Aden with similar precautions taken in the main towns up-country. The 'Volcano' spluttered and died out. Not to be outdone FLOSY started a counter series of demonstrations that were just as unsuccessful. By 14 February restrictions on movement could be lifted. There had been 66 attacks on British troops, who had to open fire on 39 occasions.

During February the British security forces had been successful in dampening the militants' ardour, but the NLF had also shown that they were a viable organization and could impose discipline on their followers. On their instructions there were no disturbances during the funerals of their members killed during the 'Volcano' rioting. But they also showed their determination to crush FLOSY, 35 of whose leading members were murdered in as many days. A bomb placed in Mackawee's house killed three of his sons. The NLF blamed the rulers. FLOSY appealed to the British for protection and many of their wealthier supporters flew off to England for safety.

March and April 1967 were months of diplomatic activity and political negotiation. In Cairo and Riyadh unsuccessful attempts were made by the British Ambassadors to persuade Arab leaders to bring their influence to bear on the NLF and FLOSY to negotiate a widening of the Federal government to include Nationalist representatives. At the same time George Thomson, Minister of State at the Foreign Office, flew out to Aden to start planning the British withdrawal with the existing Federal government. He proposed that the independence date should be brought forward to November 1967 and that a carrier task force should stay to support the new state for its first six months existence. The pill was sugared by promises of generous economic aid, but the Federal government would have none of it. Instead they called upon their friends in the Conservative Party to fight their case in Westminster for a delay in granting independence until their own security forces were stronger and for a British change of heart on the retention of some British troops and air support in the Federation under a defence agreement. They had some success. The date was put back to early 1968 and Harold Wilson gave Lord Shackleton, Minister without portfolio, the task of steering Aden to independence. He was to concentrate on the continuing efforts to bring the Nationalists and Federal ministers together into a wider and more representative successor government, and to look again at the possibility of a defence agreement.

Shackleton's efforts were not helped by the fiasco of the United Nations' Mission which was tasked to find an internationally acceptable political solution in South Arabia. Its three members from Venezuela, Afghanistan and Mali arrived in Aden on 3 April and departed five days later, having barely left their hotel. They refused to talk to the Federal government because it was not recognized by the United Nations; and neither nationalist party would talk to them unless it was recognized as the sole representative of the people of Aden. When their demands were rejected, both NLF and FLOSY set about demonstrating the degree of local support that they enjoyed and the British government's inability to keep the peace. In the five days of their stay 280 incidents occurred, 18 servicemen were hurt and eight terrorists killed. The final straw came when the Mission asked for radio facilities to put their case to the public. The Federal government initially agreed but, when the script was found to contain a denial of the government's very existence, the broadcast was cancelled. The Mission left literally shaking the dust of Aden off its feet. Its subsequent efforts to bring all parties together in Geneva were equally unhelpful in arriving at an acceptable political solution.

It was at this stage that Harold Wilson decided to adopt the methods used by Attlee to stop the internal struggle for power in India: he fixed the latest date for withdrawal from Aden as January 1968 and changed High Commissoners. Sir Humphrey Trevelyan, who had been British Ambassador in Cairo during the Suez crisis in 1956 and in Baghdad when the Hashemite dynasty was overthrown in 1958, was given Mountbatten's task of 'uniting and quitting'. There were, however, two important differences between India and Aden, apart from the obvious one of scale. Ambition to rule rather than religion divided the embattled parties, and this time there was no military under-estimate of the force needed for successful disengagement.

Trevelyan's first public statement optimistically looked forward to the establishment of a broadly based 'caretaker government'. He would end the state of emergency and release detainees if Nationalist representatives would join the government. His invitation fell on deaf ears. Neither the NLF nor FLOSY would come forward for fear of compromising themselves in Arab eyes. Instead they both made counter-demands for the immediate withdrawal of British troops, the removal of the 'reactionary' rulers, and the surrender of all authority to themselves. Nasser did try to be helpful by announcing on 2 May that his troops in the Yemen would not enter Southern Arabia after the British withdrawal; and he also gave his full backing to FLOSY as the most representative of the two nationalist movements.

Mountbatten had been able to negotiate with all parties in India. In Aden there was no wish to negotiate: only an urge to fight it out in Arab style. Unable to meet the opposition round a conference table, Trevelyan's only alternative was to try strengthening the existing Federal government politically and militarily by tackling its two main weaknesses: lack of political leadership and inadequate security forces.

To help solve the former, Trevelyan suggested to the rulers that they should stop the rotation of the chairmanship of the Federal council and appoint one of their number as Chief Minister. For the latter, ways of under-pinning the federal armed forces were looked at yet again. A defence agreement and any idea of leaving British troops and airmen behind was rejected. The main threat to the Federal government was internal. In the anti-monarchist atmosphere of the Arab world in the 1960s the rulers' chances of survival were very slender indeed. There would probably be a re-run in Aden of the Yemeni revolution of 1962 as soon as the British left. The nationalist forces would mount a *coup d'état* and appeal to Nasser for help: the Federal government would invoke their British defence treaty and also call for Saudi help. It would be difficult to stop British troops being drawn into a South Arabian civil war, a possibility which no British government would wish to risk with so little reason to stay in Aden anyway.

The outcome of Trevelyan's initial negotiations with the Federal government was a British refusal to reconsider a defence agreement but to offer more and better military equipment for the Federal armed forces, including a squadron of Hunters, extra training aircraft, more 25-pounder guns, armoured cars and automatic rifles, and a military mission to help in training. Detailed planning was put in hand for the phased withdrawal of British forces and the step by step handover of internal and external security to the Federal government. Independence day was fixed as 9 January 1968. The evacuation of the 7,200 service wives and children had begun on 1 May and was to be complete by mid-July. The decks were being cleared for a difficult withdrawal.

In the meantime, the NLF had tried to turn the Sheikh Othman and Al Mansoura townships into 'liberated areas'. On 1 June they decided to fight it out with 1st Parachute Battalion and were worsted. At least six terrorists died and five were captured in a day that the battalion christened 'the glorious 1st of June'. Both towns remained battlefields until the end, but throughout the summer and autumn of 1967 there was no doubt who held the upper hand in them.

All calculations about Aden were upset in June by the Arab/Israeli Six Day War. Nasser's 'big lie' about British and American help to the Israeli air force, told to justify the crushing defeat suffered by the Egyptians, strained previously amicable relations between British and Arab officers in the Federal government, army and police. All Arabs felt deeply humiliated by Nasser's defeat, which was only explicable in their minds in terms of Anglo-American secret collaboration with Israel. The atmosphere of suspicion was not helped by the concurrent reorganization of the Federal Regular Army and the Federal Guard into a combined force, the South Arabian Army (SAA). Tribal jealousies had been building up for some months over the selection and promotion of officers in the expanding army. On 20 June mutinies occurred in parts of the SAA and in the armed police.

The immediate cause of the mutinies was the selection of an Arab successor for Brigadier Jack Dye as Commander of the SAA.[5] The officer chosen was suspected of having better connections with Federal ministers than military competence. His selection was bitterly resented by a small group of officers, who chose to complain directly to ministers rather than through military channels. The four colonels, who led the protest, were suspended from duty. Rumours spread that they had been arrested by the British and dismissed. Early on 20 June there were disturbances in one of the SAA barracks near Khormaksar airfield on the isthmus. Some shots were fired and several buildings were set on fire, but order was restored by the Arab officers themselves without the intervention of British troops. The shots had unfortunately been heard in the nearby armed police barracks. The police, thinking the British were attacking their Arab compatriots in the army, mutinied and took up defensive positions to defend their barracks. By chance an unarmoured British 3-ton truck, carrying 19 men of the Royal Corps of Transport, happened to pass nearby on its way back to barracks from range practice. The mutineers opened automatic fire on it from very close range, killing eight British soldiers and wounding another eight. Several civilian cars were also shot up, killing a British officer, two Aden police and a Public Works Department employee.

At the request of the Federal government the mutiny was quickly dowsed by British troops, one more man was killed and 13 were wounded in the action. But it was not ended quickly enough to stop the wildest rumours of British intervention spreading to the armed police barracks in Crater, which housed 380 policemen and their families. Thinking that they would be attacked next the 140 or so men actually in the barracks at the time manned the walls and roof with rifles and machine guns. As it happened, the Royal Northumberland Fusiliers were in the early stages of handing over responsibility for Crater to the Argyll and Sutherland Highlanders. Contact had been lost with a Fusilier patrol in Crater and, fearing the worst, its company commander, Major Montcur, decided to go in and look for it. He set off in two Land Rovers with five of his own men and Major Malcolm and two men of the advance party of the Argylls. As the Land Rovers approached the police barracks, usually one of the few friendly places in Crater, they were swept with intense rifle and automatic fire. All but one of the party were killed and the vehicles set on fire.

The original patrol, which Montcur had gone into Crater to find, had meanwhile returned safely. Hearing that contact had been lost with Montcur, the patrol leader, 2nd Lieutenant Davis, volunteered to go back with some of his men and half a troop of Queen's Own Dragoon Guards in armoured vehicles. As his small force approached the police barracks, he could see the burning vehicles and bodies in the road. Coming under the same intense fire he realized he would have to call for reinforcements, so he dismounted with three men and took cover to watch the situation, while his armoured vehicles pulled back to summon help. His little group must have been attacked and over-run as they were never seen alive again. At about the same time a helicopter was brought down by rifle fire while positioning a patrol on a high point overlooking Crater, resulting in two more injuries but no deaths.

Three attempts were made to recover the bodies from the police barracks area without success. Rightly or wrongly the decision was taken to withdraw British troops from inside Crater and to draw a close cordon around it, blocking the entry roads and holding the dominating heights above the city, while the High Commissioner and the military commanders assessed the situation and decided how best to recover the initiative without enflaming the Anglo-Arab relations still further.

They were faced with a politico-military dilemma. The obvious military answer was a quick and powerful counter-attack before the mutineers and the local NLF, who had come out in the mutineers' support, could organize enough resistance to compel the use of heavy weapons with the consequential risk of civilian casualties. But to attack at once, while emotions on both sides were so enflamed, ran the risk of the mutinies spreading throughout the South Arabian Army and the armed police. There were still some 400 British wives and children living in Maalla, and another 200 or so British civilians up-country, all of whom could be placed at risk by one ill-considered and over-precipitate move. Trevelyan, with the support of his military and police advisers, took the difficult and unpopular decision not to re-enter Crater until careful preparations had been made to do so without inflicting serious casualties amongst the civilian population.

The pause did cool tempers. The South Arabian Army and the police were generally ashamed of the men who had mutinied and turned on their British colleagues. They asked to be allowed to redeem themselves by retaking Crater. Their offer could not be accepted: the temptation for NLF supporters in their ranks to consolidate Crater as an Arab capital within Aden State was deemed to be too great. Moreover, Crater was within mortar range of the vital Khormaksar airfield.

Plans for a surprise re-entry into Crater in strength went ahead briskly. The 'Spearhead' battalion[6] was called for from England and arrived within 24 hours, such was the speed of reinforcement achieved by Transport Command by 1967. With its arrival there were seven British battalions deployed in Aden, Little Aden and up-country. The Argylls and 45th Commando were given the task of dominating Crater in the meanwhile from positions overlooking the city.

During the pause an accurate Intelligence picture of the situation in Crater was built up. The telephones were still connected so information was not difficult to collect. Skilled clandestine patrolling helped with the assessment of the state of mind of the mutineers and the NLF. The chances of achieving a bloodless re-entry seemed high, but no chances were to be taken. A carefully controlled operation was planned based upon a series of report lines on which the advance into Crater could be speeded up, halted or even reversed in the light of events.

At 7 p.m. on 3 July, just a fortnight after the original mutinies, the Argylls, supported by armoured cars of the QDG, started the re-entry. They used two axes: two companies advanced along Marine Drive from the north and one from Ras Marshag on the southeast. 45th Commando, reinforced by a company from the Prince of Wales' Own, held the high points and road blocks around Crater. Under the critical gaze of the world's leading journalists, the Argylls moved in Crater to the sound of their pipes and with the red and white hackles of the Fusiliers flying from the aerials of the armoured cars. There was no organized resistance. By dawn 4 July the Union Jack was flying again over Crater. During the day the armed police agreed to co-operate and return to duty. The leader of the four colonels, whose protest had triggered the mutinies, made a remarkable public apology, saying he had never intended that his action should have led to such dire consequences and expressing his deep regret. In an equally dramatic gesture, designed to restore Anglo-Arab confidence within the security forces, the GOC, Major-General Philip Tower, inspected the armed police in Crater, drawn up on ceremonial parade. It was a tense occasion, but created the necessary spirit of reconciliation, which was to prevent Aden slipping into total anarchy before the British disengagement was complete. A judicial enquiry under the Chief Justice was set up, but never reported: time ran out.

Although military reconciliation was achieved, Trevelyan was less successful in restoring confidence in the Federal government whose credibility had been further shaken by the mutinies in *its* army and police. The need for a Chief Minister was accepted and the job was given to Hussain Ali Bayoumi, one of the few strong men left on the Federal council. His efforts to form a broadly based caretaker government were soon frustrated by NLF and FLOSY intransigence and intimidation. The United Nations Mission also became fitfully active in Geneva, but had even less success in drawing the nationalists to the negotiating table.

While all the excitement of the mutinies and their aftermath had been going on in Aden, the British withdrawal from the hinterland had been progressing relatively smoothly. By 30 June the handover to the South Arabian Army was complete and all British troops had been pulled back to Little Aden. The NLF were not slow to profit by their departure. During July and August state after state turned against its ruler and declared for NLF revolutionary governments. Most of the rulers either fled to Saudi Arabia to seek support there or retired to Europe, thankful still to be alive. The Federal government had virtually collapsed by the end of August. All that stood between the NLF and their claim to represent all the people of South Arabia was FLOSY. The South Arabian Army, under Brigadier Jack Dye's leadership had remained neutral so far in the nationalist struggle for power.

On 3 September 1967 the NLF, who had set up their headquarters at Zingibar on the coast east of Aden, claimed publicly their right to be the sole representative of the people of occupied South Yemen. Two days later Trevelyan announced that he would negotiate with the nationalist groups without specifying which. The next day, 6 September, bitter fighting broke out between NLF and FLOSY in the streets of Sheikh Othman under the incredulous gaze of 1st Parachute Battalion, who were not involved. The

South Arabian Army intervened and gave both sides until 20 September to patch up their differences and to send representatives to negotiate with the High Commissioner. Urgency was imparted to Arab deliberations by the knowledge that all British military equipment and stores would be out of Aden by the beginning of November. There were also rumours current, based on leaks from GHQ, that the British might bring their departure forward from 9 January to 20 November. Further evidence of British determination to go was provided when Little Aden was handed over to the South Arabian Army on 13 September, on schedule. Sheikh Othman and Al Mansoura were evacuated on 24 September and all British troops withdrew south of the 'Pennine Chain', a line of old defence works constructed across the isthmus during the First World War to protect Aden from Turks. It was just far enough north to keep the airfield out of mortar range.

Diplomatic efforts intensified in Cairo, Riyadh, Geneva and London during October to find a possible successor government. On 2 November the Foreign Secretary confirmed publicly what had been rumoured for some time, that British troops would complete their withdrawal by the end of November. Inter-factional fighting flared up again, during which several pointless murders of Europeans occurred as both sides tried to demonstrate their nationalist fervour. The final and decisive battles between NLF and FLOSY were fought out between 3 and 6 November. This time the South Arabian Army intervened on the side of the NLF. Qahtan as Shaabi had won. On 13 November, the British government recognized the NLF as its successor in Aden and began negotiations for the final withdrawal which was set for 29 November.

Until the very last moment there was no certainty that British troops would be allowed to leave without a fight as no one could be sure that fanatical elements among the Nationalists would not attack so as to be able to claim that they had driven the British out. A large naval task force was assembled in the bay, including the aircraft carriers *Eagle* and *Hermes*, the commando carrier *Bulwark* and the assault ship *Intrepid*. Most of the troops were flown back to the United Kingdom via Bahrein where some were dropped off to form the new British base and headquarters in the Persian Gulf. The final phase of the withdrawal was covered by 42nd Commando. The last helicopter lift flew back to the fleet at 3 p.m. on 29 November, Lt Col Dai Morgan, CO of 42nd Commando, having the doubtful honour of being the last British serviceman to leave 'the barren rocks of Aden'. Few regretted leaving. Nasser kept his word and pulled his troops out of the Yemen and perhaps had just as few regrets.

Although Britain was not, in fact, involved in the Six Day War, the fragile British economy, made all the more so by the seaman's strikes in 1966 and the dockers' strikes in 1967, failed to withstand the additional cost of the closure of the Suez Canal and the accompanying Arab oil embargo. The situation was further aggravated by the Nigerian civil war, which started in July 1967, and closed another source of cheap sterling oil. A run on the pound started and forced the Wilson government to take drastic emergency measures. Defence, as usual, was called upon to find the lion's share of the budgetary savings called for by the Chancellor of the Exchequer. In July 1967 Denis Healey published a Supplementary Statement on Defence.[7] With the ending of confrontation with Indonesia, Britain intended to halve her military presence in Southeast Asia by 1970–1, and to end it all together by the mid-1970s. Precise timings would depend upon consultations within the Commonwealth and upon progress made in building up local military forces to ensure continuing stability in the area. Even greater emphasis would be placed upon rapid military reinforcement from the United Kingdom and for this purpose a new Army Strategic Command would be established and an extra brigade would be added to the Strategic Reserve. To save foreign currency, one BAOR brigade group would be withdrawn from the Continent and housed in Britain. More troops would have been brought back had it not been for the high cost of building alternative barracks for them in England. When the withdrawal from Aden and the reductions in Southeast Asia and the Mediterranean had been carried through the strengths of the three services would be pruned. The Army would be the worst hit, losing a further 17 major fighting units (four armoured, four gunner, one engineer and eight infantry). The RAF would suffer some reductions and Bomber and Fighter Commands would be amalgamated into a new Strike Command.[8] In the Royal Navy the demise of the carriers would be hastened and greater emphasis placed on submarine warfare. The first Type 82 Guided Missile destroyer under construction would be completed, but no more would be built. Its design would be developed upwards to produce a helicopter carrying 'Command' Cruiser, and downwards to form the basis for the next generation of frigates.

Few of Healey's defence cuts could bring quick relief to the sinking pound. On 18 November 1967, Harold Wilson, who had set his face against devaluation, was forced to admit defeat and to accept a 14.3 per cent reduction in sterling's value against the US dollar. A further round of the continuing Defence Review was forced upon the government.

After devaluation the swing in public opinion against overseas commitments and in favour of entering the EEC became more marked than ever. The mood was reinforced by the realization that the Common Market was working better than most people in Britain had thought possible. Disillusion with the overseas role was matched by fear of being excluded from the opportunities offered by the expanding economies just across the Channel. The Continental school in British strategic thinking began to gain the upper hand: Maritime policies without an Empire seemed to spell economic ruin. Honouring moral obligations to Commonwealth countries was fine as long as it did not reduce British standards of living and economic expectations. The general view was that Britain should drop all pretentions to being a world power and learn to live like any of the other European middle powers.

Ten days after devaluation, de Gaulle, once more vetoed Britain's application to join the EEC, showing that finding a place in Europe was not going to be easy. Such was the power of the swing in British public opinion towards Europe that the General's veto was seen as but a temporary set back. On 16 January 1968 the conclusions of the latest round of the Defence Review were announced and subsequently summed up in the 1968 Defence White Paper published in February.[9] The salient features were: in future Britain's defence effort would be concentrated in Europe and the North Atlantic; the run-down in the Far East would be completed by 1971 and not by mid-1970s as originally intended; the British military presence in the Persian Gulf would be run down by the same date; the F 111 order would be cancelled and Transport Command scaled down; and no special capability would be retained for use outside Europe, but a general capability would be kept in Europe, including the United Kingdom, for emergency deployment overseas and to support the United Nations.

Despite protests from the governments of Malaysia and Singapore about the speed of the British withdrawal, planning went ahead for near total disengagement east of Suez by the end of 1971. In June 1968 a five-power defence arrangement was negotiated between Britain, Malaysia, Singapore, Australia and New Zealand to maintain stability in Southeast Asia after 1971. Britain agreed to contribute some six frigates or destroyers, one infantry battalion and a force of four Nimrod maritime reconnaissance aircraft and some Wessex helicopters.

The collective defence of Western Europe was the beneficiary of the withdrawal from east of Suez. All British amphibious and airborne forces were earmarked to reinforce the northern and southern flanks of NATO and other naval and air force units, returning from the Far East, were assigned to NATO as well. The Army, however, was to lose another nine major fighting units (two armoured, one artillery, one engineer and five infantry).

No new military emergency, involving British forces overseas, occurred between the end of the withdrawal from Aden in November 1967 and the withdrawal from Southeast Asia in December 1971, which could have reversed the final and peaceful phase of Britain's withdrawal from Empire. Edward Heath's victory in the general election of June 1970 made little difference. The Conservative Party was just as keen as Labour to carry Britain into the Western European club, provided reasonable terms could be negotiated for her late entry. Heath's task had been made much easier by de Gaulle's resignation. The terms offered by the EEC were accepted in mid-1971 as Britain's withdrawals from Singapore and the Persian Gulf were being completed. It looked as if Britain had, at last, become truly European and would no longer have to argue about the merits of a Continental versus Maritime strategy.

EPILOGUE

1971 to 1895

Far-called, our navies melt away;
   On dune and headland sinks the fire;
Lo, all our pomp of yesterday
   Is one with Nineveh and Tyre!
Judge of the Nations spare us yet,
   Lest we forget—lest we forget.

Rudyard Kipling's *Recessional*, 1897, Verse 3

10 ... AND BACK TO RAGS
Ulster, the Oman, Southern Rhodesia and the Falklands: 1971–1982

The Soviet Union—its policies and its military capabilities—continue to pose the main threat to the security of the United Kingdom and our response to this threat must have first call on our resources. Following the Falklands Campaign, we shall now be devoting substantially more resources to defence than had been previously planned. In allocating these, we shall be taking measures which will strengthen our general defence capability by increasing the flexibility, mobility and readiness of all three services for operations in support of NATO and elsewhere.

John Nott: *The Falklands Campaign, The Lessons*, December 1982

Three and a half centuries after James I signed the Charter of the Virginia Company in 1606 that set Britain on the road to the riches of her first empire, she was back to the rags of middle power status, having withdrawn from her second. Though relatively poorer than she had been, she was at last free to look to her own interests and to find a new place in the world unencumbered by self-imposed moral responsibilities for the welfare of a large proportion of the world's less advanced populations.

By 1971 Britain's military withdrawal from Empire was over; the political transition to a multi-racial Commonwealth was almost complete; and her third attempt to join the European Economic Community had begun. Such overseas territories that remained under British sovereignty were, for the most part, too small for an independent existence, or the majority of their people wished to remain British. The British government was prepared not only to respect but to defend those wishes as a matter of principle. In southern Africa, the problems of Rhodesia and the Republic of South Africa—the two areas where British multi-racial policies had been resisted—were already internationalized and no longer Britain's sole responsibility.

The withdrawal from Empire had gone faster than successive British governments would have wished or was generally thought desirable, but good sense had been shown in riding and, whenever possible, guiding the rising tide of Afro-Asian nationalism. Britain had held to her principles of liberal morality and the Victorian purpose of leading her Colonial people to independence as soon as they were politically, economically and militarily able to stand on their own feet. The process might have been slower had it not been for Communist hostility, American rivalry and American fears that British Colonial policies could open unnecessary doors to the spread of Communism.

In retrospect, it can be seen that whatever the speed of withdrawal, the final outcome would probably have been much the same. Britain's world mission was over. She had taught her dependent people as much as they were prepared to learn about her style of democracy, her system of parliamentary government and her way of life; and she had been overtaken and dwarfed in size, wealth and influence by the two super-powers. The US and USSR had the great advantages of vast and growing populations and contiguous land masses over which their governments could exercise effective centralized control. In contrast, the British Com-monwealth countries were not only separated by the world's oceans but also by wide differences in race, creed, culture and political ambition. Ties of sentiment, common recent history and mutual benefit have not, so far, proved strong enough to give the Commonwealth a coherent voice in world affairs. Its relevance might have been greater if world politics had remained a struggle between European powers instead of becoming an ideological war between Western democracy and Communism. In the anti-Communist battle array it is the Western Alliance, led by the United States—that amalgam of Anglo-Saxon and European tradition—which holds pride of place as right of the line. Some of the new Commonwealth countries straddle the divide between East and West, while a few prefer the Communist side. Only time will tell if the British Commonwealth as a whole has a real part to play in the world of the twenty-first century.

The withdrawal from Empire, although precipitate in historical perspec-tive, never became a route; nor did it cost as much blood and treasure as the French, Dutch, Belgian and Portuguese withdrawals, or as the humiliating American fiasco in Vietnam. Some of the credit for this must be given to the British soldiers, ably supported by their naval and air colleagues. After its first faltering steps in India and Palestine immediately after the Second World War, the British Army found the appropriate politico-military formula for British disengagement. The germ of success lay in Templer's adaptation of Mao Tse Tung's concept of the battle for the hearts and minds of the people. Templer's version was apt because it was so in keeping with the spirit of service upon which the Colonial Empire was founded in the first place. Communist subversion and rabid nationa-lism were held at bay so that, in the main, the ballot box did determine who should inherit power as most territories advanced to independence. This was no mean feat.

At the end of any significant phase in a country's history there is usually a period of slack water and confused currents before the outline of the next era can be discerned. It is far too early to suggest how Britain's post-imperial epoch will develop, but it is not too soon to start examining the trends which have emerged since 1971. The successful use of military power depends upon political will, but that will rests, in its turn, upon the assessment of the military resources and capabilities available at the time. Their existence and shape, however, are the result of decisions taken several decades earlier. For instance, it would not have been possible to fight and win the Falklands Campaign in 1982 had it not been for the decisions taken in the Watkinson/Mountbatten era of the mid-1960s to create strategically mobile Maritime forces to defend British interests beyond the NATO area in the world at large.

A number of political, military and technological trends are, indeed, discernible in the events which have taken place since 1971. In the political field the most important event was perhaps Britain's successful entry into the EEC at her third attempt. Terms were agreed in 1971 and actual accession was in January 1972. Quite how European Britain can ever become is debatable. After a shaky start, her political and economic links with the Continent have undoubtedly been strengthened, and her military thinking has become more Continental. But Britain remains an off-shore island of both Europe and the United States. Her ties with the Commonwealth have weakened. Nevertheless, though they may be gossamer thin for most of the time, they could still become bands of emotional steel in periods of crisis. The uncomfortable facts are that Britain's new European partners are still amongst her keenest commercial rivals, and her kith and kin, together with those who have espoused her way of life, circle the globe, drawing her away from Europe. Her extra-European links cannot be ignored nor can her membership of the Western European Community be exclusive.

Another political change with strategic implications brought about by imperial disengagement has been Britain's new found freedom to avoid involvement in other people's wars. She took no part in India's invasion of East Pakistan in 1971; in the Yom Kippur War between Egypt and Israel in 1973; in the final collapse of South Vietnam in 1975; in the Iranian revolution of 1979; in the Iraq/Iran War, which started in 1980; in the Israeli invasion of Lebanon in 1982 (apart from her small contribution to the United Nations Force); or in the revolutionary wars of Central America. Her only military confrontations in the 1970s have been her deployment of small forces to Belize to deter Guatamala and her support for the Sultan of Oman in his war with the Adeni-backed rebels in his southern province of Dhofar. Franco's economic and political siege of Gibraltar, which started in 1969 and continued after his death in 1975, never escalated into military conflict and was lifted peacefully in 1985.

The main trends in the military field were emerging long before the withdrawal from Empire was completed. By the mid-1960s, nuclear parity had made all-out war between the superpowers incredible. Those who wish to gain their political ends by force in the nuclear era must do so in the lower and least sophisticated bands of the spectrum of war. Subversion backed by terrorism and guerrilla campaigns has become the most fashionable, indeed the only practicable, mode of warfare. Conventional wars without the use of nuclear weapons can still be fought as has been demonstrated by Iraq and Iran, but the costs of battle winning aircraft, missiles and tanks are so high that they can only be waged in fits and starts as either side manages to accumulate enough resources to open a new offensive.

Although the British counter-insurgency campaigns of the 1950s and 1960s could be seen as peculiar to the withdrawal from Empire, three British campaigns in the 1970s suggest that they were not special at all: they were part of the pattern of warfare in the nuclear era. The first example was the IRA's terrorist campaign in Ulster, which began almost simultaneously with the final withdrawals from east of Suez and was not part of Britain's imperial disengagement. It was the continuation of the Anglo-Irish struggle that had been going on in Ireland long before the British Empire had become a reality. Although the Army used all its very extensive counter-insurgency experience, it took more troops and far longer to reduce terrorism to tolerable levels than it had done elsewhere. The IRA had three classic advantages which made its campaign so effective: support from the large Catholic minority; a nearby border over which to escape; and external financial support from the large Irish communities in the United States. The IRA's successes underline the paradox of the world's scientists' ability to spawn new weapons to keep the peace amongst the superpowers and yet total failure to find a successful deterrent to the use of the simple bomb and bullet employed to further deeply rooted political causes. As long as the nuclear stalemate lasts, political conflicts seem likely to result in variations on the terrorist and guerrilla themes.

While the Army was engaged in Northern Ireland, it was also fighting an unpublicized war in Oman, which had echoes of the imperial era as well as confirmatory pointers to the future. After the small Djebel Akhdar campaign in 1957, British officers and NCOs had been seconded to the Sultan of Oman's armed forces to enable the Sultanate to retain its independence in the harsh climate of Arab politics in the Persian Gulf. The position of Oman at the entrance of the Gulf made it an attractive target for Communist-inspired subversion. The despotic rule of the old Sultan, Said bin Taimur, helped rather than hindered the Arab nationalists. The departure of British troops from the Aden Protectorate in 1967 gave the revolutionaries a base at Hauf, close to the southern border of Oman, where a Dhofar Liberation Front was set up. Soviet and Chinese arms flowed in and by 1970 the Dhofar had, to all intents and purposes, become a 'liberated area'. Only the Sultan's southern capital at Salala and the coastal plain around it remained under his control. The Djebel country inland was dominated by the rebels, who had won the loyalty of the local tribesmen. But in July that year the Sultan's Sandhurst-trained son, Qaboos, ousted his father in a bloodless coup and put in hand a major political and economic development plan to bring his people into the twentieth century. This was made possible by the large oil revenues, which had begun to flow into the Omani government's coffers. British advisers were brought in by the new Sultan to help in the modernization of the

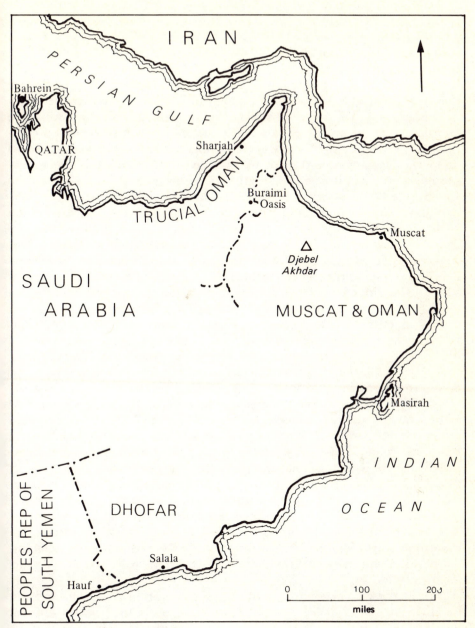

19. Muscat and Oman, 1970–5.

Sultanate at a sensible, practicable pace and to win back the ground lost to the rebels in the Dhofar by a combination of political, economic and military action.

The young Sultan's policy of raising standards of living and education with one hand while fighting the war in the Dhofar with the other paid off.

Officers and NCOs seconded from the British Army and the RAF played an important part in the latter. They were not just advisers in the American style: they held key posts within the Omani units, taking all the risks and more with their men in the traditions of the old Indian army. Brigadier John Akehurst, who was the Brigade Commander in the Dhofar during the crucial battle winning period from early 1974 to final victory in the autumn of 1975, gave six reasons for the young Sultan's success: the reforms which he instituted after the overthrow of his father; concentration on regaining the loyalty of the people of the Dhofar; joint civil and military planning and control of executive action; cutting the rebels' supply lines; air power, especially the use of helicopters; and winning the Intelligence battle. His words summarize most of the lessons of the withdrawal from Empire and set out the formula for military action in the probable environment of the post-imperial era. Small military training teams of British regular officers and NCOs, sent at the request of host countries, may well prove an effective way of projecting and protecting British interests in the twenty-first century. That the Sultanate of Muscat and Oman did not become a Communist state at the entrance to the Persian Gulf was due primarily to the wisdom of its young ruler, but the dedicated efforts of a handful of British military officers, NCOs and civilian officials made an important contribution to his success. Thirty-five lost their lives and many more were wounded in the Sultan's service.

Further variations on the guerrilla/terrorist theme were played in Southern Rhodesia at about the same time. The first nine years of UDI (1965–1974) can be looked upon as the 'sanctions busting' period. Harold Wilson's claim that sanctions would bite decisively in weeks rather than months was as wrong as Ian Smith's counter-claim that they would be 'a three day wonder'. British calculations were upset by Rhodesian ingenuity, the richness of Rhodesia's natural resources, and covert economic support from South Africa, from the Portuguese in Mozambique and from other well wishers elsewhere. In the earlier years, sanctions strengthened the white minority's resolve to slow the march towards African majority rule to a pace that, in their view, would ensure the continuation of 'responsible government' in a long process of transition. In the end, however, sanctions did play a significant part in undermining that resolve, but it took 12 years for them to do so.

Harold Wilson's negotiations with Ian Smith in HMS *Tiger* in 1966 and in HMS *Fearless* in 1968 failed because no amount of constitutional fudging and diplomatic wording could disguise the Rhodesia Front's determination not to accept African majority rule, as Ian Smith put it, 'In my life time or in my childrens'. The Front's position was not softened by Harold Wilson's addition of a sixth principle for the grant of independence: that the future Rhodesian constitution must ensure 'no oppression of the majority by the minority, or of the minority by the majority'. Lord Home, as Foreign Secretary in the Heath government, came nearest to achieving a return of the Rhodesian government to legality, but he lent too far towards Ian Smith's position. The constitution that he proposed was spontaneously rejected by the African population. The Pearce Commission, set up in 1972 to test the Home proposals against the fifth principle of acceptability to the people of Rhodesia as a whole, could only confirm its rejection.

Having foresworn the use of force, the British government was powerless to impose a solution and could only wait for the pressure of world opinion, sanctions, growing African terrorism, or some unexpected event to erode the white minority's position. The African nationalists were hardly any better placed to unseat the Smith regime by force. They were deeply divided amongst themselves in a struggle for power between and within the rival factions of Nkomo's ZAPU and Sithole's and Mugabe's ZANU. Zambia and Tanzania provided bases for the guerrillas of both parties, who received training and equipment from Eastern Bloc countries and China. Their earlier raids across the Zambezi from Zambia in the west and from the remote Tete province of Mozambique in the northeast rarely numbered more than 100 men at a time. They were easily contained by the Rhodesian security forces, which had been expanded since UDI by doubling national service from four and a half to nine months.

The unexpected did occur in 1974 when the Portuguese government in Lisbon collapsed in the left-wing *coup d'état* and Mozambique became a Marxist African state. The Rhodesia Front's position was weakened in a number of obvious ways: Mozambique became the base for Mugabe's ZANU guerrillas; the whole of Rhodesia's eastern frontier was exposed to infiltration by ZANU gangs; and the Russian and Chinese governments were encouraged to step up their efforts to exploit the opportunities opening up before them in southern Africa. The most damaging blow, however, to white supremacy in Rhodesia came from South Africa where Doctor Vorster's government embarked on a policy of détente with African states in southern and central Africa. Henry Kissenger, the US Secretary of State, gave his support to Vorster's initiative in order to head off a racial war, which could only benefit the Communist powers. In 1976 the South African President, with Kissenger's support, forced Ian Smith to accept the principle of African majority rule in a much shorter time scale by withholding further economic and military support. The Rhodesia Front had lost the first phase of the struggle to consolidate its illegal seizure of independence.

The outcome of the second or guerrilla phase of the Rhodesian conflict was never seriously in doubt. The only surprising thing about it was the length of time it took to wear down the obduracy of the Smith regime. The guerrilla infiltrations from Mozambique, and to a lesser extent from Zambia, increased month by month both in frequency, strength and standard of training of the gangs. Recruiting for the guerillas from within Rhodesia grew as ZANU's and ZAPU's efforts became more credible in the eyes of the African population. Rhodesian National Service, which had lengthened to a year in 1973, was increased to 18 months in 1976. This further expansion of the Rhodesian security forces enabled General Peter Walls, the Army commander, to begin a series of destructive counter-strikes against guerrilla bases inside Mozambique and later in Zambia. The raids, which were efficiently executed, enflamed international opinion without decisively crippling the guerrilla organizations. Inside Rhodesia, the Army and police tried all the British military techniques used in Malaya, Kenya, Borneo and elsewhere. Although they had some outstanding military successes, victory eluded them because the political half of the counter-insurgency equation was missing. Instead of winning the hearts and minds of the Africans, the population became increasingly alienated, enabling the guerrilla forces to grow, hydra like, as the months went by.

The shuttle diplomacy of Henry Kissinger, the Victoria Falls Bridge Conference in 1975, the Geneva Conference in 1976, the Anglo-American initiative in 1977, all came to grief in the myopic obstinacy of the Rhodesia Front. Although the Rhodesian security forces never lost control, the cost of the war, the effect on the economy of the absence of white managers from their firms and farms through National Service, increasing white emigration and the accumulative effects of sanctions were all beginning, by 1978, to make a settlement essential to the white community at almost any price.

When Ian Smith successfully negotiated his internal settlement in 1978, which led via the referendum in January 1979 and the general election in April, to Bishop Abel Muzorewa becoming Rhodesia's first African Prime Minister, it was Nkomo's and Mugabe's turn to become intransigent. With the support of the four 'front-line presidents' (Kaunda of Zambia, Nyerere of Tanzania, Machel of Mozambique and Khama of Botswana) they vowed to continue the guerrilla war until they had overturned the Smith/Muzorewa constitution.

By the time Bishop Muzorewa took office in June 1979, the guerrilla forces inside Rhodesia were numbered in thousands rather than hundreds. They had, at least, the tacit support of most Africans living in the Tribal Trust Lands where they were more feared than the security forces. Despite the presence of the large numbers of guerrillas inside the country intent on upsetting the internal settlement, the general elections which had brought Muzorewa to power, had been carried through in an almost carnival atmosphere in which two million Africans went to the polls for the first time. Their vote for Muzorewa was a vote for peace. It was tempting for the British, American and South African governments to treat the verdict as fulfilling the fifth principle of acceptability of the constitution to the Rhodesian people as a whole. To have done so would have been to fly in the face of Commonwealth, Afro-Asian and United Nations opinion, and could have led to a further escalation of the war. At the Commonwealth Conference at Lusaka, opened by Her Majesty the Queen in 1979, Mrs Thatcher managed to convince her fellow Commonwealth Prime Ministers of Britain's sincerity and brought all the contending parties together in the successful Lancaster House Conference, chaired by Lord Carrington, in the autumn.

The British Army, supported by RAF Hercules and Pumas, played a key role in implementing the resulting Lancaster House Agreement, which was reached in November 1979. It provided the bulk of the Commonwealth Monitoring Force that supervised the ceasefire and the concentration of the guerrilla gangs in the specified assembly areas. The Force under command of Major General John Acland, started to arrive in British and US transport aircraft on 20 December. Its total strength was only 1,548 of whom the Australians provided 150, the New Zealanders 74, the Kenyans 50 and the Fijians 24. It was a very small force to handle an estimated 13–16,000 heavily armed guerrillas, but it was intentionally so to demonstrate that it was only there to supervise and not to become another faction in the war. There were 20 rendezvous points, from which the guerrillas were to be fed to 16 assembly point camps. There they were to remain fully armed and so a threat to the Monitoring Force which certainly could not contain them if there was an absence of goodwill. The British members of the Force came straight from 44 different units stationed in the United Kingdom, Germany or Northern Ireland and found themselves within hours of arrival sitting at tables in the African bush waiting for guerrillas to walk towards them, some times in gangs of as many as 300 strong, brandishing Communist Bloc weapons. They had no way of knowing whether or not they would be murdered in cold blood. It would only require one man to lose his nerve and a whole rendezvous party might be massacred. It is a tribute to the members of the Force that its discipline, determination and good sense carried them over the difficult first hurdle of making contact with the guerrillas without any disasters.

The subsequent stages of the operation were hardly less hazardous and were made much more difficult by the logistic problems of having to provide food, tentage and transport at the assembly point camps. There was little available locally and the Rhodesian security forces were not prepared to provide anything from their own stocks. Most of the needs of the Force were flown in from Britain and the United States. In the end 22,100 guerrillas together with some 35,000 refugees arrived in the camps.[2] When the time limit for assembly was reached, after several postponements, the situation became dangerously tense. The Rhodesian security forces started to round up and, if need be, kill those guerrillas who had avoided entering the camps. Those already in the camps had the Monitoring Force at their mercy. Such confidence, however, had been established between the Monitoring teams and the guerrillas in the camps that no attempt was made to use them as hostages. This was primarily due to the British soldiers' ability to strike up friendly relations with most people and to their sense of humour which diffuses most difficult situations.

The Monitoring Force was withdrawn after the general election at the end of February 1980. Mugabe won 57 seats, Nkomo 20 and Muzorewa three. There were varying degrees of intimidation in most electoral districts. The Africans voted not so much for party policies, as for whom they thought was most likely to bring peace and end the inter-African struggle for power. Only time will tell whether Mugabe is a true Marxist or an African pragmatic nationalist who will develop a system of government more suited to the new Zimbabwe than either Westminster or Eastern-style democracy.

After the Monitoring Force had left, a British Army training team was sent out to help build and train the new Zimbabwe army, amalgamating elements of the former Rhodesian army with the ZANU and ZAPU guerrillas. Their work goes on and, like other British Army training teams in other countries around the world, is helping to strengthen Commonwealth links in a mutually beneficial way at no great cost.

In the five years since independence Zimbabwe has become a relatively stable African state in which racial bitterness has declined remarkably quickly. The white minority, though much reduced, is continuing to contribute to the growth in the economy, particularly in the agricultural sector. In 1985 the economy started to come out of decline as good rains after years of drought enabled the farmers to produce exportable surpluses, and higher prices for minerals provided more foreign currency with which to purchase spares for run down plant and to start a modernization programme.

The war itself reconfirmed most of the lessons learnt by the British Army in the withdrawal from Empire; and also the probability that guerrilla and terrorist models of warfare have overtaken conventional warfare as the most successful way of enforcing political change. The omens for continuing white supremacy in South Africa are not good.

Technological trends since 1971 have made the greatest impact of all upon British strategic thinking and military policy. Financial savings that accrued from reduction of overseas garrisons and military commitments were soon swallowed up by escalating costs. The first post-imperial Defence Review was carried out by Harold Wilson's Labour administration soon after he had unseated Edward Heath in the general election of March 1974. As usual it was a financial rather than a strategic exercise. It was carried out by Roy Mason, as Secretary of State for Defence, with Denis Healey breathing down his neck as Chancellor of the Exchequer. There was political force in the Treasury argument that the Defence vote should be pruned back from the 5.8 per cent of GNP, where it stood on completion of the withdrawal from the east of Suez, to 4.5 per cent now that the whole withdrawal from Empire and reduction of overseas commitments had also been completed. In the past, Defence had only been second to Social Security in the national financial pecking order. It made political sense to rein Defence spending back to below Health and Education.

In formulating their post-imperial strategy within the new financial constraints, the Chiefs of Staff decided they must define the critical force levels, upon which the security of the United Kingdom alone would depend in the nuclear era. Any commitments that fell outside those levels were to be treated as expendable in the process of reducing the Defence vote down to the target of 4.5 per cent GNP. It was soon clear that there would only be enough military cloth left to provide Britain with a NATO suit. Assignments to CENTO, SEATO and the Five Power Defence Arrangement for Malaysia and Singapore would have to be discontinued. Strategic reinforcement must be confined to the NATO area, and so the Army's Strategic Command would be disbanded, the RAF Transport Force pruned back, the island air staging posts like Masirah and Gan in the Indian Ocean abandoned, and the Simonstown Agreement with South Africa brought to an end. Residual forces in places like Hong Kong, Gibraltar, Malta, Brunei and the Caribbean would have to be further reduced. Even in the NATO area itself cuts would have to be made. It would no longer be possible to provide amphibious and airborne reinforcements for both the southern (Mediterranean) flank of NATO as well as for the northern (Scandinavian) flank. As a Soviet attack on Scandinavia could jeopardize the defence of the British Isles, the axe would have to fall on less vital contingency plans to reinforce the Mediterranean. In short, the outcome of the review was that Britain would, for the first time in her history, have entirely Continentally orientated forces with four tasks: manning the British nuclear deterrent; helping to defend NATO's central front; maintaining naval control of the Eastern Atlantic in conjunction with the US and other NATO naval forces; and reinforcing NATO's northern flank.[3]

Roy Mason concluded his explanatory pamphlet, *Our Contribution to the Price of Peace*, with the words:

As a result, Britain's security, which is indivisible from that of the NATO Alliance, will be undiminished.[4]

The Continental school of British strategic thinking had triumphed—at least, for a few years.

Some easing of the Continental bias in British defence policy was to be expected when the Conservatives returned to power in 1979 under Mrs Thatcher's robust leadership. This did not happen because equipment cost escalation accelerated and began to shrink Britain's newly tailored NATO suit. Even the goverment's pledge to NATO of a three per cent annual increase in the defence vote could not arrest the shrinkage. By the time John Nott became Minister of Defence in January 1981, it was clear that Britain's economy was just not growing fast enough to contain the steep rises in equipment prices. The probability that Britain's contribution to NATO would have to be cut rather than improved, as the government had intended, brought on the 1981 Defence Review.

In June 1981 John Nott published his conclusions in his *The Way Forward*. He saw Britain as having four main defence roles:

. . . an independent element of strategic and theatre nuclear forces committed to the Alliance; the direct defence of the United Kingdom homeland; a major land

and air contribution on the European mainland; and a major maritime effort in the Eastern Atlantic and Channel.[5]

After examining each in turn and looking at what could be done to reinforce NATO's flanks and to support Western interests beyond the NATO area, using the flexibility of British regular forces, he concluded that the savings needed to balance the defence budget would have to be made at the expense of the fourth role: the Maritime effort in the Eastern Atlantic and Channel. His reasoning was simple, if not simplistic. The nuclear deterrent was Britain's ultimate shield and, therefore, sacrosanct; home defence was already below the critical level and would need improving; Britain's contribution to Western European defence could not be reduced without damaging 'the military posture and political cohesion of the Alliance upon which the security of the United Kingdom depended' and so it was Britain's Maritime effort that would have to bear the brunt of his surgery.[6]

There were a number of scientific arguments that reinforced John Nott's strategic choice of weakening what was left of Britain's Maritime capability rather than her contribution to Continental defence. Surface ships—carriers, destroyers and frigates—had undoubtedly become vulnerable and expensive targets to missile attack. In general war their primary task would be to help challenge the large Soviet fleet and to escort reinforcement and re-supply convoys from North America. Submarines and Maritime air power made more scientific sense in war with the Soviet Union. Nevertheless, John Nott did acknowledge that surface ships had many roles to play in lesser levels of conflict. There was a case for shifting emphasis from surface to sub-surface in the balance of Britain's naval forces, but the preservation of the British contribution to the landward defence of Western Europe at the expense of her general naval capability was a more doubtful proposition which was to be challenged by events all too soon.

The 1982 Defence White Paper translated John Nott's theories into practice.[1] On the positive side, Trident would replace Polaris; some improvements would be made in the Air Defence of the UK and the Territorial Army; and the equipment of BAOR and RAF Germany would be up-dated. On the negative side, the Royal Navy's surface fleet would be reduced without any compensatory increase in submarine construction. The aircraft carriers would be reduced from three to two by selling the new anti-submarine warfare carrier *Invincible* to the Australians and scrapping the ageing *Hermes*. The 59 destroyers and frigates assigned to NATO would be reduced to 50. The assault ships, *Fearless* and *Intrepid*, would not be replaced and cuts would be made in the fleet auxiliaries. Amongst some of the accompanying penny-pinching measures was the withdrawal of the ice patrol ship *Endurance* from the South Atlantic.

The ink was barely dry on the draft of the 1982 Defence White Paper when the Argentinians invaded the Falkland Islands, convinced that Britain no longer had the political will nor the military resources to defend them. The very ships, which John Nott had proposed to sell or scrap, made the recovery of the Falklands practicable. They did more than just win the campaign: they re-opened the debate on the validity of Britain adopting an exclusively Continental strategy in the post-imperial era.

Looking back over the centuries of the creation and then withdrawal from Empire, it is worth asking the question, 'Who are *we*?' *We* are not just the people who inhabit the British Isles today. *We* are the people who spilled out of these islands over the last 300 years, seeking new sources of wealth in the older civilizations of Asia and a better way of life in the emptier quarters of the globe. *We* are also the heirs of the generations of British administrators, judges, soldiers, sailors and missionaries who, for better or worse, brought the British concept of good government to a third of the world's population. *We* cannot turn our backs on the past nor escape its influence. From the narrowly British point of view we must expect to be involved from time to time in areas of political instability where and when our interests or the interests of those who maintain our traditions, are in jeopardy.

Much the same conclusion can be reached when looking at the world through our recently acquired West European spectacles. There has been no slackening in the twentieth-century conflict between the Western and Communist ideologies. Few people would challenge the general assumption that the greatest threat to Western European security lies in the massive superiority of the Warsaw Pact's conventional forces, which is at present, neutralized by nuclear deterrence. As long as the nuclear balance holds, Communist pressure is likely to continue to develop around NATO's flanks and in the world beyond where nuclear weapons have less relevance, and where guerrilla and terrorist compaigns are paying the highest dividends. The end of European colonialism and the defeat of the United States in Vietnam have provided tempting precedents for Communist believers and salutary warnings for the Western democracies. It is in the remoter areas of the world rather than in Western Europe where the ideological struggle is fiercest and where military power is most likely to be needed to protect *our* interests.

At the beginning of the post-imperial era Britain is still trapped in the paradoxical position noted by Anthony Eden in 1956 of spending more on deterring the most dangerous but least likely threat to NATO's central and northern fronts than on preparations to meet the lesser, but much more probable, crises beyond the NATO area. When the continuing escalation in equipment costs enforces yet another Defence Review, the current inviolability of Britain's land and air contribution to the defence of NATO's landward frontiers should be questioned. The defence of Western Europe depends on the continuing efficiency of the West's nuclear weapons. NATO's conventional forces can only raise or lower the nuclear threshold. It may prove more sensible to rebuild Britain's Maritime intervention capability than to have British regular servicemen doing a job that would be better done by the conscript forces of our Continental allies for whom the forward defence along the Iron Curtain is vital. The withdrawal of the Rhine Army into central reserve in Western Europe so that it could be equipped and trained as a force for world-wide deployment as well as playing a useful role in European defence would, at the worst, only lead to a marginal lowering of the nuclear threshold. Indeed, it can be argued that the balance of NATO's deployment would be improved. British forces would still be just as committed to Continental defence, but their role as the principal mobile reserve would be more suited to their traditions and the geographic position of the British Isles, lying in depth behind the central and northern fronts.

There is another way of arriving at the same conclusion. It is impossible to forecast the future with any accuracy. It is the unexpected that tends to occur in military affairs because the expected can usually be deterred, provided there is the political will and sagacity to do so. The military ideal in peace time, or pseudo peace, is the creation of balanced forces able to react to the unforeseen, but only the superpowers have the resources to cover all the bands of the spectrum of war and even they have difficulty in doing so. As a middle-power, albeit a very experienced one, Britain has to be more selective in establishing a balance for her military force structure that will stand the test of time. Her forces should be as general purpose as possible with minimum specialization so that they can play a full part in Western European defence while, at the same time, being able to fight more likely and more prolonged conflicts elsewhere. This posture would be easier to achieve if such major components of Britain's defence forces were not so rigidly tied to the forward defence of a 40 mile sector of NATO's front on the north German Plain which, in any case, would be more enthusiastically defended by West German troops: men fight best for hearth and home.

Looking back over the last campaigns of the withdrawal from Empire, in which the trends of warfare in the nuclear era were clearly visible, the military maids-of-all-work have been the frigates, the infantry and the helicopters. As long as the nuclear balance lasts, conflicts are most likely to occur in the least sophisticated bands of the spectrum of war. The swing to strategic mobility in the 1960s, which was a reaction to Duncan Sandys' over-hastily convened 'Big bang' policy of 1957, served Britain well in the 1970s and early 1980s. A similar swing against the Euro-centric policies of John Nott's Defence White Paper of 1982 was started with his subsequent apologia, The Falklands Campaign: the Lessons[8] published in December 1982, but there is a long way to go before Britain regains a military flexibility comparable to the political freedom of choice in foreign policy that she has acquired by her withdrawal from Empire.

Throughout all the winds of change, which have howled around the British Empire, one thing has remained constant: the inbred fighting spirit of the British sailors, soldiers and airmen. They come from the same stock as the men who manned the broadsides at Trafalgar and the squares at Waterloo; and have so recently showed the same quality in the battles for the Falklands. They deserve a well balanced and flexible mix of Continental and Maritime strategy. From the days of Marlborough's bloody victories on the Danube and Rhine to the slaughter in the mud of Flanders, they have always suffered most from an over-emphasis on the former. The creation and withdrawal from Empire shows them at their best in the Maritime environment—sea, land and air—meeting the unexpected challenge anywhere in the world with judicious politico-military tactics which have made them some of Britain's best ambassadors.

It would, however, be appropriate to end with the last four lines of Kipling's *Recessional*:

> All valiant dust that builds on dust,
>   And guarding, calls on thee to guard,
> For frantic boast and foolish word—
>   Thy mercy on thy people, Lord.

CHAPTER NOTES
AND REFERENCES

Chapter 1

1 Nicholas Mansergh, *The Commonwealth Experience*, p. 186
2 ibid., p. 180–1

Chapter 2

1 Report on Indian Constitutional Reforms 1917
2 Quoted by H. V. Hodson, *The Great Divide*, p. 5
3 The report of the Inter-Imperial Relations Committee, Imperial Conference 1926, Section 1, para. 2
4 *Grand Strategy Series of British Official History of the Second World War*, Volume I, p. 3
5 ibid., Volume III, Part 1, p. 123
6 *Official History of Colonial Development*, Volume V, p. 4–5
7 ibid., p. 5
8 ibid., p. 5
9 *Official History of Colonial Development*, Volume V, p. 10–11

Chapter 3

1 Mansion House Speech, 10 November 1942
2 There were 565 states varying in size from Hyderabad with a population of 16 million and a fighting division of British trained troops down to minor principalities with a few thousand people and a ruler's bodyguard
3 Quoted by H. V. Hodson, *The Great Divide*, p. 163
4 ibid., p. 166

5 Tuker, *While Memory Serves*, Chapter XII, Appendix V
6 Quoted by H. V. Hodson, *The Great Divide*, p. 190
7 Mountbatten, *Report of the First Governor General of the Dominion of India*, quoted by H. V. Hodson, p. 22
8 H. V. Hodson, *The Great Divide*, p. 259
9 ibid., p. 260
10 V. Longer, *Red Coats to Olive Green*, p. 267
11 The 2nd Black Watch were the last to leave Pakistan on 26 February 1948, and the 1st Somerset Light Infantry could claim to be 'Ultimus ex India'. They left Bombay two days later after a nostalgic troop of colours through the Gateway of India
12 Lord Ismay, *Memoirs*, p. 436
13 Balfour's Albert Hall speech of 12 July 1930, quoted by Nicholas Bethel in *The Palestine Triangle*, p. 19
14 Winston Churchill, *The Second World War*, Volume VI, p. 654
15 Chiefs of Staff to General Paget (GOC-in-C Middle East) 13 May 1946, quoted by M. J. Cohen, p. 80

Chapter 4

1 *The Cold War, A Reappraisal*, p. 165–6
2 The rainy season from May to October each year was used by both sides for reorganisation for the next dry season's campaign

3 F. S. V. Donnison, *British Military Administration in the Far East 1943–46*, Appendix 7, p. 457

4 Three British, six Gurkha and two Malay infantry battalions

5 Sir Edward Gent had lost the confidence of Malcolm Macdonald, the British Commissioner-General for Southeast Asia. He had been recalled and was expected to tender his resignation. The RAF York in which he was travelling collided with another aircraft near London

6 Quoted by Anthony Short, *The Communist Insurrection in Malaya 1948–60*, p. 136–7

7 Quoted by Anthony Short, p. 220

8 Quoted by Anthony Short, p. 296

9 Harry S. Truman, *Memoirs*, Volume II, p. 445–6

Chapter 5

1 Northcote Parkinson, *Templer in Malaya*, p. 23

2 British Official History of Colonial Development, Volume V, p. 20

3 ibid., p. 22

4 ibid., p. 19

5 Antigua and Grenada 1951; Belize and Bahamas 1957; Jamaica 1960; Guyana 1962–4; Bermuda 1968; Anguilla 1969; Belize 1972–1981. Troops were also sent to Mauritius in 1965 and 1968

6 F. D. Corfield, *The History of the Origins and the Growth of Mau Mau*, p. 39

7 ibid., p. 39

8 The origin of the word Mau Mau is obscure; the literal translation is 'greedy eating'. As an onomatopaeic word it caught on, particularly among the Europeans

9 The appointment of chiefs and headmen in Kikuyu Reserves was a British-imposed administrative measure which was not natural to the tribe.

10 F. D. Corfield, *The History of the Origins and the Growth of Mau Mau*, p. 130. para. 127

11 ibid., p. 72

12 ibid., p. 130

13 The Aberdares rose to 13,000 feet and Mount Kenya to 17,000 feet

14 Report by General Sir George Erskine, 23 June 1955, para. 125–6

15 Anthony Short, *The Communist Insurrection in Malaya*, p. 354

16 Figures from Richard L. Clutterbuck, *Riot and Revolution in Singapore and Malaya*, p. 188–9

Chapter 6

1 Quoted by Herman Finer, *Dulles over Suez*, p. 434

2 Alan Bullock, Ernest Bevin quoting DO(46)27, p. 242

3 ibid., quoting CP(49)188 of 25.8.49

4 ibid., quoting CP(45)162 of 10.9.45

5 Chatham House, *Cyprus*, quoting *New York Times* of 28 July 1948

6 EOKA stood for the Greek words meaning 'National Organization of the Cyprus Struggle'.

7 *The Tripartite Conference on the Eastern Mediterranean and Cyprus*, HMSO Command 9594, October 1955

8 Anthony Eden, *Full Circle*, p. 402

9 Anthony Eden, *Full Circle*, p. 408

10 Brigadier George Baker, *The Cyprus Emergency*, RA journal, August 1958, p. 78

11 Herman Finer, *Dulles over Suez*, p. 48

12 Anthony Eden, *Full Circle*, p. 428

13 ibid., p. 440

14 ibid., p. 437

15 Philip Ziegler, *Mountbatten*, p. 537–8

16 Those who did not agree were Soviet Russia, India, Indonesia and Ceylon

17 Philip Zeigler, *Mountbatten*, p. 539

18 Herman Finer, *Dulles over Suez*, p. 189

19 André Beaufre, *The Suez Expedition 1956*, p. 74

20 Selwyn Lloyd, *Suez 1956*, p. 173–89
21 Harold Macmillan, *Riding the Storm*, p. 157
22 Herman Finer, *Dulles over Suez*, p. 446–7

Chapter 7

1 Harold Macmillan, Volume V, p. 153
2 Eisenhower, *Waging Peace*, p. 182–3
3 Harold Macmillan, *Autobiography*, Volume IV, p. 511
4 Anthony Eden, *Full Circle*, p. 371
5 Blue Streak was eventually cancelled in favour of the American air-launched Skybolt missile, which, in its turn, fell to the Polaris system in 1962. Polaris came into operational service in 1969
6 *Defence: Outline of Future Policy*, Command 124, HMSO, 1957, p. 37
7 See maps 7 and 19
8 Turk Mudafa Teskilat (Turkish Defence Organization)
9 Montgomery, 238 House of Lords Debate, 21 March 1962, Col. 579

Chapter 8

1 Command 1639, HMSO, February 1962
2 Malayan-Indonesian Relations, para. 48–9, (Malaysian government publication, 1963)
3 Quoted by J. A. C. Mackie, *Konfrontasi*, p. 125
4 *The Manila Accord*, para. 10
5 UN Final Conclusions of Secretary General regarding Malaysia SG/1593/ 13.9.63
6 Harold James and Denis Sheil-Small, *The Undeclared War*, p. 110
7 General Sir Walter Walker, *How Borneo was Won*, Round Table, January 1969, p. 20
8 Quoted by Walker in *How Borneo was Won*, p. 20

9 George Henderson had just been awarded his second George Medal
10 *The Economist*, 17 November 1962
11 Officers of the Dublin garrison in the Curragh Barracks objected to marching against Ulster in 1911

Chapter 9

1 Statement on Defence Estimates 1968, Command 3540, HMSO, February 1968
2 Statement on Defence Estimates 1966, Part 1, The Defence Review, Chapter 1 para. 2: Command 2091 February 1966
3 ibid., Part 1, Chapter 11, para. 19
4 ibid., para. 16–25
5 Brigadier Dye took over command of the FRA in 1966
6 The stand-by battalion kept at short notice in the UK for emergency deployment
7 Command 3357, HMSO, 1967
8 Signals and Coastal Command also joined Strike Command in 1969
9 Command 3540, HMSO, 1968

Chapter 10

1 Command 8758, HMSO, p. 35, para. 313
2 There were estimated to be another 200,000 in neighbouring countries
3 *Statement on Defence Estimates 1975*, Command 5976, Chapter 1, HMSO, March 1975
4 *Our Contribution to the Price of Peace*, p. 22; Ministry of Defence, August 1975
5 *The Way Forward*, Command 8288, p. 5; HMSO, June 1981
6 ibid., para. 9–31
7 Command 8529–1, HMSO 1982, published in June 1982 after the Argentinian surrender
8 Command 8758: HMSO, December 1982

APPENDIX

Independence Dates

(Territories which left the Commonwealth are shown in italics)

1 July 1867	Canada
1 January 1901	Australia
26 September 1907	New Zealand
31 May 1910	*Union of South Africa* (Republic outside Commonwealth, 31 May 1961)
31 May 1922	*Irish Free State* (Republic of Eire outside Commonwealth, 16 April 1949)
15 August 1947	India (Republic within the Commonwealth)
15 August 1947	*Pakistan* (Republic 25 March 1956; left Commonwealth 30 January 1971)
4 January 1948	*Burma*
4 February 1948	Ceylon (Republic of Sri Lanka within the Commonwealth 28 July 1972)
15 May 1948	*Palestine* mandate terminated; State of Israel proclaimed
1 January 1956	*Sudan*
6 March 1957	Gold Coast (Republic of Ghana within the Commonwealth, 1 July 1960)
31 August 1957	Malaya (joined Federation of Malaysia 16 September 1963)
26 June 1960	*British Somaliland*
16 August 1960	Cyprus (Republic within the Commonwealth)
1 October 1960	Nigeria (Federal Republic within Commonwealth, 1 October 1963)
27 April 1961	Sierra Leone (Republic within the Commonwealth, 19 April 1971)
1 June 1961	Northern Cameroons joined Nigeria
1 October 1961	*Southern Cameroons*
9 December 1961	Tanganyika (Republic within the Commonwealth, 9 December 1962)
1 January 1962	Western Samoa, joined Commonwealth, 28 August 1970
6 August 1962	Jamaica
31 August 1962	Trinidad and Tobago (Republic within Commonwealth, 1 August 1976)
9 October 1962	Uganda (Republic within the Commonwealth, 8 September 1967)

16 September 1963	North Borneo (Sabah) Sarawak Singapore } Joined Federation of Malaysia, 16 September 1963
10 December 1963	Zanzibar, joined Tanganyika to form Tanzania, 26 April 1964
12 December 1963	Kenya (Republic within the Commonwealth, 12 December 1964)
6 July 1964	Nyasaland (Republic of Malawi within the Commonwealth, 6 July 1966)
26 September 1964	Malta (Republic within the Commonwealth, 13 December 1974)
26 October 1964	Northern Rhodesia (Republic of Zambia within the Commonwealth)
18 February 1965	The Gambia (Republic within the Commonwealth, 24 April 1970)
26 July 1965	The Maldives (Republic and special member of the Commonwealth, 11 November 1968)
26 May 1966	British Guiana (Republic of Guyana within the Commonwealth, 23 February 1970)
30 September 1966	Bechuanaland (Republic of Botswana within the Commonwealth)
4 October 1966	Basutoland as Lesotho
30 November 1966	Barbados
30 November 1967	*Aden Colony and Protectorates as People's Democratic Republic of South Yemen*
31 January 1968	Nauru (Republic with special relationship with the Commonwealth)
12 March 1968	Mauritius
6 September 1986	Swaziland
4 June 1970	Tonga
10 October 1970	Fiji
18 April 1972	East Pakistan as Bangladesh
10 July 1973	The Bahamas
17 February 1974	Grenada
16 February 1975	Papua New Guinea
28 June 1976	The Seychelles (Republic within the Commonwealth)
7 July 1978	Solomon Islands
1 October 1978	Ellis Islands as Tuvalu (Special member of the Commonwealth)
3 November 1978	Dominica (Republic within the Commonwealth)
22 February 1979	St Lucia
12 July 1979	Gilbert Islands (Republic of Kirabati within the Commonwealth)
29 October 1979	St Vincent and the Grenadines (a special member of the Commonwealth)
18 April 1980	Southern Rhodesia (Republic of Zimbabwe within the Commonwealth)
21 September 1981	Belize

30 July 1980	New Hebrides (Republic of Vanuatu within the Commonwealth)
7 July 1978	Solomons
19 September 1983	St Kitts-Nevis
31 December 1983	Brunei (Monarchy within the Commonwealth)
1 November 1981	Antigua and Barbuda

Residual dependent territories in 1985

Anguilla
Ascension
Bermuda (internally self-governing)
British Indian Ocean Territories
British Antarctic Territories
British Virgin Islands
Falkland Islands and Dependencies
Gibraltar
Hong Kong
Montserrat
Pitcairn Islands
St Helena
Tristan da Cunha
Turks and Caicos Islands
Cayman Islands
Cook Islands ⎫
Niue   ⎬ associated with New Zealand

BIBLIOGRAPHY

General

Bartlett, C. J., *The Long Retreat*, Macmillan, 1972

Barnet, Correlli, *The Collapse of British Power*, Eyre Methuen, 1972

Blaxland, Gregory, *The Regiments Depart*, William Kimber, 1971

Bullock, Allan, *Ernest Bevin*, Heinemann, 1983

Cambridge Modern History, Vols. IV to XII, Cambridge University Press, 1961–1970

Carver, Michael, *War Since 1945*, Wiedenfeld and Nicolson, 1980

Churchill, Winston S., *A History of the English Speaking People*, Cassell 1957

Darby, Philip, *British Defence Policy East of Suez, 1947–1968*, Oxford University Press 1973

Eden, Sir Anthony, *Full Circle*, Cassell 1960

Eisenhower, Dwight D., *Waging Peace*, Heinemann, 1965

Fisher, Nigel, *Iain Macleod*, André Deutsch, 1973

Grand Strategy Series of British Official History of the Second World War, Vols I to VI, HMSO, 1957–1976

Kay, David A., *The New Nations in the United Nations, 1960–1967*, Columbia University Press, 1970

Keith, A. B., *Speeches and Documents of the British Dominions, 1918–1931*, Oxford University Press, 1931

Kirkman, W. P., *Unscrambling an Empire*, Chatto and Windus, 1966

Lee, David, *Flight from the Middle East*, HMSO, 1980

Luard, Evan, *The Cold War: A Reappraisal*, Thames and Hudson, 1964

Macmillan, Harold, *Autobiography*, Vols 4, 5 and 6, Macmillan, 1970–1973

Mansergh, Nicholas, *Survey of British Commonwealth Affairs 1939–1952*, Oxford University Press, 1958

Mansergh, Nicholas, *The Commonwealth Experience*, Wiedenfeld and Nicholson, 1969

Miller, J. D. B., *Survey of Commonwealth Affairs*, Oxford University Press 1974

Morgan, D. J., *British Official History of Colonial Development, 1924–1971*, five vols., Macmillan, 1980

Morris, James, *Pax Britannica Trilogy*, three vols., Faber & Faber 1978

Northege, F. S., *Descent from Power*, Allen and Unwin 1974

Oxford History of England, eight vols., Clarendon Press 1934–1962

Reeves, Thomas C., *McCarthyism*, Dryden Press, 1973

Trevelyan, G. M., *History of England*, Longmans, 1926

Wilson, Harold, *The Labour Government 1964–1970*, Wiedenfeld and Nicholson, 1971

Wilson, Harold, *Final Term*, Wiedenfeld and Nicholson, 1979

Woodcock, George, *Who Killed the British Empire?*, Jonathan Cape, 1974

Ziegler, Philip, *Mountbatten*, Collins, 1985

India

Connell, John, *Auchinleck*, Cassell, 1959

Hodson, H. V., *The Great-Divide*, Hutchinson, 1969

Ismay, Lord, *Memories*, Heinemann, 1960

Longer, V., *Red Coats to Olive Green*, Allied Publishers, India, 1974

Mansergh, Nicholas, *The Transfer of Power 1942–1947* Vols. I–XI, HMSO, 1970–1982

Mollo, Boris, *The Indian Army*, Blandford Press, 1981

Tuker, Francis, *While Memory Serves*, Cassell, 1950

Palestine

Begin, Menachin, *The Revolt*, Revised Edition, W. H. Allen, 1979

Bell, J. Bowyer, *Terror out of Zion*, St Martins Press, 1977

Bethel, Nicholas, *The Palestine Triangle*, André Deutsch, 1979

Cohen, Michael J., *Palestine and the Great Powers*, Princetown University Press, 1982

Wilson, R. D., *Cordon and Search*, Gale and Polden, 1949

French and Dutch in Far East

Donnison, F. S. V., *British Military Administration, Far East 1943–1946*, HMSO, 1956

Kahin, G. M., *Nationalism and Revolution in Indonesia*, Cornell, 1952

Lancaster, Donald, *The Emancipation of French Indo-China*, Oxford University Press, 1961

Ray, Jayanta Kumar, *The Transfer of Power in Indonesia*, Manaktalas, Bombay, 1967

Malayan Campaign 1948–1959

Campbell, A. F., *Jungle Green*, Allen and Unwin, 1953

Chapman, Spencer, *The Jungle is Neutral*, Chatto and Windus, 1949

Clutterbuck, Richard L., *The Long War*, Cassell, 1966

Clutterbuck, Richard L., *Riot &*

Revolution in Singapore & Malaya, Faber & Faber, 1973

Ovendale, Ritchie, *Britain, the United States & the Cold War in South East Asia, 1949–1950*, International Affairs, 1982

Parkinson, Northcote, *Templer in Malaya*, Donald Moore, Singapore, 1954

Short, Anthony, *The Communist Insurrection in Malaya, 1948–1960*, Frederick Muller, 1975

Sunderland, R., *Army Operations in Malaya, 1947–1960*, Rand Corporation, 1964

Thompson, Robert, *Defeating Communist Insurgency*, Chatto & Windus, 1966

Gold Coast/Ghana

Chantler, Clyde, *The Ghana Story*, Linden Press, 1971

Nkrumah, Karame, *Autobiography*, Greenwood Press, 1977

Nkrumah, Karame, *Ghana Revolution*, Allen & Busby, 1977

Kenya, Mau Mau Campaign

Barnett, Donald & Karari Njama, *Mau Mau from Within*, Magilbon & Kee, 1966

Clayton, Anthony, *Counter-Insurgency in Kenya 1952–1960*, Trans-Africa, 1976

Corfield, F. D., *Historical Survey of the Origins & Growth of Mau Mau*, HMSO, 1960

Erskine, General Sir George, *Kenya: What it is all About*, R.U.S.I. Journal 1955

Erskine, General Sir George, *The Kenya Emergency*, Ministry of Defence Library, 1955

G.H.Q. East Africa, *The Kenya Picture* locally printed 1954

Kitson, Frank, *Gang & Counter-Gang*, Barrie & Rockliff, 1960

Parliamentary Delegation to Kenya, 1954, HMSO, 1954

Cyprus, EOKA Campaigns

Baker, Brigadier George, *The Cyprus Emergency*, Ministry of Defence Library, 1957

Chatham House, *Cyprus; The Dispute & Settlement*, Oxford University Press, 1959

Crawshaw, Nancy, *The Cyprus Revolt*, Allen & Unwin, 1978

Denktash, R. R., *The Cyprus Triangle*, Allen & Unwin, 1982

Foley, Charles, *Island in Revolt*, Longmans, 1962

Foley, Charles, *Memoirs of General Grivas*, Longmans, 1964

Foley, Charles and Scobie, W. I., *The Struggle for Cyprus*, Hoover Institution Press, 1976

Foot, Sylvia, *Emergency Exit*, Chatto & Windus, 1960

Glover, J. M., *Peace Keeping in Cyprus*, British Army Review, 1965

Mayes, Stanley, *Cyprus & Makarios*, Portnam, 1960

Terrorism in Cyprus, The Captured Documents, HMSO, 1955

Egypt and the Suez Canal

Barker, A. J., *Suez, the Seven Day War*, Faber & Faber, 1964

Beaufre, André, *The Suez Expedition, 1956*, Faber & Faber, 1969

Blaxland, Gregory, *Objective Egypt*, Frederick Muller, 1966

Cavanagh, Sandy, *Airborne to Suez*, William Kimber, 1965

Chatham House, *British Interests in the Mediterranean & Middle East*, Chatham House, 1958

Connell, John, *The Most Important Country*, Cassell, 1957

Dikmejian, R. Hrair, *Egypt under Nasser*, London University Press, 1972

Dyan, Moshe, *Diary of the Sinai Campaign*, Weidenfeld & Nicholson, 1966

Finer, Herman, *Dulles over Suez*, Quadrangle Books, 1964

Keightly, General Sir Charles, *Dispatch*, London Gazette, 1957

Kyping, Sir Norman, *The Suez Contractors*, Kenneth Mason, 1969

Lloyd, Selwyn, *Suez 1956*, Jonathan Cape, 1978

Nutting, Anthony, *Nasser*, Constable, 1972

Defency Policy

Becket, Ian, F. W., and Gooch, John, *Politicans & Defence*, Manchester University Press, 1981

Defence White Papers: *Statements on Defence Estimates*, 1947–1985; *Supplementary Statements on Defence Policy*, 1967 and 1968; *Our Contribution to the Price of Peace*, 1975; *The Way Forward*, 1981; *The Falklands Campaign: The Lessons*, 1982: (HMSO 1947–1985)

Fenchtwanger, E. J., *Perspective upon British Defence Policy, 1945–1970*, University of Southampton, 1978

Healey, Denis, *Britain's Defence Review*, Survival, 1965

Martin, L. W., *The Sandys' Era*, American Political Science Review, 1962

Mayhew, Christopher, *Britain's Role Tomorrow*, Hutchinson, 1967

Owen, David, *The Politics of Defence*, Jonathan Cape, 1972

Speed, Keith, *Sea Change*, Ashgrove Press, 1982

Williams, Geoffrey & Reid, Bruce, *Denis Healey*, Sidgwick & Jackson, 1971

East of Suez Policy

Darby, Philip, *British Defence Policy East of Suez, 1947–1968*, Oxford University Press, 1973

Richards, Ivor, *Europe or the Open Sea*, Charles Knight, 1971

Round Table, *Britain's Retreat from Asia*, October 1967

Skloot, Edward, *Labour East of Suez*, Orbis, 1966

Borneo Campaign

Foxley-Norris, C. N., *Air Aspects of Operations against Confrontation*, Brasseys Annual, 1967

James, Harold, & Sheil-Small, Denis, *The Undeclared War*, Leo Cooper, 1971

Mackie, J. A. C., *Konfrontasi*, Oxford University Press, 1974

Malaysian Government White Papers on the Indonesian Confrontation, Various, Government Printers, Kuala Lumpur, 1964

Smith, E. D., *Borneo Confrontation*, Army Quarterly, 1975

Walker, Sir Walter, *How Borneo was Won*, Round Table, 1969

Aden and the Radfan

Little, Tom, *South Arabia*, Pall Mall, 1968

Paget, Julian, *Last Post*, Faber & Faber, 1969

Trevaskis, Kennedy, *Shades of Amber*, Hutchinson, 1968

Trevelyan, Humphrey, *The Middle East in Revolution*, Macmillan, 1970

Rhodesia

Hills, Denis, *The Last Days of White Rhodesia*, Chatto & Windus, 1981

Hudson, H. P. W., *Ending an Era*, Springwood Books, 1978

Hudson, Miles, *Triumph or Tragedy?*, Hamish Hamilton, 1981

Meridith, Martin, *The Past is Another Country*, André Deutsch, 1979

Wiseman, Henry & Taylor, A. M., *From Rhodesia to Zimbabwe*, Pergamon Press, 1981

Windrich, Elaine, *Britain & the Politics of Rhodesian Independence*, Croom Helm, 1978

Oman

Akehurst, John, *We Won a War*, Michael Russell, 1982

INDEX

DATE DUE

PRINTED IN U.S.A.